Assessment and Management of Mainstreamed Hearing-Impaired Children

Assessment and Management of Mainstreamed Hearing-Impaired Children

PRINCIPLES AND PRACTICES

Mark Ross
Diane Brackett
Antonia Brancia Maxon

pro·ed

8700 Shoal Creek Boulevard
Austin, Texas 78758

© 1991 by PRO-ED, Inc.

Library of Congress Cataloging-in-Publication Data

Ross, Mark.
    Assessment and management of mainstreamed hearing impaired
children : principles and practices / Mark Ross, Diane Brackett,
Antonia Brancia Maxon.
        p.   cm.
    Includes bibliographical references.
    ISBN 0–89079–458–8
    1. Hearing impaired children—Education.   2. Mainstreaming in
education—Evaluation.   3. Educational tests and measurements.
I. Brackett, Diane.   II. Maxon, Antonia.   III. Title.
HV2430.R58   1991
371.91'2—dc20   90–27495
                                                                    CIP

pro·ed

8700 Shoal Creek Boulevard
Austin, Texas 78758

10   9   8   7   6   5   4   3   2   1   91   92   93   94   95

Contents

Preface • **vii**

Acknowledgments • **xi**

1 INTRODUCTION • **1**

2 PERFORMANCE OF MAINSTREAMED HEARING-IMPAIRED CHILDREN • **19**

3 MAINSTREAMING OPTIONS AND PRINCIPLES • **67**

4 AUDIOLOGICAL EVALUATION AND AMPLIFICATION ASSESSMENT • **85**

5 COMMUNICATION ASSESSMENT • **113**

6 ACADEMIC, PSYCHOLOGICAL, SOCIAL, AND CLASSROOM EVALUATIONS • **141**

7 INDIVIDUALIZED EDUCATION PLAN • **161**

8 AUDITORY MANAGEMENT PRINCIPLES • **181**

9 AUDITORY MANAGEMENT PRACTICES • **221**

10 COMMUNICATION MANAGEMENT PRINCIPLES • **261**

11 COMMUNICATION MANAGEMENT PRACTICES • **269**

12 EDUCATIONAL AND PSYCHOSOCIAL MANAGEMENT • **303**

13 IN-SERVICE TRAINING • **321**

14 CASE STUDIES • **333**

15 SUMMING UP • **359**

Appendix A: Letter to Classroom Teacher • **371**

Appendix B: Definition of and Competencies for Aural Rehabilitation Position Statement • **373**

References • **387**

Index • **401**

126625

Preface

$\mathbf{S}$ince November of 1975, the Education for All Handicapped Children Act (Public Law 94-142) has had a major effect on special education in the United States. The first few years of its implementation saw a complete reorganization of special education, and the resulting administrative confusion and spiraling costs led to some efforts to repeal or emasculate the law. But despite these problems in implementation, the impact of PL 94-142 was, and is, basically positive.

This law is now an established fact, and federal and state initiatives currently focus on clearly defining its objectives and its operative procedures. Gaps in services are being filled. One recent development has corrected an earlier major weakness. Mandatory management provisions previously were limited to ages 2.8 to 21 years for hearing-impaired children. For this population, however, the years below age 2.8 are particularly crucial in terms of eventual communicative performance. A new law, PL 99-457 (Education of the Handicapped Act: Amendments of 1986), which took effect in 1990, requires appropriate assessment and management from birth through 3 years for all children with special needs. The actual implementation of this law well may create even more problems for those working with hearing-impaired children. These professionals now must be able to provide services to infants and toddlers, which requires competencies different from, and additional to, those needed for working with older hearing-impaired children.

Our view is that these laws simply define the parameters of management and do not guarantee them. Professional responsibilities and efforts with hearing-impaired children preceded the passage of these laws and will continue regardless of the details of statutory obligations. The essential ingredient for the successful education of hearing-impaired children is still, as in the past, the caring and informed involvement of parents and professionals. Above all, it is the spirit and intent of the law that must be the transcendent imperative; too often we have seen the clear intent of the law subverted by unimaginative bureaucrats with tunnel vision.

We are sympathetic to the concerns expressed in the Commission on Education of the Deaf's 1988 report to the President and the Congress of the United States, which points out that administrative convenience and budgetary considerations often constitute the guiding factors in the educational placement and support services provided for a particular child. The

Commission also observed that many hearing-impaired children are drowning in the mainstream. Although we have no quarrel with this distressing conclusion as it applies to *some* children, we disagree with the tone of the Commission's recommendations regarding suitable placement. Within these recommendations there appears to be an implicit assumption that mainstream placement is rarely suitable for hearing-impaired children. The intent of the original Education for All Handicapped Children Act (PL 94-142) clearly envisioned appropriate placement within a range of possible alternatives, with objectively defined criteria guiding retention or transfer. That many hearing-impaired children are placed unsuitably in mainstream educational settings is indisputable; violations of the spirit of the law, however, should move us to correct deficiencies and not foolishly create an entirely different set of problems.

Part of the problem lies in definitions. One is reminded of the old tale of the elephant and the nine blind men, each of whom define the creature by the part of its anatomy he is touching. The Commission consisted mainly of individuals whose professional and personal expertise lay with profoundly hearing-impaired children. For these children, placement in a fully mainstreamed educational setting indeed must be implemented very carefully, with due consideration given to the decision's possible negative psychosocial and educational implications. There are, however, many more hard-of-hearing children than deaf ones (as we will define them in chapter 1). For the most part, hard-of-hearing children always have been mainstreamed, although not always with the most appropriate supportive services. Because the Commission's 1988 report explicitly labels (p. xii) as "deaf" any child with a hearing impairment, including those who are hard-of-hearing, its recommendations unfortunately are flawed.

Throughout, this report contains statements and recommendations that may be appropriate to profoundly hearing-impaired children, but simply do not apply to those with lesser degrees of loss or with excellent functional use of residual hearing. (For example, the Introduction states that only about 40% of "deaf" teenagers are qualified for college.) Appropriate educational management is primarily an individualized decision; labels, however convenient, tend to mask the many and varied attributes and factors within a specific child. We must first understand the capabilities, potential or realized, of a particular child before we can plan a suitable program. We must call upon and coordinate the skills of numerous specialists and use explicit criteria to evaluate a child's progress. Such criteria must encompass psychosocial factors as well as purely academic ones. The parents' role must not only be acknowledged but seen as an essential ingredient.

Our previous book on this topic focused on hard-of-hearing children and regarded the appropriate use of residual hearing as a crucial educational tool. *Assessment and Management of Mainstreamed Hearing-Impaired Children* also emphasizes the informed exploitation of residual hearing but extends its use and advantages to children with profound hearing losses as well. Some of this latter group will develop a primarily auditory mode of functioning, some will employ audition in conjunction with vision and function in a primarily bisensory mode, while others will find only limited benefit from auditory stimulation. The focus here is on the *mainstreamed* hearing-impaired child, regardless of the degree of loss. In reality, however, most of the children who are mainstreamed will be those who have the most residual hearing, or, more accurately, those who who make the best *use* of their residual hearing, regardless of their degree of hearing loss.

When these children are very young, one cannot predict how useful hearing will be for them. Although our view holds that one is obliged to try to develop audition as the child's primary sensory channel, *this must never be taken to the point of imposing our biases when clearly another mode would be more suitable.* There has never been a professional consensus on when and how to determine auditory primacy. That the child's interests must be the deciding factor seems obvious, but various avenues toward this end are possible because so many professionals (ourselves included) are sincerely convinced of the merits of their own educational philosophy. Our goal is to exploit a child's residual hearing to its fullest extent; when it becomes obvious that the prognosis for acceptable auditory-verbal development is poor, then it is time to look for another, more suitable mode, and possibly a more suitable educational placement as well. And we must ensure that this decision is made early in a child's life.

The content level of this book assumes that the reader has had introductory courses in hearing, speech, and language. This text is not designed for persons with no, or extremely limited, pertinent academic background; rather, it is for speech-language pathologists, audiologists, and teachers who work, or are in training to do so, with hearing-impaired children being educated in the regular schools.

We cannot be effective teachers and clinicians for hearing-impaired children unless all the efforts we direct at them are permeated with a sense of urgency. When we deal with young children, time is not on our side. The early years are the most crucial in respect to later development, and it is never too soon to begin working with these children and their parents. Although we hope the information contained here will greatly assist prospective teachers and clinicians, we recognize that effective professionals are not merely purveyors of information or appliers of therapeutic "recipes." The best ones are those who truly care about the children and their parents, subordinating all other factors to this paramount value. Without both information and commitment, therapy is apt to be simply a mechanistic exercise and not a realization of human potential.

Acknowledgments

Maybe this book could have been written without the support and encouragement of our family, friends, and colleagues, but it would have been a lot harder. We are especially grateful to Helen, Art, Sjef, and Pieter for their patience, their willingness to accept our absences (even when we were physically present), and their pride in our efforts. We are additionally indebted to Helen for her careful reading and editing of our initial drafts. All the figures were completed and/or created by Bob Essman, who contributed his talent and time to ensure that all the artwork was attractive and appropriate. Finally, we want to acknowledge our deep debt to each other. In more than 14 years of collaboration, we have taught and learned from one another in friendship and respect. We look forward to more years of joint projects and continued professional growth together.

1
_____

Introduction

Hearing-impaired children should be educated in those places that offer them the greatest opportunities—psychosocial, academic, and communicative—and cause the least disruption to the integrity of their family unit. These elements must be balanced carefully and sensitively to arrive at the placement that seems best suited to a particular child. For many hearing-impaired children, most often those with the greatest hearing losses or those who also have deaf parents, the most appropriate educational placement will be a special school. The "most appropriate educational setting," therefore, is not synonymous with the "least restrictive educational setting" (LRE): "appropriate" is defined in terms of individual needs, while LRE describes the degree of involvement with normal-hearing children that the setting permits. The goal is to ensure that these two concepts are congruent for a particular child; that is, that the child is placed in an LRE most appropriate for his or her needs.

For the majority of hearing-impaired children, the most appropriate educational placement will be a mainstream one, which is the least restrictive of all educational settings. To fully appreciate this assertion, it is important to understand how we define the terms *hearing impaired, deaf,* and *hard of hearing*. Professionals charged with providing direct or supportive services for this population must understand the distinctions between these definitions in order to manage the children's habilitative needs in an intelligent and effective manner. Some of the interprofessional confusions that occur when discussing appropriate placement appear to arise from

1

different understandings of these terms. Simply put, the first step in dealing with any disorder is to understand it as well as possible.

CATEGORIES OF IMPAIRMENT

The Hearing-Impaired Child

The term *hearing impaired* here refers to any child with an auditory disorder (Ross & Calvert, 1967; Wilson, Ross, & Calvert, 1974). As such, it encompasses children with mild hearing losses as well as those with the most severe losses. We *do not* use the term as a synonym for *hard of hearing*. In the pages that follow, therefore, the term *hearing impaired* refers to the general category of children with hearing losses. Often it is convenient to employ a descriptive adjective with the term, such as "mild," "moderate," "severe," or "profound" hearing impairment. In such cases, the adjective provides sufficient distinction so that the entire term can be used appropriately. The emphasis on such distinctions here is not simply an academic or taxonomic exercise. Various diagnostic labels have a way of determining treatment and placement, and it is vital that a child's management be based on his or her characteristics and not on categorizing labels. We view the term *hearing impaired* as a generic diagnostic label and not as a description of a child's auditory functioning or capacities.

The Hard-of-Hearing Child

The *hard-of-hearing* child refers here to someone who has developed his or her basic communication skills primarily through the auditory channel and for whom audition serves as the primary communication mode. As such, it describes function rather than diagnosis, degree of hearing loss, or etiology. The residual hearing of hard-of-hearing children is sufficient, with or without amplification, to serve as the basis for their evolving speech and language skills. Although these skills are more often deficient than not, the children nevertheless are basically auditory rather than visual communicators. Thus they have much more in common with normal-hearing children than with "deaf" children, as we define this latter group. As shall be seen, this conceptual difference greatly influences therapeutic management, in that our management focus emphasizes maximizing the similarities rather than the differences with normal-hearing children.

There are many more hard-of-hearing children than deaf ones. The number of school-age hard-of-hearing children with average hearing losses between 26 and 70 dB in the better ear has been estimated as 1.6% or 16 per

1,000 schoolchildren (Public Health Service, 1964). This incidence figure is widely quoted; however, the evidence suggests that it minimizes the actual frequency of educationally significant hearing losses (which we define as speech, language, academic, and psychosocial disturbances attributable to the hearing loss).

We know that the percentage of schoolchildren manifesting a hearing disorder increases with decreasing degree of loss. We also know that hearing losses in the 15 to 26 dB range are related to academic lags in excess of 1 year (Quigley, 1978, p. 43). Using the very rigid criterion of failure to respond at 10 dB to 6 out of 14 test frequencies in either ear (250 to 8000 Hz), Sarff (1981) reports that 33% of 601 children failed the hearing screening test. Importantly, 57% of them exhibited an academic deficit of some degree (the study does not report how many of the children who passed the screening were academically deficient; one would expect the figure to be much less). Given these findings, it does appear that the percentage of children with educationally significant hearing losses exceeds 16 per 1,000 and is probably much closer to 30 per 1,000.

The estimate may even climb if we include as hard of hearing those children with unilateral hearing losses. These children often are even more "forgotten" than those with mild or moderate bilateral hearing losses (Davis, 1990), likely because of their apparently normal communication skills. Recent studies have found that approximately 24 to 35% of children with unilateral hearing loss had failed one grade in school and that an additional 13 to 41% required some special services (Bess, 1986; Oyler, Oyler, & Matkin, 1988). Clearly such children are suffering the consequences of a hearing impairment (as will be discussed more fully).

An additional factor to be considered is the increased number of premature, low birth weight, and sick infants and toddlers who survive because of advanced medical treatment. It is likely that the percentage of these children who manifest an educationally significant hearing loss will increase as time goes by. We would consider any child with an average hearing loss of 16 dB or more in either ear or a unilateral high frequency loss (Sarff, 1981) to be potentially "at risk" for manifesting deficiencies associated with the hearing loss. The reader should understand that a discussion on classification is for labeling purposes only, as such labeling cannot always be avoided. Individual children must be dealt with primarily on their own terms, not as a member of some category.

The Deaf Child

In contrast to those who are hard of hearing, the *deaf* child's development of speech and language and his or her primary avenue of communication is visually based. There is a world of difference between children who communicate mainly through a visual mode (speechreading or manual communication) and those who use audition (albeit imperfectly) as their primary sensory input mode. Professionals too often have been deceived by the apparent similarities between the two groups—after all, both have hearing losses—and have not paid enough attention to the implications of the different channels they use to process primary sensory input. Lumping these two groups of children together has been a disservice to both, but mainly to the hard-of-hearing child. There are children who are, or were, potentially hard of hearing in just about every deaf education program in the country. Given the dynamics of the self-fulfilling prophecy, these children, when classified, treated, and educated as if they were "deaf," not surprisingly function as deaf individuals (Ross & Calvert, 1967). This is not meant to denigrate truly deaf individuals in any way, but rather to emphasize that the sense of hearing is literally a human birthright. Professionals who ignore its presence and possible contribution violate an important avenue of human potential.

It is as difficult to specify the borderline between the deaf and hard-of-hearing individual as it is to divide the normal-hearing person from the hard-of-hearing one. In our judgment the only valid measure is a functional one; that is, if a hearing-impaired person can recognize verbal messages through the ear alone, then that person is hard of hearing. The hearing loss figure most often used as the borderline between deaf and hard of hearing is an average of 90 dB hearing loss in the better ear. There are bases in the literature for this figure; for example, it is at 90 dB that speech perception and production scores drop most sharply (Stark, 1974; Boothroyd, 1984). However, there are too many individual exceptions of children with greater degrees of loss functioning primarily auditorily, as well as those with lesser losses whose primary communication avenue is visual, to apply this figure unquestioningly. The nature of the auditory management a child receives from the time of initial detection often will largely determine whether the child functions as hard of hearing or deaf.

We hasten to correct the notion that deaf children, as they have been defined, cannot use their residual hearing meaningfully. We are careful to employ the term "primarily" when we refer to the major sensory channel of deaf as well as hard-of-hearing children. With even a little bit of hearing, deaf children can perceive and produce the prosodic features of speech and identify the manner of articulation of a number of phonemes (Ross, Duffy, Cooker, & Sergeant, 1973; Boothroyd, 1984). Valuable as this information is for them, however, audition nevertheless serves as very much a secondary and supplemental channel. We make this point because there are very sincere professionals and parents who sometimes give the impression that there is no such entity as a "deaf" child, that residual hearing can be "trained" in all hearing-impaired children. It does such children little good, and potentially much harm, to require from them that which they cannot give.

Demographic data indicate that the incidence of profound congenital deafness (using the 90 dB figure) is approximately 1 such individual per 1,000 births. Although changes in pre- and postnatal medical management will affect this figure somewhat, it nevertheless has remained remarkably stable over the years. As one considers the incidence of deaf and hard-of-hearing children as we have defined them, it is apparent that there are at least 16 to 30 times more hard-of-hearing children than deaf ones.

Some deaf children are mainstreamed to an extent, thus falling within the purview of this book, but proportionally they are much less so than other hearing-impaired children. In the following pages, information on deaf children will be included mainly to lend perspective to the performance and management of hearing-impaired children in general and hard-of-hearing children in particular.

The In-Between Child

The problem with neat categories is that there are too many exceptions. Obviously not every hearing-impaired child will fall neatly into one category or the other. Some children with moderate losses apparently depend less on their hearing than on their vision, while others with severe or profound hearing losses appear to use their hearing as a primary channel. And some children seem to show no overriding preference (Seewald, Ross, Giolas, & Yonovitz, 1985). Our view is that for *most* such children, understandable auditory reasons exist for why this occurs, and esoteric, abstract, and confusing diagnostic labels need not be invoked to explain these seemingly contradictory behaviors. Essentially we feel that the reasons lie in inadequate or inappropriate early auditory management; this will be developed more fully in later pages.

Nevertheless, there are children who, for whatever reason, cannot be categorized neatly as deaf or hard of hearing. They can utilize their hearing, derive much benefit from it, and even employ it as a primary channel in certain specific circumstances that offer no other choice (e.g., talking on the telephone on a restricted topic). At other times they may prefer to depend primarily on visual information for communication purposes. Many of these children apparently function in an essentially bisensory mode, effectively integrating the complementary information provided by audition and speechreading. As cochlear implants for young profoundly hearing-impaired children become more common, more of these bisensory-functioning children may appear in mainstream settings.

Performance and management generalizations about such children should be made very cautiously. Some of these children will identify and feel more comfortable with the deaf culture, some will find the hearing world more congenial, while still others will be capable of bridging the two communities. These are not the kinds of decisions professionals can, or should, make for others, as they involve factors that transcend a child's communication preference and competencies. One should keep in mind, however, that there are relatively few children in this in-between category as compared to the entire population of hearing-impaired children. With appropriate auditory management, the overwhelming majority of the hearing-impaired are, or could be, functionally hard of hearing rather than deaf or in-between.

In our judgment, a child's ability to use residual hearing for communicative purposes should serve as the overriding factor in bestowing any of the above labels. Labels should *not* be applied on the basis of an audiometric representation of the hearing loss, in spite of the significant correlation between hearing loss and function; rather, a label should be considered a *functional* description of a particular child. The discussion that follows will use all three terms—*deaf, hard of hearing*, and *hearing impaired*—frequently, not interchangeably but rather within the specific definitions that have been proposed.

EARLY DETECTION AND MANAGEMENT

Sensory Deprivation

The need to detect the presence of hearing impairments as early as possible is now widely accepted. Mechanisms for accomplishing this have varied, from mass hearing screenings of the neonatal and infant populations to "high risk" registers for children who present certain histories or conditions (American Speech-Language-Hearing Association, 1982; Hodgson, 1985). A great deal of research has been generated to determine the most cost-effective methods of early detection, and laws have been passed in some states to require early detection procedures and/or "high risk" registers. There are excellent reasons for identifying a hearing impairment very early in a child's life. An understanding of these reasons and their implications is necessary in order to imbue the efforts of those working with young hearing-impaired children with the required urgency.

The first and perhaps foremost reason concerns preventing auditory sensory deprivation. Ample evidence has shown that such deprivation can produce profound behavioral, chemical, and structural changes in the auditory system (Ruben & Rapin, 1980). Because this work has been accomplished with laboratory animals, the specific details of the effects on humans no doubt differ in some respects. Nevertheless, there is little reason to believe that human beings will not suffer analogous effects under comparable conditions of auditory sensory deprivation. Clinicians must consider the implications of the research currently available, which suggests that delay in the onset of amplification can reduce the eventual auditory processing capacity of hearing-impaired children.

Rats temporarily deprived of sound during the first few months of life demonstrate a marked inferiority in responding to differences in complex sound patterns, attributed in large part to their inability to resolve time differences. No such effect was shown in their abilities to respond to simple auditory dimensions, such as acuity thresholds (Tees, 1967; Patchett, 1977). A speech signal is a complex, patterned, acoustic event in which time differentiations are vital to its proper perception. Other studies with rats have shown that early auditory deprivation increases the latency of auditory neural responses by a factor of 2 to 3 (Clopton & Winfield, 1976) and that this sound deprivation produces histologic and other structural changes in the brainstem auditory nuclei (Webster & Webster, 1977; Webster, 1983). These nuclei have been found to be smaller, less well developed, and with fewer dendritic connections to adjoining cells. The effects of auditory sensory deprivation reduce the capability of these nuclei to process complex, time-varying signals, precisely those signals that underlie the process of speech perception.

Monaural deprivation also has been found to produce structural changes in the auditory brainstem (Clopton & Silverman, 1977; Silverman & Clopton, 1977; Evans, Webster, & Cullen, 1983; Webster, 1983). Physiologically these studies show abnormalities in binaural interactions, as well as longer latencies to click stimuli from the contralateral, nondeprived side at the level of the midbrain. In other words, monaural deprivation has been shown to affect the neurological bases detrimentally for binaural processing of auditory stimuli. Behaviorally these research findings suggest a reduced ability to localize sound sources, to select signals from a background of competing noise, and to suppress unwanted sounds.

All the research on this topic supports the general conclusion that depriving an animal of sound for some duration at an early period in its life will result in abnormalities in structure and function of the central auditory system. As stated earlier, although there is no comparable research with human beings, a clinically conservative approach must assume that similar effects may occur.

Fortunately (for this discussion, but not the children involved) there is an accumulating body of evidence with human beings on the effect of temporary and/or incomplete auditory deprivation, a kind of "natural" experiment similar to the existence of congenital cataracts with children. The reference here is to the occurrence in young children of middle-ear problems that usually, but not always, clear up as the children get older. In the last 20 years a vast body of literature has arisen on this topic, with most studies based on retrospective research. The results almost uniformly indicate some subsequent impairment of auditory-verbal based skills (see Feagans, Blood, & Tubman, 1988, for an excellent review). These results have been interpreted to suggest that there is a critical period for the acquisition of auditory learning skills, and that the hearing loss secondary to otitis media could cause irreversible damage to the ability to process auditory input (Kirkwood & Kirkwood, 1983).

The effect of even a partial sensory deprivation can be seen in such specific auditory perceptual tasks as selective attention, sequential memory, phonemic synthesis, and oral spelling (Brandes & Ehinger, 1981; Kessler & Randolph, 1979). Academic deficiencies also have been noted among children with a history of early otitis media (Zinkus & Gottlieb, 1980), as have lower verbal intelligence scores, which probably reflect linguistic rather than intellectual factors per se (Gottlieb, Zinkus, & Thompson, 1979; Brandes & Ehinger, 1981).

A number of studies also have reported phonological and linguistic deficiencies and/or developmental delays (Gabbard, 1982; Jerger, Jerger, Alford, & Abrams, 1983), with possible effects on expressive language seen as early as 1 year of age (Wallace, Gravel, McCarton, & Ruben, 1988). At least two studies on the topic have followed children with otitis media for several years and have reported that the speech, language, academic, and behavioral consequences were greater for this group than for comparable children with uninvolved ears (Friel-Patti, Finitzo-Heiber, Conti, & Brown, 1982; Silva, Chalmers, & Stewart, 1986).

The many variables associated with type of research has led some authors to suggest that the relationship between the occurrence of otitis media and performance factors has not been proven (Ventry, 1980; Paradise, 1981). Certainly caution must be exercised, but when study after study shows that children with early onset of conductive hearing impairment function more poorly than children without such histories, then the prudent clinician must assume that *something* abnormal is going on.

What this overbrief excursion into this topic should communicate is that if the auditory system is not stimulated with some critical quantity of meaningful sound at an early period after birth, then that system may display structural and physiological abnormalities that can forever limit its capacities below its original potential. Roughly speaking, the evidence suggests that the earlier and the more severe the deprivation, the greater will be the consequent effects. Given a child with a congenital hearing loss, we do not know how soon we must provide amplification to preclude these effects. All we can state with any sense of assurance is that the earlier we begin, the more likely it is that we can reduce or eliminate the occurrence of auditory sensory deprivation.

To end this section on a hopeful note, however, some restoration of auditory function should always be possible, no matter how long the deprivation has lasted. We have recommended hearing aids for congenitally, severely hearing-impaired adults, enabling them to enjoy the detection of various environmental sounds, and have found that their speech perception and self-monitoring of vocal output was improved. What is probable, however, in these instances is that if amplification had been properly used when these adults were younger, their auditory capabilities may have permitted higher level auditory processing.

Critical Period for Speech/Language Development

Related to but different than the concept of auditory sensory deprivation is that of the "critical" period for speech and language development (Lenneberg, 1967). This is the time, generally during the first 5 years of life, when the central nervous system exhibits its most rapid growth and a correspondingly heightened facility for language learning (deVilliers & deVilliers, 1978). Researchers on language acquisition agree that language growth during the first few years of life is phenomenally rapid; there is some reluctance, however, to refer to this period as "critical" because it implies that the onset of a language system at a later age is impossible. But whatever term we use, whether *critical period* or one of *heightened sensitivity*, it is clear that the normally developing child will experience the greatest growth in linguistic development in the early years.

The primary reason for attempting to preclude the occurrence of auditory sensory deprivation is to permit the auditory channel to play its natural role in speech and language development. Given the appropriate linguistic stimulation, the growing child possesses an awesome capacity to organize what he or she hears into a complex, rapidly evolving, oral language system. In the absence of an adequate auditory channel, the child would evolve a visually oriented linguistic system. In either case, children demonstrate an early capacity to develop a cognitively based and meaningful communication system. In other words, they need to communicate and thus will employ whatever sensory capabilities they have to do so. Therapeutic efforts can be most effective, therefore, when based on normal human development.

Hearing-impaired children possess the same biological capacity for learning language as do normal-hearing children. For those with a significant amount of residual hearing, the most natural and effective sensory modality is the auditory channel. Early detection and management will minimize auditory sensory deprivation and will take advantage of the readiness period for auditory-verbal development. In order to exploit the innate language learning capacity, children must hear language in relevent interpersonal situations at an early age. Because hearing loss will prevent perception of some of the acoustic cues in speech, affected children ordinarily require an increased quantity of input to attempt to partially compensate for qualitative differences. Repeated exposures to the secondary, but still salient, acoustic cues in the speech signal will permit such children to learn to take advantage of them. In brief, for most hearing-impaired children, one can take no more effective measure with regard to maximizing an auditory-based linguistic system than to employ a child's innate biological capacities as the most potent ally.

Professionals should not make the mistake of thinking that we, with all of our pedogogical efforts, are better teachers of language than these children are learners, given appropriately amplified speech inputs. These inputs permit them to learn language in a natural manner. Of course, the effective management of a hearing-impaired child is somewhat more involved than the simple provision of adequate amplification; this is, however, a prerequisite step, and one that will influence all other measures.

Overlaid Behavioral Anomalies

Hard-of-hearing children present a very confusing picture if one is unaware of the hearing loss or unfamiliar with its possible effects. On the one hand, these children are not deaf; they do hear and respond to environmental and speech sounds. On the other hand, their hearing loss prevents them from responding normally and consistently to these stimuli. To the unsophisticated observer, such unpredictable behavior often leads to judgments that these children are somewhat "odd," perhaps manifesting symptoms of minimal brain dysfunction, retardation, or emotional disturbance (Rosenberg, 1966; Ross & Matkin, 1967; Klefner, 1973).

Because of the inconsistency with which they respond to sound, hard-of-hearing children often are diagnosed later than deaf ones, and they may be fitted with amplification and receive an appropriate educational program much later than deaf children (Elliot, 1967). (One hopes that the implementation of PL 99-457 will increase awareness of hearing loss risk factors and lower the age of accurate diagnosis.) By the time a definite diagnosis of hearing loss is made and/or its effects are understood by the family, the affected child already will have lived with the burden of being considered somewhat "different" and will have been treated accordingly.

Hard-of-hearing children often display behavioral anomalies that appear co-equal with the hearing impairment (Ross, 1978b; Davis, 1981a). Professionals dealing with these children should be aware of the strong possibility that indications of other handicapping conditions may really be secondary to the continued conflict between normal expectations and inevitable performance limitations. This is not to deny that other conditions may exist—the child may indeed be "acting out" or may be developmentally delayed; however, professionals managing these children must be able to separate primary from secondary problems.

Supporting Evidence for Early Management

Until recently, only theoretical considerations and a host of anecdotal reports provided the evidence supporting early intervention. From our perspective, this evidence was, and still is, sufficiently potent to warrant our emphasis on early detection and management. However, several recent studies have directly confirmed the advantages of early intervention with hearing-impaired children.

In the first study (Watkins, 1987), subjects were separated into four groups, with 23 children in each. The first group participated in a home intervention program and also attended preschool. The second group was involved in a home intervention program only after age 2½ and attended a preschool. The third group did not receive a home intervention program but did attend a preschool, while the fourth group received neither a home intervention nor a preschool program. All children received an extensive test battery. The results showed that subjects who received a home intervention program performed better in the majority of communication and social functioning measures. Watkins also concluded that a home intervention program *combined* with a preschool program produced the best results.

White and White (1987) followed 46 prelingually hearing-impaired children from the time they entered an infant program until they were formally enrolled in a preschool program at the age of 36 months. Subjects were divided into four subgroups: (a) children of deaf parents for whom intervention was early, (b) children of deaf parents for whom intervention was late, (c) children of hearing parents for whom intervention was early, and (d) children of hearing parents for whom home intervention was late. A number of different dimensions of linguistic development were evaluated periodically. In general White and White found that early intervention had a strong positive effect on the attainment level of all the children, whether the parents were deaf or hearing. However, these effects were much more consistent with hearing parents than with deaf ones. For the children with deaf parents, early intervention appeared to foster speech skills but impede language skills. It appears that this latter group was essentially confronted with a bilingual learning situation, and that the early intervention may have produced more bilingual interference than occurred with those who began preschool at a later age. From a practical point of view, it is important to recall that the parents of over 90% of deaf children can hear.

The White and White (1987) study was one component in a very comprehensive study conducted in New York State by Levitt, McGarr, and Geffner (1987). In three other components, the subjects were 67 six-year-old children enrolled in schools for the deaf; 120 children ages 10 and 11 who were followed for 4 years; and 38 mainstreamed hearing-impaired children ages 10–14. The researchers assessed the impact of a host of variables on the children's eventual performance. In terms of factors over which clinicians and educators have some control, the one most closely related to better performance was the age at which the children received special education; children who were enrolled in special programs prior to age 3 showed, on the average, significantly higher speech and language scores than those who were enrolled later. It should be noted that the effects of hearing loss and socioeconomic variables were eliminated during the statistical analysis.

The authors (Levitt, McGarr, & Geffner, 1987) caution us that the observed relationships are correlational and not causal. The scores of *some* of the children who received early intervention were below average. However, with a few exceptions, those who *did not* receive early intervention scored below average. These results indicate that early management, although a necessary prerequisite for eventual better performance, *is in itself an insufficient condition*. This point was stressed earlier: To be maximally effective, therapeutic intervention not only must begin earlier but must continue to be appropriate in later periods as well.

Intervention Strategies

The study results just described show that the success of eventual intervention efforts may be constrained by earlier events. If the hearing loss is not detected in the very first years, if appropriate amplification is not applied soon after detection, and if the child is not enrolled in a suitable parent-infant and preschool program (Boothroyd, 1982), then likely the effectiveness of subsequent endeavors with the children will be lessened. Nevertheless, whether the child is a recipient of early management procedures or not, he or she is still with us and requires our help. There is almost always something one can do to reduce the impact of a hearing loss.

Dealing with a hearing-impaired child, one first must understand the nature and effect of the impairment, which implies a comprehensive and continuing audiological evaluation. This is in addition to the pediatric and otologic evaluations that must take place on each and every child one sees, as it is vital to resolve any medical condition that may affect a child's health or functioning. However, given the existence of either a sensorineural hearing loss or chronic middle-ear problems, the communicative, educational, and psychosocial effects of the hearing loss demand an explicit audiological focus independent of the purely medical implications.

No nonmedical intervention strategy can be maximally effective unless the child receives a comprehensive performance test battery, ordinarily including the following: (a) an evaluation of expressive and receptive oral communication skills; (b) an assessment of the child's written language skills, including morphological, syntactical, semantic, and pragmatic components; (c) the measurement of intellectual status, which must incorporate an individually administered nonverbal component; (d) an academic achievement battery; (e) classroom observations, to determine how well the child is assimilated into his or her classroom; and (f) a psychosocial estimate of home and school adjustment. For children who are already in school, it is necessary to arrange conferences with all the professionals who have contact with them. Finally, and of profound importance, conferences with the children's parents must be arranged. No one has more at stake than they do, and habilitative planning can hardly be complete without their participation. Then, on the basis of each child's unique constellation of performance and needs, the Individualized Education Plan (IEP) can be formulated as required by PL 94-142 (Nober, 1981). For infants and toddlers, the importance of the family constellation is acknowledged by the Individual Family Service Plan (IFSP) required by PL 99-457.

The first therapeutic steps in managing a hearing-impaired child revolve around auditory factors. It was, after all, the hearing loss that produced the problems, and careful auditory management can reduce their impact at the source. In other words, one does not serve these children just because they display performance limitations, but *because they display the limitations secondary to a hearing loss.* It follows, therefore, that the more effectively these children can utilize their residual hearing, the better their communication skills will be. One should not consider auditory management as just another intervention strategy, to be taken care of before moving on to the next. On the contrary, it must permeate all of a child's activities. The better the child hears the teacher, the more likely he or she will be to learn the material. Thus, the first priority in managing hearing-impaired children in regular schools is to ensure that they are using their residual hearing as effectively as possible.

We are not so naive as to believe that, even with the best audiological management, we can eliminate the problems of most hearing-impaired children. We can for *some* children, provided we begin early and do most things right. Nevertheless, for the majority, the most we will be able to do is reduce the severity and impact of their hearing loss. Appropriate audiological management is the precondition that ensures the maximum effectiveness of all other types of therapy. Audiological and educational management can proceed concurrently; "educational" in this context includes speech, language, and psychosocial factors. The point here is that audiological factors should receive the initial management focus. More often than not they will pay the greatest initial dividends in terms of a child's progress.

Therapeutic Objectives

Public Law 94-142 requires professionals to develop an IEP for all "special needs" children, which of course includes the hearing impaired. The purpose of this law is to mandate procedures intended to guarantee that each child receives the most appropriate education in the least restrictive educational setting possible. This law also demands accountability; that is, the professionals involved are required to provide objective evidence of the effectiveness of their efforts.

It is sometimes difficult to separate these primary purposes from the morass of procedures ostensibly designed to realize them. Clinicians and educators can sometimes lose sight of or de-emphasize the real objectives as they attempt to conform to the many bureaucratic and procedural demands. To a certain extent, we are all prisoners of the system (educational or otherwise) in which we operate. Nevertheless, we must keep in mind that nothing we do has much meaning if we cannot demonstrate, in some convincing fashion, that the children we work with are better off as a result of our therapeutic intervention.

Thus the comprehensive performance evaluation that each hearing-impaired child must receive and the evaluations that must be read-ministered on a regular basis. Professionals must keep track of the child's growth, or lack of it, in all the performance dimensions and relate all intervention methods to the child's current status. In this way one addresses the question of whether therapeutic efforts were responsible for any improvement or whether such would have occurred if nothing had been done. Never an easy question to answer, but it must be asked.

A corollary question also arises: Given a child's progress on one or more performance indices, what standards should be applied in evaluating his or her current status? Three standards are possible: comparing a child's performance (a) to his or her previous status, (b) to that of other hearing-impaired children, or (c) to that of normal-hearing children. No one is specifically "correct" to the exclusion of the others. Each has merit and purpose. However, one cannot communicate a child's status very well without first clarifying which standard applies when reporting a child's accomplishments.

As noted, the first standard concerns the child's performance in relation to his or her previous status on the dimension of interest (speech, language, academic achievement, or some psychosocial area). This shows how much progress the child has made in the intervening time period. Sometimes the results can be quantified in terms of months or years of growth, for example, by pointing out that scores on a receptive vocabulary test have moved from 5 years, 6 months to 6 years, 3 months in 1 calendar year, or by comparing grade equivalence scores over the same period of time.

Often the child's progress does not lend itself to easy quantification, such as when considering the complexity, appropriateness, or quality of verbal language, or when viewing a child's increased confidence and ability to engage in oral communication. Quantitative comparisons, in dimensions that lend themselves to such analysis, are the easiest to make and are very valuable. Qualitative comparisons, in dimensions not easily quantifiable, are more difficult to make but are, nevertheless, equally valuable.

Teachers and therapists should not make the mistake of ignoring a dimension because it cannot be measured or reported easily. In such cases, periodic, detailed descriptions of a child's behavior will provide the basis for future comparisons. In many respects, a child's personal growth over time is the most important standard one can apply. Basically the question is, given this particular child's potential, is he or she making the progress we would predict and hope for? This question is answered when the goal component of the IEP is completed correctly.

The second standard mentioned is less useful but still valuable. Here the child's progress is considered in respect to his or her hearing-impaired peers. In order to make this a valid comparison, one must look at studies that report performance data on *mainstreamed* hearing-impaired children (Brackett & Maxon, 1986; Davis, Shepard, Stelmachowicz, & Gorga, 1981; Shepard, Davis, Gorga, & Stelmachowicz, 1981). However, the heterogeneity of hearing losses displayed by hearing-impaired children is simply immense. One is not likely to find group data on children whose hearing losses are similar to those of the specific hearing-impaired child in question.

The data available from the Center for Assessment and Demographic Studies at Gallaudet College are sometimes helpful when using this second standard (see Schildroth & Karchmer, 1986, for an excellent review). While

these data refer mainly to children in organized special education programs, many of the subjects display hearing losses comparable to the
mainstreamed hearing-impaired children who are the focus of this book.
Thus, their performance does provide some basis for evaluating the status
of a particular child. This kind of performance comparison can assist in
placement decisions. A child may be doing quite poorly in comparison
with normal-hearing peers but much better than children with similar
hearing losses in more restrictive educational settings. Obviously the professional must consider both of these comparisons when making a placement decision for a particular child.

The last but perhaps most important standard that should be used in
evaluating a hearing-impaired child's school performance has already been
alluded to. It is one that many professionals consider "unfair": comparing
a child's performance to his or her *normal-hearing* peers. This kind of
comparison cannot be avoided if one assumes that a hearing-impaired
child can be, or is, appropriately placed in a mainstream setting.

The professional literature contains comments to the effect that separate tests and performance norms must be developed for hearing-impaired
children because they make up a separate population and must be considered on their own terms. This reasoning is specious for one basic reason.
Hearing-impaired children are anything but homogeneous in the one
dimension that distinguishes them from normal-hearing children—the
extent and history of their hearing impairments. Considering a "norm" for
a child with no measurable hearing as being the same as for a child with a
50 dB loss in the better ear simply does not make sense. Lumping all these
children together under one norm tends to lower the expected standard of
achievement to some lowest common denominator.

We have been miseducating hard-of-hearing children for years. Taking
the average performance measures of hearing-impaired children in general
and applying them to mainstreamed hearing-impaired children (most of
whom will be hard of hearing) means simply enshrining our poor results
of the past. It is not a question of being "fair" or "unfair," but only of
recognizing reality. How can teachers and therapists aspire to some measure of "normalcy" if we apply different, and lower, standards to the
expected achievements of mainstreamed hearing-impaired children? How
are informed educational placement decisions possible if we do not compare these youngsters to their normal-hearing classmates?

The point here is that all three standards are useful and all can be
applied appropriately to a particular child. It is necessary, however, to
specify the standard being used in different circumstances. On many occasions we have asked teachers and speech-language pathologists to tell us
how a child was doing, only to receive meaningless responses. To say, for
example, that a child is "doing well" says more about the teacher or

clinician than it does about the child. "Doing well" can simply mean that the child is not a disruptive presence in class. It does not describe how the child compares to his or her normal-hearing peers or whether IEP goals have been reached. When given this "doing well" response, we can almost hear the unspoken qualification, "for this kind of child." If a personal standard is being used, it should be so stated. We prefer comparisons to the generally recognized standards applied to normal-hearing children; otherwise, we are ignoring the real situation confronting a child and perhaps doing him or her a disservice by expecting too much or too little.

Personnel Considerations·

Speech-language pathologists and school-based audiologists will play a preeminent role in the management of hard-of-hearing children in regular schools. In our judgment, those who meet the American Speech-Language-Hearing Association (ASHA) standards for certification possess the requisite skills and background to serve as "case coordinators" or "case managers." The training of these specialists in the basic and clinical aspects of general communication disorders is directly transferable to the skills necessary to evaluate and manage the specific communication handicap displayed by hearing-impaired children. To be sure, additional skills and information are necessary—indeed that is the purpose of this book—and these specialists can hardly manage the entire program by themselves. However, someone who works within the public school must serve as the resident "expert" regarding the educational programming of hearing-impaired children. The ASHA Committee on Rehabilitative Audiology has outlined the competencies required by professionals who work with hearing-impaired children. In our estimation, any professional who possesses these competencies (see Appendix B) is qualified to work with mainstreamed hearing-impaired children.

Several survey studies have demonstrated the need for rigorous pre- and in-service training of speech-language pathologists in order to prepare them to work with hearing-impaired children in the regular schools (Woodford, 1987; Lass et al., 1989). About 70% of the surveyed professionals worked with hearing-impaired children, but their practical knowledge of hearing aids was unacceptably limited. Most, for example, did not know that the microphone is deactivated when a hearing aid is set on the "T" (telephone) setting. A majority did not know what caused hearing aid feedback (an audible squeal), how to check a battery with a voltmeter, or how to insert a battery in the hearing aid. Most did not look at the earmold to check for the possibility of cerumen blocking the tip. To their credit, most of the participants in the study were well aware of the deficiencies in their training and, presumably, would be receptive to the idea of an intense in-service training program.

In many regular school systems, teachers of the hearing impaired work on an itinerant basis with mainstreamed hearing-impaired children. Many of these teachers have transcended their primary training with "deaf" children and have become extremely effective in working with children whose primary receptive modality is auditory. They are clearly able to assume the case coordinator role with the mainstreamed hearing-impaired child. Whichever professional takes on this responsibility, this is the one who must coordinate the diverse contributions of a number of specialists, organize and schedule educational planning meetings, and work closely with the classroom teacher regarding the implementation of the IEP. The suggestion that one of these professionals function as the case coordinator does not imply a superior role for that person. In the schools, the classroom teacher is the central educational figure for all children enrolled in the class, "special" needs or no. Indeed, the efforts of the case coordinator, and of all the supportive and administrative personnel in the school as well, make the most sense when viewed from the perspective of the classroom teacher. The children are in the classroom for most of the school day, and if therapeutic efforts are to be most effective, it is the classroom teacher who must take the time and bear the responsibility for putting it all together.

The results of surveys conducted around the country strongly indicate the need to upgrade classroom teachers with respect to their knowledge of the impact of a hearing loss and the management of such children in their classrooms (Lass et al., 1985; Lass, Tecca, & Woodford, 1987; Martin, Bernstein, Daly, & Cody, 1988). Most of the teachers surveyed reported their willingness to include hearing-impaired children in their classrooms, but only if they were provided with substantial support and if an in-service training program were provided. Their attitude toward mainstreaming was generally positive, but the majority did not have much confidence in their current ability to teach hearing-impaired children effectively. The mainstreaming of these children can hardly be successful if the "front-line" educators, the classroom teachers, do not receive the specialized knowledge and support they require.

The classroom teacher and the case coordinator are but two of the members of the interdisciplinary team that should be organized to oversee the management of each mainstreamed hearing-impaired child. Other members may be the school psychologist, the social worker, the special educator, and the building principal; anyone, in other words, who can contribute to the management of the particular child. The combined contribution of different specialists, with varied perspectives and expertise, can far surpass any one individual's effort. And always, at every stage, the involvement of parents is crucial.

2

Performance of Mainstreamed Hearing-Impaired Children

As noted in the preceding chapter, hard-of-hearing children, who are able to use the auditory channel as a primary input mode, are 15–30 times more common than deaf children, whose primary receptive mode is visual. In the terms of the literature, however, this situation appears to be reversed. Very little performance data exists on large groups of hearing-impaired children in the regular schools, most of whom are hard of hearing. There are fragments here and there, which will be reviewed, but nothing comparable to the demographic studies on hearing-impaired children published by the Center for Assessment and Demographic Studies (formerly the Office for Demographic Studies) at Gallaudet University.

The basic reason for this deficit is that hearing-impaired children in regular school settings ordinarily are not enrolled in special programs and thus are not easily accessible for group studies. Rather, they are scattered in mainstream settings throughout the country, posing a challenge for a single public school administration to collect information regarding their performance. Indeed, it is also difficult for researchers even to determine whether such children are enrolled in particular school systems and how many there are. This is an unfortunate situation. Such data would enable relatively valid generalizations regarding these students' status and would permit a comparison of their accomplishments with those of normal-hearing children as well as with those of hearing-impaired children enrolled in special educational settings.

The answer to this information gap is not to abstract data on children with lesser degrees of hearing loss from larger studies in special education settings and to consider that the results represent fully mainstreamed children with comparable hearing losses. The picture so derived likely would portray an overly pessimistic view of the performance potential of the latter group. Generally speaking, children in special settings display greater degrees of hearing loss than do hearing-impaired children in mainstream settings. Even if one were to match the degree of loss, children in special settings ordinarily differ with respect to number of multiple problems, socioeconomic status, and ethnic background (Schildroth & Karchmer, 1986). Lacking, however, large-scale studies on mainstreamed hearing-impaired children, the discussion that follows here occasionally will review data taken from hearing-impaired children in special settings. It is important to note that their status represents the lower and not the higher end of a performance continuum.

In all the dimensions of performance considered in this chapter, one should bear in mind that for the most part research reports consider only the *average* results of a given group of children. Such data can assist in understanding the general effect of a hearing loss in a specific area but cannot validly predict the effect of this sensory deficit for a particular child. The heterogeneity of hearing-impaired children in the mainstream, in terms of their hearing losses and accomplishments, was clearly demonstrated over a period of years in the University of Connecticut Mainstream Project (Brackett & Maxon, 1986). The difference, therefore, between an average and an individual's actual performance, between group and individual data, is an important distinction for the clinician/teacher to understand. Success is not achieved because a child's scores are comparable to the average, but instead when the child reaches his or her own potential. The data in the sections that follow are presented to familiarize professionals with the *general* impact of a hearing loss, and not to define therapeutic goals for a particular child.

SPEECH PERCEPTION

The comprehension of a speech message entails more than the detection, discrimination, and identification of its acoustic components. In a conversational exchange, the listener ordinarily does not attend to acoustic/phonetic features, nor indeed does he or she even consciously focus on specific lexicon or grammar. The concern, rather, is with meaning—that is, comprehending the message the speaker intends to convey. We accomplish this feat as economically as possible, in terms of how much informational detail we need to derive from the utterance in order to understand the speaker (Boothroyd, 1978). Normal-hearing persons with a normal background of language often can grasp the meaning of an utterance using only a fraction of all the available acoustic information. They can bypass much of the acoustic, phonetic, lexical, and grammatical detail contained in a speech signal because they share with the speaker much the same intuitive grasp of the language. Speaker and listener share a learned, though usually unconscious, knowledge regarding the probabilities of phoneme sequence and occurrence, the grammatical and lexical constraints in any spoken message, and the rules underlying discourse as related to the situation and the relative status of the participants (the pragmatics of spoken English). When normal-hearing listeners are faced with ambiguity, either acoustically or linguistically, they delve as deeply as necessary into the message, right down to the basic acoustic/phonetic components, until the ambiguity is resolved. From this perspective, speech perception requires at least as much "brain work" as "ear work" (Fry, 1978).

For the normal-hearing listener, then, speech perception is usually a global process, a search for meaning. A prerequisite is shared competency in the language of the speaker. For the normal-hearing listener, this competency in general is easily and effortlessly achieved through language development mediated by audition, and it includes the ability to discriminate auditorily and identify the acoustic/phonetic features of speech (Ling, 1978a).

The hearing-impaired child is deficient in the ability to discriminate between similar acoustic elements, which consequently impairs his or her capacity to identify the acoustic/phonetic features of speech. Because of impaired hearing, such children are unable to develop the same competent and intuitive grasp of the language as do their normal-hearing peers. From the speech fragments they receive, they cannot creatively reconstruct the intended message. For them, impaired hearing serves as a "bottleneck" that reduces the amount of acoustic information delivered to their brains. They cannot, by means of a rich inner language matrix, synthesize the acoustic fragments into a meaningful message. They cannot employ their hearing to get to the global comprehension of meaning without an extraordinary focus on the foundations of perception, the acoustic/phonetic elements (Levitt, 1978). The knowledge of hearing-impaired children's ability to perceive these elements is, therefore, essential to a rational program of auditory learning. One must understand their present status in order to move beyond it.

There is no question that most hearing-impaired children have difficulty with speech discrimination tests, as supported by an abundance of clinical reports. What is not readily available, however, is controlled research that presents normative information or detailed analyses of their speech discrimination abilities. This is partly inherent in the usual condition of administering such tests. Many congenitally hearing-impaired children, particularly those with greater degrees of hearing loss, cannot be tested by conventional means because of their deficient speech and language and their inability to write responses to speech stimuli.

Precisely this problem motivated the development of closed-set picture identification tests, which do not require a verbal or a written response (Ross & Lerman, 1970; Katz & Elliot, 1978). The *Word Intelligibility by Picture Identification* (WIPI; Ross & Lerman, 1970) is a closed-set response test in which the examinee selects from a matrix of six pictures the one that corresponds to the stimulus word. In one study using the WIPI, 21 hard-of-hearing children, whose losses in the better ear ranged from 49 to 88 dB, achieved an average word recognition score of 59% (Ross, Kessler, Phillips, & Lerman, 1972). Chance scores average around 16 to 20%, and no credit is given for partially correct answers. Specific information on the nature of the perceptual errors was not obtained in this study.

Byers (1973) presents a more analytical view of the speech perception abilities of young hard-of-hearing children. This study evaluated the initial consonant intelligibility of 12 hard-of-hearing children, ranging in age from 10 to 16 years, with an average hearing loss of 41 dB. Using conventional speech discrimination measures (recorded W-22 monosyllabic word lists), the children achieved a mean score of 66%. Byers also administered the *Fairbanks Rhyme Speech Discrimination Test* (Fairbanks, 1958) at five sensation levels (10, 15, 20, 30, and 40 dB), and he analyzed the children's responses as a function of sensation level (SL). At low SLs, the scores for all the stop consonants (/p/, /b/, /t/, /k/, /g/) were poor. As the SL increased, so did the scores. The nasals (/m/ and /n/) also showed poor scores at low SLs and higher scores at increasing SLs. The semivowels /r/, /l/, and /w/, on the other hand, were highly intelligible even at low SLs. The poorest scores at all SLs were achieved with the /f/ phoneme, which is not only one of the weakest phonemes in the English language but is also of high frequency spectral composition. Surprisingly, considering its similar high frequency composition, the /s/ phoneme received moderately high recognition at all SLs. It should be noted, however, that only initial consonant errors were evaluated; other research has shown that they tend to be easier to perceive than consonants in the final position.

Table 2.1 presents an error analysis of Byers's (1973) findings, showing the most common confusions exhibited by the children. Each number represents the percentage of responses to the indicated phoneme stimulus.

TABLE 2.1 Percentage of Response to the Stimuli Phonemes for a Group of 12 Hard-of-Hearing Children

		P	T	K	F	S	H	M	N	B	D	G	W	R	L
Stimulus	P	41	16	15	7	8	7								
	T	7	59	20		9									
	K	7	7	69		9									
	F	9	7		43	30									
	S				8	73									
	H		10	10	10	12	51								
	M							59	28						11
	N							13	79						
	B						10			48	22				
	D									12	69				
	G										8	78			
	W												63	28	
	R													81	
	L														73

Note. From "Initial Consonant Intelligibility by Hearing-Impaired Children" by V. B. Byers, 1973, *Journal of Speech and Hearing Research, 16,* pp. 48–55. Copyright 1973 by the American Speech-Hearing-Language Association. Adapted by permission.

Thus, for example, on being presented with a /p/, subjects responded correctly 41% of the time and incorrectly identified the /p/ as a /t/ and /k/ 16% and 15% of the time, respectively.

As one can discern from Table 2.1, the most common errors made by the children concerned place of articulation, while the features of voicing, manner, and nasality usually were retained. For example, the voiceless plosives /t/, /p/, and /k/ were confused with each other but rarely with a voiced sound (the original data show some minor exceptions); this same effect occurred with the voiced plosives /d/, /b/, and /g/. Nasals tended to be confused with one another and seldom with other phonemes. The same finding is evident with the phonemes /s/ and /f/, which were more often confused with one another than with nonfricative sounds. Interestingly, the percentage of errors to and from particular phonemes was not always reciprocal. Thus, when the stimulus was /w/, for example, the /r/ was selected 28% of the time. When the stimulus was /r/, the /w/ was almost never chosen.

The difference in speech perception skills between hard-of-hearing and deaf children was investigated by Gordon (1987) as a component of a major longitudinal study on hearing-impaired children's development of language and communication skills (Levitt, McGarr, & Geffner, 1987). In this study, a pure-tone average of 80 dB or more in the better ear was used to distinguish deaf from hard-of-hearing children. Although the differences in speech perception between these two groups was statistically significant, with the hard-of-hearing children making fewer errors, the pattern of phonemic errors was similar for the two groups. Both groups displayed the greatest difficulty in perceiving place of articulation, less difficulty in perceiving voicing, and least difficulty in perceiving manner of articulation.

In a study composed mainly of severely hearing-impaired subjects, Boothroyd (1984) also implicated place of articulation as the feature most susceptible to the effects of a sensorineural hearing loss, followed by the perception of initial consonant voicing and initial consonant continuance. He also showed that some vowel and voicing perceptions and correct syllabic and rhythmic identification can be made even by children with profound (105–114 dB) hearing losses. Boothroyd further speculated that this performance probably represented minimal estimates of their auditory capacity. That is, if such children could be assured of appropriate early intervention procedures and consistently high-quality amplification, their auditory performance might have been even better.

The Gordon and Boothroyd studies support the questions raised on the diagnostic and performance bases for determining who is and is not a deaf child. In these studies and others (McGarr, 1987), the so-called "deaf" children were able to identify correctly acoustic stimuli of various degrees of difficulty. In other words, they were "hearing." As Boothroyd (1984) pointed out, the auditory potential of such children might have permitted them to function primarily auditorily (our definition of a hard-of-hearing person) if their auditory residuum had been employed early and effectively. Current clinical experience at a number of centers supports this observation.

Owens (1978) summarizes the findings of a number of projects on speech perception that he and his colleagues conducted over the years. This article reports on the results obtained with 550 sensorineural hearing-

TABLE 2.2 Error Probabilities of Phonemes in Initial and Final Positions

Initial Stimulus	Error %*	Final Stimulus	Error %*
s	41	s	53
p	40	p	51
k	38	z	47
d	35	k	46
θ	35	b	44
ʃ	33	t	42
b	33	f	41
t	29	θ	39
tʃ	26	tʃ	38
dʒ	26	dʒ	38
w	18	v	38
h	17	d	35
g	16	ʃ	31
f	15	g	22
v	11	n	11
l	8	l	5
r	6	m	5
		ŋ	3
		r	0

*Ss = 550 sensorineural hearing-impaired adults
Note. From "Consonant Errors and Remediation in Sensorineural Hearing Loss" by E. Owens, 1978, *Journal of Speech and Hearing Disorders, 43*, pp. 331–347. Copyright 1978 by the American Speech-Hearing-Language Association. Adapted by permission.

impaired adults who responded to the *California Consonant Test* (Owens & Schubert, 1977), a closed-set speech discrimination test designed to elicit responses in either the initial *(pin, thin, shin, kin)* or final *(leaf, leash, leap, leak)* position. The subject hears one of the words and responds by underlining one of the four possible written choices. Because of the nature of the tests used with the adult subjects, the probabilities are that a similar test administered to children would produce the same pattern of results. The ensuing discussion therefore will assume that these findings also apply to hard-of-hearing children. Table 2.2, adapted from the Owens study, gives the percentage of times errors could be expected for the different phonemes in the initial and final position in words.

126625

Some interesting generalities are evident. First, the error percentages are greater in the final than the initial position, a consistent finding in a number of other studies as well (Boothroyd, 1984; Dubno, Dirks, & Langhofer, 1982; Danhauer, Abdale, Johnson, & Asp, 1986). It is more difficult to perceive the final consonant in a word than the initial one, possibly because the final position tends to be acoustically weaker than the same phoneme in the initial position.

Second, the magnitude of the error percentage is surprisingly high. These data indicate that a subject with no contextual cues would err on the /s/ phoneme in the initial position 41% of the time and in the final position 53% of the time. As Table 2.2 shows, the error percentage exceeds 25% for 23 of the phonemes when both the initial and the final positions are considered. Inasmuch as the data were obtained with a 4-item multiple-choice response (for which chance alone would permit 25% correct answers), the magnitude of these errors is even more impressive.

Finally, as Owens (1978) points out, if errors below 20% are disregarded, 10 consonants are represented in both the initial and final positions (/p/, /t/, /k/, /tʃ/, /d/, /s/, /ʃ/, /θ/, /b/, and /dʒ/) and four are in the final position only (/f/, /z/, /v/, and /g/). Difficulties in consonant recognition, then, essentially reduce to these 14 phonemes (several others were omitted from the test because of the difficulty in developing suitable foils).

In addition to knowing what the error probabilities are for different consonants in the initial and final positions in words, it is important to understand the pattern of the substitutions made when a phoneme is perceived incorrectly. Table 2.3 shows the most frequent consonant substitutions that Owens (1978) found. Substitution probabilities less than 10% have been omitted. The response substitutions are given in decreasing order of frequency; thus, for example, in the initial position for the stimulus /p/, the largest percentage of substitutions occurred with the consonant /t/, then /k/ and /θ/. It should be pointed out that the nature of this study did not permit an analysis of the error category of "omission," which is a frequent error made by hearing-impaired children (Danhauer et al., 1986).

Comparing the data in Table 2.1 taken from Byers (1973) with the Owens (1978) initial consonant data (Table 2.3), one sees more similarities than differences. Most of the substitution errors involve consonants with different positions but the same manner of articulation. In the final position, the predominant pattern of errors relates to place of articulation. However, more manner substitution errors (e.g., fricative substitutions for plosives, and vice versa) occur here than in the initial position. Because previous data clearly pointed out that errors rarely cross the voice/voiceless boundary and that nasals are seldom substituted for non-nasal sounds, possibilities for these kinds of substitutions were not included in the Owens (1978) study.

TABLE 2.3 Consonant Errors Most Frequently Given in Response to the Indicated Consonant Stimuli in the Initial and Final Positions

Initial Stimulus	Responses	Final Stimulus	Responses
p	t k θ	p	t f k
t	p k	t	p k f
k	t p	k	t p
tʃ	t	tʃ	t k θ s
s	θ f ʃ t	s	θ f t p
ʃ	s tʃ	ʃ	f tʃ s
f	No percentages greater than 10%	f	p t s
θ	s	θ	p t k
b	v	b	ð d
d	b g	d	b v
		dʒ	d b v
		z	v d
		v	z d b

Note. Substitution errors are listed in decreasing order of occurrence. From "Consonant Errors and Remediation in Sensorineural Hearing Loss" by E. Owens, 1978, *Journal of Speech and Hearing Disorders, 43*, pp. 331–347. Copyright 1978 by the American Speech-Hearing-Language Association. Adapted by permission.

Dubno et al. (1982) essentially confirmed and extended these findings, as well as implicating place of articulation as the most significant factor affecting the speech perception capabilities of those who are hard of hearing. In addition, however, they found that the number of consonant errors was greater in certain vowel environments than others. For example, there were more errors with the high front vowel /i/ than with /a/ and /u/. This probably occurred because the high-frequency energy that characterizes place of articulation was further emphasized by the high-frequency second formant of the front vowels.

The configuration of the pure-tone threshold has a direct and consistent effect on the nature of the speech perception errors that are made. Owens (1978) reported that subjects with pure-tone configurations showing a drop at 2000 Hz had difficulty perceiving the phonemes /s/, initial /t/, and /θ/, but not /ʃ/, /tʃ/, or /dʒ/. Difficulty with the latter group occurred only when the configuration showed a sharp drop at 1000 Hz. Dubno et al. (1982) also reported additional errors with these high-frequency consonants as audiometric slope increased. This observation accords very well with data on the acoustic composition of the different groups of phonemes (Levitt, 1978). The voiceless fricatives and the initial /t/ contain most of their acoustic energy above 2000 Hz, while the affricates still display a significant amount of energy below 2000 Hz.

Reemphasizing a point made previously, although much of the data presented in this section came from studies with adults, one can reasonably assume their validity with regard to moderately and severely hearing-impaired children as well. There are bound to be differences, of course, because of the diminished language base of such children compared to adventitiously hard-of-hearing adults. However, the nature of the tests employed (closed-response monosyllable or nonsense syllable tests) minimizes language skills as a factor contributing to the results obtained, and thus permits accepting the results as reasonably reflecting the speech perception skills of most hearing-impaired children. Nevertheless, as pointed out earlier, the individual results obtained by a specific child must be the focus of any therapeutic effort, not these general findings.

Further, these analytic tests do not necessarily predict how a hearing-impaired person, child or adult, will function when confronted with a steady stream of speech. The co-articulations that occur in all running speech samples modify the acoustic product and present perceptual cues that are not present when phoneme perception is analyzed in isolation or only in a syllabic context. When exposed to large speech samples, a child can call upon many paralinguistic, contextual, and linguistic factors to aid his or her speech perception. Therefore, the greater a child's language capabilities, the better speech comprehension is likely to be, independent of the degree of hearing loss.

SPEECH PRODUCTION

Except for those with very mild deficits, children with congenital hearing losses generally will display some type of speech problem. Within broad limits, the more severe the hearing loss, the more deviant and less intelligible is the speech produced (Montgomery, 1967; Gold & Levitt, 1975; Markides, 1970; Monsen, 1978; Boothroyd, 1978; Wolk & Schildroth, 1986; Gordon, 1987). The differences between the speech of deaf and hard-of-hearing children appear to be more quantitative than qualitative. That is, hard-of-hearing children tend to make the same kinds of errors that deaf children do, just fewer of them (Gold & Levitt, 1975; Gordon, 1987), resembling in some of their productions the speech of much younger normal-hearing children (Oller & Kelly, 1974; McDermott & Jones, 1984).

The literature offers a fairly good consensus regarding the nature of speech production errors made by hard-of-hearing children. Omissions of consonants, particularly in the word-final position, apparently constitute the majority (Gordon, 1987), with the next most frequent error being substitution (although McDermott & Jones, 1984, found this relationship reversed). Accompanying the omission of the final consonant is the prolongation and nasalization of the preceding vowel. It is as if the child, realizing that "something" is there and unable to identify it accurately, alters the preceding vowel in consequence of the imperfect perception. Final consonants often are either unstressed or acoustically weak, thus not easily perceived by the hearing-impaired child. Following omissions and substitutions, distortions are the next most frequent errors in the speech production of consonants.

Examining the frequency of speech production errors by manner of production reveals that the largest number of errors involve (in order) affricates (tʃ, dʒ), fricatives (f, v, θ, ð, s, z, ʃ, h), stops (p, b, t, d, k, g), nasals (m, n, ŋ), and glides and laterals (w, r, j, l). This same order of difficulty occurs with severely hearing-impaired children (McDermott & Jones, 1984) as well as with deaf children (Gordon, 1987).

If the data are examined in terms of place of speech production, the greatest number of errors emerge with the lingua-palatal phonemes (ʃ, tʃ, dʒ, r), followed by the lingua-alveolar (t, d, s, z, n, l), lingua-dental (θ, ð), lingua-velar (k, g, ŋ), labio-dental (f, v), glottal (h), and bilabial (p, b, m, w), in decreasing order. As with manner of articulation, deaf children display the same sequence of errors but make more of them (Gordon, 1987).

The type and frequency of speech production errors are similar to, and appear to reflect, the errors made in speech perception (see Tables 2.1, 2.2, and 2.3). Consonants using tongue-tip placement, as well as fricatives and affricates, are more likely to be omitted or distorted than are other consonants. These consonants require fine-motor coordination and accurate timing, and they are developed later by normal-hearing children. Hard-of-hearing children are also prone to omit one component of an affricate (e.g., uttering /t/ for /ts/) or to distort the phoneme entirely. Although there are exceptions, the most visible phonemes, such as the bilabials and labio-dentals, are produced correctly more often than are less visible phonemes.

Other speech problems manifested by many hard-of-hearing children involve compound or abutting consonants (DiCarlo, 1968). In running speech, such adjacent phonemes should be articulated as consonant blends or affricates. The difficulty that hearing-impaired children have with these phonemes reflects deficiencies in their ability to co-articulate utterances; that is, to appropriately pre-plan the articulatory movements in running speech.

Hard-of-hearing children generally do not experience much difficulty in producing vowels accurately. In the Gordon (1987) study, only 18% of the vowels were produced in error. When errors were made, they most often were substitutions to vowels in close proximity in the vowel quadrilateral. That is, the children's vowel substitutions usually were correct in terms of tongue frontness but were wrong in terms of tongue height or tension. The most frequent vowel errors were tense-lax substitutions between the high front (ee) and high back (oo) vowels.

Hard-of-hearing children as a group do not manifest the voice quality and suprasegmental deviations that profoundly hearing-impaired children do. Those who sound more "normal" to a listener are those who use audition to monitor vocal output. Without the use of audition, it is much more difficult to develop the suprasegmental aspects of vocal output normally than it is the segmental phonemes, for which other cues (visual, tactile, and proprioceptive) can serve as alternative monitoring modes for articulatory placements. Supporting this conclusion, a study by Whitehead and Jones (1976) examined the duration of vowels in various consonant environments for normal-hearing, hard-of-hearing, and deaf children. These researchers found that hard-of-hearing children's modifications of vowel durations in different consonant environments were much more like normal-hearing children's than deaf children's. They attributed the hard-of-hearing children's ability to make these fine time distinctions in their speech to the use of audition in monitoring vocal output. It is important to note, however, that the suprasegmental dimensions of speech can be perceived and monitored even by children with the classic "left-corner" audiograms, those hearing-impaired children for whom audition does not serve as a *primary* communication mode.

West and Weber (1973) performed a detailed phonological analysis of a hard-of-hearing 4-year-old, using the child's spontaneous utterances as material. This girl had a 58 dB average hearing loss in her right ear and a 68 dB loss in the left. Half of her utterances were wordlike and intelligible, and half were not. Even those that were not understood, however, were not babble or nonsense, but were recognizable as linguistically structured units. Although this study examined the speech of only one child, interestingly the findings conformed closely to the group results of the larger scale studies reported previously.

No consonant phoneme classes were uttered correctly all the time in all contexts. Those that were fairly well established (i.e., correct over 75% of the time) were /b/, /m/, /p/, /w/, /n/, /k/, and /h/, predominantly the easily visible bilabials. Correct more than 50% but less than 75% of the time were /d/, /tʃ/, /f/, /r/, /y/, /l/, and /t/. These phonemes require greater tongue-tip control than the previous group and thus are intrinsically more difficult. These are also phonemes that a normal-hearing young child might have some difficulty articulating, although he or she would master them at a younger age than would a hard-of-hearing child. (This observation supports the notion that hard-of-hearing children show phonological development similar to younger normal-hearing children.) The last 10 consonants— /g/, /dʒ/, /v/, /θ/, /ð/, /z/, /ʃ/, /dʒ/, and /ŋ/—were not established at all at the time of the study. Most of these are also more difficult for the young normal-hearing child to produce correctly. No deviation in vowel production was reported. In summary, the child showed the expected pattern of development, gradually improving in ability to produce finer contrasts in her speech.

A host of factors, many of which are beyond control, will influence the specific errors demonstrated by a particular child. Once the child's hearing loss is detected, however, one does have some control over the quality of the total therapeutic program offered. Speech production errors (as well as the other consequences of the hearing loss) can and should be minimized by appropriate intervention. Although a later section will discuss therapeutic programs at length, it is timely to observe now that if a particular elementary-age child were to manifest the number and kind of errors just described, we would make two assumptions: either the child has not yet received therapy, or the therapy that has been offered is grossly inadequate. The speech production goal with hard-of-hearing children should be normal suprasegmental and segmental output. For more profoundly hearing-impaired children with some measurable residual hearing, the goal should be acceptable suprasegmental features and intelligible, if not normal, speech.

AUDIOVISUAL PERCEPTION OF SPEECH

Studies concerning the purely visual perception of speech—speechreading—will not be reviewed here; such data are available or can be extracted from studies having other purposes (see the impressive monograph edited by De Filipo & Sims, 1988). In our view, a focus on speechreading per se does not jibe with the reality faced by hearing-impaired children with usable residual hearing. Indeed, when speechreading becomes a main focus of therapy for such children, it actually may impede the implementation of a rational therapeutic approach.

The emphasis on speechreading for hard-of-hearing children appears to stem from not making the appropriate distinctions between the hard-of-hearing and the deaf child. In the oral education of the deaf, communication and language development through speechreading are intrinsic components of the approach. Without speechreading, oralism does not exist for the deaf child. Because historically professionals did not distinguish sufficiently between hard-of-hearing and deaf children, they tended to apply to the one a teaching method developed for the other. The practice of scheduling hard-of-hearing children for speechreading lessons then assumed credibility as a legitimate therapy approach. This is not to suggest that the practice of speechreading as the sole or primary means of receptive communication is inappropriate for many deaf children. It is, however, not appropriate as the primary means of communication for the majority of the hearing impaired (most of whom are functionally hard of hearing).

In practice what happened, and what still appears to be happening, is that the focus on speechreading occurs at the expense of capitalizing on using residual hearing, either by itself or in conjunction with visual cues (a bisensory approach). It is quite easy to devise "lesson plans" for speech-reading. At the simplest level one only has to drop one's voice while talking to a child. Ensuring that residual hearing is correctly exploited is much more difficult.

The emphasis on speechreading as a major therapeutic focus continues for a number of reasons, the most important of which would seem to be professional inertia, poor training, limited background, and inadequate motivation. There is also another good reason: The term *speechreading* (or *lipreading*) has great public relations value. The public (including administrators and parents) thinks it knows what speechreading is. A therapist who "prescribes" a course of speechreading for a child receives figurative knowing nods from this public, which reasons that this child has trouble hearing, is therefore "deaf," and therefore needs speechreading training. In other words, because the child cannot use his or her hearing very well, one must stress the unimpaired modality—vision.

Several problems reside in this line of reasoning. First, there is no convincing evidence that one can *teach* children to speechread, beyond encouraging them to focus on the lips (which is not to say that many deaf children have not somehow *learned* to speechread). Indeed, some evidence shows that innate factors play a more significant role in speechreading than previously believed. This evidence suggests that ability to speechread may be related to the speed with which a visual sequence (lip, tongue, and jaw movements) is converted to neural messages and transmitted to the brain. Shepard, Delavergne, Frueh, and Clobridge (1977) found a correlation of .93 between the latency of a visually evoked electrical potential in the brain and speechreading ability. Later studies have extended and confirmed this initial result, with a multiple correlation of .84 between speechreading and a number of visually evoked waveforms (Samar & Sims, 1983; Shepard, 1982). Thus speechreading may be one of the many faculties for which human beings ordinarily show a wide range of innate capacities, restricting the efficacy of specific training.

Second, the dependence of a hard-of-hearing child on the visual aspects of a speech message varies according to the extent of the hearing loss, the nature of the amplification system being worn, and the masking effects of ambient noise in different environments. Rarely does such a child meet with communicative demands in which residual hearing cannot be utilized at all, particularly if there has been an effort to provide a good signal-to-noise ratio with an appropriate amplification device (see chapter 9). Speechreading training that omits the auditory signal is not only unrealistic, it may tap a different skill from that required for comprehending simultaneous visual and auditory clues. The amount of information received in a conversational situation changes continually. On rare occasions only visual cues are available; at other times complete comprehension can be achieved through the auditory channel alone. A good point of departure in any training situation is replicating the real world as much as possible. Therefore, the most plausible training situation is one in which a child receives audiovisual messages with varying types and levels of competing noise.

Finally, as was alluded to earlier, speechreading actually emphasizes the less efficient modality with regard to developing and comprehending language. Audition, not vision, is the channel through which human beings most efficiently demonstrate their biologically determined capacity to receive and generate the spoken word (Liberman, Cooper, Shankweiller, & Studert-Kennedy, 1967). When great emphasis is placed on the visual by-products of the spoken word, audition gets relegated to a supportive role, and children who are exposed to such a program become primarily visual rather than auditory communicators.

Visual cues (speechreading) *should* be employed to enhance a hearing-impaired child's total perception of speech. As a matter of fact, it is essential that these children use their eyes to complement the information they receive through their ears. The point is simply that the auditory channel, whenever possible, should be the dominant one. A great deal of evidence demonstrates that audiovisual reception is clearly superior to that obtained by any single modality (Garstecki, 1988).

Erber (1974) reported on four studies demonstrating that for severely hearing-impaired children the mean advantage of audiovisual perception over speechreading alone ranged between 19% and 28%. Ross, Kessler, Phillips, and Lerman (1972) reported the same advantage to be 20% for 26 such children. Ling, Leckie, Pollack, Simser, and Smith (1981) compared audiovisual reception to that obtained by a single modality for 24 children with an average hearing loss of 102 dB in the better ear. These subjects had auditory development continually stressed in their training program. Ling et al. found an audiovisual improvement of 20% compared to the score obtained through speechreading only. Possibly these children could discern the acoustic/phonetic characteristics of speech and not just the time-intensity pattern, contrary to prevailing belief in view of the extent of their hearing losses.

It is important to make a distinction between unimodal and bimodal recognition scores and the development of language via a single or a combined sensory modality. The foregoing evidence is unambiguous as to the advantage of audiovisual *recognition* of speech. But whether language *development* can occur through, or is fostered by, such bisensory inputs remains unknown. Some recent evidence (Dodd & Burnham, 1988) suggests both that bisensory processing is a normal feature of normal child development and that the implications of this fact for the hearing-impaired child must be addressed. These investigators found that normal-hearing children as young as 4 months were aware of the synchrony between lip movements and speech sound, and even children as young as 10 weeks preferred to focus on the face of someone speaking their own language rather than a foreign language. Dodd and Burnham suggest that speechreading cues are an integral part of the speech perception process, and that "phonological information, whether perceived by eye or by ear, is combined into one processing code" (1988, p. 57). For these authors, this implies the need to employ an audiovisual mode in training hearing-impaired children because such a combination can provide more information than either mode separately.

Without minimizing the potency of audition in the training of hearing-impaired children, the possibility that language development can be fostered by an audiovisual approach certainly appears exciting, particularly when considering the severely and profoundly hearing-impaired child. Further, recent research with children and adults using cochlear implants and vibrotactile systems supports this possibility (Boothroyd, 1988), as do the perceptual processes underlying bimodal reception.

In the earlier review of the typical speech perception errors that hearing-impaired people make, it was noted that their greatest difficulty arises in perceiving consonants with different places, though the same manner, of articulation (Tables 2.1 and 2.3). Thus, for example, the stop-plosives /t/ and /k/ often are confused with /p/, and vice versa; /b/ and /g/ with /d/, and vice versa; and the voiceless fricatives /th/ and /f/ with /s/. Rarely do auditory errors cross the voice/voiceless boundary in cognate phonemes (e.g., between /t/ and /d/). This, together with the following observation, suggests that nature has provided us with an excellent opportunity to use vision and audition complementarily, with one modality providing the cues not readily available in the other.

Consider some typical homophenous (look alike on the lips) groupings: /b, p, m/; /f, v/; /θ, ð, ʃ, dʒ/; /t, d, n, s, z, k, g/ (Binnie, Montgomery, &

Jackson, 1974; Jackson, 1988). Research findings show that *visual* errors take place *within* and not *between* groups. That is, visually it is very difficult to detect differences in the movements of the phonemes within each category. Conversely, *auditory* errors are rarely made *within* a group because each is comprised mainly of phonemes that differ in voicing and manner of production, features relatively easy to hear. The errors made visually, in other words, are not generally those made auditorily, and vice versa. For example, in the word *fan* the /f/ could be confused auditorily with an /s/, but visually the /f/ in *fan* is quite distinct from /s/. The /n/ sound is confused auditorily with /m/, but never visually. If a severely hearing-impaired child, then, just heard the word *fan*, it could be confused with *sam* or *san*. With vision, however, the correct word would be apparent.

Almost perfect recognition is potentially possible therefore when visual and auditory cues are combined, at least for adults. The situation is not quite so promising for congenitally hearing-impaired youngsters, whose complementary use of visual and auditory cues is, of necessity, tied to the status of their language competencies. That is, if such a child does not know the meaning of a word, he or she will hardly be able to recognize it, even if all the features are perceptually salient. This reintroduces the speculative point made earlier: Can such bimodal saliency underlie or improve the *development* as opposed to the *recognition* of language? Considering the evidence that Dodd and Burnham (1988) are accumulating, as well as the complementary nature of the visual and auditory cues in speech, the possibility certainly exists and should be considered in planning a therapeutic program.

In practice, hard-of-hearing children seem to depend on vision only as much as is necessary for them to understand a message. When presented with an optimal auditory signal, as should occur with an FM auditory training system, these children tend to keep their eyes on their books or their work or, if taking a test, on their paper. They soon discover that they can depend on their auditory channel alone and do not continually require additional visual information.

When the acoustical situation is not optimal, as when using hearing aids in a noisy classroom, these children tend to keep their eyes on the speaker while the message is being presented. Only when the speaker has finished do they look down at their books or papers. Hard-of-hearing children learn, mostly quite unconsciously, that in such circumstances they require visual cues in order to understand the message. (This observation does not apply only to hard-of-hearing children. In such environments normal-hearing individuals, too, must depend more and more on visual clues as the acoustics become progressively degraded through noise or other distortions [Sumby & Pollack, 1954]). Thus the task with hearing-impaired children is to maximize the auditory possibilities available to them, and only then to encourage the complementary use of visual cues; the latter alone, however, is never a substitute for appropriate auditory management.

LANGUAGE ABILITIES

Vocabulary

Many hard-of-hearing children seem to function well in simple face-to-face communication, appearing to have no problem in comprehending the speaker and in making appropriate responses. However, during a conversation the participants select from their personal repertoires those language structures that seem appropriate to the situation, continually adjusting to the situational demands. Thus in extended conversations, particularly those involving abstract topics, the hearing-impaired child's language skills are seen to be much less flexible than those of normal-hearing peers. The skilled listener will soon detect pervasive language problems, one of the most important and underestimated of which relates to vocabulary knowledge.

Although the literature on the vocabulary status of hard-of-hearing children is not extensive, the studies that do exist are mutually supportive and accord very well with clinical impressions and experiences. Using the *Ammons Full-Range Vocabulary Test* (Ammons & Ammons, 1948), Young and McConnell (1957) found that 20 hard-of-hearing children (mean loss 51 dB) scored significantly lower than 20 comparable children with normal hearing. Their finding that no hard-of-hearing child did better than any of the normal-hearing subjects was particularly discouraging. One would hope, inasmuch as this study was conducted more than 30 years ago when amplification devices were much less accepted and available, that today such a complete dichotomy would not result. Our own experience (Brackett & Maxon, 1986) has revealed that *some* hard-of-hearing children perform better than *some* of their normal-hearing peers. Currently available therapeutic interventions give added cause for cautious optimism.

Markides (1970) reported a typical vocabulary status for hard-of-hearing and normal-hearing children. Using the Ammons test, he found a 2-to-3-year lag in the vocabulary development of hard-of-hearing subjects as compared to normal-hearing peers (which should be compared to the much larger gap found with educationally "deaf" children). Similar results regarding vocabulary status were found by Hamilton and Owrid (1974), with one interesting extension. These researchers evaluated three groups of children, persistent conductive hearing losses (average 32 dB in the better ear), mild sensorineural hearing losses (average 38 dB), and normal-hearing controls. Whereas the average vocabulary scores of the hearing-impaired groups was poorer than the normal-hearing group (as expected), children from higher socioeconomic backgrounds did better than those from lower socioeconomic backgrounds. Nonverbal intelligence test scores were the same for both groups. The superior results on the verbal tests related to the reading habits of the parents; that is, their better reading habits were associated with higher verbal scores for their children. The researchers concluded that the effect of hearing impairment is exacerbated in lower sociocultural backgrounds. Not surprisingly, it appears that parental expectations and parental examples can profoundly alter the consequences of a hearing loss.

The vocabulary deficit of hard-of-hearing children is also evident in a landmark study conducted by Davis (1974). She administered the *Boehm Test of Basic Concepts* (Boehm, 1967) to 24 hard-of-hearing children with hearing losses ranging from 35 to 70 dB in the better ear. The Boehm test consists of 50 picture displays, which represent verbal concepts selected from basic kindergarten, first-, and second-grade material. The test content includes vocabulary designed to assess a child's ability to identify space, time, quantity, and other concepts. Davis's results show that hard-of-hearing children's ability to recognize and respond appropriately to age-graded test vocabulary decreases as they get older. The scores for half of the 6-year-olds did not exceed the 50th percentile; the other half scored at or below the 10th percentile. Only 22% of the 7- and 8-year-olds scored at average levels, while 67% of the 7-year-olds and 83% of the 8-year-olds scored at or below the 10th percentile. In other words, as the hard-of-hearing children got older, the vocabulary gap relative to normal-hearing children increased. Table 2.4 presents the verbal concepts that these subjects found most difficult.

It is difficult to really get a "feel" for the vocabulary deficits exhibited by hard-of-hearing children only by looking at numbers, whether the latter represent percentages, chronological age gaps, or other criteria. More pertinent vocabulary problems are ignored than addressed by this quantitative approach. Much normal conversation is made up of idiomatic or metaphoric expressions, slang, and colloquialisms—in other words, combinations of words whose meanings cannot be sought in a literal translation of the individual words. All hearing-impaired children (the deaf more than the hard of hearing) have difficulty with word combinations that do not literally convey their dictionary meanings. Such expressions change with age, time, and place, and the hearing-impaired child has trouble "staying with it" or "going with the flow."

Synonyms present another example of vocabulary that causes difficulty. Such children often learn, or are taught, a single meaning for a word

TABLE 2.4 Percentage of Hard-of-Hearing and Normal-Hearing Children Responding Correctly to Indicated Verbal Concepts

	Hard of Hearing	**Normal Hearing**
Not first or last	58	100
Right	58	87
Forward	58	100
Above	58	100
Widest	54	100
As many	54	93
Beginning	54	87
Third	50	93
Left	45	87
Few	45	87
Always	45	87
Skip	41	87
Equal	41	87
Between	37	100
Separated	33	100
Medium-sized	29	93
Least	25	100
Pair	20	73

Note. From "Performance of Young Hearing-Impaired Children on a Test of Basic Concepts" by J. Davis, 1974, *Journal of Speech and Hearing Research, 17,* pp. 342–351. Copyright 1974 by the American Speech-Hearing-Language Association. Adapted by permission.

or, conversely, just one word to express a general concept (e.g., for bipedal locomotion, only the word *walk*, whereas normal-hearing individuals might use *amble, creep, dawdle, stride, hike, trudge, ramble, march, tramp,* or *traipse* to express nuances of the same basic concept).

Hearing-impaired schoolchildren frequently will have trouble with certain kinds of academic tasks, not because of the work itself but because they do not understand the vocabulary (and sometimes the syntax) of the directions. The vocabulary contained in Table 2.4 turns up frequently in directions for completing academic tasks. Obviously, success poses quite a feat for a child when he or she cannot even understand the instructions.

The problems are not over after the directions are explained (in simpler language, by example, through pantomime, etc.). Many of these children experience inordinate difficulty with academic (content area) vocabulary, which usually appears in the fourth or fifth grade. Teachers can assume that most of this new vocabulary either is already familiar to normal-hearing children or that there is sufficient linguistic context for them to comprehend meaning. Neither of these assumptions necessarily holds true for most hearing-impaired children, whose initial vocabulary development derives largely from the language addressed (and explained) directly to them, in already familiar contexts. These children do not hear or understand the incidental language that flows around them at home or at school. The normal-hearing child is immersed in the center of an extended language sphere; the hearing-impaired child, for the most part, perceives speech signals only from a small portion of that sphere. Using context to figure out the meaning of a new word is also very difficult when the language context itself is insufficiently understood. The mainstreamed hearing-impaired fifth-grader, suddenly exposed to words such as *photosynthesis, chlorophyll, ecology, producers, consumers, ecosystems, carnivore, omnivore,* and *herbivore* (all taken from a fifth-grade science text) can be easily overwhelmed and fall further behind, in both vocabulary and content, as the years progress.

Syntax

The syntactical performance of hard-of-hearing children does not differ as clearly as deaf children's from that of normal-hearing children (Quigley, 1978). The differences between hard-of-hearing and normal-hearing children appear in degree rather than in kind, with little difficulty evident for older hard-of-hearing children in the simpler syntactical constructions. As the reader will recall, this is the same impression one receives when evaluating the speech production development of hard-of-hearing children. The hearing loss apparently depresses the normal developmental growth pattern. Deviations, when they occur, seem due to insufficient and inadequate input at an appropriate developmental stage, with the children then using their linguistic rule-generating ability to create functional, though deviant, strategies for language comprehension and production. This interpretation is supported by two studies that specifically evaluated the linguistic capabilities of hard-of-hearing children and one that compared hearing-impaired children in self-contained educational settings (hearing losses 80 dB or greater in the better ear) with mainstreamed children (about half of whom had hearing losses less than 80 dB).

Wilcox and Tobin (1974) used a sentence repetition task to evaluate the syntactical performance of 11 hard-of-hearing children (average hearing loss 61 dB; mean age 10 years). The study set up three experimental conditions: (a) repeating 1 of 12 sentences while looking at a picture depicting the event, (b) recalling a sentence after being shown the appropriate picture, and (c) repeating the sentence without being shown the depicting picture. Set in third-person singular, the verb constructions selected for study were present tense, auxiliary (be + -ing), auxiliary (have + -en), auxiliary (will), passive, and negative passive.

As expected, the hard-of-hearing children not only performed significantly worse than the normal-hearing subjects, but they also showed a much wider range of competence. This unusually wide range in syntactic performance levels has been noted in other studies as well (Levitt, 1987). None of the normal-hearing children in the Wilcox and Tobin (1974) study experienced much difficulty with any of the verb constructions. Of the six syntactic features evaluated, the hard-of-hearing children diverged most sharply from their normal-hearing counterparts with the auxiliary (have + -en) and the negative passive.

Wilcox and Tobin point out that in both these instances a word can be omitted without a resulting ungrammatical sentence. In the example "Mary has picked the flowers," the child can ignore the word *has* and interpret the sentence as a instance of a simple past tense. The same situation occurs in the negative passive, such as "The glass was not dropped by Mary." In this example, the *not* can be omitted, leaving a simple passive sentence in the past tense. In this latter construction, two simultaneous transformational rules occur, one for passive and one for past tense. Hard-of-hearing children apparently have a great deal of difficulty applying two grammatical rules simultaneously, as do younger normal-hearing children. A relatively small percentage (16%) of the hard-of-hearing children's responses were completely ungrammatical, lending support to the delay rather than deviant hypothesis regarding linguistic development in hard-of-hearing children.

Davis and Blasdell (1975) compared the performance of hard-of-hearing and normal-hearing children in comprehending sentences that contain medially embedded relative clauses. Their subjects were 23 hard-of-hearing children, ranging in age from 6 to 9 years and in average hearing losses from 35 to 70 dB. The children listened to a sentence with an embedded medial clause (e.g., "The man who chased the sheep cut the grass") and then selected one of four associated pictures. Additionally, they used the same surface structure to create sentences conveying different meanings (e.g., "The sheep that chased the man ate the grass").

As had Wilcox and Tobin (1974), Davis and Blasdell found that normal-hearing children made the same kind of errors as hard-of-hearing children, though fewer of them. A wider range of scores was observed again with the hard-of-hearing children. Response analysis showed that such children adopted a processing strategy that shifted their attention to the latter part of the sentence to cull the underlying meaning. Thus they would point to the picture of a man cutting the grass when the sentence "The sheep that chased the man ate the grass" was read. Another of their strategies was to interpret the sentences in contiguous fashion, using the closest subject/verb and object sequence in processing a sentence for meaning. Thus, when the previous sentence was read to them, they would interpret it to mean that the man ate the grass.

This behavior accords with the strategy used by young normal-hearing children who display the same difficulty processing embedded relative clauses as do older hard-of-hearing children. The hard-of-hearing subjects' responses appeared uncertain. In addition, faced with an apparently confusing sentence, they would produce responses that did not make semantic sense (e.g., the man ate the grass) but that they thought were required of them by the examiner. The hard-of-hearing children in the Davis and Blasdell study misunderstood complex sentences 49% of the time. This is a very serious problem in schoolwork, but one not usually manifested in social conversational utterances (how often do we use medial embedded phrases in our speech?).

The difficulty in processing complex sentences becomes quite evident when these children must utilize their deficient language skills for academic tasks. Quigley, Smith, and Wilbur (1974), for example, report that relative clauses appear regularly in the second primer of a typical reading series used in regular schools. Hard-of-hearing children's problems with this type of language structure undoubtedly accounts for a large portion of their academic problems.

As a component of Levitt, McGarr, and Geffner's (1987) major longitudinal study of hearing-impaired children's language and communication skills, Levitt (1987) reported on the results of syntactic comprehension tests for two groups of children. One group encompassed deaf children enrolled in special education settings and the other comprised both deaf and hard-of-hearing children enrolled in a mainstream setting. This latter group, of course, draws the primary concern of this book, but their performance can be appreciated best when placed in a perspective that includes both other hearing-impaired as well as normal-hearing children.

Both groups of children received the *Test of Syntactic Abilities* (Quigley, Steinkamp, Power, & Jones, 1978), a paper-and-pencil test that includes a large number of syntactic forms and error types. Fewer differences emerged between the two groups' total scores than had been anticipated, although the average results clearly favored the mainstreamed group. The higher scoring mainstreamed children achieved well above their peers in the special schools, while the poorer scoring mainstreamed children achieved only slightly higher levels than the deaf children in the special schools. These results cannot be explained simply as a function of hearing level, as a relationship between syntactic scores and hearing level was evident only for the children with the mildest hearing losses (50 and 60 dB). Higher syntactic (and speech production) scores were produced by those children who received early special education, had deaf parents, and possessed measurable high-frequency hearing (which suggests that high frequencies may make an underestimated contribution to the *development* of speech and language in addition to the *recognition* of a known message).

The Levitt (1987) data display a wide range of scores in all syntactic dimensions for both groups examined. Also noteworthy was the overall slow rate of improvement for the children in the special schools over the 4-year course of the study. Because the mainstreamed children were evaluated for only 1 year, their progress over time could not be ascertained. The syntactic forms that gave both groups of children the most difficulty were those that required combining sentences either by relativization or complementation, followed by problems with the verb system and pronomilization. This does not suggest that their performance for other syntactic forms was normal; their scores in all syntactic areas were poorer, sometimes much poorer, than those obtained by normal-hearing children.

The children in the special schools who scored the lowest at the inception of the Levitt study made no improvement in the more difficult syntactic forms over the 4-year period. These children used syntactical forms marked by deviancy, particularly as they got older. Levitt (1987) points out that delay and deviance are not independent entities, but appear to be closely related. For children with poorer language capabilities, it appears that, given sufficient language *delay*, attempts to communicate more complicated messages will produce a *deviant* language structure.

Mainstreamed children with *relatively* good language skills show developmental patterns similar to that displayed by normal-hearing children. That is, the language development of this group of hearing-impaired children appears to be delayed rather than deviant, at least for the less difficult syntactic forms. It is doubtful, unfortunately, that the syntactic capabilities of the poorer achieving children in both groups will ever reach normalcy at any age.

ACADEMIC ACHIEVEMENTS

Studies concerning the academic achievements of hearing-impaired children, in either mainstream or special settings, show these children *on the average* behind their normal-hearing peers (Steer et al., 1961; Kodman, 1963; Quigley & Thomure, 1968; Hine, 1970; Hamp, 1972; Peckham, Sheridan, & Butler, 1972; Paul & Young, 1975; Trybus & Karchmer, 1977; Brackett & Maxon, 1986). The findings are consistent, and valid generalities can be drawn by reviewing only several representative studies. What perhaps may be more useful to this discussion, however, are some of the observations that can be made from a careful review of these studies. Before beginning, though, it should be stressed again that the relatively poor accomplishments of hearing-impaired children in the mainstream are not preordained or inevitable. Given the kind of management program presented in this book, there is every reason to anticipate academic performance within the normal range.

In 1963 Kodman reported on the educational status of 100 hard-of-hearing children enrolled in mainstreamed settings. These subjects all fell in the normal range of intelligence and had hearing losses in the better ear between 20 and 65 dB. On the basis of their age, these children should have been placed in the sixth grade. Their actual placement, however, was in the middle of the fourth grade. Inasmuch as these 100 children repeated, on the average, 1½ grades, there were 150 extra grades repeated by just this group. Multiplied by the number of similar such children in the country, this situation represents a significant economic impact on society (in addition to the personal cost of academic failure). Even though Kodman's subjects were placed a grade and a half below their age level, their academic achievements, as indicated by performance scores, were even poorer than their placements. These children demonstrated an average 2- to 3-year lag in academic achievements.

This figure of 2 to 3 years comes up time and again, and probably can be considered mainstreamed hearing-impaired children's average deficit in settings providing inadequate support services (Hine, 1970; Hamp, 1972). Of the 100 children in the 1963 Kodman study, only 35 wore hearing aids and only 24 received speech and language therapy. Although one now would expect a greater percentage of hearing-impaired children in regular schools to be wearing hearing aids, this is not necessarily the case. Reporting on the percentage of children in the Iowa public schools who wore hearing aids, Davis (1981b) found such usage among only 20% of the children with 30–50 dB sloping losses, 48% of those with flat losses of 30 to 50 dB, and 81–88% of those with more severe losses. These figures all should have been closer to 100%. But even among the children who were using aids, the chances are that approximately one third of the devices were not operating or were functioning poorly.

The same pattern of academic retardation can be seen in a study conducted 5 years after Kodman's. In this study, Quigley and Thomure (1968) evaluated the academic performance of all the hearing-impaired children in a medium-size Illinois city. Out of a group of 173 children, 116 were administered audiometric and IQ evaluations, and several subtests of the *Stanford Achievement Test* (SAT). Age ranges were fairly equally distributed, except for a sharp drop in the number of hearing-impaired children enrolled in the schools after age 15. The researchers speculated that these children tend to drop out of school when they reach the legal age, probably because of the severity of their academic problems. (This seems a credible explanation, further supporting the need for urgency in managing our hard-of-hearing children. In addition, the high percentage of hearing impairments among delinquent and prison populations also demonstrates how the cost to society of mismanaging such children may extend beyond the purely "academic.")

The results of the Quigley and Thomure study are reported in terms of the hearing level of the student's better ear, and several interesting findings emerge. There is a definite pattern of academic retardation, even for children with unilateral hearing losses. On the SAT, these children were behind an average of 1 year in word meaning, while the average of the various subtests (paragraph meaning and language) showed a deficit of about three fourths of a year. The hearing-loss category of 15–25 dB in the better ear showed an average subtest delay of a little more than a year, with each succeeding category demonstrating an additional gap of approximately a year until the scores level off at about 3 years' average academic retardation. The children in all hearing-level categories performed more poorly in the word meaning subtest than in any of the others. This measure is basically a vocabulary test, and the results support the previous comments regarding hard-of-hearing children's vocabulary problems.

The 116 children evaluated in this study also showed an average grade placement gap of a little more than a year, which was close to Kodman's (1963) earlier findings. Only 5 of the 116 children wore hearing aids. If one considers only the children in the more severe categories (27 dB hearing loss or more in the better ear), 20 of them were potential hearing aid candidates. This evidence of audiological mismanagement was mirrored in a similar lack of other support services. The availability of such services has increased since this study was reported, but the glaring need for improvements is still apparent in schools where hearing-impaired children are enrolled.

Over a 4-year period Paul and Young (1975) monitored the academic performance of 58 children with mild to moderate sensorineural hearing losses (average of 40 dB). The *Metropolitan Achievement Test* (Durost, Bixler, Wrightstone, Prescott, & Balow, 1971) battery was administered four times during this study. A child was considered an "academic success" if his or her achievement scores increased by at least 6 months each academic year, with no more than a 1½-year gap between the actual and expected grade-level scores. Despite this very lenient criterion, more than a third of these children placed in the "failure" category. The results are even worse than they appear because the children's academic performance was related to grade level but not to age; that is, these subjects may well have been older than their normal-hearing classmates.

A particularly discouraging aspect of this study was the fact that half the teachers did not think the children's academic problems had anything to do with their hearing losses, although they all knew the children had hearing problems. This finding further illustrates the conflicts faced by less severely hearing-impaired children that were discussed in chapter 1. Because these children seem to "hear," and can and do respond appropriately much of the time, their teachers and other important individuals in their lives develop certain normative expectations regarding their ability to communicate. When their responses appear unpredictable or irrelevant to the stimulus, or when they seem to "tune out" or ignore a speaker, they frequently are penalized for engaging in deliberately provocative and negative behavior.

Such children find themselves in a bind. On the one hand, because of their normal appearance and superficially normal communicative behavior, it is assumed they will act within a certain framework of expectations. On the other hand, because of their hearing losses, with the attendant language problems and greater sensitivity to negative classroom acoustical conditions, it is impossible for them to do so. Schools must devise strategies for resolving this contradiction. Paul and Young (1975) developed an in-service program that oriented classroom teachers to the hard-of-hearing child. This approach proved effective in dispelling some of the myths and misinformation associated with these children.

The unilaterally hearing-impaired child is the classic object of misunderstanding because of the unsuspected impact of a hearing loss. These children are consistently rated as having "greater difficulty in peer relations, less social confidence, greater likelihood of 'acting out' or withdrawn behavior in the classroom, greater frustration and need for dependence on the teacher, and more frequent distractibility" than normal-hearing children (Bess, 1986, p. 54). In his summary article, Bess points out that 35% of the 60 children he evaluated failed at least one grade in school. Moreover, the children with severe to profound hearing losses in the impaired ear were more likely to have failed a grade and to have obtained lower Verbal IQ scores than children with somewhat better hearing in the affected ear. As pointed out in chapter 1, one should not underestimate the impact of even a "mild" hearing loss.

In the course of a 6-year in-service training program, Brackett and Maxon (1986) collected data on the accomplishments of mainstreamed hearing-impaired children. The 142 children in this study received support services from speech-language pathologists and teachers of the deaf who were enrolled in the program. At ages 11, 13, 14, 15, 16, and 17, over 80% of the children were older than their classmates, most by only a year or so but some by 2 or 3 years. Beyond this gap, the older hearing-impaired children were advanced from grade to grade on the basis of "social promotions," regardless of their performance in class.

Such academic failure is not preordained. Mainstreamed hearing-impaired children of normal intelligence fail when effective remedial measures are the exception rather than the rule. Although a moderate or severe hearing loss certainly will affect a child's performance, teachers and clinicians can reasonably expect to reduce the academic lag that these children so often experience. The results of some exemplary management programs definitely provide grounds for cautious optimism. McClure (1977) reported on 14 mainstreamed children with moderate (56–70 dB) and severe (71–89 dB) hearing losses who were the recipients of an early auditory management program. These children achieved average reading scores and low average spelling and mathematics scores. The data were adjusted to enable comparison with normal-hearing children of the same age rather than grade, therefore taking into consideration the fact that 9 of the 14 children were older than their normal-hearing classmates.

In a paper delivered at the 1986 A. G. Bell Association convention, Olmstead recapped the results of the mainstreaming program conducted by the Carleton Board of Education in Ontario. Subjects' hearing losses ranged from mild to profound. Of the 72 children in the total program, 49 were fully mainstreamed (with support services available). Of these 49 children, the academic performance of 27 of them (using reading scores as the criterion) was at or above grade level; the performance of 10 was slightly delayed, and 6 were delayed by 2 or more years. The children's performance in mathematics was even better.

A recent article by Geers and Moog (1989) showed good reading and writing performance for a group of 100 orally educated, mainstreamed, profoundly hearing-impaired 16- and 17-year-olds. The mean grade level for their reading comprehension was eighth grade—not normal, but superior to what typically has been found with "deaf" youngsters.

These latter studies provide excellent examples of what could be, rather than what generally exists. There is no doubt that we can do better than we are doing. Academic delay for hard-of-hearing children is not inevitable. Professionals working with them can be assured that their devoted and informed efforts can really pay off in ways that they can see and appreciate.

RELATIONSHIP OF HEARING LOSS TO PERFORMANCE

Some professionals working with hearing-impaired students seem reluctant to accept the notion that a child's academic and communicative performance may be related to severity of hearing loss. We have heard this reluctance expressed by very effective teachers, those who understand how to use a child's residual hearing to its fullest extent. Many of the children they work with perform very well, sometimes better than those with lesser degrees of hearing loss, and therefore degree of hearing loss may appear an almost irrelevant consideration.

However, recognizing that many children with severe and profound hearing losses can obtain excellent results does not mean that degree of hearing loss is unimportant or that there is not some general relationship to performance. In fact, most of the literature on the topic shows a significant, but far from perfect, relationship between performance and degree of hearing loss.

What these studies demonstrate are the consequences of ineffective management conditions, the results of which reflect the relatively undiluted impact of the hearing loss itself upon achievement. If congenitally hearing-impaired children were not fitted with hearing aids, if preschool programs were not available, if there were no differences in personal and family characteristics—if, in other words, the isolated impact of the hearing loss itself could be examined, then one could predict a very high relationship between degree of hearing loss and academic and communicative accomplishments. But, of course, this is the point; children *do* differ in all these respects. The less than perfect relationship that exists between degree of hearing loss and performance testifies to the possible impact of management and personal factors on a child's accomplishments (Levitt, 1987). It is therefore reasonable to assume that a *low* relationship between degree of hearing loss and performance indicates the beneficial influence of these factors, and a *high* relationship implies less than optimal personal and/or management factors. In other words, severely and profoundly hearing-impaired recipients of an optimal management program should function as if their hearing losses were less severe.

In terms of speech production intelligibility, the research data agree: the greater the hearing loss, the poorer the performance. Montgomery (1967) examined this general relationship in detail and identified the hearing level at 2000 Hz in the better ear as the most significant factor underlying speech production intelligibility. Boothroyd (in Stark, 1974, p. 45) corroborated the importance of 2000 Hz in a population of "deaf" students. Negative correlations of .62, .68, and .71 between average degree of hearing loss and speech production intelligibility were found by Markides (1970), Jensema, Karchmer, and Trybus (1978), and Monsen (1978), respectively. Levitt (1987) similarly found a high negative relationship; however, he also showed that children who received an early management program, were mainstreamed, became postlingually deafened, or demonstrated the presence of high-frequency residual hearing all performed better than the average in speech production intelligibility. As Wolk and Schildroth conclude in their large-scale analysis of surveys conducted by Gallaudet University: "A student's degree of hearing loss, when differentiated as less-than severe, severe, and profound, is the strongest and most consistent correlate of speech intelligibility" (1986, p. 152).

Many investigators have pointed out that whereas a "good" audiogram is a reliable predictor of intelligible speech, a "bad" audiogram does not predict either good or bad speech (Monsen, 1978; Stark, 1974). As one would expect, a lesser degree of hearing loss apparently permits some natural development of speech, whereas a more severe hearing loss requires an explicit program of management for the development of intelligible speech. The same relatively high relationship exists between speech perception and degree of hearing loss (Stark, 1974, pp. 52–57) that exists with speech production intelligibility. That is, the greater the child's hearing loss, the poorer his or her speech perception skills (Boothroyd, 1984).

Not as obvious as the foregoing relationships is that between degree of hearing loss and academic and language abilities, although the trend is also clear. In a comparison of the language or academic skills of deaf and hard-of-hearing children, the hard-of-hearing children achieve the higher scores (Brannon & Murry, 1966; Brannon, 1968; Hamp, 1972). When the relationship between degree of hearing loss and academic and linguistic skills is evaluated for hearing-impaired children in general, the children with the lesser degree of loss also perform on average superiorly (Hine, 1970; Pressnell, 1973; Jensema, 1975; Davis, 1974; Ross, 1976; Trybus & Karchmer, 1977; Gemmill & John, 1975).

Table 2.5, one of the reports of the Center for Assessment and Demographic Studies at Gallaudet University (Jensema, 1975), presents a comprehensive review of this relationship for 6,871 hearing-impaired children enrolled in special education settings. As noted in the table, the data are presented as age deviation scores. These statistics compare a particular child to the average score obtained by other hearing-impaired children, not normal-hearing children. Note the progression from better scores to poorer scores as hearing loss increases, particularly in vocabulary and reading comprehension. Note, too, the relatively wide standard deviations at each data point, illustrating, again, the diversity of accomplishments one finds among hearing-impaired children. They cannot by any means be considered a homogeneous group.

This same pattern of results was observed in a demographic study conducted in British Columbia on 383 school-age hearing-impaired children (Rogers, Leslie, Clarke, Booth, & Horvath, 1978). The subjects' hearing losses ranged from less than 44 dB in the better ear to profound. Their results showed vocabulary and reading comprehension scores declining as the severity of hearing loss increased, but no decline in mathematics scores

TABLE 2.5 Relationship Between Degree of Loss and Academic Achievement

Hearing Loss in ISO dB	N	Vocabulary		Reading Comprehension		Math Concepts		Math Computation	
		Mean	S.D.	Mean	S.D.	Mean	S.D.	Mean	S.D.
Normal (<27 dB)	64	1.28	1.27	0.78	1.11	0.50	0.89	0.19	0.86
Mild (27 to 40 dB)	140	0.85	1.36	0.65	1.30	0.58	1.11	0.28	1.04
Moderate (41 to 55 dB)	367	0.59	1.10	0.51	1.16	0.39	0.98	0.24	0.92
Moderately Severe (56 to 70 dB)	775	0.22	1.06	0.18	1.11	0.16	1.02	0.08	1.02
Severe (71 to 90 dB)	1838	–0.03	0.94	0.02	0.97	–0.04	0.98	–0.02	0.98
Profound (>90 dB)	3464	–0.16	0.88	–0.12	0.87	–0.09	0.94	–0.04	0.96
Unknown	223	0.14	1.08	0.00	1.07	0.11	1.08	–0.07	1.07
All Students	*6871*	*0.00*	*0.99*	*0.00*	*0.99*	*0.00*	*0.99*	*0.00*	*0.98*

Note. The data are presented in age deviation scores, with a score of 1.00 representing the 84th percentile, and a score of –1.00 the 16th percentile. These data compare hearing-impaired children to other hearing-impaired children, and not to normally hearing children. From *The Relationship Between Academic Achievement and the Demographic Characteristics of Hearing-Impaired Children and Youth* (Series R, No. 2) by C. J. Jensema, 1975, Washington, DC: Gallaudet College, Office of Demographic Studies. Copyright 1975 by Gallaudet College. Reprinted by permission.

(computation, application, and concepts). With regard to academic abilities, a hearing loss evidently levels its greatest effect on areas requiring the greatest degree of language competence.

In the 4-year longitudinal study conducted by Levitt, McGarr, and Geffner (1987), the first observed pattern of relationships between hearing level and communication skills was confirmed at the conclusion of the study. Speech production and speech perception skills related more highly to hearing levels than did linguistic accomplishments. As the researchers interpreted the relationships between hearing level and language skills, they concluded that although a hearing loss is an obstacle to normal linguistic performance, "it is primarily the steps taken to remedy the situation that are critical to the child's acquisition of language" (Levitt, McGarr, & Geffner, 1987, p. 86). That is, the effects of the hearing impairment can be overcome at least partially by beginning special education and auditory management (the proper use of amplified sound) at an early age.

In reviewing the relationship between hearing level and performance, therefore, it is apparent that variables other than hearing loss affect performance. Hearing-impaired children display the same range of attributes as do normal-hearing children, and these in turn influence their accomplishments much the same way. Add to this the impact of various degrees of hearing loss, and the diversity in hearing-impaired children's performance becomes wide indeed.

Tables 2.6, 2.7, and 2.8 illustrate some of these personal variations in performance. The data in Table 2.6 compare children of similar hearing levels and age but different performance scores. Tests were administered with hearing aids in a sound-treated room. The first two children, M.M. and M.L., both have profound hearing losses; however, M.M. makes good use of residual hearing, while M.L. does not. In any modality, M.L.'s reception of speech is very poor. As one can see, his receptive language scores are very delayed; yet in spite of displaying the language skills of a preschooler, he has been placed in the eighth grade and is expected to function at grade level.

The second pair of subjects, J.V. and A.D., have severe to profound hearing losses, and both have relatively good combined (speechreading and audition) speech reception scores. J.V., however, shows better speech, language, and syntax usage, and is placed only one grade below expected grade level. This shows how hearing-impaired children of similar ages and hearing levels vary in their performance, the same as normal-hearing children. Teachers and clinicians, then, must invoke factors other than the hearing losses to explain these variations in performance.

Table 2.7 presents a picture of two children with differing degrees of hearing loss but similar ages and performance levels. J.T. has considerably poorer hearing than D.M., but both function in much the same way. These cases exemplify how the degree of hearing loss does not predict an individual child's performance.

As pointed out earlier, children with better hearing levels usually demonstrate higher performance scores. That there are exceptions can be see in Table 2.8. In spite of having significantly more residual hearing, T.P. scored more poorly than M.G. in all language-related tests. Although both children are in the same grade, T.P. requires more support and invites more

TABLE 2.6 Children With Similar Hearing Levels and Ages but Different Performance

Child	Ear	500	1K	2K	Age	Grade	PPVT*	TACL	Aud/Vis	Aud	Vis	Speech Intell
M.M.	R	100	110	110	13	7	–6yr 2mo	6–10	88%	84%	68%	Fair
	L	105	110	120								
M.L.	R	100	100	110	14	8	–10yr 4mo	3–5	38%	10%	24%	Poor
	L	100	105	115								
J.V.	R	75	95	100	14	7	–5yr 3mo	6–11**	75%	36%	72%	Good
	L	85	95	NR								
A.D.	R	85	90	100	14	6	–7yr	6–6	84%	4%	64%	Fair
	L	85	90	95								

*Peabody Picture Vocabulary Test, deviation from chronological age
**Ceiling score on the Test of Auditory Comprehension of Language

TABLE 2.7 Children With Different Hearing Losses but Same Age and Performance

Child	Ear	500	1K	2K	Age	Grade	PPVT*	TACL	Aud/ Vis	Aud	Vis	Speech Intell
D.M.	R	70	65	75	12	7	–1yr 4mo	6–11**	90%	76%	40%	Good
	L	75	75	80								
J.T.	R	95	90	90	12	7	–6mo	6–11**	100%	70%	70%	Good
	L	95	110	NR								

*Peabody Picture Vocabulary Test, deviation from chronological age
**Ceiling score on the Test of Auditory Comprehension of Language

TABLE 2.8 Children of Same Age With Different Hearing Losses and Different Performance

Child	Ear	500	1K	2K	Age	Grade	PPVT*	TACL	Aud/Vis	Aud	Vis	Speech Intell
M.G.	R	95	100	100	10	4	−2yr 11mo	6–11**	80%	76%	64%	Fair
	L	100	105	110								
T.P.	R	45	55	60	10	4	−5yr 10mo	5–2	92%	92%	40%	Good
	L	45	55	65								

*Peabody Picture Vocabulary Test, deviation from chronological age
**Ceiling score on the Test of Auditory Comprehension of Language

concern about the appropriateness of her academic placement. What these data demonstrate is that while a hearing loss may constrain academic and communicative achievements, it does not throw up an insuperable obstacle.

EFFECT OF EDUCATIONAL SETTING ON PERFORMANCE

Special education in the United States received a severe challenge in 1975 with the passage of the Education for All Handicapped Children Act, Public Law 94-142. One of the important educational emphases of this law requires that children be educated in the least restrictive educational setting possible. For hearing-impaired children, the most restrictive educational setting is a residential school, and the least restrictive is full mainstreaming in the local regular school. One must ask if there is any educational merit to this provision. Does enrollment in a local school bring more benefits than problems for the average hearing-impaired child? The least restrictive educational setting is not necessarily *the most appropriate* one for a particular child. Mainstreaming hearing-impaired children, however, is an established fact, and this section will draw on the literature pertaining to both deaf and hard-of-hearing children, in special and regular settings, in an attempt to isolate the influence of the educational setting on performance.

Experience has long noted that hearing-impaired children in regular schools speak more intelligibly and perform better on language and academic achievement tests than their counterparts in more restrictive educational settings. However, as the literature has pointed out repeatedly (Jensema, 1975; Jensema et al., 1978; Jensema, Karchmer, & Trybus, 1978; Allen & Osborn, 1984; Wolk & Schildroth, 1986; Allen, 1986), hearing-impaired children in regular and special schools differ on a number of other demographic variables as well. The better performance of those in the regular schools may simply reflect these other variables rather than educational placement. Moreover, other preselection factors may be operative as well. These children may be in regular schools *because* of their higher performance, which preceded the educational placement, and thus this initial status accounted for their later superiority.

Although demographic and initial performance factors undoubtedly explain much of the superior performance in mainstream settings versus more restrictive ones, unfortunately no data document this oft-repeated assertion. To our knowledge, no studies have compared the performance of comparably hearing-impaired children in special and mainstream settings at the time of enrollment. No matter how pertinent these demographic and initial performance factors, the preponderance of evidence reviewed in this section suggests that, all other factors being equal, the educational setting itself can influence academic and communication accomplishments.

The first consideration must be of educational placement as a function of degree of hearing loss. Ross (1976) reported on the hearing levels and the academic and communication performance of children placed in various educational settings under the aegis of a single school for the deaf. The study noted that the children in the self-contained classes had an average hearing loss of 97 dB, those in resource rooms in regular schools had an average loss of 83 dB, while those who were fully mainstreamed with supportive services had losses averaging 76 dB. Although the children were assigned to the different placements on the basis of communicative and academic functioning rather than degree of hearing loss, the result was that those with lesser hearing loss were placed in the least restrictive settings. Both Reich, Hambleton, and Houldin (1977) and Allen and Osborn (1984) reached this same conclusion. Wolk, Karchmer, and Schildroth's (1982) large-scale survey study looked at the number of hours hearing-impaired children were integrated with others of normal hearing. These researchers found that children with lesser degrees of hearing loss were integrated for more hours than were those with greater degrees of loss.

The Center for Assessment and Demographic Studies at Gallaudet University (Jensema et al., 1978) has collected extensive data documenting this observation from 945 children in programs all over the country. Table 2.9 is drawn from these results. Looking across the top row (residential school, residential students), one sees that only 7.2% of the students had hearing losses of 70 dB or less; 27.5% had losses of 71 to 90 dB, and the remaining 65.3% had losses of 91 dB or more. In the bottom row (All part-time services, which includes fully integrated students), the trend completely reverses. Here 57.3% had hearing losses of less than 57 dB, 24.2% fell between 71 and 90 dB, and only 18.5% had losses greater than 91 dB. The intermediate programs show the expected gradations between these two placement extremes.

As the observation that children with less severe hearing losses are enrolled in less restrictive settings only confirms what one would expect, it is much more pertinent to ask whether such enrollment stimulates personal and educational advantages beyond those usually occurring in a more restrictive setting, and then whether these possible advantages reflect the influence of the setting or just initial placement decisions. There are some data and clinical observations that can be applied to this question.

In the previously described report that plotted academic achievement as a function of hearing loss, Jensema (1975) also analyzed the effect of

TABLE 2.9 Program Placement by Degree of Loss

Type of Program	< 70 dB		71 to 90 dB		> 91 dB	
	N	%	N	%	N	%
Residential school Residential students	24	7.2	93	27.5	220	65.3
Residential school Day students	5	7.4	18	26.4	45	66.2
Day school	23	16.1	35	24.5	85	59.4
Full-time classes	73	26.7	85	31.1	115	42.1
All part-time services	71	57.3	30	24.2	23	18.5

Note. From *The Rated Speech Intelligibility of Hearing-Impaired Children: Basic Relationships and a Detailed Analysis* (Series R, No. 6) by C. J. Jensema, M. A. Karchmer, and B. J. Trybus, 1978, Washington, DC: Gallaudet College, Office of Demographic Studies. Copyright 1978 by Gallaudet College. Adapted by permission.

program placement on academic achievement. As he points out, one could predict that children enrolled in different types of programs would perform differently (as they did) simply because of the known differences between their demographic attributes. However, even after correcting for some of the major demographic factors (e.g., degree of hearing loss), differences in academic achievement as a function of program type still were clearly evident.

Table 2.10 was adapted from the Jensema (1975) study, organized from most restrictive at the top to least restrictive at the bottom. The categories reported in the study have been modified, inserting the "Resource Room" category between the "Full-Time Special Educational Class" and the "Part-Time Educational Class." The category "Other" refers to children who are in regular classes full time, receiving only that extra support available to other special children in the school.

As in Table 2.5, the results here are reported as age-deviation scores, with the addition that the influence of certain key demographic variables has been eliminated statistically. Note that the children enrolled in the top two categories ("Residential School" and "Day School") are performing slightly below average for the hearing-impaired population, whereas the children in the "Full-Time Special Educational Class" (housed in a regular school setting) are at an average level. As educational setting categories

TABLE 2.10 Age Deviation Scores in Four Areas of Academic Achievement as a Function of Educational Setting

Type of Special Program	N	Vocabulary		Reading Comprehension		Math Concepts		Math Computation	
		Mean	S.D.	Mean	S.D.	Mean	S.D.	Mean	S.D.
Residential school	3073	-0.09	0.82	-0.06	0.78	-0.10	0.84	-0.09	0.84
Day school	1018	-0.13	0.91	-0.14	0.82	-0.11	0.91	-0.11	0.86
Full-time special educational class	1975	0.04	0.90	-0.01	0.93	0.02	0.89	0.02	0.91
Resource room	192	0.19	1.07	0.22	0.97	0.17	0.93	0.13	0.92
Part-time special educational class	392	0.24	1.09	0.37	1.05	0.31	0.99	0.28	0.98
Itinerant program	215	0.69	1.23	0.71	1.20	0.56	1.02	0.42	0.94
Other	29	0.95	1.53	0.82	1.45	0.51	1.09	0.49	1.04

Note. The influence of degree of loss, age at onset of loss, number of additional handicapping conditions, presence of mental retardation, and reported ethnic background was corrected for in these data. In all areas of academic achievement, the children's performance tends to improve as the program type moves from the more to the least restrictive setting. From *The Relationship Between Academic Achievement and the Demographic Characteristics of Hearing-Impaired Children and Youth* (Series R, No. 2) by C. J. Jensema, 1975, Washington, DC: Gallaudet College, Office of Demographic Studies. Copyright 1975 by Gallaudet College. Adapted by permission.

become less restrictive, the children's performance surpasses the average scores for hearing-impaired children. These data strongly suggest that, other factors being equal, children enrolled in a less restrictive educational setting will outperform their peers in a more restrictive setting. Jensema (1975) rightly cautions that other, unaccounted for variables may be responsible for the differences noted in Table 2.10; however, considering the important variables statistically eliminated in the analysis, the large number of subjects, the clear trend of the data, and the often random nature of initial educational placement during this period, one also can interpret the results as indicating that the setting itself may be the ingredient that contributes to the improved performance.

The salutary effect of educational placement on performance also emerges in a later report by the Office of Assessment and Demographic Studies (Jensema et al., 1978). In this study, speech intelligibility ratings of hearing-impaired children were related to a number of demographic variables, including the degree of hearing loss and program type. Table 2.11, taken from this study, shows the relationship between the rated speech intelligibility of hearing-impaired children by program type and by degree of hearing loss. Note that in the first column, for the students with a less than 70 dB hearing loss in the better ear, the judged speech intelligibility was poorer for the students in the residential school, both day and residential, than for the students in the other placement categories. The converse is true for the children with the most severe hearing losses (greater than 91 dB): their speech intelligibility ratings were higher for those in day and integrated settings than for children enrolled in residential schools, particularly for the residential students.

One could argue, as do Jensema et al. (1978), that within the less severe hearing loss category (less than 70 dB), more students in the residential school had hearing losses at the upper range of the category, and thus it may have been the lesser degree of hearing loss that was responsible for the better speech of students in the part-time services group. This is valid, given the fact that the hearing loss data were reported in only three general categories. However, this argument is not possible for the children in the more severe hearing loss category (more than 91 dB); here, also, the children in the less restrictive educational settings displayed higher speech intelligibility ratings. In brief, the data strongly suggest that something positive is going on in the less restrictive settings, related either to higher expectations (using normal-hearing children as role models and communication partners) or to more stringent speech and audiological management.

If these latter were the only studies reporting such findings, a cautious interpretation would certainly be in order, considering the implications for education and placement. Other reports, however, also have demonstrated the superior performance of hearing-impaired children in a mainstream

TABLE 2.11 Percentage of Students with Intelligible or Very Intelligible Speech (as Rated by Teacher) by Program Type and Degree of Loss

Type of Program	<71 dB %	71 to 90 dB %	>91 dB %
Residential school Residential students	67	45	17
Residential school Day students	80	68	31
Day school	91	54	26
Full-time classes	85	62	24
All part-time services	90	51	39

Note. From *The Rated Speech Intelligibility of Hearing-Impaired Children: Basic Relationships and a Detailed Analysis* (Series R, No. 6) by C. J. Jensema, M. A. Karchmer, and B. J. Trybus, 1978, Washington, DC: Gallaudet College, Office of Demographic Studies. Copyright 1978 by Gallaudet College. Adapted by permission.

setting, *even when other demographic factors are considered.* As part of a larger study done in England, Hamp (1972) compared the reading scores of 87 hearing-impaired children in a residential program to 53 children with similar degrees of hearing loss enrolled in a day school. Hamp found reading score differences ranging from a half to almost a full year in favor of the day students and attributed them to the higher standards and expectations within the integrated day setting. The study also considered the influence of the family, finding this positively related to reading achievement, regardless of setting.

In an unpublished study conducted some years ago at the Willie Ross School for the Deaf, 10 children in self-contained classes were compared to 10 who were fully integrated in their local schools. The subjects were matched as closely as possible with regard to age and degree of hearing loss. The results, given in Table 2.12, showed that the two groups differed significantly on all the tests administered. In keeping a balanced perspective, one should note that although better than the results of their hearing-impaired peers in a self-contained setting, the mainstreamed students' scores still fell far behind those of of their normal-hearing peers.

In an extensive Canadian study, Reich et al. (1977) assessed the academic, speech, and psychosocial status of elementary and secondary hard-of-hearing students enrolled in different mainstream programs for different

TABLE 2.12 Relative Performance of Two Groups (N = 10 in Each Group) of Hearing-Impaired Children

	Self-Contained	**Mainstreamed**
Age	8.6 yrs	8.5 yrs
Pure Tone Average	82.1 dB	80.0 dB
Peabody Picture Vocabulary Test	3.8 yrs	4.10 yrs*
Goldman-Fristoe Test of Articulation	66.4	80.1*
Preschool Language Scale: Receptive	4.9 yrs	6.1 yrs**
Preschool Language Scale: Expressive	4.4 yrs	6.3 yrs**

*Significant beyond the 0.05 level
**Significant beyond the 0.01 level

periods of time. The elementary level involved a total of 154 subjects: 77 (average hearing loss 42 dB) were fully integrated; 42 (average loss 54 dB) were fully integrated and also received extra services from an itinerant teacher of the deaf; and 36 (average loss 63 dB) were in special hard-of-hearing classes within the regular public schools. Forty subjects were enrolled in secondary schools: 12 (average loss 41 dB) were fully integrated; 17 (average loss 47 dB) were fully integrated and also received services from an itinerant teacher of the deaf; and 11 (average loss 69 dB) were partially integrated, evidently in a resource room arrangement.

These researchers' findings corroborate and extend the results of the studies reviewed previously. In academic performance (reading and language), the fully integrated children performed at or above grade level, whereas the children receiving itinerant help or enrolled in special classes were a year or more behind their classmates. Of course, as the children with greater hearing losses were in more restricted programs, these findings align with those reviewed previously and are not surprising. The same relationship was noted in the speech intelligibility ratings.

More pertinent to the concern here, however, are Reich et al.'s subsequent analyses and interpretations of their data. They reasoned that if integration is beneficial, then children should demonstrate relatively more progress the longer their enrollment in integrated programs. If, however, their superiority is the *cause* rather than the *result* of integration, then those who have been integrated for shorter periods should perform as well as those who have been integrated longer. Other demographic variables were equated as much as possible for this analysis.

The Reich et al. analysis suggests that the longer children were enrolled in a regular program, the more their relative performance improved. This was also true for the children in the itinerant program, who progressed *relatively* more in language and speech the longer they were in the program. The setting itself, in other words, somehow acted as a stimulant (or a goad) for increased performance. These researchers also found that the students in the (more restrictive) hard-of-hearing classes fell further behind in reading the longer they remained in those classes. Similar trends in academic and speech performance occurred at the secondary level.

One possible flaw in this generally rosy picture appeared at the secondary level: Reich et al. (1977) state that personal and social problems may be more severe for hard-of-hearing children in integrated rather than restrictive educational settings. Although the Reich et al. data supporting this contention are only tenuously suggestive at best, we would agree that considering the psychosocial implications of mainstreaming must form a central criterion in evaluating the placement's possible success. Improved communicative and academic ability do not outweigh intact self-esteem and social adjustment.

At about the same time this preceding study was conducted, another was under way at the other end of Canada analyzing the academic performance of 383 hearing-impaired children as a function of their academic settings (Rogers et al., 1978). Subjects were enrolled in regular schools, day classes in regular schools, classes situated in regular schools but administratively attached to a school for the deaf, classes on the campus of a school for the deaf, and special classes for problem children. During the analysis, the effect of degree of hearing loss was eliminated statistically in the same way and for the same reason as in the study conducted by the Center for Assessment and Demographic Studies (Jensema et al., 1978). With the effect of hearing loss statistically partialled out, the results in the two language-related areas (vocabulary and reading comprehension) showed better performance by the children in the regular schools than by those enrolled in any other setting. The scores for the children in the most restrictive setting (classes on the campus of a school for the deaf) were the poorest in these two areas.

Recently, as part of a larger study, Geers and Moog (1989) evaluated reading and writing skills in an orally educated group of congenitally and profoundly hearing-impaired 16- and 17-year-olds. (The other two groups in the larger study were educated in total communication programs.) The hearing losses of the 100 subjects exceeded 85 dB in the better ear and averaged 100 dB. Eighty-five percent of the students were mainstreamed for all or most of the day, and half of these had been mainstreamed by age 12.

The mean grade level for these subjects in reading comprehension was eighth grade. Thirty percent of them achieved average reading levels at or above 10th grade, and only 15% averaged 3rd-grade levels (which was the average reported by Schildroth & Karchmer, 1986, for hearing-impaired children of this age group). In spite of their achievements, however, most of the students did not achieve levels comparable to normal-hearing adolescents of the same age and socioeconomic status. The predictive measures that related most highly to the reading and writing scores were spoken language ability, hearing ability (including speech perception factors as well as degree of hearing loss), and participation in early intervention programs. Mainstreaming itself did not contribute significantly to the subjects' overall literacy. There is no way to know whether mainstreaming fostered spoken language competency, which in turn could have affected the literacy measures. However, one can legitimately conclude that these profoundly hearing-impaired mainstreamed adolescents could utilize their residual hearing, speak intelligibly for the most part, and perform academically far beyond the average accomplishments of segregated hearing-impaired children with comparable hearing losses.

This issue has deserved lengthy review here because of its importance in the current educational scene. The data suggest, hearing loss and other demographic variables aside, that the academic and spoken language achievements of mainstreamed children tend to be higher than those of comparable children in more restrictive educational settings. However, this conclusion is based on *average* performance; for a particular child, the decision must come down to the "most appropriate" educational setting and not simply the "least restrictive." As to why the group data show superior performance for children in the mainstream, one can only make some informed speculations.

In observing these children in self-contained classes, noting their own expectations and the standards of their teachers, one often perceives a lower expected performance as compared to hearing children of the same intelligence and background. The "norm" in a special class is derived, consciously or unconsciously, from the average performance of the children within it. Almost always this norm seems much lower than what is possible. Until quite recently, most teachers of the deaf have had little contact in their training or experience with normal-hearing children. Moreover, many did not not fully appreciate, because of inadequacies in their training, the potential of properly utilized residual hearing. Their efforts with children who had significant residual hearing were patterned, in reality if not in principle, on experiences and expectations based on the most profound hearing losses. A self-fulfilling prophecy was thus set in motion: By expecting their potentially hard-of-hearing children to achieve within the range expected of deaf children, teachers tended to modify their standards in accordance with their reduced expectations.

The situation is quite different for the hearing-impaired child enrolled in a regular class with normal-hearing children. The regular classroom teacher, not having much experience with hearing-impaired children, tends to expect from them academic achievements within the range of accomplishments manifested by normal-hearing children. Regular teachers do not know that the average reading score of a deaf high school graduate is "supposed" to be around the fourth grade. When the "special" child, who appears otherwise bright and motivated, falls too far behind his or her classmates, the teacher becomes concerned and puts the pressure on. Or perhaps the student, seeing what the other children are achieving, applies the pressure to him- or herself. Parents also get involved when their child's performance lags too far behind normal-hearing classmates. Many parents, too, are not aware that hearing-impaired children are "supposed" to be unable to function in a grade-appropriate manner.

Paradoxically, those teachers who have *not* been trained to work with hearing-impaired children may effect more positive changes in academic performance than those who have. This is not to imply that regular teachers do not require the supportive assistance of special teachers, speech-language pathologists, and educational audiologists; expectations alone will not lead to improved performance. However, the higher standards and expectations of a mainstreamed setting, *coupled* with the contributions of a support team, will lead to increased performance for most hearing-impaired children.

These comments have particular meaning for children with the most residual hearing. Although some deaf children have been mainstreamed successfully, the process and the problems are much more involved for them. Placing a deaf child with poor oral skills in a fully integrated setting, with inadequate or no support services, concocts a recipe for disaster. If the child is isolated, unhappy, and unable to benefit from the classroom instruction, one has not arranged the "most appropriate" setting; this in fact serves to sacrifice a *child* for the realization of theoretical *principles.*

PSYCHOSOCIAL STATUS

The foregoing discussion underscores how and why the psychosocial implications of a mainstream setting for a particular child must form a major consideration in judging the suitability of such a placement (Ross, 1978b). A decision maker would be remiss in his or her responsibilities to these children if such implications are ignored in order to achieve the presumed advantages to academic and communicative performance that can be stimulated in a mainstream setting.

Older hearing-impaired children, in particular, frequently feel like outsiders among their normal-hearing classmates. Often they are the only ones in the school with a hearing loss. They may not know anyone else with a hearing impairment and, oddly, may not fully appreciate their own handicap (i.e., abnormal hearing is "normal" for them). Many such children, particularly those who have not come through good early management programs, resent the fact that they must wear hearing aids. Adolescence may bring active rebellion against wearing aids or frequency modulated (FM) auditory training systems. Identity problems may occur for functionally hard-of-hearing youngsters, as they are neither normal hearing nor deaf. Although such problems are not necessarily inevitable and can be alleviated, they must not be ignored.

Very little research exists on the psychosocial status of hearing-impaired children in regular schools, and what little there is seems inconclusive and often contradictory. This is a very difficult area to research, as results depend heavily on factors such as the availability of teacher and parent support programs and the subjects' socioeconomic and educational backgrounds. The extant data do permit at least one cautiously optimistic generalization regarding the elementary-age hearing-impaired child: social maladjustment and self-esteem problems are not inevitable (Elser, 1959; Kennedy, Northcott, McCauley, & Williams, 1976; Reich et al., 1977). The hearing-impaired children reported on in these studies are not indistinguishable from normal-hearing children—differences, of course, do occur. The point is, at least as we evaluate the literature and our own experiences with many such children, that these differences fall within an acceptable range of behaviors. This perspective does not deny the existence of potential and actual problems, but rather affirms that they can be resolved or reduced with proper management.

Hearing-impaired children appear to depend more on their teachers for mediating classroom activities than do normal-hearing children, who rely more heavily on their peers (Kennedy et al., 1976). This is understandable when one considers the difficulty these children frequently experience in following classroom discussions. As they get older and more influenced by peers (just like other "normal" adolescents), their personal and social problems may increase (Reich et al., 1977). However, these are only general tendencies. The psychosocial adjustment of any particular child reflects many personal and social variables and can be assessed correctly only on an individual basis. Solutions, too, will be highly personal.

The preceding should illustrate that whereas the hearing loss per se may increase the likelihood of negative psychosocial behaviors, they are not preordained. Moreover, because existing studies describe *group* behaviors, they seem almost irrelevant to individual children as we know them. The psychosocial status of a hearing-impaired child is best assessed through an *individual* evaluation—talking to him or her and the parents, asking about friends and after-school activities, and observing the child in the classroom, cafeteria, and during recess. In the face of so many individual variations and permutations, generalizations regarding *the* psychosocial status of *the* hearing-impaired child are impossible.

3

Mainstreaming Options and Principles

The advent in 1975 of Public Law 94-142 introduced the concept of mainstreaming to the general public. Previously the education of handicapped children fell primarily to professionals working in segregated, often residential schools. That local school systems were responsible for providing a free, appropriate education in the "least restrictive environment" to all handicapped children (ages 3–21 years) was considered a landmark decision. Then, in 1990, the children not provided for in this original legislation were included with the enactment of PL 99-457. This newer law mandated states' responsibility for the assessment and management of handicapped and (in some cases) "at risk" 0–36-month-olds.

For the school-age, hearing-impaired child, PL 94-142 opened the possibilities of educational placements with normal-hearing children. In fact, the idea of mainstreaming hearing-impaired children was accepted and carried out fairly quickly, resulting in the closing or significant reduction in size of some schools for the deaf, especially those with an "oral" tradition. Perhaps the reason for this quick integration of hearing-impaired children into regular education settings was related to the mistaken notion that it could be easily accomplished. The naivete that led to large-scale transfer of these children out of the settings in which they received a great deal of individual attention, had special amplification equipment, and were taught by specifically trained instructors was, in retrospect, overwhelming.

Had regular-education administrators given more consideration to the effects of hearing loss, perhaps they would have been a bit more judicious in the sudden full mainstreaming of hearing-impaired children within their school districts. Armed with more knowledge they would have realized that mainstreaming meant far more than just placement in a class with normal-hearing peers. The model presented below summarizes the effects of congenital/early onset hearing loss on the developing child, which must be understood thoroughly in order to fully realize the ramifications of mainstreaming:

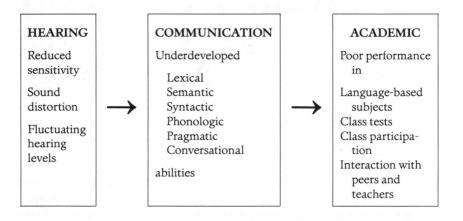

The communication demands placed on hearing-impaired children in regular education settings are quite different than those within segregated schools and/or special programs. The following list details the communication skills and abilities needed in a regular education classroom, without which hearing-impaired children cannot participate fully in a mainstream setting:

1. Comprehend verbally presented material (vocabulary, concepts, syntax).

2. Comprehend written material (vocabulary, concepts, syntax).

3. Ask questions with appropriate language and intelligible speech.

4. Answer questions, verbal/written, with appropriate language and intelligible speech/spelling.

5. Take written tests, understanding the directions as well as the content.

6. Take oral tests, receiving and understanding the directions as well as the content.

7. Follow oral directions through hearing and use of speechreading or through total communication.

8. Follow written directions.

9. Abide by the rules of the classroom and display acceptable interactive and participation behaviors.

10. Follow class discussion, receiving and understanding its content.

11. Participate in class discussions, using appropriate language and intelligible speech.

In order to decide on the appropriate educational setting for a particular hearing-impaired child, some of the issues related to PL 94-142 must be explored.

LEAST RESTRICTIVE ENVIRONMENT (LRE)

Many educators have taken "least restrictive environment" (LRE) to mean only one thing: placing a child in a regular education class within his or her home school. They thus treat this placement as the ideal setting and goal for all handicapped children. Certainly there are hearing-impaired children who can and do function quite well in mainstream settings, particularly when they receive such support services as speech and language management and classroom amplification. However, full mainstreaming is *not* the appropriate placement for all hearing-impaired children. Therefore, LRE should be given a somewhat different interpretation.

When determining appropriate educational placements, the restrictiveness in question does not apply to the particular site in which the child functions. Rather, it refers to the limits placed on the child's potential in a given classroom. For example, a child who is capable of relying on residual hearing (while using an FM system), has appropriate language and speech skills for receiving the academic material, and participates in class discussions would be restricted by an educational program that did not exploit these capabilities. Conversely, the child who must use total communication would be restricted by a placement that required the use of hearing alone, without a method for ensuring that academic information is received (perhaps through the use of a sign interpreter). A 12-year-old hearing-impaired child should not be placed in a regular-education seventh-grade class without special services if his or her language level is that of an 8-year-old.

Thus the environment that is least restrictive is the one that is most appropriate for the child. That key word, *appropriate*, should be the foundation on which a child's educational program is based. LRE, therefore, can have a variety of operational definitions, all of which depend on the needs of the particular hearing-impaired child.

EDUCATIONAL PLACEMENT ALTERNATIVES

Knowing that LRE does not mean only full mainstreaming, educators must become familiar with the placement options for hearing-impaired children. These alternatives, from segregated settings to full mainstreaming, do not imply, in any sense, a value hierarchy. Instead, the settings should be considered lateral, with free movement among them. As a result of the evaluations and recommendations contained in the Individualized Education Plan (IEP; see chapter 7), a child's placement, including special services, may be changed to better accommodate his or her needs; for example, a student who spends full days in the regular classroom one year may require part-time placement in a resource room the next. The critical point is for the involved professionals, parents, and child to feel comfortable with such a change and not view it as a "demotion" or failure on anyone's part. Placement options must be kept open, with no one considered any better than another. Table 3.1 displays the various placement options that should be considered when developing the IEP for school-age, hearing-impaired children.

Even if it has not been set as the goal for placement, full mainstreaming often has been misinterpreted. Some educational administrators, for example, believe it means placement in the home school in a chronological age–appropriate, regular-education classroom with no support services. Although the term *full mainstreaming* implies regular-education classes, the need for support services must also be presumed. In the case of hearing-impaired children, some services (including auditory and speech and language management, conducted by the appropriate professionals) should always constitute an integral part of the IEP, even for the child performing at or above grade level.

Full mainstreaming, therefore, allows the hearing-impaired child to participate in all the academic and special classes in which his or her classmates participate. This child is placed in the regular-education classroom, generally at or perhaps one grade below that appropriate for chrono-

TABLE 3.1 Educational Placement Alternatives for School-Age Hearing-Impaired Children

Mainstreaming Type	Settings	Academics	Services*
Full	Home school Centralized school	All in regular education class with regular education teacher	Auditory, Language, FM, Speech, Tutoring, Amplification monitoring
Partial	Home school Centralized school Program for hearing-impaired	Some in regular education class, some in resource room or class for hearing-impaired or one-to-one instruction	Same as above
Social (lunch, recess, gym)**	Home school Centralized school Program for hearing-impaired School for the deaf	All in special education class or resource room or class for hearing-impaired with special education teacher	Same as above

*Depends on the individual child; the majority are candidates for FM systems and language management services
**Requires a great deal of flexibility and the ability to handle the logistical problems of transportation

logical age, and receives academic content from the regular-education teacher. Typically this child uses special classroom amplification (a wireless FM system) instead of personal hearing aids and receives educationally related language management. Such a student usually can function in communication situations that require maximal use of residual hearing and spoken language. Some children who rely on total communication also can function quite well in a full mainstream setting when the services of a classroom interpreter are provided.

Full mainstreaming also implies complete integration with normal-hearing peers, both academically and socially. Therefore, although the child will need to spend part of the day in the one-to-one setting required by language management, he or she should not be removed from all opportunities to interact socially with peers. Some creative planning can assure inclusion in most recesses and "special" activities (gym, music, art).

Partial mainstreaming is the appropriate educational option for the hearing-impaired child who cannot handle all of the academic material in the regular-education class, but who is able to function at grade level for several subjects. For example, a hearing-impaired child may study math, spelling, language arts, and reading with the regular-education teacher and then go to a resource room for social studies and science.

When developing the IEP for a partially mainstreamed child, the planner needs to know which subjects must be specially scheduled (in a small group or one-to-one setting). This placement allows for interaction with normal-hearing peers for some academics and "specials" as well as for regular social "breaks"—recess and lunch. Provision for classroom amplification and language management are always an integral part of the partially mainstreamed child's educational programming.

Another means of implementing partial mainstreaming comes through a special program for the hearing-impaired housed in a public school. In this situation, although the hearing-impaired child may not be in the home school, he or she is in the local or regional school district and attends some regular academic classes and "specials" with normal-hearing peers. The time spent outside the regular-education classroom is spent in a class or resource room specifically for the hearing impaired, and the academic material is presented by a teacher of the hearing impaired. The curriculum used in this class for the hearing impaired does not differ from that of the regular education class but has been modified for the child's level. As with the other placement alternatives, support services must be coordinated with the regular-education curriculum.

Table 3.2 presents suggestions for facilitating full or partial mainstreaming. As can be seen, the skills and potential that the child brings to the educational setting comprise only part of the picture. The school's facilities and capabilities for modifications play an equally important role. Although necessary modifications may not be present initially, they can be integrated into the facilities by the time the hearing-impaired child enters the system. For example, favorable classroom noise levels can be achieved through a combination of physical modifications and the use of classroom amplification. Child-related factors, such as speech intelligibility, are less easily modified. Eventually, however, with good management, changes can be effected.

TABLE 3.2 Child- and Setting-Related Factors That Facilitate Mainstreaming, Preschool through High School

Dimension	Facilitating Factors
CHILD	Has age appropriate behaviors: classroom, social, interactive.
	Fits into an established group in the selected class with respect to language and academic performance.
	Can coordinate maximal use of auditory cues via personal and school-worn amplification with any necessary visual cues.
	Can speak intelligibly to classroom teachers and to normal-hearing peers.
	Has the receptive language skills necessary to comprehend classroom material and conversational exchanges.
	Has the expressive language skills necessary to participate in class discussions and to communicate with teachers and peers.
	Can integrate socially into a peer group.
	Wants to participate in a mainstream program.
	Has parents willing to have their child mainstreamed.
	Can assume some responsibility for own education.
	Is adaptable and able to handle changes in routines.
SETTING	Classroom teacher receptive to having a hearing-impaired child in the room, including working closely with support personnel.
	Relatively small class size, allowing for individual attention.
	Favorable listening conditions in classroom, with relatively low noise levels.
	Appropriate support services readily available.
	Classroom teacher willing to make modifications in teaching style.
	Classroom teacher willing to use an FM system.
	School administrator willing to fund all necessary services.
	Valid performance IQ measures updated for the child.
	Teachers given time for in-service training.
	Role of case manager recognized and appropriate time allotted to carry out this function.
	Services of a speech-language pathologist available for intensive daily programming if necessary.
	Wireless FM system available for the child's use.

Social mainstreaming (see Table 3.1) is the label given to placing a hearing-impaired child in regular-education classes for special activities (art, music, etc.) and for lunch and recess with the same group of normal-hearing children. All academic subjects, however, are taken outside of the regular-education classroom. The full spectrum of special services also is necessary for children who are socially mainstreamed.

There are several different settings in which socially mainstreamed children can study academic subjects, including a special-education resource room, a class for the hearing impaired within the home school district (local or regional), or a special school. This last option requires presenting all of the academic material in a special setting in the morning and then transporting the child to his or her home school for lunch and an afternoon of specials. Any of these options can be difficult to implement, particularly if there is only one hearing-impaired child in a district, but they are certainly not impossible.

Another educational option, not presented in Table 3.1, entails placing the hearing-impaired child in a school for the deaf, either on a daily or residential basis. This setting provides no contact with normal-hearing peers or regular educators. All aspects of academic and social programming are conducted by professionals trained to work with the hearing impaired. One typically selects this option for children with minimal usable residual hearing or for those with multiple problems who need the special techniques that cannot be provided in any regular-education setting. The majority of hearing-impaired children do not require the kind of programming offered in schools for the deaf.

MAINSTREAMING PRESCHOOL CHILDREN

Preschool hearing-impaired children also should be afforded several educational placement alternatives. As presented in Table 3.3, young children also can benefit from full and partial mainstreaming. It is most important for hearing-impaired preschoolers to spend time with normal-hearing peers so they can be exposed to good child language and speech models. This ideal implies, of course, that the majority of the other children in the integrated program should have better language skills than those of the hearing-impaired child. Certainly the major benefit of a mainstream preschool program would be lost if the hearing-impaired child had the best language skills in the group.

Preschool programs must be observed carefully before selecting one for a particular child. As early intervention programs continue to grow, especially with the arrival of PL 99-457, there will be a tendency to enroll

TABLE 3.3 Preschool Educational Mainstream Programming Alternatives

Mainstream Type	Description	Demands	Services
Regular pre-school (full mainstreaming)	Participate in all activities with normally hearing peers.	Produce intelligible speech. Understand routine activities, directions. Follow simple stories. Interact verbally with peers and teachers.	FM when appropriate Language management Auditory training Speech training
Integrated pre-school (partial mainstreaming	Participate in some activities with normally hearing peers. Taken out for special instruction with other hearing-impaired children.	Interact verbally with peers and teachers. Able to receive through auditory and visual channels.	FM when appropriate Language management Auditory training Speech training

hearing-impaired children in them. Early intervention and preschool programs designed for developmentally delayed children tend to employ a curriculum with a reduced level of linguistic input, making them considerably less beneficial for the child with a hearing loss. Hearing-impaired preschoolers need enriched, not reduced, linguistic input. The team that will decide on a placement for a particular young hearing-impaired child must ensure that such a setting is the most appropriate *for that child*. Children should not be placed in a program just because it exists.

Regardless of the placement, the preschooler's need for special classroom amplification should be considered. Unlike the fairly obvious need in classes for older children, the benefit of special school amplification in preschool programs must be determined on an individual basis. Whether using hearing aids or an FM system, one must monitor the child's amplification on a daily basis. The need for language management at this age is also mandatory, and can be conducted by the school district's own speech-language pathologist or one who is privately contracted. Regardless of how they are funded, auditory training and language development are integral parts of the hearing-impaired preschooler's programming. Depending on the child's age, all aspects of the program should be included either in the IEP (age 2 years, 8 months or older) or the Individual Family Service Plan (IFSP) required by PL 99-457.

SERVICE OPTIONS FOR EDUCATIONAL PROGRAMMING

Regardless of the specific educational plan, successful school placement requires that a hearing-impaired child have access to a variety of services. Brackett and Maxon (1986) identified the interdisciplinary services that any hearing-impaired child might need during his or her school career. Their list, presented in Table 3.4, indicates the wide range of assessment and management procedures that one must consider. Although not all children will require all the services listed every year, the development of an appropriate IEP demands that the potential need be considered each year for every single hearing-impaired child. Table 3.4 also demonstrates that the age of the child and the management setting will affect the need for a particular service. For example, electroacoustic immittance measures are definitely used (D) for all three age groups and take place in a center-based (C) setting. Assessment of written language is not applicable (N) to the two younger groups, but age-appropriate techniques (A) should definitely be used (D) for the oldest group, and such an assessment will take place in the educational (E) setting. (Later chapters will show how one can implement the various components of this service alternatives list.)

The assessment components of Table 3.4 imply that the way to determine the skills and potential that a hearing-impaired child brings to an educational program is by assessing all of the skills necessary for success in school. Figure 3.1 displays a model for developing an educational program based on the results of the interdisciplinary assessment. This model, originally presented by Maxon and Brackett (1987), shows the need for a careful evaluation of all areas before determining specific management services. Through the assessment components, the individual team evaluators document the hearing-impaired child's strengths and weaknesses. The multi-

TABLE 3.4 Variety of Services That Should Be Available for Hearing-Impaired Children in Regular Education Placements, Preschool Through High School.

Assessment Considerations			
	Age (years)		
Services	**0–2.11**	**3–5.11**	**6+**
1. Audiological and amplification evaluation			
Unaided measures: (C)			
pure tone air and bone conduction	TA	DA	D
sound field warble tones	T	N	N
speech recognition thresholds	TA	TA	DA
speech awareness thresholds	T	TS	TS
speech discrimination	TAS	TAS	TS
Electroacoustic immittance measures (C)	D	D	D
Aided measures: (C)			
sound field warble tone thresholds			
hearing aids and FM system	DA	DA	D
sound field speech awareness			
hearing aids and FM system	TAS	TS	TS
sound field speech discrimination			
hearing aids and FM system	TAS	TS	TS
Electroacoustic analysis of amplification hearing aids and FM system (C)	D	D	D
Written report from audiologist to parents, school, agencies, physicians, etc. (C)	D	D	D
2. Comprehensive communication evaluation			
Auditory capabilities (CHE)			
minimal abilities	D	D	D
preferred mode of speech reception	D	D	D
dependance on audition	D	D	D
Comprehension of spoken language (CHE)			
vocalization (quality and use)	D	N	N
word level	D	D	D
sentence level	T	D	D
connected discourse	N	D	D
Speech production intelligibility (CHE)	D	D	D

TABLE 3.4 (Continued)

Services	Age (years) 0–2.11	3–5.11	6+
Assessment Considerations			
Self-monitoring of speech (CHE)	D	D	D
Written language (CE)			
grammar/syntax	N	N	DA
word use	N	N	DA
content	N	N	DA
Written reports to parents, school, agencies, etc.	D	D	D
3. Educational evaluation			
Readiness (CHE)	N	D	N
Reading skills (CHE)			
vocabulary	N	DA	D
comprehension	N	DA	D
word attack	N	DA	D
Arithmetic skills (CHE)			
calculation	N	DA	D
word problems	N	DA	D
In-depth diagnostic evaluation for possible learning problems (E)	N	TA	D
Written report to parents, school, agencies, etc.	N	D	D
4. Psychosocial evaluation			
Developmental (CHE)	D	DA	A
Social adjustment (CHE)	D	D	D
Formal IQ measures (E)			
performance	N	DAS	DS
verbal	N	T	D
Parent/child interaction (CHE)	D	D	D
Written report to parents, school, agencies, etc.	D	D	D

TABLE 3.4 (Continued)

Assessment Considerations			
Services	**Age (years)**		
	0–2.11	**3–5.11**	**6+**
5. Observations			
Child/adult interaction (CHE)	D	D	D
Child/child interaction (CHE)	D	D	D
Child participation (CHE)	D	D	D
Environmental modifications (CHE)	D	D	D
Learning strategies used (CHE)	D	D	D
Use of hearing aids (CHE)	D	D	D
Use of FM system (CHE)	D	D	D
Analysis of noise sources (HE)	D	D	D
Visual distractions/interference (HE)	D	D	D
Use of aide/interpreter (E)	N	DA	D

Management Considerations			
1. Audiological			
Improving environmental acoustics (HE)	D	D	D
Recommendation for and use of amplification (CHE)			
hearing aids	D	D	D
FMs	T	D	D
Daily amplification troubleshooting (CHE)			
hearing aids	D	D	D
FMs	D	D	D
Assessing amplification use (CHE)			
hearing aids	D	D	D
FMs	D	D	D

TABLE 3.4 (Continued)

Management Considerations			
		Age (years)	
Services	0–2.11	3–5.11	6+

2. Communication

Direct service focusing on   (CHE)

preverbal	D	N	N
lexicon	DA	D	D
comprehension	DA	D	D
production	DA	D	D
conversational skills	DA	D	D
speech production intelligibility	DA	D	D
receptive modality	DA	D	D

Vocabulary and content for

home involvement	D	D	D
social interaction	D	D	D
educational setting	D*	D	D

3. Educational

Favorable S/N (CHE)	D	D	D
Home support (H)	D	D	D
Teacher expectations (E)	D*	D	D
Coordination of regular and special educators (E)	D*	D	D

Preview/review reinforcement   (HE)

vocabulary	N	D	D
concepts			

Classroom amplification (E)	D*	D	D
Teacher behaviors (E)	D*	D	D
paraphrase content			
direct discussion			
use visual aids			
check comprehension			

Visibility of speaker (E)	D	D	D
Buddy (E)	N	N	D

TABLE 3.4 (Continued)

Management Considerations			
	Age (years)		
Services	**0–2.11**	**3–5.11**	**6+**
Notetaker (E)	N	N	TA

In-class support personnel   (E)
   aide
   interpreter
	DS*	DS	DS

Academic support (E)	N	N	DS
4. Psychoeducational			

Parent education/counseling   (CHE)
   hearing loss and its effects
   amplification
   impact of noise
   communication development
   parent expectations
   language stimulation
   signal-to-noise information
   general development
	D	D	D

Child counseling   (CHE)
   self-esteem
   career opportunities
   sex education
	N	A	DAS

Extracurricular activities (HE)	D	D	D
5. In-service training (CHE)	D	D	D

Key: A = use age-appropriate techniques; C = center-based; D = definitely need to use/apply; E = educational setting; H = home-based; N = not applicable; S = modify for skill level; T = try, need depends on child/setting; * = day care

disciplinary team then synthesizes this information under the direction of the case manager, so that a clear profile of the child's overall performance and capabilities can be determined. As the assessment components include both formal evaluations and observation of classroom interactions and performance, the team should be able to develop an educational program that not only meets the needs of the individual child but takes into

FIGURE 3.1   Model for developing an educational program from interdisciplinary team evaluation.

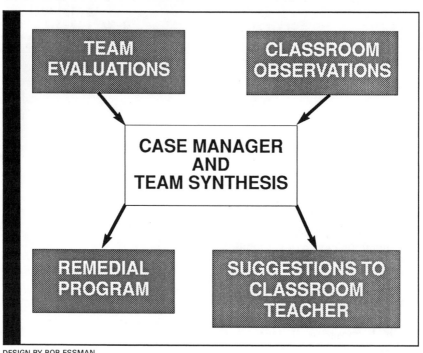

DESIGN BY BOB ESSMAN

consideration the concerns of the parents and the regular-education personnel.

The range of hearing loss and of language, speech, and academic skills exhibited by hearing-impaired students in regular-education settings is considerable (Davis, Shepard, Stelmachowicz, & Gorga, 1981; Shepard, Davis, Gorga, & Stelmachowicz, 1981; Brackett & Maxon, 1986; Maxon & Brackett, 1987). The fact that one cannot predict these children's academic performance solely from knowledge of the degree of hearing loss only serves to make selecting an appropriate educational placement more difficult (Maxon & Brackett, 1987).

As the hearing-impaired child's placement moves further away from full mainstreaming, more professionals become involved in carrying out the services. The greater the number of services included in a child's IEP, the greater the need for coordination, to avoid duplication, to reinforce the use of the class curriculum, and to fulfill the requirements of the IEP.

Therefore, a school-based professional must be selected as the case manager. That person should be designated in the child's IEP and will become responsible for taking on the role of coordinator.

The case manager is not necessarily chosen because of special credentials. Rather, the candidate needs to be on-site daily, have a good understanding of the effects of hearing loss on school performance, be knowledgeable about amplification and the effects of noise on listening, and be able to function as a coordinator without worrying about "turf" issues. In general, the role of case manager is taken on by the school's speech-language pathologist or, when available, by a school-based audiologist or school-based teacher of the hearing impaired. This individual must be able to work well with all of the direct-services providers, regular education personnel, school administrators, and, of course, the child and his or her family.

Although not mandated by PL 94-142, a team of service providers will evolve because of the nature of hearing impairment and the educational significance of its effects. Therefore, it makes sense to borrow a transdisciplinary team approach from PL 99-457, regardless of the child's age. Professionals who have worked with hearing-impaired children soon become aware that no one person is equipped to provide all of the necessary services. Speech, language, and hearing professionals must be willing and eager to work with other professionals who have complementary skills.

4

Audiological Evaluation and Amplification Assessment

Because the communicative, linguistic, academic, and social problems exhibited by hearing-impaired children evolve from the loss itself, the audiological evaluation, which defines the type, configuration, and degree of hearing loss, becomes the first and indispensable component of a comprehensive assessment. A thorough assessment of amplification should follow, adding vital detail to the picture. The number of such evaluations conducted each year is determined by the child's age and specific needs. In general, children over the age of 6 are evaluated on an annual basis, while those between 3 and 6 should be checked semiannually. Younger hearing-impaired children (0–24 months) should have an audiological evaluation every 4 months.

AUDIOLOGICAL EVALUATION

Pure Tone Measures

Pure tone air and bone conduction threshold testing comprise the typical basic measure of hearing status, providing information about type and degree of hearing loss across frequency for each ear. Air conduction and bone conduction measures commonly use a conventional, hand-raising technique; however, younger and multiply handicapped children require modification of these conventional test procedures and response modes.

For the younger child who will accept headphones and can perform a motor task to indicate hearing the pure tone, one can employ a play audiometry technique to yield a complete air and bone conduction audiogram. When a play audiometry technique is too difficult for the child, a visual reinforcement paradigm (in which an appropriate response, such as turning the head in the direction of the tone, is reinforced with a visual stimulus like a moving, lighted toy) typically becomes the method of choice. Presentation of warbled tones (rather than pure tones) in the sound field (through the loudspeakers) can be used for children of any age who will not accept headphones. Regardless of the response mode selected for a particular child, when audiometric thresholds are obtained in the sound field, only better ear responses are being measured; if one ear has better hearing, it is the hearing in that ear that will be represented on the sound field audiogram.

The information derived from pure tone (or warble tone) tests provides a general framework for estimating the potential problem areas that affect speech, language, and academic performance, and forms a basis for determining the specific amplification characteristics that may benefit the child. Even though individual ear pure tone information is better, binaural amplification can readily be prescribed when only sound field information is available (Maxon, 1982).

One also can use the pure tone audiogram to monitor any change in hearing level when thresholds are plotted chronologically. Beginning with the first reliable, individual ear test, thresholds can be recorded on a form such as that in Figure 4.1. Keeping this type of record in the child's file permits a view of air conduction thresholds over time, allowing for any deterioration in threshold level to be noted. Such an occurrence should prompt an otological or other medical evaluation. Even if medical intervention does not halt or reverse the progression, awareness of it enables parents and professionals to begin coping with the ramifications of the change in hearing status.

The relationship of air and bone conduction measures as displayed in Table 4.1 indicates the type of hearing loss the child demonstrates. Middle ear disease or structural abnormalities will result in a *conductive hearing loss* that will fluctuate with the medical condition. Structural conductive etiologies, such as malformed ossicles, are congenital, while the others, such as middle ear fluid, typically are acquired. Audiometrically, a conductive hearing loss will show thresholds within normal limits for bone conduction and below normal limits for air conduction. This comparison of air

FIGURE 4.1 Form for cumulative record of air conduction thresholds.

Cumulative Record of Air Conduction Thresholds

Client Name _____   File Number: _____

Date	Right									Left									Audiologist
	250	500	1000	1500	2000	3000	4000	8000		250	500	1000	1500	2000	3000	4000	8000		

Comments:

TABLE 4.1 Hearing Loss Types

Type	Audiometric Results	Etiologies*
Sensorineural	Air conduction and bone conduction thresholds show an equal hearing loss. High frequency thresholds tend to be poorer than lower frequencies. Speech discrimination scores show effects of high frequency loss. Normal tympanometry.	Genetic factors Pre-, postnatal infections Anoxia, trauma
Conductive	Air conduction thresholds show a hearing loss and bone conduction thresholds are within normal limits. Low frequency thresholds tend to be poorer than high frequencies, or the hearing loss is "flat." Speech discrimination is good. Tympanometry is abnormal.	Middle ear effusion Structural abnormalities
Mixed	Air conduction thresholds show a hearing loss. Bone conduction thresholds show a hearing loss but are better than air conduction. Tympanometry is abnormal.	Any combination of the above

*Some examples of etiologies that are common to children.

and bone conduction thresholds is not the only way to determine the type of hearing loss. Immittance measures also document the status of the middle ear.

A pure *sensorineural hearing loss* is the result of damage to the cochlea or eighth cranial nerve (CN VIII), and may be congenital, acquired, or progressive in children. When displayed on an audiogram, air conduction and bone conduction thresholds show a hearing loss of approximately equal degree. Generally, sensorineural hearing losses are greater in the higher frequencies and so have a more negative effect on the perception of speech sounds.

Some children with a permanent sensorineural hearing loss also acquire, as a result of middle ear disease, a conductive component. This condition is referred to as a *mixed hearing loss*. The degree of hearing loss will fluctuate with the middle ear condition, becoming worse as the conductive component increases. The audiogram of a child with a mixed etiology demonstrates a hearing loss by bone conduction (representing the sensorineural component) and an even greater loss by air conduction (reflecting the additional effects of the conductive component).

Speech Audiometry

Speech audiometry is a necessary component of every audiological evaluation. These measures permit a better understanding of the overall effects of the hearing loss on a child's everyday functioning. In dealing with a wide range of ages and hearing losses, however, it is frequently necessary to modify the traditional procedures. Descriptions of the conventional procedures and some suggestions for modifications follow.

Speech recognition thresholds (SRTs) are used to gain an overall estimate of the child's hearing loss and to check the validity of the pure tone thresholds. The SRT is defined as the lowest hearing level at which the child can hear 50% of the two-syllable, spondaic words (e.g., *cowboy, hotdog, toothbrush*) used as stimuli. Results correlate highly with the *pure tone average* (PTA) loss at 500, 1000, and 2000 Hz, particularly in the two better frequencies (i.e., where the hearing loss is least).

SRTs also can help the audiologist understand how well a child with a sloping hearing loss uses residual hearing. If the SRTs of such a child agree more closely with the pure tone thresholds at the lower audiometric frequencies (250 and 500 Hz), where hearing is better than at the middle and higher frequencies, this suggests good potential for making effective use of that low-frequency residual hearing. That is, this child has the ability to extract numerous acoustical cues for speech from the low-frequency components of the speech signal.

Typically one obtains an SRT by systematically varying the intensity of spondaic words and having the child repeat them until reaching the intensity level that yields only a 50% correct response. Because semantic familiarity with the stimuli is necessary, spondee word lists for children have been developed (Martin, 1987). If a child's language status does not permit oral responses, he or she may point to representative photographs, drawings, or objects. These same techniques are appropriate for the child with unintelligible speech. Even if a child will not accept headphones, a sound field SRT may be obtained and compared to the sound field warble tone results.

Some hearing-impaired children cannot participate in an SRT task because of their limited ability to use residual hearing. These children know that speech is being presented, but they cannot make out the words. An estimate of their SRTs can be derived by obtaining a *speech awareness threshold* (SAT). For SAT measures, the child needs only indicate that speech is heard, not what is heard. It has been demonstrated (Chaiklin, 1959) that the SAT (the lowest intensity level at which a child indicates detecting speech 50% of the time) is approximately 10 dB better (lower in intensity) than the SRT, and so an SRT level can be predicted from the SAT.

Infants, toddlers, and some other young children who cannot provide an SRT will readily participate in an SAT task when an appropriate reinforcer is used. Therefore, a child with limited language skills (due to chronological age, developmental age, or hearing loss) who has participated in conditioned play, visual reinforcement, or behavioral observation audiometry also can participate in an SAT procedure.

The measurement of an SRT can be very important in identifying problems with a particular group of school-age children. Those who present a pure tone hearing loss but have considerably better SRTs than would be predicted from the PTA may have a non-organic hearing loss. These children seem to find comfort in the attention they gain from exhibiting problems that do not have a physical basis. They may do so rather than go to school or participate in a particularly unpleasant task. Children who have had some experience with hearing loss (either personally, with a transient middle ear condition, or with a hearing-impaired family member) may display this pseudo-loss of hearing.

This problem should not be minimized, as it is crucial to know when a hearing loss is non-organic and to determine its underlying cause. Without establishing the functional nature of the problem, the child may endure repeated and unnecessary otological examinations, be fitted with hearing aids, and even undergo exploratory middle ear surgery.

Speech discrimination tests offer the audiologist a great deal of useful information. The purpose of such testing is to determine how well an individual can perceive the various speech sounds when words are presented at a comfortable listening level. Typically, the poorer a person's high-frequency hearing, the poorer the discrimination score. The audiologist's initial decision in such testing pertains to the specific type of test and procedure to employ.

In conventional procedures, the examiner reads or plays a prerecorded list of 50 monosyllabic words, presented in a carrier phrase. The list is delivered at a predetermined sensation level (30, 35, or 40 dB SL re: SRT), and the child must repeat exactly what is heard. A percent correct score is obtained with any error in response scored as "incorrect." Because the words used should be in the examinee's vocabulary, the lists developed for adults (PB-50, W-22, Harvard lists, consonant-nucleus-consonant [CNC], consonant-vowel-consonant [CVC]) may be inappropriate for children, especially those with limited language skills. Regardless of chronological age, for children with intelligible speech and reduced vocabulary, the PB-Kindergarten lists of monosyllabic words are more appropriate than the adult lists.

When an oral response is not possible, or if the child's vocabulary falls below that of an average normal-hearing 5-year-old, one cannot employ conventional procedures; the situation requires alternative response protocols and test stimuli. Two such standardized tests of speech discrimination ability are *Word Intelligibility by Picture Identification* (WIPI; Ross & Lerman, 1970), a closed-set, picture-pointing word identification measurement with an age 3 vocabulary level, and the *Northwestern University Children's Perception of Speech* (NU-CHIPS; Elliot & Katz, 1980), a similar, somewhat easier test. These instruments can give an accurate estimate of speech discrimination in the young hearing-impaired child.

For children with even lower language levels than those suitable for the WIPI or NU-CHIPS, one can make an informal assessment of unaided residual hearing use by having the child follow simple commands, point to familiar objects, or indicate the presence of sounds in Ling's five-sound test (Ling, 1976). These sounds, /ɑ/, /i/, /u/, /s/, and /ʃ/, can be delivered to the child at an appropriate intensity level and he or she can indicate (see preceding on SAT) having heard them. Absence of response denotes that the particular speech sound is not audible.

When possible, speech discrimination tests should be administered to each ear separately, at an appropriate intensity level. Research has demonstrated (Davis & Silverman, 1960) that one obtains optimal speech discrimination scores at 30–40 dB above the SRT. For children with normal hearing or mild hearing losses, a presentation level of approximately 45 dB HL (normal conversational speech level) provides good information. When the severity of the child's loss precludes this relatively low intensity, a higher suprathreshold level is necessary. If known, the child's *most comfortable loudness* (MCL) level should be used; that is, the intensity level at which speech sounds most comfortable. However, as readily obtaining MCL measures is difficult with younger and limited-language children, in these cases a 30–40 dB sensation level (intensity above the SRT) is appropriate to measure speech discrimination.

The following suggestions present variations of typical procedures that the examiner can carry out in addition to regular testing and thus obtain more information about the hearing-impaired child. The information so derived helps determine realistic goals for educational placement and all other aspects of managing hearing-impaired children.

1. *Phonemic scoring for speech discrimination.* A speech discrimination score typically is obtained by scoring whole-word correctness. However, Duffy (1967) and Markides (1978) suggest that one should score speech discrimination tests for phoneme correctness rather than, or in addition to, whole-word correctness. By analyzing each error and comparing it to those

expected from the configuration of the hearing loss, it is possible to determine how well a child makes use of residual hearing. If the degree and configuration of the hearing loss reduce or eliminate specific acoustic cues for speech, a child cannot be expected to correctly perceive the phoneme that the cue distinguishes. For example, a child with a moderate high-frequency loss should have difficulty hearing the acoustic cues that distinguish /f/ and /s/, but not /b/ and /p/. When the audiologist provides phoneme-specific error information, those errors can form the basis of auditory management. In brief, this method of scoring agrees with the major purpose of the evaluation; that is, assessment should help clarify the direction and goals of management.

2. *Effects of language.* Chapter 5 discusses the need to ensure that problems in speech perception do not confound the measurement of language status. When the audiologist assesses speech discrimination, however, he or she must consider the opposite issue; that is, test material should be selected to ensure that deficient language (e.g., vocabulary) does not negatively affect results, yielding a reduced discrimination score. If a child is unfamiliar with a particular stimulus word, whether it occurs in a closed-set, picture-pointing test or in an open-set, monosyllabic word discrimination test, he or she probably will not perceive it correctly, giving the appearance of a more severe speech perception problem than actually exists. As it is difficult to separate out the relative impact of language on speech discrimination testing after the assessment is complete, the audiologist must be aware of and take into account a child's vocabulary, comprehension, and syntactic abilities when determining the appropriateness of a particular test.

The PB-K lists and tests such as the WIPI and NU-CHIPS came about in an attempt to circumvent problems associated with assessing speech discrimination in children with reduced language levels. By modifying some of the conventional methods of administering these tests, the effects of language skills on speech discrimination can be determined during the testing. With the WIPI, for example, when a child gives an incorrect response, the examiner can point to the correct picture and ask the child to label it. If he or she cannot do so, perhaps the stimulus item is not in the child's lexicon. On the other hand, if the stimulus picture is identified correctly, one can assume that the child knows the word but perceived it incorrectly during testing. When scoring these items, the latter would be considered an error of speech discrimination, while the possibility of reduced vocabulary would be noted in the former. Either way, the audiologist's report should include clinical impressions of the impact of the hearing-impaired child's language on the assessment of speech discrimination.

3. *Assessing older hearing-impaired children.* Tests like the WIPI and NU-CHIPS can create problems when used with older hearing-impaired chil-

dren. Although such examinees may not have the requisite skills for the language and response modes of conventional tests, low-vocabulary, closed-set tests may be too easy for them and overestimate their speech discrimination abilities. Clinical experience has shown that when used with older children, WIPI scores can be significantly higher than those obtained on an open-set monosyllabic word list. In one extreme example, a child scored 80% on the WIPI and 16% with the PB-K lists.

The audiologist must consider how age-level factors might interfere with the validity of speech discrimination tests. In an attempt to overcome this problem, Ross and Randolph (1987) developed the *Auditory Perception of Alphabet Letters* (APAL) test, in which the names of letters are used as stimuli, and the child responds by pointing to, repeating, or fingerspelling the correct letter. The APAL is considered a closed-set test, in that responses are limited to the 26 letters of the alphabet; however, the probability of correct guessing is theoretically reduced. Due to the simple nature of the stimuli and children's familiarity with alphabet names, the effects of language abilities should be minimal.

4. *Comfortable and uncomfortable loudness levels.* Measurements of most comfortable loudness (MCL) and threshold of discomfort (TD) are valuable, often overlooked dimensions of a hearing-impaired child's auditory abilities. The simplest way to measure MCL entails using speech stimuli and establishing the intensity level the child indicates as most comfortable for listening to speech. Note that the MCL is not a precise point but a range, and that the audiologist's instructions and specific measurement methods may affect the results. It is possible, however, to arrive at a moderately repeatable and valid estimate of MCL by alternately increasing and decreasing the level of speech and asking the child for a judgment of the most comfortable presentation level (Martin, 1987). Once obtained, speech discrimination can be measured at the MCL.

The TD can be vital when selecting hearing aids. Clinical observation has shown that children whose hearing aids deliver uncomfortably loud sound will either reduce the volume and therefore the full benefit, or will reject the devices altogether. The procedure used to find MCL, however, does not work well for determining TD. To measure the latter, speech intensity level must be increased slowly until the child signals that it is becoming uncomfortable. The audiologist must provide careful instructions for this procedure, as its basic intent is to determine the highest intensity level the child will tolerate. The resulting level will help define the output limits of the child's hearing aids and FM system.

Modification of standard clinical procedures for measuring MCL and TD helps when testing hearing-impaired children; however, any audiologist who tests many children, particularly younger ones, knows that reliable measurements are unlikely. Obtaining MCL and TD require judgments difficult for any young child to make accurately, and for those with reduced language levels that affect their ability to understand the exact nature of the task, it is even harder. As children mature cognitively and linguistically, the possibility of measuring MCL and TD improves.

Immittance Measurements

Middle ear measurements have become a routine part of a complete audiological evaluation. A very large and comprehensive body of literature also has developed, especially as some schools have added tympanometry to their hearing screening programs. Rather than delving into the research literature, however, the discussion here will concentrate on observations and suggestions related to the management of hearing-impaired children.

As mentioned previously, children with sensorineural hearing loss are as likely to develop middle ear disease as are normal-hearing ones. For these hearing-impaired children, the effectiveness of their hearing aids and wireless FM systems will be significantly reduced when this occurs because of the change in hearing levels associated with middle ear conditions.

Immittance measures are particularly crucial for children with severe or profound (i.e., greater than 60 or 70 dB) sensorineural hearing loss. Because of the output limitations of bone conduction oscillators on clinical audiometers, one cannot measure bone conduction thresholds at levels greater than 60 dB HL. Further, as bone conduction measures reveal the status of the cochlea, the inability to measure above 60 dB prevents an audiologist from determining if cochlear hearing levels exceed that figure. These limits prevent determining the presence of an air-bone gap and, therefore, the presence of a conductive component for a child with severe to profound air conduction thresholds.

The best way to determine middle ear status is through clinical acoustic immittance measurements, a relatively quick and easy process that accurately describes any problems such as middle ear effusion (fluid). These measures derive from the fact that the normal middle ear impedes a certain amount of energy flow when a sound is delivered toward it. Acoustic immittance allows the examiner to measure the presence of abnormally high impedance of sound through the middle ear, indicating pathology. Three such measures are commonly used: *tympanometry*, which determines how well the system transmits energy as air pressure changes in the ear canal; *static immittance*, which determines the effects of the tympanic membrane and the middle ear cavity; and *acoustic reflex thresholds*, which determine the minimum intensity levels at which the middle ear muscles contract.

When making clinical immittance measurements, the bridge or meter incorporates a probe that is placed in the external ear canal. The probe's components allow for several functions, the first of which directs a probe tone (typically 220 Hz) toward the tympanic membrane. As with the introduction of any sound, the probe tone then travels through the rest of the auditory system, with some sound reflected back from the eardrum toward the probe. The amount of sound that is transmitted and reflected depends on the impedance (stiffness) of the middle ear system. A very stiff system will have a high impedance, causing more of the probe tone to be reflected away from the eardrum and back toward the probe. The probe microphone then relays information about the intensity of this reflected tone back to the immittance bridge/meter, and the impedance of the system is determined. The probe also allows the user to manipulate air pressure in the examinee's external ear canal (usually varying from +300 mm/H_2O to –300 mm/H_2O) by means of an air pump.

By measuring the reflected probe tone and by varying the air pressure, tympanometry allows the audiologist to determine the compliance (as opposed to impedance) of the middle ear system and to measure indirectly the pressure in the middle ear cavity. Because the eardrum is most flexible (compliant) when the air pressure in the middle ear cavity equals that of the external ear canal, the audiologist can determine the pressure in the middle ear cavity by varying the air pressure in the external canal and finding the point at which the eardrum is most compliant.

Typically a tympanogram is plotted by displaying air pressure (mm/H_2O) along the horizontal axis and relative compliance along the vertical axis, describing the effect of changing the air pressure in the ear canal on the relative compliance of the eardrum while defining air pressure status in the middle ear cavity. By comparing the clinically obtained tympanograms to existing classifications (Katz, 1985), one can determine the status of the middle ear, including the presence of abnormalities. Figures 4.2–4.6 depict the classifications of tympanograms (Types A, Ad, As, B, and C) as categorized by Jerger (1970).

The assessment of static immittance will corroborate the tympanometry results because the stiffness of the middle ear system also can be determined by measuring the volume from the probe through the middle ear cavity. The stiffer the middle ear (e.g., because of the presence of fluid), the smaller the measured volume. The normal range of static compliance is 0.33 to 1.66 cubic centimeters (cc). Any volume less than 0.33 cc indicates an extremely stiff middle ear system, while any volume greater than 1.66 cc suggests abnormal compliance.

Volume measures can be confounded by certain common ear canal and/or tympanic membrane conditions as well as by inaccuracies in measurement. A very low volume measure, for example, can be caused by

FIGURE 4.2 Type A tympanogram, indicating normal middle ear status.

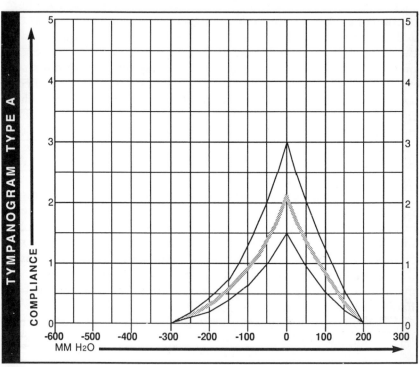

DESIGN BY BOB ESSMAN

impacted cerumen in the ear canal. In that case, the volume being measured is that between the probe and the cerumen itself. Otoscopic inspection prior to placing the probe in the child's ear should reveal this possibility. Alternatively, a very small volume measure coupled with a flat tympanogram may result from placing the probe improperly, either against or facing the ear canal wall. Here the volume being measured involves only the area from the probe to the wall. Removing and replacing the probe should alleviate the problem.

Very large volume measurements can be obtained when there are patent (open) pressure-equalizing tubes in place. In this situation the hole in the eardrum allows for measurement through the membrane itself, resulting in a much larger than normal cavity. Otoscopic inspection and knowledge of the child's medical history would reveal the presence of the

FIGURE 4.3 Type Ad tympanogram, indicating very compliant tympanic membrane.

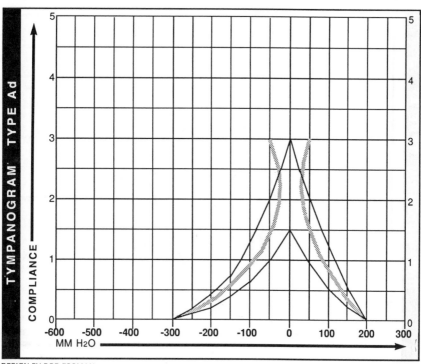

DESIGN BY BOB ESSMAN

tubes prior to testing. This and the other examples indicate that otoscopic examination should precede any immittance measurements.

The third common immittance measure, acoustic reflex thresholds, can reflect the status of the middle ear and provide some information about the type of hearing loss. The two middle ear muscles, the stapedius and the tensor tympani, protect the inner ear from damage caused by loud sounds by reflexively contracting in response to these sounds and thus stiffening the whole middle ear system. For example, when the stapedius muscle contracts, it tightens the ossicular chain, which in turn stiffens the eardrum, reducing the amount of sound reaching the inner ear. The stiffening (reduction of compliance) of the eardrum can be measured readily by the change in reflection of the probe tone; that is, as the eardrum stiffens, more of the probe tone is reflected. Because the stapedial reflex is bilateral, a loud sound introduced to one ear will cause the stapedius muscles in both

FIGURE 4.4 Type As tympanogram, indicating stiff tympanic membrane.

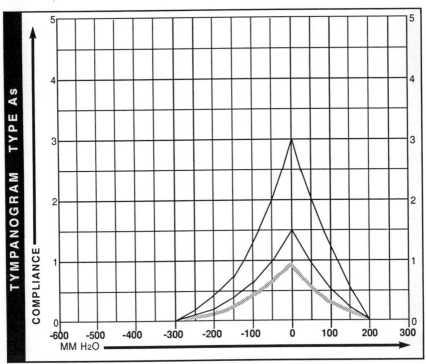

DESIGN BY BOB ESSMAN

ears to contract. Therefore, the reflex can be measured either by presenting a sound via a headphone to the ear without the probe (contralateral) or through the probe itself (ipsilateral).

The lowest intensity level at which the reflex can be observed (through the change in tympanic membrane compliance) provides diagnostic information. For normal-hearing children with no middle ear pathology, reflexes should fall within normal intensity limits (70–90 dB). Children with pure conductive hearing loss can have either elevated reflexes (thresholds obtained at higher than normal intensity levels) or absent reflexes (no reflex observed at the intensity limits, typically 110 dB). The higher or absent reflexes occur because the middle ear system of a conductively impaired ear is quite stiff to begin with, and any contraction of the middle ear muscles will not readily cause any increase in stiffness as it would in a normally compliant ear.

FIGURE 4.5 Type B tympanogram, indicating very stiff middle ear system.

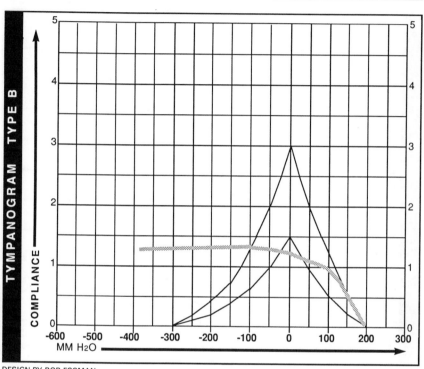

DESIGN BY BOB ESSMAN

Children with sensorineural hearing loss also typically will have elevated or absent reflexes, depending on the degree of hearing loss. The presence of the hearing loss interferes with the acoustic reflex because the amount of sound (sensation level) reaching the cochlea is not as great in an ear with a hearing loss, making the muscle less likely to contract. In ears with milder degrees of sensorineural hearing loss, reflexes generally can be elicited with higher than normal intensity levels. Severe and profound hearing loss usually results in absent reflexes because the stimulus cannot be made loud enough to cause contraction of the muscles. Exceptions are seen in children with tolerance problems that may be associated with severe hearing losses, but who have "normal" reflex thresholds.

Table 4.2 shows the possible immittance results obtained for different types of hearing status. Because immittance measurements are really a gauge of middle ear status, tympanometry results should be the same for

FIGURE 4.6   Type C tympanogram, indicating negative middle ear pressure.

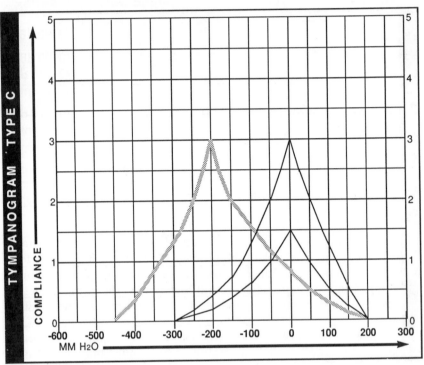

DESIGN BY BOB ESSMAN

children with normal hearing and those with sensorineural hearing loss in which the middle ear is normal. The conductive component of a mixed hearing loss causes the tympanometry results to look like those of a pure conductive hearing loss, reflecting problems in the middle ear.

Immittance measures permit easy determination of the status of the middle ear for each ear individually. Even if the child does not accept headphones, the probe can be hand held, or a screener that utilizes a hand-held probe and surface seal can be used. Whatever is necessary in that regard, immittance measurements are always included in a routine clinical audiological evaluation. They should also be conducted when a hearing-impaired child (a) suddenly begins to show some behavioral changes, even if they are not apparently auditory, or (b) suddenly demonstrates acoustic feedback (whistling) from his or her amplification. The child who begins to show disruptive behavior may be responding to a reduction in auditory

TABLE 4.2 Patterns of Immittance Results

Hearing Status	Tympanogram Type	Static Compliance	Stapedial Reflex
Normal	A	0.33–1.66 cc	70–90 dB
Sensorineural hearing loss	A	0.33–1.66 cc	70–90 dB, 90–110 dB, or absent*
Conductive hearing loss	As, Ad, B, or C	<0.33 cc or lower end of normal	90–110 dB or absent*
Mixed hearing loss	As, Ad, B, or C	<0.33 cc or lower end of normal	90–110 dB or absent*

*No reflex is measured at the intensity limits of 110 dB.

information and may be unable to express it in any other way. Immittance measurement can help isolate the problem. In the case of acoustic feedback, the presence of middle ear fluid will cause the tympanic membrane to be stiffer and therefore reflect sound back toward the earmold, increasing the chance of amplified sound leaking out and causing the whistling noise.

Because immittance measurements do not require a voluntary response, they can be used successfully with young children and older infants. The major caution regarding the latter concerns the validity and reliability of these measures when used with infants younger than 7 months of age (Cone & Gerber, 1980). As a newborn or young infant's external ear is very compliant and the tympanic membrane is not positioned at its adult angle, true measures of impedance of the middle ear system may not be obtained. Research in progress indicates possibly overcoming this problem through a different probe tone frequency (Gravel, 1990).

AMPLIFICATION ASSESSMENT

The discussion at this point assumes that (a) the hearing-impaired child has come to the audiological assessment after a proper hearing aid evaluation has been conducted and appropriate, binaural amplification has been provided, and (b) that the personal hearing aids were recommended with classroom amplification coupling in mind (see chapter 9 for a discussion of the wireless FM auditory system). The routine audiological assessment should include electroacoustic and behavioral evaluations of a child's personal hearing aids and wireless FM system.

Electroacoustic Analysis

Electroacoustic analysis entails measuring the performance characteristics of the child's amplification system under carefully controlled and specified conditions, according to the 1982 American National Standards Institute (ANSI) specifications for hearing aids. The purpose of such an analysis is to compare the performance of the unit (hearing aid and FM system) to the specifications supplied by its manufacturer. In addition, some aspects of amplification performance, such as distortion, can be assessed only through an electroacoustic analysis.

The instrumentation for performing these analyses consists of a small soundproofed box in which a loudspeaker is mounted. The hearing aid in question is connected to a 2 cc cavity (approximating the dimensions of the average adult ear canal and middle ear) coupled to a measuring microphone. The audiologist places the hearing aid inside the soundproofed box with the microphone positioned above the loudspeaker. A signal then is produced by the loudspeaker, picked up by the hearing aid microphone, amplified by the hearing aid, and transmitted though the 2 cc coupler to a response indicator. The resulting display presents the difference in sound pressure levels between the input signal produced through the loudspeaker and the output signal produced by the hearing aid. The kind of information provided by the electroacoustic analysis includes gain (the amount of amplification provided by the specific hearing aid), SSPL-90 (the maximum output that the specific hearing aid can produce), frequency response characteristics (the amount of gain provided at the various frequencies), and distortion measures. The audiologist compares these results to the guidelines provided by the manufacturer to determine if the amplification is functioning properly.

An electroacoustic analysis should be performed (a) when the hearing aid is first delivered to the child, (b) at the regularly scheduled audiological evaluations, (c) when behavioral and subjective measures suggest a problem, (d) when the child and/or a caregiver suggest(s) a problem, and (e) when changes in auditory response cannot be attributed to any other problem.

The audiologist should maintain a cumulative record of these analyses (see Figure 4.7) in the hearing-impaired child's file, so that any changes in electroacoustic characteristics will be immediately obvious. Such a record

FIGURE 4.7 Form for cumulative record of aided thresholds.

Cumulative Record of Hearing Aid Performance

Client Name _____ Hearing Aid Make and Model _____

Date Obtained _____ Receiver _____ Output Setting _____

Tone Setting _____ Other Findings _____

(1) Gain obtained by subtracting input SPL from output recorded in a basic frequency response measure.
(2) All conditions of measurement (e.g., input SPLs, tone and output settings) should be standardized as much as possible so that record reflects changes in the response of the amplification.
(3) Total harmonic distortions measured at use gain with 70 dB input.

Date	Input SPL		GAIN													OUTPUT													Total Harmonic Distortions		
		250	400	630	1000	1600	2000	2500	3150	4000	4750	5600	6700	250	400	630	1000	1600	2000	2500	3150	4000	4750	5600	6700	500	800	1600

Comments:

documents variations in amplification performance that may not be readily apparent in behavioral measures or in the child's self-reports. It pinpoints problems that may be overlooked in daily troubleshooting sessions, problems that may not be noted at the low-volume levels necessitated by the normal hearing of the person conducting the troubleshooting. Whenever the hearing aid or FM system does not perform according to the manufacturer's specifications, it should be repaired or replaced.

The child's routine amplification evaluation should include an analysis of the FM system. This can be carried out in the same way as the hearing aid analysis, but separate analyses must be performed for both the environmental microphones and the transmitter. In the case of a traditional, two-channel system, one must assess both channels. When the child is using direct audio input or a teleloop, care must be taken to evaluate those coupling systems as well.

Behavioral Amplification Analysis

Measuring the performance of a hearing aid or an FM system, as it is worn by a child, provides the most valuable information one can obtain for estimating the suitability of that device for a particular child. Certainly electroacoustic analysis must supplement such behavioral measures, but the final judgment about a hearing aid or FM system's appropriateness can best be made while the child is using the device. Not only do the physical dimensions of a child's ear canal affect the amount of sound actually delivered to the ear, but earmolds create some changes in the acoustic signal, particularly when the molds have been modified (Cox, 1979).

In fact, deliberate modification of earmold acoustical characteristics offers one of the best tools audiologists have in refining the electroacoustic performance of a hearing aid (i.e., the amplified signal that the child receives). At present, the way that earmold characteristics influence performance is most often measured clinically by using sound field techniques. The increasing use of probe microphone measures will provide very specific information about the signal being delivered.

A behavioral amplification evaluation should start with unaided sound field warble tone measures. During sound field measures the stimulus is presented through a loudspeaker with the child seated 3 feet away. These measures typically are conducted in quiet so that the resulting information demonstrates the child's optimal responses.

The audiologist then repeats the same measures with the hearing aids in place, either individually or binaurally. The primary purpose of the entire audiological evaluation derives from this step. From the information obtained (i.e., the functional gain), one can judge the suitability of a particular amplification system (i.e., the hearing aid or the receiver of an FM auditory system) for a particular child. When making functional gain measures with the FM system, the audiologist should obtain warble tone thresholds via the environmental microphones and then the transmitter, with the microphone suspended approximately 8 inches from the loudspeaker (as it would be in the natural use condition).

Some controversy exists regarding this latter means of measurement because the advantages of an FM system cannot readily be demonstrated under those conditions; however, that is not the purpose of this measure, which is to determine the strength of the transmitter at close range as compared to the environmental microphones at a "typical" distance (i.e., to ensure that the transmitter is yielding better thresholds than the environmental microphones because of the built-in intensity advantage and the proximity of the transmitter to the sound source).

After measuring the functional gain, it is important to demonstrate the effect of amplification on the hearing-impaired child's ability to receive and perceive speech. By measuring aided speech discrimination, one can make general determinations about how well a child can handle normal conversational or comfortably loud speech. These measures should be carried out for each hearing aid individually, binaurally, and with the FM system.

However, several problems relate to measuring aided speech discrimination. The clinical situation offers optimal listening conditions (quiet, close to the sound source), which provide little information that can be directly applied to an auditory training program. One way of getting the information necessary to develop such a program involves comparing the aided warble tone thresholds to aided speech discrimination results that have been scored in a particular way. Generally when speech discrimination is assessed, a word-correct percentage score is obtained; by using phoneme scoring, however, one can devise a more accurate description of acoustic cue perception.

In this technique, the stimulus is presented in an auditory-only mode at a normal conversational level. The examiner instructs the child to repeat exactly what he or she has heard, then records the response and analyzes any errors. The acoustical characteristics of the incorrect response phoneme are compared to those of the stimulus phoneme with respect to the child's aided audiogram. In this way, one can evaluate the error in terms of acceptability based on usable aided residual hearing. A very careful plan of auditory management then can be developed (Maxon, 1982). Although obtaining aided warble tone measures may be a common practice among clinical audiologists, phoneme scoring is not. Therefore, a clinician wishing to employ this technique for developing an auditory training program may have to request it from the audiologist, or do it him-

or herself. (A more thorough discussion of this procedure can be found in chapter 9).

In addition to any auditory assessment of receptive speech discrimination, it is sometimes beneficial to evaluate a child's ability to receive visual-only and combined (visual + auditory) presentations. These techniques determine the child's preferred mode of sensory input and assess his or her ability to synthesize the visual and auditory aspects of speech. By assessing all three possible speech reception modes, judgments can be made about the child's use of residual hearing, his or her ability to use visual cues when (if) necessary, and the benefit gained from the combined use of auditory and visual cues. The clinician can then develop an appropriate auditory management program.

As an example, consider a child with a moderate, bilateral, gradually sloping sensorineural hearing loss who has speech discrimination scores of 42% (auditory only), 64% (visual only), and 88% (combined). Taken out of context, the score of 88% in the combined mode would suggest that the child has little difficulty in perceiving the various speech sounds, but this is true only as long as the speaker can be seen. The more critical implication is suggested by the auditory-only score: residual hearing is not being used maximally. In this instance, auditory training would focus on increasing auditory skills, particularly emphasizing the sounds that are acoustically available when this child uses amplification. Without the audiological information, however, it would be difficult for the school clinician to know the child's skills and potential.

The results obtained by measuring speech discrimination in the three modalities also have impact for the classroom teacher. They can be used to explain, for example, why it is not possible for a given child to listen to a lecture and take notes simultaneously, or to emphasize why a teacher must make certain presentation modifications (e.g., not talking while writing on the blackboard). Careful explanation of the implications of these results should clarify the realities of classroom listening for the hearing-impaired child.

Another nonstandard technique for determining a child's preferred modality for speech reception has been evaluated by Seewald (1981) and by Maxon and Brackett (1987). This method uses a specially produced, videotaped version of the WIPI that enables the child to hear one word on the audio track while simultaneously seeing the speaker saying a different word on the video track. For example, the speaker is depicted saying "ball" on the video track while "bowl" is presented on the audio track. By comparing the child's auditory-correct responses to the visual-correct responses, one can determine his or her preferred modality. Unfortunately, this videotape was not commercially available at the time of this writing.

It is sometimes necessary to demonstrate the difference between a child's aided and unaided speech discrimination scores. This may be particularly true for children with mild hearing losses because they may "get by" without amplification. Comparisons of percent correct scores obtained at normal conversational levels (45 or 50 dB HL), with and without amplification, will provide an estimate of the benefit that amplification affords.

Probe Microphone Measurements

Electroacoustic characteristics of hearing aids and FMs make use of a standard 2 cc coupler for comparing a particular device's performance to that specified by the manufacturer. When the audiologist wants to determine the true acoustic signal being delivered to a child's ear through that device, however, those electroacoustic measures are lacking.

The 2 cc coupler is used in hearing aid analyzers because it simulates the characteristics of the adult human ear canal, including areas of resonance. For the young hearing-impaired child, whose ear canal is smaller, using a coupler to predict the amplification being afforded is problematic. As the resonance characteristics of the child's ear differ from those of an adult's, interaction with the signal produced by the hearing aid will yield different results. A clinical technique was developed to overcome the problems in estimating functional gain from a coupler response. Actually these problems occur even with adults, because of the changes in ear canal resonance caused by the insertion of the earmold during normal hearing aid use. Probe microphone measures allow one to determine the exact sound being delivered to an individual's eardrum after that sound has been amplified and modified by the hearing aid, earmold, and ear canal (Lairidsen & Nielsen, 1981).

In probe microphone measurement, a small silicone tube from a microphone is inserted into the ear canal, and measurements are made of the resonance characteristics by delivering a sound (sweeping from 125 to 8000 Hz) to the ear via a loudspeaker. After making these open-ear measures, the hearing aid/FM is coupled to the ear in the normal fashion with the small probe tube remaining in place. Once again the examiner measures the signal present in the ear canal, using the same method so an in situ gain can be found. These two sets of information then allow the audiologist to determine the characteristics of the signal delivered through the whole amplification system, taking into account the ear canal resonance and the effect of earmold insertion.

Probe microphone measures offer a potential tool for testing the young child on whom it is difficult to get threshold-specific and subjective information. (Note that very young children, even those who are good hearing aid users, may object to the insertion of the probe microphone because it must be placed well into the ear canal.) For example, the results can help determine if the rejection of a specific hearing aid relates to inappropriate gain in a specific frequency region not indicated by the electroacoustic analysis or to the functional gain measures. The caution here is that "objective" techniques are not meant to replace the "subjective" ones. Rather, they should supplement the behavioral methods that demonstrate the use a particular child makes of amplification.

COMMUNICATING RESULTS

The audiological and amplification evaluation provides information for audiological and auditory management and for the educational aspects of such management. In order for school personnel to develop an appropriate IEP, the clinical audiologist must disseminate the assessment results and then follow through on recommendations. The professionals involved in the daily education of a hearing-impaired child must be sure they have received the report and understand the implications for management. They also must be comfortable asking for further evaluation when necessary and for clarification of any confusing issues.

By writing an effective report and then following up with a school visit (or phone call) and an explanation, the clinical audiologist can alleviate some of the "communication breakdown" known to occur between clinics and schools. It is important to ensure that the audiological reports are shared among all relevant personnel. Further, parents must have a copy of the written report so that they know the status of their child's hearing and amplification performance. (In cases where the school is funding the evaluation and wants to use the results for planning management, it may be necessary for the parents to obtain the report from the director of special education.) When parents are aware of assessment results, they are more likely to be informed participants in the education of their child.

Communication with the parents also should extend beyond the written report. The audiologist must share the results of the evaluation immediately after completing it and be available for questions and discussion, particularly if the report contains language with which the parents may be unfamiliar. The older child, too, should be included in the discussion of the results, especially as they relate to hearing status and performance.

The report of the initial evaluation is, of necessity, more comprehensive than those compiled after follow-up evaluations. The initial report should include information regarding probable etiology (perhaps obtained from the child's physician), age of detection, all communicative behaviors (auditory responsiveness, speech and language status, gesture utilization), interpretive discussion of the audiometric results, initial counseling attempts with the parents, type of amplification system recommended, and provisions for an intensive follow-up in a parent/child program.

For the purposes of this discussion, devoted to the hearing-impaired child who has already been identified, the following outline[1] provides the general components of an audiological and amplification reevaluation and report. Though no one such evaluation will include all these steps, all hearing-impaired children must be managed on their own terms with consideration given to their individually planned program.

Components of a Comprehensive Audiological and Amplification Reevaluation

I. Unaided Measurements

  A. Basic procedures
    1. Pure tone air and bone conduction thresholds
    2. Immittance measures
  B. Speech procedures
    1. Speech thresholds
      a. Speech recognition thresholds
      b. Speech awareness thresholds
    2. Speech sound identification (discrimination)
      a. Word identification—open set, word repetition
      b. Word identification—closed set, picture pointing
      c. Sound identification—closed set

II. Amplification Assessment

  A. Child's aided performance
    1. Sound field warble tone thresholds with personal hearing aids (individual ear and binaural)
    2. Sound field warble tone thresholds with wireless FM system (environmental and transmitter microphones)

---

1 From "The Hearing-Impaired Child in Regular Schools" by A. B. Maxon and D. Brackett, 1987, *Seminars in Speech and Language, 8,* pp. 393–413, Copyright 1987 by Thieme Medical Publishers. Adapted by permission.

      3. Sound field speech sound identification at normal conversational level (45–50 dB HL) when possible
        a. Individual ear and binaural with personal hearing aids
        b. Environmental and transmitter microphones with FM system
      4. Auditory-visual and visual-only speech sound identification when appropriate
        a. With binaural personal hearing aids
        b. With FM (environmental and transmitter microphones separately)
  B. Electroacoustic performance of amplification systems: hearing aids, FM environmental microphones, FM transmitter microphone
      1. Frequency response characteristics
      2. Saturation sound pressure level (SSPL 90)
      3. Reference test gain
      4. Harmonic distortion

III. Evaluation Report

  A. Background
      1. Review of child's past hearing and amplification status, including any reported changes since last evaluation
      2. Description of child's present programming/management, including implementation of previous recommendations
      3. Current concerns regarding amplification, earmolds, classroom management, etc.
      4. Description of child's progress communicatively, academically, and socially
      5. Purpose of present evaluation
  B. Results
      1. Unaided results, including type and degree of child's loss, with any changes noted
      2. Immittance measurement results, including implications for middle ear status and effects on child's performance
      (This is particularly important if the results suggest the presence of a conductive component.)
      3. Speech audiometry measures, especially speech discrimination, with implications for child's performance
      4. Techniques used to obtain all results, including difficulty in testing and/or any measures that could not be made
      5. Aided results, including performance with personal and school-worn amplification, and discussion of functional gain and speech discrimination
      6. Implications for management, including what child can and cannot detect (e.g., high-frequency phonemes such as /s/ and /t/)
      7. Implications for child's speech and language performance, classroom performance, and auditory training
      (Some audiologists do not feel comfortable making such statements; however, if an audiologist is working regularly with hearing-impaired

children and direct service personnel are depending on the results, such implications must be provided.)
8. Electroacoustic data regarding hearing aid and FM performance compared to manufacturer's specifications
9. Any probe microphone implications, including suggestions for changes in amplification, earmolds, and settings
   (If new earmolds are needed, either because of feedback or to modify the acoustic properties of the mold, this information should be included here. If the audiologist has taken ear impressions, the person or procedure for delivering the new earmold to the child must be specified.)
C. Needs
   1. If child does not have an FM system, present any problems with listening in noise, at a distance, etc.
      (School personnel and parents must understand that aided speech discrimination results were obtained in quiet, 1 meter from the loudspeaker, and that discrimination is likely to decrease with poorer listening conditions.)
   2. Recommendation for a wireless FM system (when appropriate), in cooperation with child's case manager
D. Impressions and recommendations
   1. Summarize results and recommendations made previously
   2. Include supplemental details of amplification recommendations, such as funding source, place of purchase, and follow-up plan
   3. Specify how and by whom recommendations will be implemented
   4. Comment on particular problems to consider in future evaluations
E. Disposition
   1. Note status of follow-up, including dates for reevaluation, other evaluations, etc.

Very importantly, the information provided in the report should describe the child and his or her performance in ways that will have meaning for school personnel. It should spell out the impact of the hearing loss and aided performance on classroom performance, and describe the amount of speech available to the child under both optimal and less than optimal conditions, thus enabling the teacher to make any necessary modifications. Of particular significance are the aided results, which will demonstrate that neither hearing aids nor the FM system will provide "normal" hearing, although they can improve the situation greatly.

5

Communication Assessment

Maxon and Brackett (1983) describe the mainstreamed population of hearing-impaired children as dependent on auditory input for receiving speech, while also demonstrating a significant delay in receptive vocabulary that impacts on their class performance. Their hearing losses range from mild to profound, but as a group they are competent communicators, able to send and receive messages on familiar topics that are intelligible to their teachers and peers. And when matched for hearing loss, mainstreamed children clearly exhibit oral communication skills superior to those of their hearing-impaired peers in self-contained settings (Reich, Hambleton, & Houldin, 1977; Schildroth & Karchmer, 1986). However, when these children enter the mainstream setting, it is important for them to be compared with their normal-hearing peers (Brackett, 1982; Moeller, 1988; Thompson, Biro, Vethivelu, Pious, & Hatfield, 1987).

In selecting a mainstreamed setting as the primary educational environment, the hearing-impaired child is expected to receive his or her academics primarily through a spoken language system. With this in mind, it seems logical to assess the child's communication abilities through the input mode in which he or she functions in the classroom. However, some professionals disagree with this approach to assessment, believing that hearing-impaired children will perform poorly if required to receive test items via spoken language. Their argument includes the point that the speech and language skills being sampled may not be visually or audi-torially salient for the child. But if the goal is to assess the reality of the situation, then one must measure the mainstreamed child's ability to deal with the language system used in the classroom.

Much of the opposition to using speech and language tests standard-ized on normal-hearing children comes from professionals who fear that poor scores will be interpreted as indicative of low learning potential, and thus may prevent the children from having access to the mainstreamed setting. However, when scores on a communication evaluation are inter-preted in conjunction with academic and psychological information, it becomes clear that the test results reflect only a small area of the child's development, with all other areas commensurate with chronological age. In this total picture, the communication scores describe the primary deficit in need of remediation.

The few such tests that are standardized on hearing-impaired children are useful in comparing the child against him- or herself and for informing the parents of the child's communicative status relative to the total popula-tion of hearing-impaired students of a similar age and degree of hearing loss. However, the fact that mainstreamed children score in the upper 10th percentile of tests that have been standardized on a hearing-impaired population offers little help toward developing a remedial program that addresses a mainstreamed child's deficits.

TEST SELECTION AND GENERAL PROCEDURES

The evaluation tools for communication assessment consist of standard-ized tests, nonstandardized procedures, and structured observation within the educational context. No one test can adequately describe the scope of strengths and weaknesses. An evaluation must be based on the skills a child needs to handle the communicative demands of the classroom. Examples of the complexities of classroom interactive language follow:

1st grade: "Who can show us where we live? Who can show us where Connecticut is?"

2nd grade: "Who can tell us the story of what happens when you add three numbers together?"

7th grade: "Now in that exercise you had to pick out the adverb and tell what verb it modifies."

10th grade: "If I say 'I'm waiting for _____,' do you want a direct object pronoun or an indirect?"

Even though the nature of the information being presented or elicited varies according to the child's academic level, the complexity of the syntax and the topic-specific vocabulary remain consistently difficult throughout. These students require techniques for analyzing discourse, such as determining to whom or to what the pronoun refers in the previous clause or sentence. Comprehension of the words and syntax used in questions is essential, as traditional teaching elicits information through a question/answer format. Taking in these features is complicated by the rate, loudness, and clarity of the actual presentation as well as the availability of visual input. These interactive language skills must be examined, together with those skills necessary to understand and produce written language. Written language increases in importance throughout the grade levels. Underlying all of these skills is the child's ability to receive the speech signal through visual, auditory, or combined modalities.

Many of the assessment tools used to diagnose communicative deficits in normal-hearing children can be employed with hearing-impaired children as well, provided that the examiner understands the limitations imposed by the hearing loss. Perhaps the major factor limiting the applicability of these tools is the need to prevent the peripheral speech perception effects of a hearing loss from contaminating the results. The influence of these contaminating factors represents the norm of the child's communicative functioning and thus provides valuable information on the child's functional ability. On the other hand, it is necessary to isolate (as much as possible) the effects of speech perception deficits from the language measures in order to develop an appropriate educational plan based on the child's specific strengths and weaknesses.

The communication assessment is performed not only to develop individual remedial programs and to monitor a child's progress, but also to help regular educators gain insight into the communication problems of hearing-impaired children. By considering the purpose of a communicative assessment, the examiner can evaluate a test's potential usefulness and build a test battery. A specific test battery is not prescribed for all children due to age differences and large variations in spoken language skills. Above all, tests have little value unless their results can be applied to improving the child's communicative performance through a remedial program or through transmission to the classroom teacher.

The sections that follow divide spoken language into its input (speech reception and language comprehension) and output components (expressive language and speech production) and describe an approach to communication assessment that addresses parallel skills across these components. This approach assumes, when dealing with hearing-impaired students, that a breakdown can occur in any or all of the input/output aspects of the model. Speech reception, language comprehension, language expression, and speech production should be evaluated at the word, sentence, and paragraph level, with special emphasis on how the deficit is manifest in the classroom.

Regardless of the kind of testing being done, certain procedures should be followed to ensure that the hearing-impaired child is not penalized for not hearing the stimuli:

1. The child's amplification should be checked immediately preceding the evaluation to be sure that it is functioning at optimal levels. If the child uses classroom amplification (FM unit) that employs a microphone, the examiner should wear it to eliminate any interference from background noise.

2. The test environment should be as quiet as possible, located away from obvious noise sources (e.g., band room, cafeteria, gym, playground), and free of visual distractions.

3. The test environment should be well lighted from overhead. If the room has a window, the child should be seated opposite the examiner, with his or her back to the window. This seating arrangement eliminates glare, which can interfere with speechreading the examiner's face.

4. Instructions should be given while the child watches the examiner's face and accompanied by an explanation or demonstration. Having the child paraphrase the directions ensures comprehension of the task.

5. When verbal test stimuli are presented, the child should be watching the examiner's face and repeating back what was heard.

6. If the test requires verbal responses, written responses should be allowed when speech intelligibility is a problem.

SPEECH RECEPTION

Typically assessments of normal-hearing students begin with the assumption that the examinee makes responses based on accurately received stimuli. On the contrary, any assessment of hearing-impaired children requires careful description of their speech reception capabilities because the latter impact greatly on further test performance and function. Through the evaluation of these receptive skills it is possible to (a) determine the child's primary channel for receiving speech, (b) document the negative affect of background noise and speaker distance on speech reception, and (c) ascertain the appropriateness of the pattern of misperceived phonemes relative to the child's hearing loss.

The basic component of speech reception testing is a list of familiar words, preferably phonetically balanced, presented live voice under varying listening conditions. The child responds to each word by repeating it verbatim (if his or her speech is adequate) or by giving the designated nonverbal response (writing or picture pointing).

With children for whom the traditional phonetically balanced word lists prove too difficult, either because of age or language level, one can adapt the procedure by using the *Word Intelligibility by Picture Identification* (Ross & Lerman, 1970) measure or the *Northwestern University Children's Perception of Speech* (Elliot & Katz, 1980) test, both of which are designed for children under 5. When even these words exceed the knowledge base of the very young child, a list of familiar words obtained from the child's parent or teacher can serve the same purpose. Although the phonetic content of such a list would be far from standard or representative, it would allow for comparisons of function under varying listening conditions.

Because the word lists are administered live voice in a face-to-face fashion, a number of variables undoubtedly influence the procedure. Unless a sound level meter is available to monitor intensity levels, the child's scores possibly will reflect variations in the speaker's voice. One should take special care to keep the voice at the same level in the distance conditions, as it is a natural reaction to raise the intensity when speaking to a person beyond the typical 3-foot conversational distance. When using visual-only and combined modalities, the presenter should avoid exaggerated mouth movements.

It is possible to analyze the child's speech reception capabilities in isolation, without being restricted by his or her speech production proficiency. A nonverbal response mode such as pointing to pictures or indicating an answer graphically allows bypassing the child's speech skills. Although this approach enables comparisons among various listening conditions, it does not provide insight into how the child auditorily self-monitors. By utilizing a verbal response, the examiner can analyze the acoustic pattern of the errors relative to the stimuli and explore the interrelationship between speech perception and speech production. Critical to this procedure is a knowledge of the child's articulatory skills when spontaneously producing sounds in words. For example, if the child produces the /k/ in *cat* when looking at the picture or when imitating a full-face model but repeats *tat* when given an auditory-only model to imitate, then it is the perception of the auditory cues for /k/ that are lacking when listening through an impaired ear.

Two different approaches to scoring can be used to analyze the results of the speech reception testing. A whole-word approach yields a percent-correct score for each listening condition tested, but it does not allow for patterns of errors to emerge. For example, after hearing the word *please*, a response would be tallied as incorrect if the child said "pleat" (1 phoneme incorrect) or "true" (4 phonemes incorrect). The first response represents a closer approximation of the stimulus word, with the vowel and two of the three consonants correct. The second response deviates much further from the stimulus and, as such, represents a greater mistake. Yet under the whole-word scoring procedure, each response would receive the same score—1 wrong (see chapter 9 for an in-depth discussion).

A more detailed analysis becomes possible by scoring each of the phonemes in the child's response that corresponds to those in the stimulus word. For example, responding to a list of 25 phonetically balanced (CVC—consonant-vowel-consonant) words, a child could obtain a perfect score of 75 if he or she produces all the phonemes correctly. (If the words contain blends, then each phoneme in the blend must be counted, potentially increasing the maximum score beyond 75.) The AB Isophonemic Word Lists (Boothroyd, 1984), which consist of 10 words with all sound categories included, lend themselves to this phonemic analysis. In this case, a total score of 30 would indicate that all the phonemes in the CVC words are correct. Further analysis is possible of the percentage of vowels correct ($^*/10$) and the percentage of consonants accurately perceived ($^*/20$).

Primary Modality

To assess the relative contribution of the visual and auditory modalities for speech reception, the word lists should be presented by speechreading alone, listening alone, and with speechreading and listening combined, while holding all other factors such as distance and noise level constant. The child should be seated at a comfortable conversational distance from the speaker (usually 3 feet) in a quiet room. The examiner presents the lists at the same intensity level while turning the student's amplification off for the speechreading condition, eliminating visual cues (by covering the mouth or having the child shut his or her eyes) for the auditory condition, and maximizing both auditory and visual cues for the combined condition. The scores obtained in the combined look/listen mode should be higher than those obtained in either single-modality condition, confirming the complementary contribution of speechreading and audition on the speech reception of hearing-impaired listeners.

Comparing the single modality scores enables the examiner to gain some insight into whether a child depends primarily on one input channel, and to observe the relative contribution of each modality toward combined reception. If it is possible to enhance the functioning of the poorer modality where clearly there is room for improvement, then the effect would be to increase combined modality reception.

Consider two children with very similar hearing who both achieve combined reception scores of 84%. Superficially, it would appear they are functioning in a comparable fashion. However, the single modality scores of the first child were 30% for speechreading and 62% for listening, while the second child achieved a speechreading score of 60% and a listening score of 32%. Considering the disparity in the speechreading and listening scores and the comparable hearing losses, the clinician must seek the reason for the disparity.

The classroom teachers of hearing-impaired children have an immediate need for the information reflected by these scores. Many teachers believe that if the child wears a hearing aid, no further action on their part is necessary. They also think that if a child can see the teacher's lips, he or she can follow the classroom discussion and lessons just through speechreading. The improvement noticed in combined reception (visual and auditory) over single modalities often results in teachers being more willing to make modifications in teaching style in order to maximize the students' reception of speech. Minor teaching changes such as no longer talking while writing on the blackboard or while holding a pencil in one's mouth can dramatically enhance speech reception for these hearing-impaired children, who are so dependent on hearing to function in the classroom.

Interference

Due to the negative acoustic conditions in the average classroom (see chapter 8), most hearing-impaired students face an educational environment that is poorly adapted to their listening needs. When these conditions couple with the variability of speaker (teacher) distance from the child, the negative effect is intensified. Presenting the word lists under simulated classroom conditions can convey to the teacher the effects of noise and speaker-listener distance on the child's receptive capacities.

As demonstrated in Figure 5.1, the lists are presented auditory-only under two distance conditions: 3 feet to simulate conversational distances, and 8 to 10 feet to represent typical teacher-student distances. At each location, the examiner presents the lists in quiet (no obvious background noise) and in noise. To reflect the composition of classroom noise most accurately, the noise source should be a tape of multiple talkers, either commercially produced or self-generated in a cafeteria or large group setting. The tape recorder playing the noise (N) should rest 3 feet in front of the student, directly across from the speaker/presenter (SP) and in front of the hearing-impaired student (HI). Ideally the speaker's voice and the noise should register 65 dB SPL on a sound level meter at the child's ear, replicating normal conversational levels at 3 feet. If such measurement is not possible, then a subjective estimate of equal loudness between the speech and noise should be made by more than one person. (Once the intensity level has been established, mark the volume control on the tape recorder so that the same level can be set at the next evaluation.)

FIGURE 5.1 Location of noise (N), speech (SP), and hearing-impaired listener (HI) for close (A) and far (B) distances during structured speech reception testing.

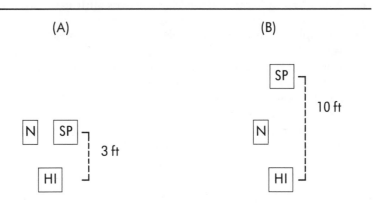

When the distance condition (B) is attempted, the speaker (SP) should move back until 10 feet from the student (HI), holding constant the intensity of the speech and the noise level (which stays in the same position at 3 feet). This condition most closely approximates the typical "lecture class," in which noise from equipment, children, and desks occurs closer to the child (and therefore is louder) than the primary speaker.

The examiner should employ a special set of conditions with children who have unilateral hearing losses or who are unilaterally amplified. The placement of the noise tape becomes critical as one tries to interpret these results. Typically children with residual hearing in one ear have enormous difficulty when noise occurs primarily on the side of their good ear, as it monopolizes the ear and effectively masks the speech. Noise on the poorer ear side incurs less interference because the better ear is left free to attend to the speech. For these unilaterally impaired children, it is important to alternate the location of speech and noise for both the close and far distance conditions. Such results can help determine classroom seating placements and whether an assistive listening device should be considered.

Error Patterns

To further explore the child's use of residual hearing, the examiner can analyze his or her listening errors and relate them to the degree and configuration of the hearing loss, as in the following example:

Stimulus	Response	Errors
ship	shik	/k/ for /p/ (voiceless plosive)
thatch	fax	/f/ for /th/ (voiceless fricative);
		/ks/ for /ch/ (voiceless affricate)

These sample errors show that all the misperceived sounds are voiceless plosives and sibilants, which suggest the child does not hear the high-frequency cues that characterize these features. The next step is to examine the aided audiogram to determine if the child has access to these high-frequency cues when using amplification at conversational levels (see chapter 9). If amplification cannot provide the acoustic information, then these errors can be expected. If, however, this high-frequency information is audible to the child and not being used, these errors are unacceptable and should be included as stimuli in the remedial program.

A second example will elaborate the benefits of examining error patterns:

Stimulus	Response	Errors
hide	hine	/n/ for /d/ (nasal for plosive)
fib	fip	/p/ for /b/ (voiceless for voiced)
food	seek	/s/ for /f/ (place error);
		/i/ for /u/;
		/k/ for /d/ (voiceless-voiced error)
hen	hin	/I/ for /E/
choose	chow	/au/ for /u/;
		/-/ for /z/

Here the child misperceived three vowels, interchanged voiced and voiceless consonants, and substituted a nasal for a stop-plosive. The child's aided audiogram shows that he has access to the speech frequencies through 1500 Hz at a conversational level, but he can hear the high frequencies only at loud intensity levels. Therefore, the phonemes that rely primarily on cues falling in the lower speech frequencies, such as voicing, nasality, and vowels, should be perceived correctly. Knowing this, auditory perceptual training is indicated for this child because his errors are inconsistent with his aided hearing.

Sentences and Paragraphs

While the information gained from isolated words is useful, reality requires evaluation of longer speech units—sentences and paragraphs. However, these are employed less frequently as stimuli because to select appropriate examples requires an intimate knowledge of the child's language competence. It is unrealistic to expect children to repeat or comprehend sentence-length material that falls outside their language knowledge. To determine the linguistic appropriateness of the sentences selected, the examiner should present them first in a simultaneous visual/auditory condition. If the child can repeat them at the 100% level, then linguistically similar sentences can be used to assess functioning under auditory-only or visual-only conditions while varying listening environments.

The addition of linguistic context should result in more words received correctly in the sentence than in the isolated word test. It is not unusual for a hearing-impaired child with a 40% word recognition score and strong language skills to repeat 90% or more of the words in a sentence. A picture-pointing response can be added to analyze the child's comprehension of the stimulus sentence after it is repeated. Within the closed set, the child should be able to combine acoustic cues available auditorially with the linguistic context to determine the answer. Depending on his or her intended purpose, the examiner can present the sentences within the modality paradigm (Aud, Vis, Aud+Vis) or under optimal (Close/Quiet) or negative (Close/Noise, Far/Quiet, Far/Noise) listening conditions.

Speech reception of paragraph-length material adds the factor of retention to the linguistic complications raised during sentence testing. When paragraphs are presented, the examinee must perceive the lengthy acoustic signal, comprehend the meaning of each sentence as well as the interrelationship among sentences, and retain the meaning across the entire group of sentences. Because only paragraph material well within the child's linguistic competence is utilized, responses become indicators of the ability to receive connected discourse under visual and auditory modalities as well as varying environmental conditions. Two response modes are possible: pointing to pictures that answer content questions, or paraphrasing the content of the paragraph. As with the sentences, the child must be able to respond at close to the 100% level, using combined visual and auditory input, before the examiner can use the paragraphs for determining primary modality or functioning under less than optimal listening conditions.

In many ways paragraph stimuli provide the most information regarding how a child functions in an educational setting. Paragraphs require accurate reception, processing, and retention of content in order to produce accurate responses, much like when the teacher asks the class to repeat the content just included in a lecture.

COMPREHENSION OF SPOKEN LANGUAGE

Context plays an important function as children are learning the meanings of words. Situational clues enable children to attach meaning to words and sentences as they occur. Initially very dependent on gesture, movement, eye gaze, routine, and associated objects, children begin to require less contextual support as they acquire the full meaning of the word. Early in the language acquisition process, meaning is also conveyed by the paralinguistic context. The speaker's intent and sentence type are carried by pitch, rate, stress, intensity, and intonation contour. Combined with the situational context, these paralinguistic elements offer the earliest aspects of meaning to infants and continue to play a large role with older children in grasping the meaning of words.

The young child's meaning for a word represents just a small part of the fuller meaning obtained by adulthood. As normal-hearing children listen to a word used in a variety of linguistic contexts, they add subtleties to their initial knowledge until, approaching their teen years, they begin to acquire the full adult version of the word.

Hearing-impaired children, however, function within the narrow-meaning system for a longer period of time. Their restricted ability to receive speech reduces their opportunities to observe the "word" in all its situational and linguistic contexts. Additionally, when the hearing-impaired student learns a word in a particular context, he or she may experience difficulty understanding the word without its contextual support. Therefore the growth of word meaning is slow, often not developing fully until the student begins to expand it through reading.

Word Level

Tests of single-word receptive vocabulary frequently are used with normal-hearing children as a measure of intelligence since scores correlate highly with the scores obtained from other intelligence tests. Such tests should never be employed as an IQ measure with hearing-impaired children. A receptive vocabulary test reveals only a quantitative estimate of a hearing-impaired child's understanding of single words when speech is the presentation mode.

To obtain the most accurate information on a child's word knowledge, one must verify the appropriate functioning of the child's amplification (chapter 9) and then administer the test under optimal listening conditions, preferably face-to-face in a quiet room. The examiner may need to repeat the stimulus item if the child does not look and listen at the initial presentation. The student should be asked to repeat each of the words prior to pointing at the picture. If the word is mispronounced, the examiner should help the child say it correctly, or as well as possible, before he or she makes a choice so that the selection is based on receiving the correct word. A sample sequence goes as follows:

1. Examiner says "paints."

2. Child repeats "pants" and begins to point to clothing.

3. Examiner says "Listen again. *Paints.* "

4. Child repeats "paints" and points to the action picture.

When using tests designed for normal-hearing children on the hearing-impaired population, some procedural changes are required. One problem with a test format that presents stimuli in isolation is that it eliminates all opportunities for applying contextual clues (Moeller, 1988). This format particularly affects the understanding of verbs, which rarely are heard out of context. While normal-hearing children have little difficulty with this setup, hearing-impaired children, masters at developing alternative strategies for comprehending words via contextual clues, display their weak skills.

The age-equivalent score used on word level tests facilitates explaining to parents the gap that exists between their child's chronological and receptive vocabulary age. For example, a 10-year-old hard-of-hearing child who attains a 7 year, 8 months score on the *Peabody Picture Vocabulary Test* (PPVT-R; Dunn & Dunn, 1981) shows a gap of 2 years, 4 months compared to the average normal-hearing child. The age-equivalent score, however, provides no indication of the normal deviation of scores around the chronological age (McCauley & Swisher, 1984a). The child's percentile rank denotes how the score falls relative to all the other same-age children in the normative sample. A percentile of 35 denotes that the scores of 65% of normal-hearing children the examinee's age fall above his or her score, and 35% fall below.

Beyond these numbers, however, this type of testing can yield information on specific error patterns, such as with nouns (*shoe, dog, bus*), verbs (*sewing, submerge, descent*), categorizations (*weapon, transportation, appliance*), and occupation titles (*chemist, chef, sentry*). By observing and questioning the child regarding his or her incorrect choices, the astute examiner can discern the examinee's strategies for dealing with unfamiliar material. The child may be utilizing the process of elimination (if the answer is definitely not foil #1, #2, or #3, then it must be #4) or associative clues (selecting a picture of *store* to represent the word *mercantile*, based on the familiar word *merchant*) to arrive at the response.

When explaining results to the classroom teacher, it may be possible to relate the child's test performance to potential difficulties in comprehending orally presented content material in the classroom. Subjects such as science and social studies may present particular difficulties because of the rapidity with which new vocabulary is introduced. This vocabulary deficit may explain apparent behavioral problems in the classroom, such as inattention or disruption of nearby activities; the child is being bombarded with words that he or she does not understand. For example, consider the following question from a sixth-grade drug test given to an 11-year-old hearing-impaired girl: "A tiny amount of cocaine can produce a sensation causing serious personality changes in the person who takes it. (T) or (F)" On the basis of her PPVT scores and the speech-language pathologist's long involvement with her, it was possible to underline the words she would have difficulty understanding. The girl knew the concept being tested with this question but simply did not understand the question itself. If there were just one or two new or difficult words in the question, she could perhaps comprehend its intent by the total context and then answer appropriately.

Tests that assess the breadth of word knowledge through multiple meanings, verbal absurdities, synonyms, and antonyms are available for use with the school-age hearing-impaired child. These measures require the student to demonstrate flexibility of word knowledge in tasks that mirror what takes place within classroom activities. Two patterns emerge that provide insight into the scope of the student's word knowledge. The first has the student creatively addressing these tasks as long as the stimulus word is familiar. This is the student who says "How do you expect me to tell you the opposite when I don't even know the meaning?" The second type of student knows more words, but each has a narrow meaning. Typically, hearing-impaired students receive higher scores on these tests of in-depth word knowledge than on isolated vocabulary tests, due to contextual support and less restricted answers.

Sentence Level

Because words rarely occur in isolation, it is important to assess the hearing-impaired child's understanding of words as components of phrases and sentences, with endings attached that transform their meaning. Comprehension at the phrase or sentence level requires an awareness of the relationships expressed between words, a knowledge of the effect of word order on meaning, and a semantic understanding of morphological endings.

Standardized testing enables an examiner to assess a hearing-impaired child's comprehension of the morphological and syntactic rules of spoken English. The word, phrase, or sentence is presented orally, and the child responds by pointing to the picture that best represents the stimulus. As with all other tests requiring oral presentation, the examiner often must modify standard presentation practice to ensure that responses accurately reflect a child's current language status and are not simply errors in speech reception (Moeller, 1988). Hearing-impaired children may have difficulty hearing the endings attached to words because they are unstressed and tend to be composed of high-frequency speech elements, which are the most difficult for them to hear.

The sentence level testing may be administered in two different ways: by presenting the morphological markers at a normal rate and intensity—as with a normal-hearing child—or by increasing the intensity at which the markers are presented. The decision to administer the test with one or both methods should be made prior to the testing session, and so noted on the test form. Interpretation of results varies according to the mode of presentation. If the test is administered at a normal rate and intensity, the results only suggest the child's functional ability to comprehend the markers in a normal conversational situation. Under these conditions, it is not possible to determine whether the incorrect responses reflect a lack of knowledge of the grammatical marker or simply that the salient acoustic information was not perceived.

When presenting the marker in its intensified form, the results reflect the child's linguistic performance under more optimal conditions. A high score emphasizes the need to ensure that the child receives an optimal amplified auditory signal. A low score indicates the need for language remediation activities in addition to amplification changes.

Proper interpretation of sentence level testing can help explain a hearing-impaired child's classroom performance. The classroom teacher must be made aware of the child's ability to understand specific syntactical and morphological forms, as this may increase understanding of the child's social behavior, affect expectations for academic performance, and signal the need to modify the oral presentation of instructional material.

Paragraph Level

Paragraph comprehension requires understanding the elements within sentences as well as between sentences. Cohesion of thought, reference as established through the pronoun system, and time displayed through verb tense are all factors that must be considered when processing paragraph material.

Paragraph comprehension testing, only recently addressed in communication assessments, is used to simulate the linguistic demands made on a hearing-impaired child during a classroom lesson or during an extended conversation. The examiner reads a paragraph to the child, who then must respond by answering content questions or by paraphrasing the main ideas. The paragraphs and questions are read clearly and without special emphasis on content words. To optimize reception, the child should be seated close (3 feet) to the examiner in a quiet room and should maintain visual contact with the speaker's face. If the child's attention wanders during the paragraph reading, testing stops until he or she returns to a look-and-listen receptive mode.

The examiner in need of testing material can adapt already existing paragraphs, such as the *Test of Auditory Comprehension* (TAC; Farrar et al., 1976) subtests 8 and 10, which are equated for vocabulary and syntactical complexity. In this case each paragraph is followed by five questions related to content. Answers should be elicited first without the assistance of the response pictures in order to determine exactly how much the examinee understood. Once the set of possible answers is visible, the child may be able to use partial information to make an educated guess.

A similar approach involves paragraphs of graded difficulty. As the paragraphs become more demanding, including inference and more abstract concepts, one can document the child's change in understanding by the number of questions answered correctly. Grade-equivalent scores can be obtained and compared to the child's actual grade placement.

The areas of comprehension discussed so far have covered primarily structural aspects. However, another critical factor to address is receiving and comprehending conversation. Children must make certain obligatory responses based on their understanding of the previous turns in the conversation. For example, they must continue the conversation in the tense designated by the previous utterance as long as the same topic is maintained. If a change in time is necessary, then it must be signified by time delineators in the new utterance. Topic also is maintained from utterance to utterance unless otherwise indicated by a participant. If the previous utterance comes in a question format, then the respondent needs to answer or in some way acknowledge the question before proceeding with a new topic. As a listener or a respondent, the child must actively process the speaker's utterance in order to anticipate an appropriate point for a topic change or for taking a turn.

Hearing-impaired children have difficulty applying these conversational rules due to poor reception and comprehension skills. At present, however, there are no tests to assess the conversational aspects of communication. The examiner must engage the child in interactive exchanges to determine his or her competency in applying the rules of discourse. However, interaction only with adults produces a skewed sample of the child's functional ability. If possible, one should attempt to observe the child interacting with his or her peers and family members.

PRODUCTION OF SPOKEN LANGUAGE

While receptive language competence is critical for academic success, a child's expressive ability impacts most profoundly on social interactions.

Many people will judge his or her general skill development and knowledge by focusing on speech and language production. Instead of delving into the level of understanding that the child exhibits, these individuals use a child's inefficient speech/language production as the primary indicator of communication development. By jumping to this inaccurate conclusion, conversational partners may simplify their speech inappropriately for the child's level of understanding.

In order to parallel the assessment of comprehension skills, the areas of vocabulary, morphology/syntax, and language use at the word, sentence, and paragraph level must be sampled during the production portion of the evaluation. Such information helps teachers form realistic expectations regarding a child's ability to ask questions, formulate answers to the questions of others, and in general participate in class discussions. To function successfully in mainstreamed settings, hearing-impaired children require facility in spoken language, to engage peers in social interactions, to take turns in a conversation, and to adapt to listener status.

Hearing-impaired children vary greatly in their speech production abilities. The more they depend on their hearing, the closer will their speech production errors reflect the availability of acoustic speech cues. Typically these children delete the high-frequency, unvoiced consonants that are critical for expressing plurals, present and past tense, negative contractions, and possession. In assessments the examiner must be sure that these sounds (which comprise the morphological endings) are in fact produced, as the anticipation of a response may lead the examiner to perceive the critical element when it has not actually been articulated. For example, when the child produces a past tense verb in an obligatory context, care should be taken to ensure that the phonemes denoting past tense (/t/ or /d/) are audible and not just presumed to be there by the listener.

A child whose spoken response cannot be understood should be allowed to write it down. This, however, should be the last resort rather than the first response mode attempted. If the examiner allows written responses, interpretation of results must reflect the fact that while the child may have acquired specific vocabulary or grammatical elements, he or she cannot transmit the information orally. Thus, in a classroom setting this child might perform effectively in a written mode, but he or she might be inaccurate in answering questions orally.

When production tasks require analyzing a group of words or sentences for their commonalities, semantic intactness, or grammaticality, it is important to ensure that the examinee has received the stimuli accurately. As with reception and comprehension testing, the most effective presentation mode begins with immediate repetition of the stimuli by the child, with correction given until the repetition is recognizable as the original stimuli. When an acceptable imitation is not forthcoming despite attempts at correction, the stimuli can be written.

Word Level

To add to the vocabulary information obtained during comprehension testing, further analysis of a child's word knowledge can extend to performance in a forced naming task and in providing definitions. Forced naming requires the child to recall and produce the word that best corresponds to a picture. At the lower levels, the target words are direct labels for the objects or actions depicted. Higher level stimuli offer less direct correspondence between the picture and the target word, and the child must rely on inference in order to select the correct picture. The following examples illustrate this increasing complexity:

Target Word	Picture
cow	cow
jewelry	ring, earring, bracelet, necklace
measurement	scale, ruler, yardstick, protractor

Unlike receptive vocabulary tasks, which depend on the child's deficient auditory system for reception of the stimulus words, expressive vocabulary tasks utilize the intact visual system for interpreting the pictures. This explains why receptive vocabulary scores may appear poorer than expressive vocabulary scores, contrary to what is expected with normal-hearing children.

Additional tasks give a glimpse of a child's semantic knowledge. Words can be *defined* by explaining their meaning or by "telling all you know about a word." Determining which word *does not belong* to a group of other words further delineates the limits of meaning for that word. Sentences that *misuse* a word can help determine if the child recognizes incongruity in meaning and knows how to fix the sentence by substituting the correct word. *Opposites* require the child to understand subtleties in word meaning in order to recall the precise word that offers an antonym to the stimulus. *Multiple meanings* can be explored by using the word's different meanings in sentences or by giving an explanation. All of these task options require that the student know the meaning of the initial stimulus before flexibility in its use can be explored. Typically scores on tests of semantic knowledge correlate closely with single-word vocabulary scores.

Children with deficient vocabulary skills often resemble those with word recall problems, as both must spend time searching for the appropriate word to fill a slot in a sentence. It is critical to know whether the problem entails word knowledge or word recall because the applicable reme- diation techniques would be very different. The child with a deficit in expres- sive vocabulary has difficulty naming specific objects or locations and typically will substitute general terms such as *it, this, these, that,* or *over there.* However, given a choice of possible responses, the child may be able to select the correct answer. If an expressive vocabulary deficit exists (as with most hearing-im- paired students), then intervention should address improving the child's quan- tity and quality of word knowledge. With word recall problems, strategies for recalling already familiar words become the focus of remedial activities.

Parents often react incredulously when confronted with the vocabu- lary deficit and will respond, "Of course he knows what a ____ is—we talked about it yesterday." They typically confuse *exposure* to the word in a situa- tion with actual *mastery* of the word. After exposure, the child may be able to recognize the word when it is presented in an oral or written context, but he or she likely cannot access it expressively, to use in appropriate contexts. In the classroom environment, children must select specific words to describe phenomena, actions, or objects; vague, general answers and descriptions are inadequate.

Sentence Level

Analysis of the semantic and syntactic complexity of sentence level mate- rial can be based on samples derived from a variety of formats: elicited, prompted, and spontaneous. *Elicited* samples are based on the premise that certain grammatical forms will occur when framed in a grammatical context that obliges the speaker to use the particular structure (e.g., fram- ing a reply in past tense because the previous speaker's question was posed in past tense). In addition to obligatory grammatical contexts, certain conversational contexts require one to maintain the topic asserted by the previous speaker. Other obligatory contexts derive from the intent of the previous speaker's utterance: questions require answers, commands require actions, and statements require verbal or nonverbal acknowledgments.

Therefore, when analyzing a child's sentence production, it is impor- tant to look at utterances in the context in which they were elicited. A sentence may look grammatically correct in isolation but be used incor- rectly in its elicited context. For example:

Isolation	*Elicited Context*
"He goes home."	Q: "Where did he go next?"
(grammar correct)	A: "He goes home."
	(Incorrect verb tense used)

Tests using this obligatory context format, such as the *Structured Pho- tographic Elicited Language Test–II* (SPELT-II), assume that the child has heard and attended to the salient features in the previous utterance and responds accordingly. As with any test on which poor speech reception interferes, the examiner may need to repeat the stimuli. The initial presentation is made with the critical element spoken at a normal rate and loudness. The child's response to that reflects performance under typical listening conditions and should be interpreted as such. The targeted features next should be emphasized by an increase in loudness and stress to ascertain the child's optimal performance in obligatory contexts. An example follows:

First Presentation	*Second Presentation*
Q: "What did the boy do next?"	Q: "What *did* the boy do next?"
A: "He jumps off the bars."	A: "He jumped off the bars."

Prompted test formats provide the child with the form/word to use, allowing the examiner to determine whether meaning is retained when the child inserts the form/word into a unique sentence. For example, given the word *when*, the child is expected to produce a sentence with a clause that denotes time. This approach samples the elements of English that are less likely to appear spontaneously, such as adverbs (e.g., *heavily*), subordinate conjunctions (e.g., *although*, *since*), and complex verb forms (e.g., *would have jumped*).

Other tests, such as the *Grammatical Analysis of Elicited Language* (GAEL), employ a more directly prompted format. In effect, the student is given an example of the targeted grammatical construction and asked in the next prompt to use it with different vocabulary. For example, the examiner selects two test elements, the boy doll and the chair, and says "The boy is sleeping on the chair" while carrying out the action. Next, the examiner demonstrates the girl doll jumping on the table and asks the student to describe this action. (The target construction here is "is _____ing"). A prompted sample is designed to bypass the problems experienced in obtaining a representative spontaneous sample. The stimuli and forms are provided, leaving little for the child to do except memorize the form and insert the vocabulary. The prompted nature of this elicitation technique cannot replace a spontaneous sample in which the speaker has a specific intent that is expressed through self-selected vocabulary and syntax (Moeller, 1988).

An analysis of spontaneous sentence production requires a representative sample that adequately reflects the child's grammatical capability. The specific sampling procedure as well as the rapport between examiner and child can greatly affect the sample obtained. The following principles have been used successfully in order to elicit adequate spontaneous language samples:

1. Use conversation without pictorial support if at all possible. If pictures must be used, select those that allow the following kinds of ques-

tions: "What happened before this action occurred?", "What are the people saying to each other?", and "How do you think ____ is feeling?"

2. Role playing can permit a conversational format without falling into a traditional question-and-answer routine. For example, ask the child to pretend to be a police officer giving a ticket, or a waitress working in a restaurant, or a mother fussing at her child for tracking in mud.

3. Tell an elaborate story about a true or hypothetical situation, then have the child follow with his or her own. For example, starters such as "Do you know what happened when I went . . . ?" or "If I were a king, I would . . ." can initiate elaborate fantasies.

The main point here is not the technique but rather the need to elicit a representative language sample. The quality of the analysis depends totally on the adequacy of the sample. Without a good sample, there is no point in proceeding any further with the analysis. The transcription of the child's tape-recorded language sample can be improved by repeating ambiguous utterances immediately after the child says them. It is easier to understand a child in person than through a recorded version of the same speech. Therefore, during the audiotaping, when the third person singular is marked by an /s/ that is weak or indistinct, the examiner may say "That's right, he walks up the stairs." Taking notes of such occurrences for later transcription also helps.

The examiner can analyze the sample informally by describing the errors apparent on a visual examination of the written transcript. The errors can give information on the grammatical form being attempted but produced inaccurately. For example, if the child attempts to use a complex construction such as "If I were a king, I would wear a crown" (which begins with a subordinate conjunction and requires using a conditional verb form), the examiner should acknowledge the attempt even if it contains errors ("If I were a king, I will wear a crown"). In this case the child could have chosen a simpler construction and produced it correctly ("I'll be a king. I'll wear a crown"), but instead attempted the more complex emerging structure.

While this approach may be the most expedient, it does not provide the quantitative information required by most school systems for placement or planning purposes. For these purposes, the sample also can be analyzed through one of the standardized methods, in which certain grammatical forms receive a score indicating semantic and syntactic accuracy. Such an analysis yields a total score for the sample that one can compare to the scores of normal-hearing children of various ages. Additionally the examiner can tabulate the child's performance over time to document his or her rate of progress, using either the total score or those for individual categories of grammatical elements, such as verbs, conjunctions, and pronouns, as the baseline.

Paragraph Level

Because little of what is said is expressed in the form of isolated words or single sentences, the evaluation must tap the child's ability to produce paragraph-length utterances typical of storytelling, classroom lectures, explanations, or narratives. Paragraphs require all the knowledge inherent in sentence production and more; that is, each sentence must relate grammatically in some way to the sentence that precedes it. Not only are verb tenses governed by the "time" established at the beginning of the paragraph, but prior reference also influences the use of personal and demonstrative pronouns. In addition to the structural aspects of paragraph production, one must consider organizational factors. For example, the events should be sequenced in a logical order and presented with sufficient detail so that the uninitiated can follow the story line. If the interactants share experiences, then the detail can be reduced. The ability to produce a cohesive paragraph increases with age during the elementary school years.

The examiner can use the spontaneous sample obtained for the sentence level evaluation for the paragraph analysis if the child can be persuaded to tell an extended story or provide a narrative about some ongoing activity. Several techniques can facilitate this effort:

1. Tell the child an elaborate story using no more than four pictures, taking care to use dialogue ("Then he said '___' ") and advanced clauses. Then ask the child to retell the story in his or her own words. Typically the child will attempt to use the advanced forms that he or she heard but, due to the length of the story, will not remember the story verbatim. Therefore, what is produced will be the child's version of what has been said. Although this technique yields an extended paragraph, it does not provide any information on the organizational aspects of paragraph construction because the child generally follows the adult's format.

2. Give the child a topic to tell about (and later to write about) or let him or her select one. General topics such as "favorite television shows" or "sports events" produce samples characterized by simple sentences. A better approach is to ask the student to retell *the latest episode* of a favorite television show or describe *how to play* a particular sport. Children generate the most complex grammatical and organizational formats when they must describe a situation that made them angry, embarrassed, scared, or nervous.

Language Use

Finally, some estimate is needed of how effectively children use and understand language in its social context; that is, how well they employ the correct forms to establish contact with others, influence actions, secure desired objects or experiences, and obtain information. Learning to use language requires a sensitivity to both the demands of the social context and the people in it (such as how and when to take turns speaking). This does not come naturally; such skills require a significant amount of linguistic exposure in different situations. As do their normal-hearing counterparts, hearing-impaired children must interpret the differences between "Is that door open?", "Don't you ever shut the door?", "The door is open", "Why don't you ever close the doors?", and "Shut the door!" when spoken by parents or teachers in different circumstances. In addition they need to adapt the language and emotional content of their speech to the listener's status, linguistic ability, and knowledge. They must learn "peer" language. Hearing-impaired children frequently do not know the latest slang expressions, or understand jokes, riddles, or verbal analogies, all of which acts as a barrier to their effective use of language, particularly with their peers in social contexts.

The examiner can gain an insight into these usage deficits by observing the child in natural situations and by interpreting responses to simulated experiences depicted pictorially. Newly available tests sample some of these abilities and provide ways to quantify them. Simon (1979) has developed a comprehensive checklist to assist the examiner in focusing attention on the myriad factors included under the label "usage."

WRITTEN COMPREHENSION/PRODUCTION

Comprehension

It is desirable to gain some insight into a child's comprehension and use of written language as a correlate to his or her spoken language performance. Reading comprehension subtests can yield important information about children's knowledge of written words, sentences, and paragraphs. Because such scores are translated into grade equivalents, however, they are somewhat difficult to compare to the age-equivalent scores of most communication assessments. Yet, in combination with the evaluations previously suggested, these tests delineate specific problems in handling written language, a skill essential to all classroom activities.

Missing from the typically used academic achievement tests is an exploration of children's ability to comprehend specific linguistic structures in written form. Tests such as the *Test of Syntactic Ability* (TSA) utilize fill-in-the-blank or multiple-choice (the correct word to fit in a sentence, the only grammatical sentence out of four, or the best conjoined sentence of four) formats to assess the understanding of written syntax. This instrument assesses the student's ability to understand, in print, the morphological endings, negation, conjunctions, determiners, question formation, verb processes, pronominalization, relativization, complementation, and nominalization. The results indicate how much the context of a written sentence can assist the student in predicting meaning. When compared to the student's comprehension of these same structures when spoken, it is possible to ferret out those errors that may relate to speech reception.

Production

Classroom tests on knowledge of subject matter or language constructs often demand competent written language performance (essay questions, fill-in-the-blanks, etc.). It is therefore important to distinguish between a hearing-impaired child's possible deficiencies in written language and his or her knowledge of the academic material.

Many hearing-impaired children exhibit wide discrepancies between spoken and written language skills. If they have acquired spoken language through oral means, those skills probably will far surpass their writing ability. This pattern corresponds closely to that of normal-hearing children, who learn to speak before they learn to read or write. Because reading and writing derive from language knowledge, one would expect this relationship between the child's spoken language and writing skills.

Analysis of a written language sample resembles the analysis of oral narratives previously described: either an informal perusal of the grammatical and syntactic complexity, or a standardized procedure that yields a score. Regardless of technique, the paragraph's organization and cohesion also should be assessed.

The examiner can obtain the written sample at the same time as the spontaneous spoken language sample in order to get the most direct comparison. Once the child has "told" the story, he or she can write it, and then look it over for errors. After the written story is complete, the child should read it aloud exactly as written to check for additional errors. A child who depends on hearing to monitor speech should notice the constructions that do not "sound" right when read aloud. This ability to recognize errors while "proofing" the story aloud offers a useful strategy to apply to written work in the classroom.

Hearing-impaired children experience particular difficulties in translating their knowledge of oral grammar to the written page. Their written errors are characterized by omissions of morphological endings, auxiliary verbs, and contractions. Typically they write in simple sentences in place of the more complex forms evident in their speech. Bridging the gap between spoken and written language represents a challenging goal for these children, but capitalizing on their strong auditory-based language skills expedites the process.

SPEECH ARTICULATION/INTELLIGIBILITY

Speech assessments must describe not only the kinds of errors a child makes but also the intelligibility of his or her speech to listeners with varying levels of expertise in listening to hearing-impaired children. This is of critical importance in the regular classroom, where the student must participate in a variety of instructional and social verbal exchanges. If listeners must repeatedly request restatement of utterances, they may find the task of "listening" laborious and lose interest in deciphering what the hearing-impaired student has to say. Additionally, frequent requests for clarification can so frustrate the hearing-impaired student that he or she simply stops trying to communicate orally with unfamiliar partners.

The consistency and accuracy of articulatory productions are influenced by auditory perceptual skills as well as oral-motor sequencing abilities. Therefore any analysis must address the relationship between perception and production and the ability to produce sounds in rapidly changing phonetic environments.

Regardless of the procedure used to obtain a sample of the phoneme repertoire, the results must be compared to the student's auditory perceptual capabilities. Specifically, the examiner must compare each production error to the perceptual errors recorded during the perception testing. If a child spontaneously produces a phoneme incorrectly, but perceives it correctly (listening only), then hearing can be utilized to remediate the production by comparing the error to a correctly produced adult model. The child who exhibits this kind of error pattern is not using his or her hearing effectively to self-monitor. If the child displays the same error in perception as in production, one can assume that the error is the residual effect of hearing a distorted signal. Training in improving perception and production simultaneously would address this pattern of errors most effectively.

Syllable Level

The most comprehensive assessment procedure for evaluating the speech production skills of hearing-impaired children was developed by Ling (1976). Although designed primarily for children with severe and profound hearing losses, the test also applies to children with lesser degrees of hearing loss. Ling's evaluation consists of a phonological analysis (using the stimuli recorded during the language sampling procedure) and a phonetic level evaluation. The phonological evaluation documents which speech patterns are consistently present, inconsistently used, or absent in a spontaneous sample. During the phonetic level evaluation, each vowel is repeated in isolation and in rapidly alternating patterns with widely different vowels; consonants and consonant blends are repeated in isolated syllables with the /a, ee, oo/ vowels in repeated syllables, alternating syllables /ba-be-ba-be/, repeated syllables /ba-ba-ba-ba/, and with varied pitch.

The difference between the phonological and phonetic analyses may suggest that speech production breaks down when coarticulation influences sound production or when the child spontaneously produces the sounds. Conversely, a change in the other direction may signal that, although the production of individual sounds is poor, in connected speech the imprecise articulation interferes less with intelligibility.

Word Level

Many of the tests traditionally used by speech-language pathologists to assess speech production skills apply to measuring these same competencies in the hearing-impaired child. Although these tests are designed to elicit spontaneous production of targeted words with normal-hearing students, hearing-impaired subjects may require modifications based on their unfamiliarity with the vocabulary of the target word (e.g., *vacuum*). Comparing spontaneous and imitated production can help identify habitual versus optimal skills. These traditional tests have the advantage of ready availability in most public school systems.

Sentence Level

Many hearing-impaired children can produce all sounds correctly in syllables and words, but evidence breakdown when the sounds are produced in sentences. Thus it is important to assess sound production when the words are used in sentences. One approach involves telling the child a story with pictorial support, then having him or her retell the story with the assistance of the same pictures. Targeted words constitute a major focus of the story and are featured predominantly in the pictures. The difference in articulatory performance at the word and sentence level provides direction for the therapy program. If the child's phoneme production is similar at the word and sentence level, then it would be appropriate to work on mastery of sounds in words.

Most children in fully mainstreamed environments depend on their hearing for speech and language acquisition. For the majority, the elements of voice, stress, pitch, and rhythm fall within normal limits. However, the occasional student who exhibits deviant vocal qualities needs these elements evaluated. Traditionally these suprasegmental features are assessed by a rating procedure, in which the examiner judges the child's utterances during structured and unstructured tasks. The *Fundamental Speech Skills Test* (FSST; Levitt, Youdelman, & Head, 1990) provides a more objective view of these features by utilizing a series of tasks that sample the underlying speech processes. The procedure, although reliant on examiner judgment for adequacy of response, samples breath control, pitch stability, and repeated sequences of alternating syllables. Most useful are the tasks constructed of monosyllabic words, multisyllabic words, phrases, and sentences that vary in number of syllables, stress pattern, and intonation contour.

Intelligibility

Beyond the detailed analysis of a hearing-impaired child's articulatory deficiencies lies the need to gain some overall estimate of the child's intelligibility. Even a child with a severe articulation deficit can produce intelligible speech, and children with superficially similar speech results can manifest quite a variety of speech intelligibility ratings. Functional assessment of speech intelligibility comprises an important dimension of the overall assessment of hearing-impaired children. These students may have a lot to say, but if peers and teachers cannot understand them, they will not have the opportunity to talk or, worse yet, will be discouraged from doing so. Such children often will avoid classroom discussions or responding to a teacher's questions.

The National Technical Institute for the Deaf (Subtelny, 1975) has developed a 9-point rating scale for speech intelligibility, but it lacks sufficient definition in the intelligible speech range to delineate satisfactorily the speech production deficiencies of mainstreamed hearing-impaired children. The *Speech Intelligibility Evaluation* (SPINE; Monsen, Moog & Geers, 1988) represents a more recent approach to gauging speech intelligibility. Here the student identifies pictures of objects, the names for which share a common distinctive feature and vary minimally from each other (e.g., *church, shirt, chair, share*). The examiner, who cannot see the picture, writes down the word the child says. The child then shows the examiner the picture so the accuracy of the production can be ascertained.

The number of words the examiner perceives correctly yields a speech production intelligibility score.

The information provided by the communication assessment should be useful in describing the child to regular school personnel. It should indicate the impact of speech and language functioning on classroom performance and enable the teacher to make necessary modifications.

6

Academic, Psychological, Social, and Classroom Evaluations

After completing the audiological and communication assessments, several evaluations remain in the multidisciplinary assessment battery to complete the picture of a student's ability to function in mainstream settings. The educational evaluation documents the student's present academic achievement level relative to other students in the equivalent grade. The psychological evaluation provides a measure against which the child's performance on all other testing can be compared to determine if he or she is performing at expected levels. By analyzing the student's social adjustment and self-esteem, feelings regarding the appropriateness of the mainstream placement become evident. Finally, to corroborate the test results, the examiner needs information on how the student functions socially and academically in the classroom relative to his or her peers.

Table 6.1 summarizes the schedule of multidisciplinary evaluations required in order to manage a student's program effectively. Depending on

TABLE 6.1 Schedule of Multidisciplinary Evaluations for Preschool and School-Age Hearing-Impaired Students

Assessment	Frequency	Age (years)		
		0–2.11	3–5.11	6+
Audiological and amplification	>2x/yr	x		
	2x/yr		x	
	1x/yr			x
Communication	2x/yr	x	x	
	1x/yr			x
Educational	1x/yr	x	x	x
Psychosocial	>1x/yr	x		
	1x/yr		x	
	<1x/2yrs			x
Classroom observation	1x/yr	x	x	x

the availability of trained personnel within the school system, it may be possible to perform one or more of these evaluations at the child's home school. If not, the case manager should arrange for the evaluations at outside agencies. These evaluations should not be considered perfunctory or a routine activity; they provide the vehicle by which parents and teachers can monitor the student's progress and redefine the management program to reflect ever-changing needs.

ACADEMIC ACHIEVEMENT EVALUATION

Achievement testing provides a standardized means of documenting a hearing-impaired child's present educational status. For a child just entering a mainstream educational setting, it allows comparison of his or her performance with that of potential classmates to determine if he or she has the entry skills necessary for success. Once a child attends regular education classes, there is a critical need to reassess the placement periodically and to monitor educational progress. Achievement test results should not be viewed in isolation but rather in conjunction with audiological, communication, and psychological evaluation results to formulate a complete picture of functional skills.

School systems vary in the frequency of academic achievement testing, the specific tests selected, and the personnel designated to administer the tests. Optimally, hearing-impaired children should be scheduled for achievement testing on a yearly basis, even though the school system may not be required to do so that frequently for normal-hearing children. Careful annual testing allows one to plot the child's academic progress relative to previous scores and to normal-hearing peers.

Achievement tests typically are administered to an entire class. Group administration, however, makes it difficult to ensure that hearing-impaired children can hear and understand the directions. Whenever possible, these children should be tested individually, or in small groups, to minimize any complications arising from difficulties hearing and understanding the examiner. This adaptation—individual administration of standardized testing—should be stated on the IEP.

The level of mainstreaming in the child's program as well as his or her communicative proficiency factor into deciding whether tests normed on hearing-impaired or normal-hearing subjects are more appropriate. Whenever possible, the same achievement test given to the normal-hearing students should be administered to the hearing-impaired children as well. The latter's grade equivalency and percentile ranking scores then can be compared directly to the scores achieved by normal-hearing peers. An additional score shows the child's standing, on each of the subtests, relative to his or her actual classmates. If for any reason the conditions for administering a standard achievement test are altered (e.g., extended time), these modifications should be noted and results interpreted accordingly. (Extended time frequently is afforded these children because they take longer to process the language used in the questions.) If a particular aspect should be altered every time, then this should be indicated under the test modification section on the IEP.

When a standard test is not appropriate, one can use a version of the *Stanford Achievement Test* (SAT; Madden, Gardner, Rudman, Karlsen, & Merwin, 1973) specifically adapted for the hearing-impaired population. Through a screening procedure, the examiner determines the level at which to administer the language-based subtests. Due to existing language deficits, it is not unusual for a hearing-impaired student to need the subtests that rely heavily on language and reading (vocabulary, reading comprehension, math word problems) administered several levels below that chosen for the more analytic tasks. The adapted SAT provides a way of both comparing the hearing-impaired child to other hearing-impaired children of the same age, and deriving a grade equivalent based on the performance of normal-hearing children.

The educational evaluation can be the most difficult to arrange for personnel reasons. The average school system may not have an educational evaluator with expertise in evaluating hearing-impaired children. On-site professionals can do the job as long as they implement the modifications noted in chapter 5 and give due consideration to the impact of the hearing loss when interpreting the results.

A number of achievement tests assign the same descriptive label to subtests that require widely different responses and may actually tap different underlying skills, which complicates interpretation of results. As an example, consider four commonly used achievement tests: the *California Achievement Test* (CAT; Tiegs & Clarke, 1970), the *Iowa Test of Basic Skills* (ITBS; Hieronymus & Lindquist, 1974), the *Metropolitan Achievement Test* (MAT; Durost, Bixler, Wrightstone, Prescott, & Balow, 1971), and the previously cited *Stanford Achievement Test* (SAT). Each of them purport to measure vocabulary, three by requiring the child to read a stimulus word and select from among four choices the word with the same meaning; on the fourth test (SAT), the teacher dictates the word, adding speech reception difficulties to the equation. Table 6.2 expands this example across spelling, vocabulary, and language subtests.

Classroom teachers must be informed about the effect of the subtest format and presentation style on the child's test performance. The evaluation process is not complete until these interrelationships and their implications for the child's day-to-day school behavior and performance are explored and transmitted to the teachers.

In general one expects the hearing-impaired child to perform well on the analytic, concrete subtests, such as math computation and spelling, which are presented with a minimum of language. However, as all the tests are presented primarily through reading, any problem the child has in understanding the written word has the potential to impact negatively on many subtests. Depressed performance will be noted on any subtest that depends heavily on reading and/or that taps language (vocabulary, math word problems, grammar, sentence/paragraph comprehension). Therefore, a typical hearing-impaired child's profile on achievement testing will resemble that shown for the SAT in Table 6.3. The amount that the score is reduced relative to the performance of same-age classmates depends primarily on the student's overall language skills and secondarily on the presence of additional handicapping conditions.

An atypical profile for a hearing-impaired child would display depressed skills on the concrete, analytic subtests as well as the language-based subjects. Although based on such a profile one could draw no conclusions about the factors interfering with learning, the atypical pattern should act as a signal for additional investigation into the student's learning style.

Some time prior to the scheduled administration of the achievement test, the examiner should review the vocabulary typically included in test

TABLE 6.2 Variation in Subtest Content Across Achievement Tests

Subtest	CAT	ITBS	MAT	SAT
Spelling	Select word from among four choices to fill in the blank	Identify correct spelling for dictated word	Write correct spelling for dictated word	Identify misspelled word from a set of four
Vocabulary	Pick synonym from among four choices after reading word	Pick synonym from among four choices after reading word	Pick synonym from among four choices after reading word	Find synonym following dictated word
Language	Select word from among four choices to fill in the blank	Select grammatically correct sentence from among three choices	Perform various usage and capitalization, punctuation tasks	Show knowledge of relationships between sentence parts

TABLE 6.3 Typical and Atypical Performance Profile on the Stanford Achievement Test

Typical Profile		Atypical Profile	
Subtest	Grade Equivalent	Subtest	Grade Equivalent
Vocabulary	Below	Vocabulary	Below
Reading Comprehension	Below	Reading Comprehension	Below
Word Study Skills	On Grade	Word Study Skills	Below
Math Concepts	On Grade	Math Concepts	Below
Math Computation	On Grade	Math Computation	Below
Math Application	Below	Math Application	Below
Spelling	On Grade	Spelling	Below
Language	On Grade	Language	Below

instructions with the child. A child's performance can be affected negatively by the complexity of language in the written or oral directions. Some children may benefit from practice in test taking so that they understand what certain test formats require, especially fill-in-the-blank and multiple choice. As the purpose in administering these tests is to assess a child's knowledge of academic content, and not his or her grasp of test directions or a particular question format, a preview will increase the likelihood that the results do indeed help satisfy the purpose.

PSYCHOLOGICAL EVALUATION

Planning a child's educational program naturally requires some estimate of intelligence; it is important to know if communicative, academic, and social skill development is commensurate with potential to learn. However, many of the concerns raised regarding academic achievement testing also apply to psychological assessment. As most school psychologists have had limited experience evaluating hearing-impaired children, they may be unaware of the modifications in presentation of test materials that ensure a child's score truly reflects his or her learning potential (see chapter 5).

Schools commonly administer group intelligence tests at regular intervals throughout a child's school career. These tests can penalize the hearing-impaired child unduly when they combine verbal and performance items to obtain a single IQ score. Because the psychological evaluation lays the foundation for all the other testing, it is important that the hearing-impaired child be tested individually by a qualified psychologist.

In selecting IQ tests appropriate for hearing-impaired children, one should use those that permit separation of the verbal and performance portions, each of which can be broken further into a number of subtests. The scores the child achieves on the performance section of an IQ test give the best estimate of his or her intelligence. However, inadequate attention to verbal variables can affect the validity of this component. The hearing-impaired child's score on the verbal portion of an IQ test should not be reported as his or her "verbal IQ"; it can be reported as a verbal score, but one that reflects language knowledge and not learning potential. Reporting a full scale IQ that averages the combined verbal and performance scale scores will penalize the hearing-impaired child; a low verbal score averaged with a superior performance score causes a marked depression in the overall results and distorts interpretation. Consider the following examples:

Score: Full Scale IQ = 90 (average of Verbal IQ = 60 and
    Performance IQ = 120)

Interpretation: Child is functioning at low levels and should be placed in lower track. Low expectations.

Score: Verbal IQ = 60, Performance IQ = 120

Interpretation: Child has superior learning potential with a serious deficit in language. High expectations with support.

No one should accept a full scale IQ score as representing a hearing-impaired child's intellectual status.

During the psychological testing, the examiner must be alert to the possible presence of other problems in addition to the hearing loss. It is tempting but somewhat simplistic to routinely ascribe a child's poor achievements to the presence of a hearing loss. The child may be developmentally delayed as well, or exhibit specific perceptual or language disabilities that are unrelated to the hearing loss.

In order to determine the presence of an additional learning handicap, it is important to analyze the pattern of verbal and performance subtest scores and compare them to the typical pattern expected from hearing-impaired children without additional problems (see Table 6.4). The hearing-impaired child appropriately placed in a mainstream setting should exhibit a profile in which the performance subtests are elevated relative to the verbal score. The more closely the child's communication skills match age-appropriate levels, the less obvious the difference between the verbal

TABLE 6.4 Evolution of Verbal and Performance Scores Over a 2-Year Period (Normal Range = 10±3)

Original Profile		Two Years Later	
Subtest	**Score**	**Subtest**	**Score**
VERBAL		VERBAL	
Information	8	Information	10
Comprehension	5	Comprehension	8
Similarities	3	Similarities	6
Arithmetic	7	Arithmetic	7
Vocabulary	2	Vocabulary	4
PERFORMANCE		PERFORMANCE	
Picture Completion	14	Picture Completion	14
Picture Arrangement	15	Picture Arrangement	15
Block Design	11	Block Design	11
Object Assembly	13	Object Assembly	13
Coding	9	Coding	9

and performance scores on the intelligence test. One measure of language growth is the reduction in the difference between these scores over time. Because the performance IQ score remains relatively stable over time, a decrease in the difference generally reflects changes in the verbal score.

An examination of Figure 6.1 shows how easily some verbal-performance subtest patterns could be confused with each other, resulting in misdiagnoses and inappropriate placements. The normal-hearing student with a language learning deficit (C) presents, on the psychological test battery, like the student with a hearing loss (D). In both cases, the reduced verbal subtest score reflects the degree of language delay/deficit. Regardless of etiology, there is a reduction in the gap between verbal and performance scores when language competence increases. The hearing-impaired child who shows additional learning problems (F) has an overall test profile that mirrors that of a developmentally delayed child (E), yet functionally they are easily differentiated.

Additional clues signalling the interference of perceptual or learning problems emerge in the profile of subtests that comprise the intelligence test's verbal and performance sections. In persons with normal learning potential, one typically sees a fairly even distribution of scores across the subtests. When a specific learning deficit is present, one or more of the performance subtests may be depressed, resulting in a scattered profile. Here as in other evaluations, one must be mindful that when a hearing-impaired child is multiply handicapped, it is very important to separate out the affects of the individual conditions; each must be dealt with on its own terms while trying to minimize the compounding effect of the other factors.

A comprehensive review and analysis of appropriate psychological tests and their necessary adaptations for the hearing impaired can be found in Boyle (1977) and Heller (1990).

SOCIAL ADJUSTMENT EVALUATION

Fostering social integration is one of the reasons for placing a child in a mainstreamed setting. Through daily social interaction with normal-hearing peers, hearing-impaired students are exposed to and thus ultimately will learn age-appropriate social behaviors. In addition, through these social interactions the hearing-impaired child can learn the social language and conversational rules that govern verbal exchanges.

Numerous scales or checklists exist that purport to estimate a child's feelings of self-esteem or adjustment; most are designed to be filled out by

FIGURE 6.1 Patterns of verbal and performance test scores in differential diagnosis.

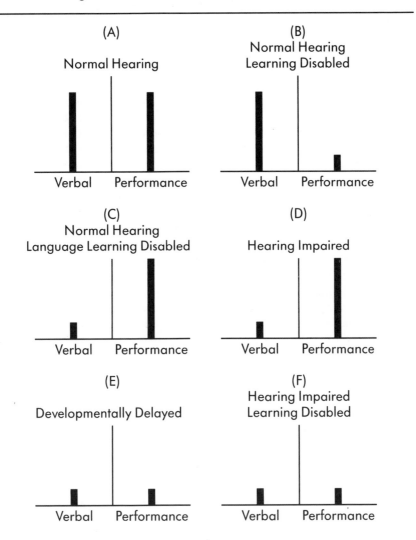

parents or teachers. Even though the adult responses do not reflect the child's self-analysis, they do provide a way of comparing how the child is perceived at home and in school settings. These parent-reports offer a useful addendum to the psychoeducational battery as they corroborate or negate the results of objective testing. If a discrepancy exists between the parent's perception of the child's skills and the actual tested skill level, then further testing is required to resolve the differences. Perhaps the parent underestimates the child's skills and in so doing keeps the child dependent. Conversely, the child can develop feelings of self-doubt when the parent overestimates the child's skills and thus sets up a situation in which failure is inevitable.

The school psychologist can provide some indication of self-concept and self-esteem. The child may be asked to draw a person, draw themselves, or draw a family, after which the psychologist analyzes the completed pictures according to set criteria. As long as the instructions are clear, this approach can yield basic information on the child's feelings about him or herself. The technique of asking a hearing-impaired child to describe abstract drawings or shapes to elicit insights into self-esteem generally has been unsuccessful because the child has to use a deficient language system to generate and produce the answer.

Traditional assessments of social adjustment and self-esteem require reacting to oral or written statements that relate to typical problems identified in the normal population. There has been some attempt to modify the response mode of these tests for hearing-impaired students, using faces with varying expressions to denote gradations of agreement or a container that gradually fills to represent "never to always." The underlying problem, however, lies with the statements themselves. Because these children enter the test situation with a poor language foundation, they react to the statements based on a flimsy understanding of what is being asked. Thus the results obtained from such an assessment lack reliability.

It is possible to obtain an indicator of self-esteem and social adjustment by having the child's teacher indicate which statements on a formal test of social/emotional status pertain to the child as he or she functions in class. The scores reflect the teacher's perception of the child's social problems and as such may differ greatly from the child's own view of the situation. The other children in the class can provide some insight into how effectively the hearing-impaired student is integrated into the class by each indicating which two classmates he or she would like to interact with. The sociograms that result tally how often the hearing-impaired child is selected as a desirable social partner.

In an effort to address these issues, Maxon, Brackett, and van den Berg (1991) have developed a procedure that uses cartoons accompanied by simplified linguistic statements to assess feelings of isolation, introversion, and independence. With the support of pictures, examinees indicate that the statement "never" (empty cup), "sometimes" (cup half full), or "always" (full cup) applies to them. Research with this procedure has shown differences in the responses of normal-hearing and hearing-impaired children on these factors.

CLASSROOM PERFORMANCE EVALUATION

An on-site visit to a child's classroom permits observation of all aspects of academic, social, and communication demands as they interact in a spontaneous situation. Table 6.5 delineates the child-, teacher-, and setting-related factors that one can observe in a classroom and lists the questions/ concerns that the observer should address. The areas sampled include participation in classroom activities and discussion, social and verbal interaction with peers and teachers, adaptations in the classroom presentation, equipment use, and environmental modifications.

When addressing the child-related questions, the observer should ask the teacher if the behaviors in evidence typify the child's daily function. Just as the teacher may be on "company" behavior, so, too, the child may be trying to demonstrate optimum performance. He or she may try to utilize newly acquired speech sounds, vocabulary, or grammar, or try to impress the observer with knowledge of the content material by excessive handraising. Although many feel that this unrealistic view of the child functioning in the classroom renders the observation useless, as long as one considers that the classroom situation will vary from day to day, much information can be gleaned from an on-site observation. If the observer views a situation in which all aspects of teacher and child interaction are at optimal levels, then he or she can assume that all parties are aware of their responsibilities and how to implement them; that is, when not under scrutiny, the potential exists for a beneficial situation, even though, realistically, not always at such a high level. Conversely, when the interaction and involvement in the classroom appears less than optimal under the observed condition, then one can assume that the typical situation is worse.

When focusing on the teacher-related factors, the same assumptions of best versus typical situation should apply. Even if the child is called on more frequently, the FM microphone is used optimally, and the discussion is directed, the observer gets to see if the teacher knows what to do when functioning under the best conditions. Maintaining this level presents a different issue, which cannot be determined in a single visit. Asking the child a specific question regarding the use pattern of the FM or the presence of classroom modifications may illuminate the issue of daily implementation.

The pattern of interaction established between the teacher and child can provide the observer with additional information on the frequency and quality of the interactions. If the interaction occurs with fluency and accuracy despite any of the linguistic and speech deficits that the child exhibits, then it is clear that the teacher has called on the student regularly and developed an efficient method of conveying and transmitting informa-

TABLE 6.5 Components of a Classroom Observation

Dimension	Factor	Questions/concerns
CHILD	Participation in activities	Can the child follow the discussion? Does the child become involved in activities? Does the child volunteer answers? Does the child know who is talking? Does the child attempt to follow activities? Does the child follow instructions or look at his/her neighbor's paper? Does the child know the information when he/she is called on?
	Peer interaction (verbal and social)	Is the child part of a group, socially isolated, or with one child at a time? Does the child make social overtures? Do peers accept the social initiations? What does the child do when he/she is not understood? What does the child do when he/she does not understand?
	Learning strategies	Does the child repeat information to himself/herself to aid recall? Can the child take notes? Does the child monitor the lecture and ask questions as misunderstandings occur? Does the child ask for help?
	Child-teacher interaction (verbal and social)	Does the child attend to the teacher when he/she speaks? Does the child gain the teacher's attention in an acceptable fashion (call name, raise hand)? Have the child and teacher worked out a way to communicate effectively? When breakdown occurs, does the child have strategies for clarifying what has been said?
TEACHER	Teacher-child interaction (verbal and social)	Does the teacher call on the child frequently? Does the teacher encourage child's questions? Does the teacher understand the child's speech?

TABLE 6.5 (Continued)

Dimension	Factor	Questions/concerns
		Are the teacher's expectations appropriate for the child's functional levels?
		Does the teacher act embarrassed when he/she cannot understand what the child has said?
		Does the teacher effectively employ the interpreter?
		Does the teacher respond similarly to all the students' answers, or is special attention given to the hearing-impaired child?
	Presentation modifications	Does the teacher repeat or rephrase?
		Does the teacher check on the child's comprehension of pertinent information?
		Does the teacher use visual aids?
		Does the teacher give oral assignments or tests?
		What is the rate, pitch, and loudness of the teacher's voice?
		Does the teacher ensure that the child can see and hear optimally?
SETTING	Amplification	Does the child indicate when the system is malfunctioning?
		Does the teacher turn the microphone on/off appropriately?
		Does the teacher resent using classroom amplification?
		Does the child resent using classroom amplification?
		Is a system in place for the child to indicate that the FM microphone is not activated?
		Does the teacher effectively use the FM microphone during group activities, seatwork, and class discussions?
	Noise sources	Are there internal/external noise sources?
		Where does the child sit in relation to the noise source?
		Does the room contain any sound-absorbent material?

TABLE 6.5 (Continued)

Dimension	Factor	Questions/concerns
		Where does the child sit relative to the teacher? peers?
	Visual distractions	Does the lighting cast shadows on the teacher's face? Does the glare from the window shine in the child's face? Does the teacher maintain a full-face presentation during board writing, demonstration, and the use of visual aids?
	Layout	Are the desks arranged to allow for maximum visibility and audibility? Is the child seated at a desk that allows him/her to see and hear optimally? Is the interpreter placed so the child can easily view the teacher too?

tion. When the interaction remains awkward after the first months of school have passed, the teacher needs assistance in finding the student's strengths.

The setting is one of the few aspects of the classroom learning situation that remains fairly stable over time. Each room has its own set of acoustics resulting from nonabsorbent flooring, ceiling material, and other reverberant surfaces. The biggest variations occur in the amount of background noise, generated internally by different classroom activities and externally by shifts in hallway and playground populations. (The strategies that the teacher uses to accommodate these conditions are reported under teacher observations.)

In approaching any teacher regarding the schedule for classroom observation, the on-site observer must stress that the focus of the observation is the hearing-impaired child as he or she interacts with peers and teachers during educational and social activities. Teachers in no way should be made to feel as if their competency is being assessed or questioned.

It is impossible to determine the appropriateness of a student's classroom performance unless he or she is observed interacting with teachers and peers in a natural setting. Any discrepancy between a child's performance during the evaluations and his or her observable classroom behaviors can provide important diagnostic information. It may take several observations during different activities to truly get the feel for a child as a participating member of the classroom. For example, observing only during seatwork provides just a limited sample of classroom behavior. However, this observation together with those made during a reading group and a general class discussion, as well as in gym, math, and social studies classes, helps confirm whether the comprehensive performance assessment accurately reflects the child's performance in a natural situation.

Taking into consideration the time constraints for most evaluators, a single observation in the elementary classroom can be scheduled to overlap several different kinds of activities. When a child moves to different learning environments during the day, as in junior and senior high school, observations should be conducted in as many of the content areas as possible, but at least the language-based subjects or any areas that the child indicates are problematic.

The observer's task then extends to ascertaining the match between test performance on the multidisciplinary evaluations and the learning behaviors observed in the classroom. Certain behaviors could be predicted from the evaluation alone that may or may not show up in the classroom. When behaviors are expected and then do not occur (e.g., good grades on math tests but poor performance during in-class participation), the child needs work on generalizing his or her skills into real-life situations. When the test performance is poorer than the academic proficiency level observed in the classroom, the child may not be familiar enough with classroom concepts to store them in long-term memory for future retrieval.

In addition to matching classroom performance with test results, the observer must determine the potential causes of particular behaviors. Often the teacher will have formed an inaccurate rationale as to why a certain behavior continues to occur. For example, it is not unusual for a teacher to report that "____ is cheating on tests by looking at other students' papers, indicating that he doesn't know the material." Although a plausible explanation, other factors can provoke an apparently negative behavior like this, such as not hearing the instructions or not understanding what the questions ask. Table 6.6 lists some frequently reported negative classroom behaviors and the in-depth questions the observer must ask to get to the root of the problem.

The accuracy with which causative factors are determined affects the kind and quality of management that is implemented. For example, if the reason behind the cheating is lack of confidence, the child needs social remediation; if it is unfamiliarity with the content material, then increased academic support or improved homework reinforcement can be implemented. Remediation must reflect cause.

TABLE 6.6 Possible Causes for Negative Classroom Behaviors

Behavior	Analysis
"Borrows from his neighbor's paper"	Does he understand the content material? Does he work so slowly that he usually does not finish in time? Has he given so many wrong answers in the past that he expects failure? Did he understand the instructions or the task required? Does he lack the motivation to try the work on his own?
"Doesn't participate in classroom discussion"	Does he know the information requested by the teacher? Is he reticent about speaking because of poor speech intelligibility? Has he learned failure from attempts in the past?
"Circles all the answers rather than underlining them as instructed"	Did he hear the instructions? Did he understand the vocabulary and grammar in the instructions? Was he looking at the worksheet rather than visually attending to the teacher during instruction?
"Stares into space while the lesson is being presented"	Does he hear the teacher? Is he bored with the topic or presentation? Is he familiar with the material, or is it all above his head? Is he fatigued with the effort of listening and needs to tune out for a short while? Is he unable to concentrate due to lack of sleep the night before?
"Doesn't know what page he is supposed to be on"	Did he hear the instructions? Did he pay attention as the page number was stated? Did he "mishear" the number (13 for 30)?
"Gets good grades on independent seatwork but fails the tests"	Does he "borrow" from his neighbors' papers? Is the format of the test different from the worksheets? Is the language used in the test questions more complex than that on the worksheets? Does he know how to study for exams?

INTERPRETING ASSESSMENT RESULTS

Each performance evaluation must be interpreted in conjunction with all of the others rather than viewed as a separate entity. The initial audiological evaluation documents the extent of hearing impairment and generates amplification recommendations for personal and school use. Ongoing evaluations monitoring hearing levels reassess these amplification systems on a regular basis, check on the effectiveness of the school-based amplification monitoring program, and analyze the listening environment. The speech-language evaluation determines the child's understanding and production of spoken language, speech reception through auditory and visual channels, and intelligibility of speech, and predicts the impact of the communication deficit on academic performance. The educational evaluation documents academic achievement in reading, language, and math, and checks for signs of additional learning disabilities. The fourth evaluation, psychosocial, determines the child's potential for learning and his or her degree of social adjustment within the mainstreamed setting.

Programming decisions based on only one or two of these assessments operate on a distorted, incomplete picture of the child's strengths and weakness. If viewed only educationally, the child who is a good reader presents in a positive light; however, socially he may be weak due to poor spoken language skills. Using only the audiogram, one easily could make incorrect assumptions about the same child's potential for learning spoken language. On cursory review, an audiogram depicting a severe hearing loss would signal the need for a specialized placement in a language-based class. Weighing the impact of the hearing loss against the student's tested communicative, academic, and social skills, however, could support or negate such an assumption.

Through multidisciplinary evaluations, a profile of strengths and weaknesses emerges that can be synthesized into the goals that form the Individualized Education Plan (IEP). One way the cross-disciplinary results can be organized is according to the general parameters assessed (see Table 6.7). Another approach categorizes results by the stimulus used; for example, all subtests assessing word level skills, regardless of modality, could be grouped together to look for any commonalties (see Table 6.8). As hearing-impaired students usually perform best with a linguistic context to assist in determining meaning, such a grouping typically would show all the word level testing yielding lower scores than the tests that use sentences or paragraphs as stimuli.

Alternative strategies for organizing test results include by test format (fill-in-the-blank, multiple-choice, open-ended) or by presentation modality (auditory only, visual only, or auditory/visual combined). One also can apply multiple strategies to the same data. For example, further dividing

TABLE 6.7 Organization of Evaluation Data by Parameter

Parameter	Discipline	Evaluations
SPEECH RECEPTION	Audiology	Speech reception threshold Speech recognition
	Communication	Speech reception/noise Speech reception/distance Visual enhancement Reception of words, sentences, paragraphs

VERBAL COMPREHENSION	Communication	Vocabulary
		  Associations
		  Absurdities
		Sentence
		  Grammar
		  Syntax
		Paragraph

	Education	Vocabulary (reading) Passage (reading) Math word problems Science (reading) Social science (reading)
	Psychology	Information Verbal problem solving Vocabulary Associations
WRITTEN LANGUAGE	Education	Vocabulary (reading) Passage Language
	Communication	Written grammar Written paragraph

the verbal comprehension category into test format may help determine if style of presentation impacts on a child's understanding.

Data organization and interpretation can be accomplished informally during the interdisciplinary meeting that generates the IEP. Here each professional involved can present his or her test results and relate them to the preceding description of the child's strengths and weaknesses. Further,

TABLE 6.8 Organization of Evaluation Data by Stimulus

Stimulus	Discipline	Evaluation
VOCABULARY	Communication	Comprehension (spoken) Production (spoken) Production (written)
	Education	Vocabulary (reading)
	Psychology	Vocabulary
SENTENCE	Communication	Comprehension (grammar) Comprehension (syntax) Production (grammar) Production (syntax) Production (written)
	Education	Language (grammar)
	Psychology	Information Verbal problem solving
PARAGRAPH	Communication	Comprehension (spoken) Production (spoken) Production (written)
	Education	Comprehension (reading)

parental input at the meeting can provide an additional dimension of insights derived in the less-demanding home environment. Alternatively, the case manager can categorize the results beforehand, for review by all the participants at the IEP meeting.

Obviously, the more a child's communicative performance and academic skills approach the level of his or her classmates, the more easily and successfully he or she will participate in all facets of the regular classroom. However, a child should not be prohibited from undertaking the challenge of a mainstream experience based on depressed vocabulary scores. With an academic support system in place, as long as a child's other skills are age/grade appropriate and his or her self-esteem is high, a delay of 2 to 3 years in vocabulary will not unduly hinder effective mainstreaming.

Determining the appropriateness of an educational placement demands looking at the child's skills not in isolation, but in conjunction with the setting in which he or she is or will be asked to function. If the environment has a well-organized, specifically adapted support system in place, then the supplemental help will make up for any spotty entry skills.

When the available academic support is at best minimal, then the child will require more advanced skills, to prepare for class and review material without assistance.

The bridge that allows the multidisciplinary team to translate assessment results into a well-developed management program is the IEP. Through careful individual planning, all of the information presented in the preceding chapters can be considered and applied appropriately.

7

Individualized Education Plan

The federal government enacted PL 94-142 to ensure quality public education for all handicapped children in the least restrictive environment appropriate for their level of functioning. From this law has come the mechanism for ensuring individually designed programs, quality assurance safeguards, and due process procedures—the Individualized Education Plan (IEP). Since its introduction in 1976, the IEP has evolved into a useful document for tailoring, in writing, the unique components of a child's educational program and the skills thereby to achieve.

As noted in the previous chapter, the IEP is generated by professionals and parents following a comprehensive multidisciplinary evaluation. Within the formulation of the IEP the child's deficit areas shape and focus the remedial program and classroom management. This approach requires the participating professionals to discuss their evaluation results, determine the common elements, generate a comprehensive profile of the student's needs, and jointly determine appropriate management.

The law clearly establishes the parents' role in designing and approving the special education plan and provides the legal vehicle through which they can appeal if they are not satisfied with the outcome. Parental responsibilities do not end with the development of the initial IEP, as the plan should be reexamined at least yearly to document progress and review the required services.

The Individualized Education Plan is built on standard components, regardless of the exact format that the particular school system chooses. Of particular relevance for the mainstreamed hearing-impaired student are the following:

1. *Classification of handicapping condition:* deaf or hard of hearing

2. *Extent of participation in regular education:* full mainstreaming or part-time mainstreaming for specific subjects

3. *Related services:* speech and language management; academic support; remedial reading

4. *Service providers:* name, title, and goal responsibility

5. *Special equipment:* FM unit

6. *Management needs:* preferential seating; use pattern for FM unit; extended time for standardized tests; individually administered standardized tests; coordination time for special and regular education staff; daily amplification monitoring program; interpreter; notetaker; acoustically adapted environment

7. *Level of performance:* speech reception, language comprehension, expressive language, speech production

8. *Annual goals:* speech reception, language comprehension, expressive language, speech production

9. *Short-term objectives:* instructional materials; evaluation timetable

10. *Participants in the planning conference:* parents and multidisciplinary team

CLASSIFICATION OF HANDICAPPING CONDITION

Even though the labels "hard of hearing" and "deaf" are descriptors of function, educators often use them to classify children according to hearing loss. The classification assigned a student may not be worth arguing about *unless* (a) the label excludes the child from particular services or (b) the child somehow does not measure up to a predetermined level of function attributed to the label. Stipulations in the educational guidelines may require students to carry the specific label of "deaf" in order to be placed in self-contained classes or "hard of hearing" in order to receive support services in the home school. In either case, an explanation of the label would be necessary in order to obtain appropriate services.

EXTENT OF PARTICIPATION IN REGULAR EDUCATION

The student's degree of participation in mainstreamed education must be reassessed each year to determine how well the regular classroom accommodates his or her academic needs. A level of participation appropriate in the early elementary years may no longer meet the student's needs in middle school or high school. A successful mainstream placement occurs most commonly in the early grades, when one teacher is responsible for the child's education. All in-service and consultative services can be directed to this one teacher, who spends the entire day with the same group of students and thus can be quite sensitive and responsive to individual needs.

Beginning in middle school, however, the student faces departmentalized classes with four or more different teachers per day. Each teacher must present a specific curriculum, with less time spent on individualizing the presentation. Some hearing-impaired students require a more self-contained program during these years in order to master the academic requirements. Conversely, students educated in self-contained classes during the earlier grades may have shown sufficient progress to warrant more involvement in regular education for some subject areas.

When a mainstreamed placement is selected, the IEP must delineate in detail the role of the regular classroom teacher. This should be done whether the student's participation is to be fairly minimal (limited to social experiences only) or quite complete (including studying academic subjects in the regular classroom). If the student is placed in the mainstream setting in order to participate in all aspects of the learning experience, then the classroom teacher is fully responsible for planning and implementing the expected curriculum for the grade. Such a student needs sufficient entry skills to learn from the lessons as presented to all the students in the class. Further, he or she will fall under the same grading scheme and class requirements as the other students. Any questions or confusion on the teacher's part regarding tests, homework, and expected performance should be resolved before the mainstream placement begins.

A student just entering a mainstreamed setting for the first time often benefits from a short transition period from the smaller supportive setting to the more pressured regular classroom environment in which the expectations are altered. The classroom teacher should be informed as to the purpose and supported in his or her efforts, so that he or she can set appropriate expectations and report back to the referral source regarding the appropriateness of the placement.

MANAGEMENT NEEDS

Management needs are those adaptations (e.g., preferential seating, extended time on tests, etc.) required to make the learning environment accessible to the mainstreamed hearing-impaired student so that his or her annual goals can be achieved. Such needs are derived from the student's performance in the multidisciplinary evaluations. Hearing-impaired students have two kinds of special learning requirements: those that enhance the visual reception of speech, and those that optimize the auditory reception of speech. These needs must be written into the IEP; they provide the basis for legal recourse if the program does not proceed according to plan.

The first step in visually enhancing speech reception involves adapting certain aspects of the environment. Ensuring that the classroom is well lighted and that the teacher's face is illuminated without window backlighting allows the student to make use of speechreading cues. The classroom seating arrangement should allow the hearing-impaired student visual access to his or her classmates. This may require seating the student near the front right or left corner, which brings the rest of the room into view when the child turns to see who is speaking. It is critically important to remain flexible, adapting the seating plan as the visual demands of the activity vary.

If necessary, an interpreter (oral, cued speech, sign language) can ensure that the child receives the teacher's utterances. The interpreter's role, however, must be clearly defined regarding issues of tutoring, direct translation versus paraphrase, and classroom responsibilities.

A notetaker should be provided when students are responsible for the material discussed during classroom presentations. The grade at which a notetaker becomes necessary depends on the educational philosophy of the school and the specific teacher. Normal-hearing classmates of proven ability to extract important information from class discussions can serve in this capacity. Student helpers should be given special carbonized paper to facilitate the notetaking process, or a system for photocopying the notes should be established. Some incentive also should be built in, to keep the quality of the notetaking service high.

It is possible to optimize auditory speech reception by modifying the acoustic characteristics of the listening environment. The addition of any sound-absorbing materials can dramatically reduce the amount of class-room noise that might interfere with what is being said (see chapter 8 for details).

Further, preferential seating keeps the distance between teacher and student minimal, resulting in optimal auditory reception. In the usual procedure, the student is seated in the front of the room (first or second row) to access the full intensity of the teacher's voice. As long as teacher and student remain in the assigned places, optimal intensity is maintained. Due to variations in teaching style and subject demands, however, teachers may move around the room, utilizing all the counter, desk, and writing surfaces available to them. While these movements may heighten student interest level, they pose a dilemma for preferential seating. Further, visual accessibility should not be compromised by these seating arrangements.

To further offset negative conditions, classroom listening devices should be recommended for students with even the mildest of hearing losses, and the IEP should describe their use in detail. Although there is a section on the IEP form for listing the special equipment needed to implement the plan, there is no place to describe its use. Too often children are instructed to use their FM units only in one-to-one therapy or in the resource room. However, this contradicts the intended application of an FM system, which is most useful in noisy situations or where a large distance lies between speaker and listener. To avoid misunderstandings, it is important to designate on the IEP when the device *must* be used as well as when the choice is optional. For the sensitive junior high or high school student, specifying that the device need not be worn in the hallway between classes could ease a potentially uncomfortable or embarrassing situation.

Modifications in the administration of standardized testing also fall under "Management Needs" (or, in some cases, within a special section of the IEP). The procedures specified could include, for instance, the extent to which the student participates in city and statewide testing, the allowance for additional time in test taking, and the one-to-one administration of tests. By extending the time limits of standardized tests, hearing-impaired students are not penalized for needing more time to comprehend and process the test items, and their scores then reflect their actual abilities.

Individualized administration of standardized achievement tests ensures that students understand the instructions and, in cases where the stimulus is presented orally, that they accurately receive the item. Depending on individual teachers' examination procedures, further testing variations may be necessary. For example, if a teacher insists on giving math tests orally from the back of the room (thus eliminating visual input and severely reducing the child's access to speech), the student should be allowed to leave the classroom during these examinations and be tested on a one-to-one basis by the academic support personnel.

CONSIDERATION OF SERVICES

Due to the heterogeneity of the hearing-impaired population with regard to auditory, communicative, academic, and social skills, one cannot prescribe specific services based on age or degree of hearing loss. Instead, the checklist described below delineates the full range of services that might be needed by a student with a hearing loss. Whether a service is appropriate for a particular child can be determined only by a thorough evaluation of the child's skills in and out of the classroom. At the planning meeting, the full range of services (see Figure 7.1) should be considered for inclusion in the IEP, omitted only when the child's performance rules out the need.

The frequency and length of the various sessions, as well as the number of students involved in services such as speech/language therapy, academic support, and remedial reading, also must be specified. Service sessions should be scheduled at least twice a week if progress is to occur. This level of frequency allows new material to be introduced, reinforced, and absorbed in a short period of time. The rate at which new forms generalize into everyday function increases if parents are included in the learning process. At the junior high and high school levels, the length of sessions corresponds to the school day "period" (usually 40 to 50 minutes). At the elementary level, half-hour sessions are more typical. Thus when the IEP specifies two weekly sessions, the total time actively involved may be as little as an hour a week, very little when one considers the all-encompassing effect of the hearing loss.

One-to-one involvement is recommended for some or all of the child's speech/language therapy sessions. Unlike many language- or speech-disordered children, the hearing-impaired student exhibits multiple communication and academic deficits in need of attention. Further, groups generally are composed of students with a common deficit, and group sessions focus on this element (to the exclusion of other individual deficit areas). Individual sessions allow the professional to manage multiple problem areas simultaneously, thus effecting greater change within a given time limit and maximizing the time that the child is taken out of the classroom. Group sessions, however, can be a useful adjunct by affording the student an opportunity to develop turn-taking and conversational skills and to monitor the speech of others. Group size should be limited to a maximum of three participants so that the child can monitor everyone's input.

FIGURE 7.1 Checklist of services for mainstreamed hearing-impaired children.

	Considered	Needed
Audiological and amplification evaluation		
Communication evaluation		
Educational evaluation		
Psychosocial evaluation		
Classroom evaluation		

	Considered	Needed
Analysis of classroom listening environment		
Classroom listening system (FM unit)		
Amplification monitoring program		
Speech-language therapy		
Academic support/tutor/resource room		
Remedial reading		
Classroom aide		
Interpreter		
Notetaker		
Social-emotional counseling		
Career counseling/job readiness		
Parent support group		
Extracurricular social activities		
In-service training		
Alternative educational placement		

One-to-one sessions are optimal if the child needs a highly individualized academic support program. It is impossible to introduce the vocabulary for a classroom topic and reinforce previously introduced classroom concepts when the "group" does not have the same needs or has discussed similar topics in the classroom. Group academic support typically results in the teacher presenting a different curriculum than the children are exposed to in the mainstream classroom. Thus instead of receiving support in academic subjects, the student may be burdened with additional work. Although the child obviously could benefit from this additional instruction, it should not supersede the requirements of the mainstream classroom.

If there was one "best" way to implement a successful education program for a hearing-impaired child, and if children across the country had equal access to the same level of service, the administrator's job would be greatly simplified. As this is not the case, of course, administrators, parents, and team members have had to creatively design programs within the economic and geographical constraints of their region. It is possible to deliver services with widely different formats, even to two students with identical profiles, and through each program effectively address the goals and objectives of the IEP. However, the known, established program, which is comfortable, less time-consuming, and relatively free of stress, does not always present the best or only delivery system for achieving desired results. The parents and planning team must remain open to less conventional alternatives. Certain factors should be considered when deciding which service delivery model will best meet the needs of the child and the social educational environment in which he or she learns:

1. *The child's attitude.* Children highly motivated to learn, who take independent action in learning settings, will likely succeed in the regular classroom with supportive help. Students who are aware of their deficits and ready to seek out answers require a less intense level of supplementary services than those who learn content material only when "spoonfed." The latter present a poor risk for handling the competitive mainstream setting.

2. *Home reinforcement.* In some cases home reinforcement can reduce the necessary level of in-school supplemental services, thus keeping the child in the classroom for several additional periods per week. Parents who maintain their continued involvement throughout the school years and learn techniques for working effectively with their child can be outstanding assets. Before enlisting them in this capacity, however, they need to feel confident in their ability to effectively implement the daily reinforcement program. Many parents feel uncomfortable when put in this role, opting instead for the school to assume the entire responsibility. A critical factor in considering home involvement is the parent's English language fluency. If the home language is other than English, then the parents will have diffi-

culty reinforcing the language-based subjects and interpreting the instructions. In such cases, an older sibling, a relative, or an interested neighbor often can provide the necessary support.

3. *Availability of interdisciplinary team.* An interdisciplinary team is required to implement all the services a mainstreamed child may need. Professional team members can include an audiologist, speech-language pathologist, teacher of the hearing-impaired, guidance counselor(s), and tutor. The extent to which any of these professionals become involved depends on the services the child requires and the team member's availability.

Often, the management team does not include the regular educator (or does so only minimally). When one considers that mainstreamed hearing-impaired children spend at least 3 hours per day, 600 hours per year, in an academic setting where the classroom teacher has primary responsibility for teaching them content material, this lack of involvement is deplorable. Even if these children received daily academic support services and speech/language therapy management, they would have contact with special educators only 280 hours per year. Yet most often the special educators, not the regular educators, participate in the IEP meetings.

Although federal law requires that parents be asked to attend these meetings, they are often considered to be ancillary rather than functioning members of the team. Service providers may view parents as adversaries rather than co-participants with important additional information. They often are relegated to rubber-stamping a program predetermined by the professionals, who instead should capitalize on parental expertise with the child. While excluding parents may expedite the IEP development meeting, their acceptance and *commitment* to the program can often decide its success or failure. If parents understand and rally to the program as outlined in the IEP, they likely will reinforce the remediation at home.

4. *Attitudes toward mainstreaming.* Some school systems exhibit negative attitudes toward mainstreaming children with problems within the regular educational setting. Such resistance can come from prior negative experiences, administrative directive, lack of experience, or concern that necessary personnel are not available to help these children function academically, socially, and communicatively with unimpaired peers. These systems prefer to send their special education students to regionalized programs that are specifically designed for children with particular handicapping conditions.

Other school systems, though, willingly commit to maintaining these special education students in their home schools by utilizing available staff resources. Contrary to expectations, it is often the small town with no organized program for the hearing-impaired that implements an effective management plan, relying on outside agencies to supply direction and in-service training. However, with no teacher of the hearing-impaired to provide academic support and perhaps only an over-extended itinerant speech-language pathologist, it remains questionable if it is possible to provide a quality program with the personnel who are available.

However, many highly individualized programs have been implemented by support personnel who, with some consultant in-service programs, provide exactly what a child needs even though they do not possess the "correct" professional credentials. Having external services available eliminates many of the organizational and staffing problems encountered by smaller school systems; yet it also can present obstacles for parents who want their child to receive unique programming at his or her home school.

Even when the IEP recommendation describes a specific level of service, generally there will be some choices regarding its implementation. When deciding how to carry out a mainstream/academic support program, the team must tackle multifaceted issues such as home school versus centralized school, and itinerant services versus resource room. Nothing can replace the benefits of going to school in the neighborhood and having classmates who live within "playing" distance. In this scenario, the student might receive speech-language management two times a week and academic support three times a week from itinerant service providers. A special problem here is the lack of sufficient time for the itinerant staff, who most often leave immediately after a lesson for commitments at another school, to coordinate the remedial work with the classroom teachers. On the other hand, though the regular educators at the home school might be naive about the problems of making subject matter accessible to a hearing-impaired student, they could approach this challenge without preconceptions that can negatively color interactions with the student.

An alternative option would have the student educated in a centralized school (outside the local district) that contains the full continuum of services for hearing-impaired students, from self-contained classes to full mainstreaming. Related services would be delivered by a speech-language pathologist familiar with the needs of hearing-impaired students and by a teacher of the hearing-impaired attached to the resource room program. Aside from the familiarity of the support staff regarding the needs of hearing-impaired students, the regular school staff in such a setting also would be better prepared and more experienced. As long as that prior experience was positive and the teacher's past efforts were well supported by the remedial staff, such a background could work in the child's favor. However, if the teacher had worked primarily with marginally mainstreamed students, or those who lacked the skills to handle the academic material, the previous experience could lower his or her performance expectations with regard to the newest hearing-impaired student.

The decision between these two options is a difficult one. Careful discussion of each alternative's negative and positive aspects should lead to informed choices for the year in question. Critical to the decision is the fact that it applies *only* to the year in question. Each year will require reassessing the method of implementing the program, adapting to the child's social-emotional, communicative, and academic growth.

5. *Costs of mainstreaming*. Economic factors further complicate the selection of the service delivery model. In a town/city experiencing financial hardship, the administration might be less willing either to spend the money necessary to adapt the present program with the help of consultants or to send the student to a regionalized program. It is difficult to delineate the costs of mainstreaming a student because the child's functioning contributes to the equation. Utilizing on-site professionals may cost less but requires a coordinator to ensure that all program components are in place, that they are functioning optimally, and that continuing education about hearing loss occurs regularly. When the planning team selects an already established program, the responsibility for implementation and monitoring shifts from the school system to the program. On the negative side, this does not allow the sending town/city to have input on policy and curriculum issues.

All these child and school factors must be considered when deciding on a service delivery model, as no one approach is right for each student or school district. The challenge lies in finding the best match between the student's motivation level and the school's economic needs and attitude.

LEVEL OF PERFORMANCE

Every IEP must state the child's present level of all aspects of performance. These statements (based on the results of the comprehensive performance evaluation) must objectively and quantitatively describe the child's present accomplishments. Vague, generalized statements are not acceptable. The results of all standardized tests should be reported in age- or grade-equivalent scores, percentiles, or raw or standard scores. Standardized tests, however, only sample some of the dimensions of communicative performance; they do not completely define the child's overall communicative capacity. In an IEP, the description of a child's performance also should include results from non-standardized assessments, essential mechanisms for understanding a child's linguistic system and devising personalized intervention strategies.

The evaluation data should be grouped according to the following factors:

1. *Physical.* For the hearing-impaired child, the audiological testing results document his or her sensory deficit. A well-constructed summary of the child's unaided and aided performance as measured by the audiologist thus enables anyone reading the IEP to understand the source of the child's problems. The audiological results present only the first step. A more functional description documents the child's functional use of hearing for speech reception at the sound, word, sentence, and paragraph level, as assessed in the communication evaluation. The perceptual error patterns evident during testing should be reported briefly, and interpreted in light of their appropriateness for the child's aided hearing. Change in perceptual function due to the interference of background noise and speaker/listener distance also should be noted in this section, as it will be addressed when auditory management is discussed.

Additional information here should include a description of the child's ability to insert the earmold, and to maintain and troubleshoot personal and classroom amplification; an evaluation of the amplification monitoring program; and an acoustic analysis of the learning environments.

2. *Academic.* The description of the child's academic achievements should highlight specific strengths and weaknesses as these will become the focus of the academic support program. In addition, the presentation of all language and speech results will establish the child's present level of performance in communication and will suggest its impact on academic and social performance.

3. *Social.* The social parameters of evaluation data include those directly related to the child (self-esteem, acceptance of hearing loss, social adjustment, and classroom and social behavior) as well as relevant family conditions (expectations, provision of home reinforcement, and liaison between clinic, school, and home).

ANNUAL GOALS

A logical progression from multidisciplinary evaluation through interpretation to goal development allows all the identified deficits to be addressed in the written goals. Unlike many children with communication disorders, the hearing-impaired child experiences weaknesses in all aspects of communication, which in turn impacts on social and academic skill development. Therefore, the goals generated by the speech-language pathologist, audiologist, special education personnel, and the regular educator should jointly address the child's discernable deficits. IEP written goals must reflect behaviors that realistically can be accomplished in 1 year. Given the deficit pattern typically exhibited by mainstreamed hearing-impaired children, goals should address speech reception, language comprehension and expression, speech intelligibility, reading comprehension and related language-based academic areas, and social adjustment.

OBJECTIVES

Once the service delivery model has been selected and the management needs identified, the service providers write objectives for each of the identified deficit areas and designate a timetable for evaluating the student's performance. Each annual goal typically requires multiple objectives to ensure addressing in the IEP all the deficits described in the evaluation section. Objectives need to specify the following:

1. Modality of presentation (visual only, auditory only, combined, total communication; cued speech; written)

2. Stimuli (phoneme, syllable, word, sentence, paragraph)

3. How child will demonstrate knowledge (select object, point, repeat, write)

4. Level of achievement expected (60–70% for new skill; 90–95% for carryover)

Table 7.1 displays the sort of goals and objectives that logically evolve out of the stated levels of performance. This example uses behaviors typically encountered in the hearing-impaired population (preschool through secondary level, with widely varying hearing losses). Each of the numbered "Short-Term Objectives" corresponds to a similarly numbered behavior under "Level of Performance."

After generating the objectives, the direct service provider selects instructional materials that will facilitate learning within the designated time period. Although one cannot predict all potentially useful remedial activities, written descriptions of anticipated activities give parents an opportunity to confirm previously useful methods and point out others that are contraindicated because of the child's previously demonstrated learning style.

The final section of the IEP specifies the evaluation tools that will assess the child's progress in learning the targeted skills. Although some skills are assessed readily through standardized testing, others require the examiner to tally the occurrence of the target in spontaneous conversation to determine if the designated achievement level has been attained. In general, progress should be assessed at least annually so that changes in the IEP will reflect new levels of performance.

Achievement summaries describe the quality of the student's skill acquisition as it pertains to the particular objective. If the student has not achieved the skill to the level specified on the IEP (60% of the time when 90% was targeted), then the achievement summary should so indicate, with the recommendation that the objective continue to be targeted on the next IEP. As the IEP is generated yearly, objectives can include the acquisition of new skills as well as carryover of old skills (from the previous IEP) into spontaneous use.

Parental signature indicates agreement not only with the services, goals, and objectives, but also the timetable stated in the text. If agreement cannot be reached on all sides, an appeal will be made and a due process hearing scheduled. The Impartial Hearing Officer presiding over the hearing makes a decision that can be accepted or rejected. If this hearing does not produce a mutually satisfactory solution, a binding decision will be sought in court proceedings. However, a skilled mediator usually can resolve most service delivery disputes before this last step occurs. Resolution may require both parties (parents and school) to compromise on controversial issues.

TABLE 7.1 Examples of IEP Goals and Objectives

Level of Performance	Annual Goal	SPEECH RECEPTION Short-Term Objectives	Evaluation	Date	Achievement Summary
Listening only: 1) Is aware when amplification is turned off but not when severe distortion is present	To improve the child's ability to use her aided hearing for the reception of speech	XX will correctly indicate the quality of the amplified sound when asked during daily troubleshooting at 60% accuracy			
2) Is able to perceive differences in number of syllables in babble but not in real words		XX will recognize the number of syllables in two and three syllable words listening alone at the 80% level			
3) Is able to identify pairs of words differing only in the vowel, except /ee,oo/ and Ih,Eh/		Given an auditory only presentation, XX will respond by picture pointing, repeating back, or carrying out an action to pairs of words differing only in the vowel /ee,oo/ and Ih, Eh/ at 90% level of accuracy			
4) Is able to answer content questions about sentence material but not two or more sentences together		After a single auditory-only presentation, XX will answer content questions pertaining to 2,3, and 4 sentence paragraphs containing familiar vocabulary at 75% level			
5) Is not aware when other children are talking unless her name is called		In a group setting, XX will, after alerting to the voice, locate the person talking by visually scanning the group for the person engaged in conversation 60% of the time			

TABLE 7.1 (Continued)

LANGUAGE (COMPREHENSION)

Level of Performance	Annual Goal	Short-Term Objectives	Evaluation	Date	Achievement Summary
1) Has basic labels but lacks specific vocabulary for directions	To demonstrate one year's growth in the comprehension of spoken language	XX will indicate understanding 50 words and phrases extracted from the instructions in her textbooks at 90% level			
2) Understands how to make verbs into past tense, but is unsure of when to use past tense		Given an obligatory past tense context, XX will use a past tense verb 95% of the time			
3) Responds appropriately to who, what, and where questions, but gives wrong information for when, why, and how come		XX will respond with the information requested to when, why, and how come questions at 65% level			
4) While listening to a familiar story told by an adult, she can not provide the next logical event without question prompts		XX will indicate her understanding of an orally presented short story by answering questions, providing the next event in sequence, and filling in dialogue at 75% level of accuracy			
5) Instead of indicating when she has not understood what has been said, she either nods her head or has a blank face		Given an unintelligible or ambiguous utterance, XX will indicate her confusion by requesting clarification which specifically indicates that part of the utterance that was misunderstood			

TABLE 7.1 (Continued)

Level of Performance	Annual Goal	LANGUAGE (EXPRESSION) Short-Term Objectives	Evaluation	Date	Achievement Summary
1) With prompting will produce two word combinations	To demonstrate one year's growth in expressive language	XX will spontaneously formulate two to three word combinations for the purpose of labeling, commenting, making requests, and questioning 80% of the time			
2) Uses general terms (this, that, thing) rather than specific labels in spontaneous speech		Given the spoken word, XX will demonstrate through defining or using in a sentence, her understanding of 250 (at a minimum) science, social studies, and math words extracted from her textbooks at 80% level			
3) Uses present progressive and irregular past tense, but eliminates the unstressed /t/ and /d/ for regular past tense		Given an obligatory context for past tense, XX will spontaneously use /t/ and /d/ to mark past tense at 75% level			
4) Sentence formation is simple but accurate, with few complex or compound structures attempted		Given the subordinate conjunctions After, Before, If, Although, Since, While, When, XX will produce a complex sentence with correct verb agreement between clauses at 65% level			

TABLE 7.1 (Continued)

SPEECH PRODUCTION

Level of Performance	Annual Goal	Short-Term Objectives	Evaluation	Date	Achievement Summary
1) Has excellent control of suprasegmental features of speech, such as rhythm, rate, pitch, and intonation contour, with the exception of syllable number	To improve speech intelligibility	Will repeat back the correct number of syllables in three and four syllable words given an adult model, with 80% accuracy			
2) Makes consistent errors on the voicing feature for the plosives /k,g/, /t,d/, and /p,b/		Will demonstrate accurate voice onset time for the plosive cognates /k,g/, /t,d/, and /p,b/ at the word level, with 80% level of accuracy			
3) Following a model, she easily produces the /s/ in words and as a morphological marker, but it is not used spontaneously		Will self-correct /s/ as it occurs spontaneously in words and as a morphological marker during a 15 minute time period with 95% accuracy			

PSYCHOSOCIAL

Level of Performance	Annual Goal	Short-Term Objectives	Evaluation	Date	Achievement Summary
1) Enjoys the company of other children but seems to be led astray or leads the others into unacceptable behavior	To demonstrate age-appropriate social behavior	Given peer/peer interaction, child will demonstrate or suggest socially acceptable behavioral alternatives at 75% level			
2) Uses aggressive means of interacting with her peers in situations where negotiation is the socially acceptable alternative		Will demonstrate her verbal negotiation skills during role playing activities which mirror potential situations in the classroom at 85% level			

TABLE 7.1 (Continued)

Level of Performance	Annual Goal	ACADEMIC Short-Term Objectives	Evaluation	Date	Achievement Summary
1) Reading is at age level for concrete material with breakdown occurring when inference is required	To achieve age level reading and writing skills	Will demonstrate understanding of inference in grade level paragraphs at 85% level			
2) Has difficulty interpreting the information being requested in essay questions		When presented with essay questions that require the student to *describe*, *compare and contrast*, or *list*, the student will provide a well-organized answer which accurately addresses the question, at 60% level			
3) Can do math calculation at grade level, but performs poorly on math word problems		Given math word problems containing the words *same as*, *less than*, and *more than*, the student will apply the correct mathmatical calculation 75% of the time			

8

Auditory Management Principles

The first and indispensable objective in the auditory management of hearing-impaired children is to provide the maximum salient speech-acoustic information appropriate to their hearing losses for as many hours a day as possible. All other technical/organizational details and considerations follow from this objective. Other management considerations are of course relevant and important, but they must derive from the full exploitation of a child's residual hearing. Indeed, only when the auditory objectives are met can the child realize the full benefits of other therapeutic approaches. Such therapy, then, should *supplement* an auditory management approach, not attempt to *substitute* for one.

By capitalizing on these children's residual hearing, one is, in a sense, heading off some of their problems at the source; that is, appropriate amplification can mitigate the impact of the hearing loss. In order for these children to learn their lessons effectively in the classroom, they have to hear them, and the better they hear them, the more they are going to learn. These sentiments may appear simplistic, but no factor has been so sadly lacking from hearing-impaired management practices as the auditory one, and yet no program can hope to be truly successful unless founded on appropriate auditory management. The sections that follow will consider

FIGURE 8.1 Auditory management model.

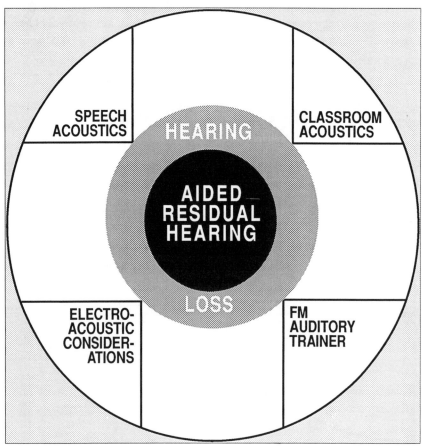

DESIGN BY BOB ESSMAN

audiological management from the perspective of the simple model presented in Figure 8.1.

The interactions of speech acoustics, classroom acoustics, and amplification systems with the specific hearing loss creates the final product, the child's aided residual hearing. Note, however, that this product offers simply the raw material of auditory learning and provides no guarantee that a child will make the most of it. This is the *detection* level in the auditory developmental hierarchy, the others being *discrimination* (the ability to discern the difference between two sounds), *identification* (the aplication of a linguistic label to a particular sound), and *comprehension* (the ability to understand running speech). The potential for development in all of these higher level auditory functions is constrained by the first factor. The child, in other words, cannot effectively employ his or her residual hearing unless he or she receives the greatest possible degree of relevant acoustic information.

SPEECH ACOUSTICS

Because the sound of speech forms the basis of auditory management, the prospective teacher/clinician must become generally familiar with its acoustic and perceptual properties. Figure 8.2 presents a static view of the acoustic spectrum of the speech signal as plotted on an audiogram. The average intensity of the speech signal is about the 40–45 dB hearing level

FIGURE 8.2 Acoustic spectrum of the speech signal (HL scale).

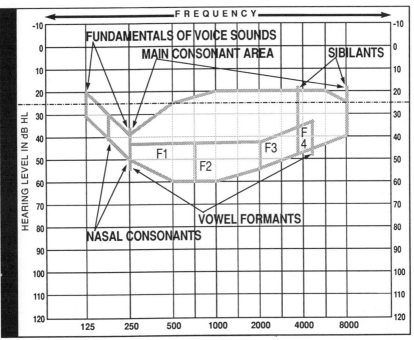

DESIGN BY BOB ESSMAN

(HL), with peaks generally 12 to 15 dB above and troughs some 18 to 25 dB below. The average intensity spread of a speech signal at any given instant in time usually is given as 30 dB; however, when considering normal intensity inflections over time, this figure is frequently exceeded. As a goal for presenting an amplified sensation level to a child, however, the 30 dB figure represents an optimal value.

Generally speaking, the vowels are comprised of lower frequencies than consonants. Strong sibilant consonant energy extends to 8000 Hz and beyond. The first vowel formant extends to about 800 Hz for adult males, while the second, third, and fourth formants extend to 2000, 3000, and 5000 Hz, respectively. These are only approximate locations and hold true only for males. Women and children produce higher formant locations than do males (see Table 8.1).

Figure 8.2 also shows the acoustic cues provided by nasal consonants. A speaker produces this energy when the port leading to the nasal cavity is open and the sound coming from the larynx is free to resonate in the nasal cavity. This very low frequency energy may serve as an important cue in the perception of certain speech features, particularly for a child with a profound hearing loss. Figure 8.3 configures the same information on a sound pressure level (SPL) rather than a hearing level (HL) scale.

To clinicians accustomed to viewing audiograms, plotting the speech spectrum on an SPL scale may appear an unnecessary complication. The ultimate convenience, however, of viewing all the necessary dimensions of acoustic performance on the same reference level becomes apparent. For example, the electroacoustic performance of a hearing aid ordinarily is plotted on an SPL scale, as is the acoustical condition of a classroom. Moreover, given the prevalence of selecting hearing aids in accordance with their electroacoustic parameters (Ross & Seewald, 1988), teachers/clinicians should become at least generally conversant with the SPL scale and its relationship to the familiar audiogram. (In a later section on the electroacoustic performance of hearing aids, we will plot some of the same information on both scales.)

Table 8.1 displays the average values of the fundamental frequencies and the frequency locations of the first three formants of 10 American English vowels. Considering the results for male speakers as the base, one can see that the fundamental frequency of a woman's voice is approximately 85 to 90 Hz higher, and that of children is a full octave higher.

The vowel /i/ is composed of both the lowest first formant (270 Hz) and the highest second formant (2290 Hz). The fact that many hearing-impaired children with high-frequency hearing losses often confuse /i/ with /u/ is explained by the similarities between their first formants. The first formants (F1) of /i/ and /u/ are quite close in frequency, and because the F2 of /i/ may be inaudible, many children will confuse the two vowels.

TABLE 8.1 Fundamental Frequencies and Formant Characteristics of 10 American English Vowels

	i	ɪ	ɛ	æ	a	ɔ	**ʊ**	**u**	ʌ	3˞
FUNDAMENTAL FREQUENCIES (Hz)										
Men	136	135	130	127	124	129	137	141	130	133
Women	235	232	223	210	212	216	232	231	221	218
Children	272	269	260	251	256	263	276	274	261	261
FORMANT FREQUENCIES (Hz)										
F1 Men	270	390	530	660	730	570	440	300	640	490
Women	310	430	610	860	850	590	470	370	760	500
Children	370	530	690	1010	1030	680	560	430	850	560
F2 Men	2290	1990	1840	1720	1090	840	1020	870	1190	1350
Women	2790	2480	2330	2050	1220	920	1160	950	1400	1640
Children	3200	2730	2610	2320	1370	1060	1410	1170	1590	1820
F3 Men	3010	2550	2480	2410	2440	2410	2240	2240	2390	1690
Women	3310	3070	2990	2850	2810	2710	2680	2670	2780	1960
Children	3730	3600	3570	3320	3170	3180	3310	3260	3360	2160
FORMANT RATIOS										
F2/F1 Men	8.48	5.10	3.47	2.61	1.49	1.47	2.32	2.90	1.86	2.76
Women	9.00	5.77	3.82	2.38	1.44	1.56	2.47	2.57	1.84	3.28
Children	8.65	5.15	3.78	2.23	1.33	1.56	2.52	2.72	1.87	3.25

Note. From "The Acoustics of Speech Production" by H. Levitt in Auditory Management of Hearing-Impaired Children (M. Ross and T. G. Giolas, Eds., p. 70), 1978, Baltimore, MD: University Park Press. Copyright 1978 by H. Levitt. Reprinted by permission.

FIGURE 8.3 Acoustic spectrum of the speech signal (SPL scale). From *Statistical Properties of Speech Signals* (p. 942) by D. L. Richards, 1964, Stevenage, Hertshire, England: IEE Publishing Department. Copyright 1964 by the IEE Publishing Department. Reprinted by permission.

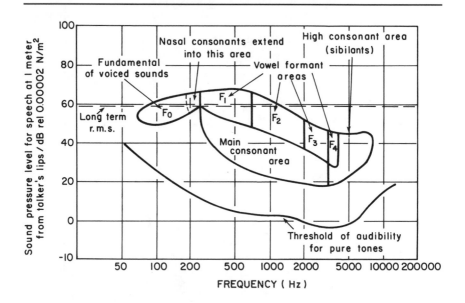

The table does not show the bandwidth of the formants, which naturally constitute a greater range than the single frequency shown. On average, the bandwidth of the first formant is approximately 50 Hz, with higher formants producing progressively larger bandwidths. Therefore, a hearing-impaired child may be able to perceive at least part of a formant band and use that information for vowel discrimination and identification.

The unimpaired listener makes the correct perception of vowels by the relative position of the formant frequencies. That is, formant relationships are such that the ratio of F1 to F2 for a specific vowel remains fairly constant for all speakers, but is different across vowels. For example, the ratios (F2/F1) of the vowel /i/ emerge as follows:

$$\text{Men: } 2290/270 = 8.48$$
$$\text{Women: } 2790/310 = 9.00$$
$$\text{Children: } 3200/370 = 8.64$$

As one can see, the ratios stay relatively constant across speaker group. However, the ratios between two different vowels are quite different:

$$/i/: 1990/390 = 5.10$$
$$/u/: 1020/440 = 2.32$$

This information helps explains how listeners can perceive the same vowels for men, women, and children despite very different absolute formant locations. In identifying a specific vowel, the task is not so much to detect all its energy, but just enough to ascertain the formants' relative positions.

Table 8.2 lists the normal sensation levels (SL) of 34 English phonemes. For the most part, the phonemes' normal SLs and the levels they must attain to be recognized are quite close. Some phonemes require a slightly higher than normal SL for recognition, while others (notably the /θ/) can be recognized when the *average* energy falls below the threshold of audibility. (The latter observation supports the earlier point that representing a speech signal with a single intensity level can be misleading.) In this instance, presumably the *peak* energy in the phoneme cues the appropriate perception. In the column of averages, one can see that the range between the weakest phoneme in the English language /θ/ and the strongest /ɔ/ covers about 25 dB. These two phonemes differ not only in intensity, but quite a bit in their frequency characteristics (see Table 8.3). When electroacoustically adjusting an amplification system, one of the goals is to make both of these phonemes audible; if accomplished, in both the intensity and frequency dimensions, then likely the remaining phonemes of speech also will be audible.

The spectra of fricative consonants appear in Table 8.3. Note the high frequency composition of these phonemes, particularly the /s/ (which has little energy below 3500 Hz). Until quite recently hearing aids rarely provided usable amplified sound beyond approximately 3000 Hz. Therefore, /s/ was inaudible to hearing-impaired children, even those with a significant amount of residual hearing in the frequency range of 3000 Hz and above. Even with the many improvements in hearing aid technology, it is still difficult to make the high-frequency phonemes audible for children with severe and profound hearing losses (Ross, in press).

The ability to hear /s/ has language as well as phonological implications because this phoneme carries morphological and syntactic information, such as plurals ("lamp" vs. "lamps"), possession ("Mark's marbles"), third person singular construction per se ("She walks home") and in differentiating present from past ("She puts it away" vs. "She put it away"), and conventional contractions ("it is" vs. "it's"; "let us" vs. "let's") and colloquial speech ("What does it mean?" vs. "What's it mean?"). As many other examples are possible of the morphological role of /s/, ensuring the auditory perception of this phoneme, when possible through residual hearing in the high frequencies, becomes a high priority clinical objective.

TABLE 8.2 Relative Levels of Speech Sounds as Heard by the Normal Ear

Speech Sound		Relative Sensation Level (dB)	Relative Level Re Threshold of Recognition (dB)	Average (dB)
ɔ	(sought)	26.0	26.0	26.0
ɑ	(calm)	25.6	26.0	25.8
ɑɪ	(sigh)	25.5	26.0	25.8
ɑʊ	(now)	25.2	26.0	25.6
oʊ	(soap)	25.6	24.9	25.3
a	(half)	23.4	26.3	24.9
æ	(sat)	25.2	23.2	24.2
ʊ	(foot)	23.1	24.1	23.6
ε	(set)	24.4	19.5	22.0
eɪ	(day)	19.3	24.2	21.8
ɝ	(third)	22.0	21.5	21.8
u	(food)	21.9	20.3	21.1
ɪ	(sit)	18.6	21.5	20.1
l	(low)	19.5	18.6	19.1
i	(seat)	15.4	22.3	18.9
ŋ	(sing)	14.9	19.8	17.4
ʃ	(shed)	14.9	19.2	17.1
tʃ	(child)	13.2	15.7	14.5
n	(no)	12.8	12.7	12.8
dʒ	(jump)	9.7	15.7	12.7
m	(me)	11.4	11.1	11.3
t	(ten)	10.1	12.4	11.3
g	(gate)	8.9	12.9	10.9
k	(key)	9.8	11.3	10.6
ð	(then)	10.2		10.2
d	(den)	4.9	13.8	9.4
h	(home)	9.9	7.7	8.8
z	(zero)	7.6	7.6	7.6
b	(bend)	4.8	9.7	7.3
p	(pen)	6.6	7.4	7.0
v	(vine)	7.4	6.1	6.8
f	(fine)	9.6	3.7	6.7
s	(said)	8.4	4.1	6.3
θ	(thin)	4.7	-2.8	1.0*

*As relative levels are shown, the least intense sound, /θ/, was chosen as the reference and its average level was set arbitrarily to 1 dB.

Note. From "The Acoustics of Speech Production" by H. Levitt in *Auditory Management of Hearing-Impaired Children* (M. Ross and T. G. Giolas, Eds., p. 76), 1978, Baltimore, MD: University Park Press. Copyright 1978 by H. Levitt. Reprinted by permission.

TABLE 8.3 Spectral Range and Shape of the Fricatives

Phoneme	Spectral Range	Spectral Shape
/f/	1500 to 7500	Rather flat over range
/s/	3500 to 8500	Little energy below 3500 Hz, peaks at around 4200, flat to 8500
/ʃ/	1600 to 7000	Little below 1500 Hz, peaks at 2200, 2800, and 4000
/θ/	1400 to 8000	Flat spectrum

The acoustic composition of the other consonants appears in Table 8.4. Generally these have lower frequencies than the fricatives but higher than the vowels. Because the majority of hearing-impaired children display better hearing acuity at the lower than the higher frequencies, and because it is much easier to reproduce the lower frequencies with a hearing aid, one can easily ensure detection of the lower frequencies after arranging detection of the higher ones. The teacher/clinician's knowledge of the speech signal's acoustical composition permits auditory training/learning activities at a somewhat higher level than simply requiring a child to differentiate between the sounds of bells and drums.

Table 8.5 provides another overall view of the acoustics of speech (Gerber, 1974). Here one sees the relationship between different bands of speech and the percentage of speech power and intelligibility contained in those bands. Although these data derive from adults with normal language development and not congenitally hearing-impaired children endeavoring to learn language, the basic relationships (confirmed by many studies) enable one to appreciate the intrinsic capacity of the different bands of a speech signal to convey perceptual information. Note that the low frequencies, under normal circumstances and for normal-hearing adults, carry little of the intelligibility of speech but much of its power. These relationships confirm the importance of making as many of the high frequencies audible to hearing-impaired children as their hearing losses permit.

In digesting this point, one should not assume that the lower frequencies are useless. On the contrary, they help identify the speaker's emotional state (Ross, Duffy, Cooker, & Sergeant, 1973), assist in monitoring vocal output, enhance oral speech perception in the bisensory mode, and provide some important spectral cues to children whose residual hearing is limited to the low frequencies. The value of the suprasegmental aspects of

TABLE 8.4 Frequency Bands for Consonants as a Function of dB HL

Consonant	1	2	Frequency Bands 3	4	Intensity (dB)
r (err)	600–800	1000–1500	1800–2400		46
l (let)	250–400		2000–3000		43
sh (shot)			1500–2000	4500–5500	41
ng (wing)	250–400	1000–1500	2000–3000		41
ch (chat)			1500–2000	4000–5000	38
n (no)	250–350	1000–1500	2000–3000		37
m (me)	250–350	1000–1500			35
th (that)	250–350		2500–3500	4500–6000	34
t (tap)			2500–3500		34
h (hat)			1500–2000		32
k (kit)			2000–2500		34
i (iot)	200–300		2000–3000		36
f (for)				4000–5000	34
g (get)	200–300		1500–2500		33
s (sit)				5000–6000	32
z (zip)	200–300			4000–5000	31
v (vat)	300–400			3500–4500	31
p (pat)			1500–2000		30
d (dot)	300–400		2500–3000		29
b (bat)	300–400		2000–2500		29
th (thin)				about 6000	28

TABLE 8.5 Relationship Between the Percentage of Speech Power and Speech Intelligibility Contained in Various Frequency Bands

Frequency Range (Hz)	Speech Power %			Intelligibility %		
62 to 125	5	⎫		1	⎫	
125 to 250	13	⎬ 60	⎫	1	⎬ 5	
250 to 500	42	⎭	⎬ 95	3	⎭	
500 to 1000	35		⎭	35		
1000 to 2000	3	⎫		35	⎫	⎫
2000 to 4000	1	⎬ 5		13	⎬ 60	⎬ 95
4000 to 8000	1	⎭		12	⎭	⎭

Note. From *Introductory Hearing Science* (p. 244) by S. Gerber, 1974, Philadelphia, PA: W. B. Saunders. Copyright 1974 by the W. B. Saunders Co. Reprinted by permission.

speech (intonation, stress, duration, and rhythm) conveyed by the low frequencies should not be underestimated. When begun early, some profoundly hearing-impaired children can employ residual low frequency remarkably well, sometimes beyond what is theoretically possible. However, the high frequencies receive emphasis at this point only because in the development of hearing aids, and in too much routine clinical practice, the high-frequency acoustic needs of children still developing language have not been stressed sufficiently.

The discussion up to this point has provided a simplistic and static view of a dynamic dimension. Speech is quintessentially the product of dynamic articulatory activities, with the majority of its acoustic/perceptual clues derived from phonetic assimilation and co-articulation, which occur rapidly and change in *time*. Thus a static framework of speech acoustics omits the predictable acoustic modifications that occur in different phonetic environments and influence the entire process of speech perception. Many of these dynamic cues for speech perception are available to hearing-impaired listeners (Pickett, 1980), and thus although a complete exposition is not feasible, several of paramount importance and relevance should be noted at least briefly.

Second and third formant transitions (the latter hold less importance for children with hearing losses) directly reflect the movement of the articulators to and from the consonant restrictions preceding and following each vowel. Each such movement to and from a particular consonant constriction for a specific vowel entails a unique simultaneous movement

FIGURE 8.4 Representation of formant transitions, by manner of articulation (columns) and voicing/nasality (rows).

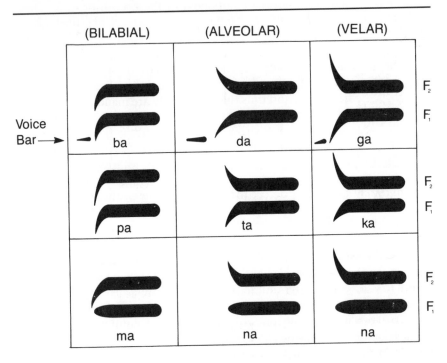

KEY: Vertical dimension = frequency
Horizontal dimension = time

of several articulators. These co-articulatory movements modify the resonance characteristics of the entire vocal system in a characteristic fashion for each combination of vowel and consonant. Acoustically, these are seen as rapid frequency shifts in time to and from the steady-state formant values given in Table 8.1.

Figure 8.4 contains a schematic representation of formant transitions. The columns show the manner of articulation and the rows display voicing and nasality. Within each box the vertical dimension represents frequency and the horizontal indicates time. The spacing between the formants would change for different vowels; only the /a/ is shown here. Other real-life cues are the simultaneous onset of voicing and the second formant transition for voiced phonemes, and the delay in voicing for the voiceless phonemes (the voice-onset-time) compared to its voiced cognate.

As speech ordinarily is syllabic, with consonants and vowels following each other in the normal flow, these rapid frequency shifts—or formant transitions—make up a normal component of the speech process. These transitions serve as powerful cues for perceiving the place of articulation of the consonants, particularly the stop consonants, which hearing-impaired people typically have a great deal of difficulty perceiving.

The spectral energy (bursts of energy related to the rapid release of the articulation) of these stop consonants is fairly high frequency (though not as high as the fricatives), and thus they frequently are inaudible, or audible in only a limited fashion, to a child with a high-frequency hearing loss or one who wears a hearing aid with a limited high-frequency range. As the characteristic frequency movements over time of the second formants are of lower frequency than the burst energy of the plosives, a child can identify the presence of specific consonants that cannot be heard. That is, the child may be able to detect the frequency shift in the vowel formant even though the high-frequency energy of the particular consonant is not itself audible. Readers can verify this effect by uttering nonsense syllables such as /eep/, /eet/, and /eek/, or /ap/, /at/, and /ak/, and not exploding the final consonant but simply placing the articulators in the proper position. The /ee/ and /a/ will sound slightly different each time because the movements toward each of the different consonants uniquely modify the oral cavity, the acoustical consequences of which can be perceived.

Co-articulation affects not only the frequency composition of vowels (as in formant transitions) but also their duration in different consonant environments. Perhaps the most audible of these effects, and the one that should be most available to hearing-impaired people, is the relative prolongation of vowels preceding voiced consonants as opposed to their voiceless cognates. For example, when saying "hit" and "hid," the vowel preceding /d/ is noticeably longer than the one preceding /t/.

Unique phonological effects abound in normal speech. The nature of the articulatory process forces us to modify our movements and articulatory gestures in a fairly predictable fashion. Thus, in using the morpheme /s/, it is voiceless after a voiceless sound and voiced (/z/) after a voiced sound. The duration of phonemes changes uniquely depending on their position in a word and the number of them occurring in a blend.

Thus many of these characteristic acoustic modifications, of secondary importance to a normal-hearing person, can take on primary significance for a hearing-impaired person. That is, a speech signal incorporates multiple acoustic cues for the correct perception of speech sounds. Using any or all of them, however, depends on speech being made audible. Even the judgment of a lack of sound, such as when a child cannot detect a high-frequency fricative, relies on perceiving the audible acoustic frame of such phonemes. Silence in such a situation also has characteristic duration and can be of value in the perceptual decision. Although no one can know how well a hearing-impaired child will be able to utilize residual hearing, unless the amplification device makes a speech signal sufficiently audible, that child's chances will be greatly reduced by poor auditory management and not just by poor hearing.

CLASSROOM ACOUSTICS

The speech signal a teacher produces must travel a certain distance in the classroom before it reaches the hearing-impaired child. Therefore, the acoustic conditions existing in the classroom will affect the quality of the speech signals the child receives. If the room is noisy and reverberant, much of the speech energy will be masked or otherwise distorted before it reaches the child. If the child sits some distance from the speaker, these effects will be greater than if he or she is closer.

That classrooms are typically noisy places needs little elaboration here. It is often surprising, however, to find out just how noisy they are. The average sound pressure level (SPL) found in several studies indicates that children must learn in noise levels exceeding 60 dB SPL (Paul & Young, 1965; Sanders, 1965; Webster & Snell, 1983; Markides, 1986). In the course of the UConn Mainstream Project (a 6-year in-service training program conducted in the Communication Services Department at the University of Connecticut and funded by the U.S. Office of Special Education and Research), existing noise levels were measured in 45 classrooms in which hearing-impaired children were placed and in 62 rooms where individual speech-language tutoring took place. The results are shown in Table 8.6.

The researchers took these measures during normal school activities using both the "A" and linear scales of a sound level meter. These scales differ mainly in that the linear scale (or "C" network) gives equal weight to all the frequencies being measured. The curve of the "A" scale weighting network, on the other hand, resembles the SPL threshold curve of the normal ear. The values obtained with the "A" scale, therefore, usually are less than those obtained with the linear scale because the "A" scale is less responsive to low-frequency energy. As a matter of fact, the difference in decibel levels between these two scales offers a good informal way to determine the level of low-frequency ambient sounds.

These results support the common observation that poor acoustic conditions exist in classrooms. The mean results are bad enough, but when one considers the magnitude of the standard deviations, it is apparent that fully a third of the classrooms demonstrated ambient noise levels in excess of 70 dB SPL. (Remember that these measures came from actual classrooms

TABLE 8.6 Average Noise Levels and Standard Deviations in Rooms in Which Hard-of-Hearing Children Were Placed

Location	Number	"A" Scale dB	S.D.	Linear SPL	S.D.
Classrooms	45	60	7	64	8
Speech rooms	62	49	9	55	10

where hearing-impaired children supposedly were being educated.) Ambient noise levels should be compared to the goal of achieving sound levels of about 35 dB on the "A" scale (in empty classrooms with normal activity in adjacent areas).

Another form of noise, reverberation, can pose even greater detriment to speech perception than noise produced by other sources. Reverberation is defined as the prolongation of sound after the source has ceased vibrating and is a function of the type of surfaces in a room. Concrete, ceramic tiles, wooden walls, and hard ceilings reflect most sound energy, while porous surfaces (rugs, drapes, corkboard, acoustical tiles) absorb much more. The longer the reverberations continue (i.e., the longer the reverberation time), the greater the detrimental effect on speech perception in the classroom.

Reverberation time is defined as the length of time required for a specific sound to decrease 60 dB after the source has ceased. A good figure to strive for in regular classrooms is an average (125, 250, 500, 1000, 2000, and 4000 Hz) reverberation time of .4 seconds (Nabalek & Robinson, 1982; Neuman & Hochberg, 1983). A number of factors can affect the specific figures measured (Klee, Kenworthy, Riggs, & Bess, 1984), including the stimuli employed in the measurement (speech babble produces higher figures), the size and dimensions of the classroom (we can tolerate more reverberation in a large room), and whether the classroom is occupied (people absorb sound, but little kids absorb less sound).

When the reverberation time exceeds about .4 seconds, speech perception for hearing-impaired individuals begins to suffer considerably. The strongest elements in the speech signal, usually the vowels, overlap in time and mask the later arriving, weaker consonantal speech elements. That is, the reflections of the vowels (the indirect sounds) will arrive at a person's ears or hearing aid microphones at the same time as the unreflected consonants (the direct sounds). As already noted, these high-frequency consonants are particularly important for speech understanding, and thus one should expend every effort to reduce reverberation time. Actual classroom reverberation times have reached an average of 1.2 seconds in some studies (Ross, 1978a; Klee et al., 1984).

The comprehension of speech in a classroom is affected less by the absolute levels of the noise and reverberation times than by the speech-to-noise ratio (the intensity level of the speech compared to the level of the background sounds). When the intensity level of the direct speech signal (prior to its first reflections) reaching a child or a hearing aid microphone is much greater than the noise and reflected sound energy in the same location, speech perception is enhanced. When it is not, the child cannot utilize his or her residual hearing effectively, no matter how carefully the hearing aids have been selected. Indeed, of all the factors that can affect speech perception, the speech-to-noise ratio (S/N) is perhaps the most important.

All studies investigating the actual signal-to-noise ratios in classrooms consistently have found ratios of +1 to +5 dB; that is, speech levels only 1 to 5 dB greater than the background noise level (Sanders, 1965; Paul & Young, 1965; Ross & Giolas, 1971; Markides, 1986). Although normal-hearing children may be able to function adequately under such conditions (an arguable proposition), hearing-impaired children cannot. The evidence clearly shows that hearing-impaired individuals are susceptible to greater absolute and relative effects on speech perception than normal-hearing people under the same conditions of noise and reverberation (Tillman, Carhart, & Olsen, 1970; Gengel, 1974; Finitzo-Hieber & Tillman, 1978; Dirks, Morgan, & Dubno, 1982; Boney & Bess, 1984). This effect is apparent in Table 8.7 (data from Finitzo-Hieber & Tillman, 1978).

Note in this table that in every condition of noise and reverberation, separately and in combination, the scores of the hard-of-hearing children are poorer and become relatively worse as the listening conditions deteriorate. For example, with no reverberation, the scores for normal-hearing children drop 35% (from 95 to 60) when the signal-to-noise ratio is reduced from +12 to 0, and the scores for hard-of-hearing children drop 46% (from 88 to 42). That is, the hard-of-hearing children not only demonstrate poorer speech perception scores under the most favorable conditions, but their score reduction under unfavorable conditions is greater. This observation affirms that the speech perception scores of hearing-impaired children are *relatively* affected by noise and reverberation more than those of normal-hearing children.

Under the poorest acoustical conditions (reverberation time = 1.2 seconds, S/N = 0—not at all unusual in classrooms), the scores of the normal hearing drop 47% (77 to 30), as do those for the unaided hard of hearing. With hearing aids, however, because of the imposition of reduced fidelity signals compared to the unaided conditions, the scores drop even more, to a horrendous low of 11.

TABLE 8.7 Speech Discrimination Scores for 12 Hard-of-Hearing Children Under Noise and Reverberant Conditions

Reverberation Time (sec.)	Signal-to-Noise Ratio (dB)	Normal Hearing	Unaided Hard of Hearing	Aided Hard of Hearing
0.0	quiet	95	88	83
	+12	89	78	70
	+6	78	66	60
	0	60	42	39
0.4	quiet	93	79	74
	+12	83	69	60
	+6	71	55	52
	0	48	29	28
1.2	quiet	77	62	45
	+12	69	50	41
	+6	54	40	27
	0	30	15	11

Note. From "Room Acoustics Effects on Monosyllabic Word Discrimination Ability for Normal and Hearing-Impaired Children" by T. Finitzo-Hieber and T. W. Tillman, 1978, *Journal of Speech and Hearing Research, 21,* pp. 440–458. Copyright 1978 by the American Speech-Hearing-Language Association. Reprinted by permission.

Boney and Bess (1984) found the same effects on speech perception in a study of minimally and mildly hearing-impaired children that used noise and reverberation levels typically found in regular classrooms (+6 dB S/N and .85 reverberation time). Their results also indicate that the combined effects of noise and reverberation on speech recognition scores were much greater than the individual effects, particularly for the hearing-impaired children. Additionally, they point out that these listening conditions also affected children with normal hearing, albeit less than those with impaired hearing.

Obviously one cannot ignore the probable implications of poor classroom acoustical conditions for the speech recognition performance of hearing-impaired children. If *recognition* scores for known vocabulary are affected detrimentally, one can safely assume negative consequences for the auditory *development* of speech and language. It follows that one must make every effort to reduce the classroom noise and reverberation levels for hearing-impaired students. The most efficient (and ideal) procedure for improving these conditions is to sound-treat the entire classroom, through the services of a knowledgeable builder or, in difficult cases, an architectural acoustician.

Certain practical measures are obvious, however (Olsen, 1977, 1988), and can be readily implemented in many classrooms. Rugs on the floors and acoustical tiles on the walls and ceilings (preferably a dropped, low ceiling) will make an immediate and discernible difference in the classroom's existing acoustical conditions. Drapes over windows and liberal use of corkboard can help when installation of acoustical tiles on the walls is not possible. Further, creative teachers have fashioned interesting designs of colored egg cartons on the walls, with both decorative and acoustical results. (Care must be taken, however, not to create a fire hazard along with the acoustical improvements.)

Classroom noise sources must be identified and steps taken to eliminate or reduce them (in spite of occasional temptations, we do not recommend eliminating the primary source of noise in classrooms—the children). Air conditioners and heating systems can be major offenders, and one can reduce the noise they generate without impairing their operating efficiency. Overhead projectors, gaps under the doors, windows opening onto busy thoroughfares—the list of actual and potential noise sources can be extended almost indefinitely. The first and most important step, however, toward decreasing excess classroom noise and reverberation levels is to increase the sensitivity of classroom teachers and administrators to the deleterious impact of these conditions.

Often it is not possible to significantly reduce the absolute levels of noise in a classroom, but much can be done to maximize the audibility of the teacher's voice. Possibly the most important such procedure that teachers and clinicians can employ is simply to decrease the distance between their mouths and the microphone of the child's amplification device (hearing aids or FM auditory training systems). Figure 8.5 graphically illustrates this phenomenon.

The figure assumes an average speech signal of 66 dB SPL 3 feet from a speaker, and 60 dB SPL of ambient noise equally distributed throughout the classroom. (In hearing level terms, i.e., on an audiometric scale, these values would be approximately 20 dB less, i.e., 46 and 40 dB HL, respectively; the same relationships exist regardless of the particular reference level employed.) As one can see, the signal-to-noise ratio substantially increases as the distance between the speaker and the microphone/child decreases. As the distance between the source (teacher) and the recipient (microphone/child) is halved, the speech level increases by 6 dB and the S/N grows to +12 dB. As the distance is halved again (to the 9-inch location), the signal increases to 78 dB and the S/N to +18 dB. Finally, at the 4½-inch location, the S/N is a positive and acceptable 24 dB.

FIGURE 8.5   Effects of distance on audibility.

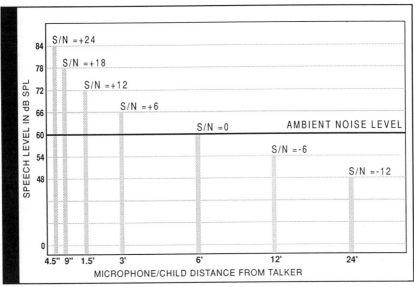

DESIGN BY BOB ESSMAN

Hearing-impaired people in general require approximately a 15 dB more favorable S/N than normal-hearing people in order to reach the limits of their auditory capabilities (Dirks et al., 1982). Figure 8.5 demonstrates that this can be obtained easily by locating the microphone of the amplification device closer to the speaker. There is no magic about these figures and the underlying concept—the intensity of a speech signal increases or decreases by 6 dB as the distance from the source is doubled or halved. Called the inverse-square law (and strictly applicable only in free-fields and anechoic chambers), it also applies in classrooms at locations close to the source of a sound. Noise levels, on the other hand, tend to be equally distributed in a room (except, again, at locations close to the source). This concept underlies the main advantage of an FM auditory training system, which will be elaborated on in chapter 9.

ELECTROACOUSTIC CONSIDERATIONS

The auditory management model next takes in electroacoustic considerations. Choosing the term *electroacoustic* as opposed to *hearing aids and auditory trainers* emphasizes our primary concern with the performance characteristics of these devices rather than their name, cost, and appearance.

It is imperative that hearing-impaired children be provided with the most advantageous electroacoustic characteristics possible, and that these in turn be monitored carefully and continuously. As hearing losses differ, so must the recommended parameters of amplification performance. Knowledge of the relationship between electroacoustic characteristics and speech intelligibility as well as the ability to modify them have increased tremendously in recent years. The clinical impact of this knowledge, however, is still imperfectly realized.

The fact that a child wears a perfectly functioning hearing aid offers no reason to assume that its pattern of amplification is optimal for that child. To do so would confuse a box (the hearing aid) with its content (its electroacoustic characteristics). One would hardly accept, for example, the notion that a visually impaired child could be fitted satisfactorily with eyeglasses taken from containers labeled "near-sightedness," "far-sightedness," "amblyopia," "astigmatism," and so on. It is not unreasonable for a teacher, clinician, or parent to seek assurances from the child's audiologist that the hearing aid in use provides an appropriate amplification pattern.

Professionals working with hearing-impaired children should develop a working knowledge of the advantages and disadvantages of the hearing aids suitable for children, an understanding of the various electroacoustic characteristics by which hearing aids are described, an appreciation of the implications of these characteristics as they concern the speech signal processed through hearing aids, and the skill to appropriately supervise hearing aids' daily operation. Subsequent sections will cover these topics and demonstrate their relevance to the concept of aided residual hearing.

Physical Components of Hearing Aids

No matter the type, all hearing aids consist of the same basic components. All must contain a microphone to convert the air-borne sound waves into electrical impulses and an amplifier to increase the magnitude of these impulses. Some include tone-control circuits, which can modify the hearing aid's frequency response, and just about all have a volume control (although some of the smallest models do not have room for this feature). All hearing aids must have a way of converting the amplified electrical signal back into sound. In hearing aid parlance, this component is called a *receiver* (actually it is a miniature loudspeaker). Requiring a means of obtaining electrical power, all hearing aids include batteries. Finally, the amplified sound has to be delivered into a person's ear, accomplished through an earmold. Although while strictly speaking the latter is not a hearing aid component, it is an important part of the entire acoustical system (as well as the most frequent problem area).

One component common to many hearing aids is the telephone coil, or "T" switch, originally developed to permit hearing-impaired people to use the telephone more effectively. When activated, the coil detects the magnetic field emitted by a telephone, which is then amplified by the hearing aid and converted into sound by the receiver. When the "T" switch is on, the microphone ("M") is usually off. With the "T" switch activated, the characteristics of the amplified sound produced by the entire system usually change. The inclusion and function of "T" switches become very important as one considers certain alternative ways of coupling an FM auditory training system to a personal hearing aid.

Types of Hearing Aids

There are four general types of personal hearing aids suitable for children: body aids, behind-the-ear (BTE) aids, in-the-ear (ITE) aids, and some members of the CROS (contralateral routing of offside signals) family.

Body aids are larger and generally sturdier than other types of hearing aids, and their controls are relatively easy for young children to manipulate. Because of their size, batteries last longer in body aids than in other types. Modern body aids also incorporate a number of controls that can modify their electroacoustic characteristics. Feedback (acoustic squeal) presents less of a problem with them than with ear-level hearing aids because of the greater distance between the microphone (located on the body) and the receiver—the "loudspeaker" of the aid—at the ear. That is, there is less likelihood that this microphone would pick up the sound that escapes from the ear, which then would be reamplified by the hearing aid, commencing the feedback cycle and causing audible squeal.

Because the child wears the microphone on his or her body, the speech signal is not detected at the normal ear-level location; further, the microphone also is frequently covered with layers of clothing, which can muffle high-frequency reception. The microphone rubbing against the child's clothing produces "clothing noise"—that is, audible sounds that act as both a masker of speech and an annoying distraction. In addition, the influence of the child's body itself produces a "body baffle" effect. The location of the aid on the body results in some attentuation of the higher frequencies, and a slight enhancement of the low frequencies, compared to the manufacturer's specifications. Moreover, body aids generally show poorer responses at the higher frequencies than BTE and ITE hearing aids because the latter incorporate more efficient receivers. There is, however, no intrinsic engineering reason why body aid receivers could not be made more efficient.

Body aids require that the nub of the hearing aid receiver be snapped into the retaining ring of a standard earmold. This effectively precludes manipulating the shape of the earmold for possibly advantageous acoustic effects (as will be discussed). The use of binaural amplification is possible with body aids, but less physically convenient than with ear-level hearing aids.

Body aids may be recommended for some infants with profound hearing losses, when feedback and/or retention problems are likely with BTE aids, and when deformities of the pinna prohibit their use. Occasionally, too, an older child with a profound hearing loss will benefit from the extra low-frequency boost produced by the aid's body baffle effect. Body aids are somewhat in disrepute at the present time, but mainly for cosmetic reasons (Ross & Madell, 1988). Choice of a hearing aid, however, should be dictated by performance and not cosmetic factors whenever possible.

In later discussions of FM systems (see chapter 9), it will be noted that the FM receiver in a self-contained system functions essentially as a body hearing aid. Most of the preceding comments apply, but with several exceptions. The FM receiver usually is worn outside the clothing and so is not muffled by external apparel, and two microphones permit convenient binaural use, though still not as effectively as BTE aids (Maxon & Mazor, 1977).

Behind-the-ear aids incorporate all the electroacoustic possibilities found in body aids and, unless limited by feedback, are capable of delivering high SPL signals to the ear. Because of the close proximity of the microphone and the receiver (both are located in the hearing aid case), however, feedback can present much more of a problem than with body aids. Battery life also is relatively short, though much greater than some years ago. The BTE aid's controls can be difficult for young children to manipulate, and the internal settings are often so minute so as to present a problem to the middle-aged audiologist with presbyopia (a magnifying glass is a good investment). "Wind noise" can be quite disturbing when wearing these aids outdoors on a windy day; the turbulence occurring at the borders of the hearing aid case are amplified by the hearing aid. This amplified turbulence can become quite loud and annoying, often to the point of precluding effective outdoor communication.

The BTE aids are worn at ear level, the normal location for perceiving sound. This permits the interposition of the head between the hearing aid microphones, the acoustical effects of which are important for realizing some dimensions of binaural listening. Some BTE aids come with directional microphones to replicate more closely the normal ear's localization capacities. The latter will favor the detection of signals arriving from a 45-

degree arc in front and will suppress to a certain extent those arriving from the rear. Cosmetically, children find BTE aids more acceptable than body aids, often to the point of refusing to wear anything else. (This cosmetic consciousness carries a heavy price when children object to wearing an FM system because the receiver is visible on the body.) The shell earmold employed with BTE hearing aids can be altered physically in ways that modify the acoustic characteristics of the entire hearing aid/earmold system.

BTE aids can contain powerful telephone coils, an important component for certain modes of coupling an FM system to a personal hearing aid. Other BTE hearing aids permit direct electrical coupling to the output of an FM system, which allows a child to wear his or her own hearing aid as an integral component of the FM system. Because of the often unforeseen necessity of coupling an FM unit to a BTE, either through magnetic induction (via the telephone coil) or the direct audio input, every BTE hearing aid recommended for a child should include these features. Many modern BTE aids also include automatic signal processing (ASP) capabilities, which for the most part reduce the low-frequency amplification of the hearing aid as the low-frequency input signals increase.

Recent years have seen a proliferation of different *in-the-ear hearing aids*, ranging from one that completely fills the concha to mini-canal aids deployed fairly deep in the ear canal. Although the present discussion will confine itself to the full concha ITEs because of their greater fitting flexibility, there is no intrinsic reason why some older children could not be fitted satisfactorily with the newer generations of these aids.

The full ITE hearing aid contains all its electronics in essentially an earmold. That is, the entire hearing aid—microphone, amplifier, receiver, battery, and various other controls—sits within the body of the earmold, permitting the pinna to play their normal physiological role in sound reception. Contrary to some previous thought, the pinna are not just more-or-less ornamental appendages hung on the sides of our heads. They act as slight obstacles to high-frequency sound emanating from the rear and assist in binaural reception and localization of speech (Preves & Griffin, 1976a–d).

Current models of ITE aids offer a wide range of fitting possibilities and, from an electroacoustic perspective, are suitable for a wide range of mild and moderate (and even some severe) hearing losses. Some include ASP circuits as well as some capability to modify the aid's frequency responses and output SPL. Although telephone coils can be incorporated in ITE aids, they are rarely powerful enough for a moderately or severely hearing-impaired person to use effectively on the telephone or in conjunction with an FM system.

Currently ITE aids cannot be considered appropriate for young children because of the need to reset the aid in another earmold as the size of the ears increase. As with the newer generation of smaller ones, ITE aids can be considered a viable alternative to BTEs for some teenagers whose head growth has slowed. Before such a decision is made, however, one must determine whether the cosmetic attractions of these smaller aids require too much compromise in terms of desirable amplification patterns and other features.

The *CROS (contralateral routing of offside signals) hearing aid* presents an amplification option for children with nonfunctional hearing in one ear and, preferably, a mild, high-frequency loss in the better ear. The basic CROS design entails placing a microphone, inserted within the case of a BTE, behind the nonfunctional (or "bad") ear. The signal from this microphone is sent to the amplifier/receiver in the "good" ear via a wire around the back of the neck, or by a radio wave. In essence the aid is separated into two parts, one part with the microphone and the other with the rest of the aid's components. In a CROS fitting, the "good" ear typically does not require amplification in its own right.

The acoustic signal emanating from the hearing aid receiver in the "good" ear is coupled to the ear via an open or a nonoccluding earmold, which does not impede the direct reception of sound. Only the signal reaching the microphone placed by the poor ear is amplified, and only enough to overcome the obstacle the head ordinarily imposes between the bad and good ears. A CROS arrangement thereby enables a wearer to be aware and to respond to speech directed to either ear, although it is actually perceived only in the better one.

The preceding is not a binaural arrangement. It can best be conceptualized as a "V" connection, with the tips of the "V" representing where sound is detected and the bottom representing where the sound is being directed. For some children, in some conditions, a CROS arrangement can be quite helpful, particularly where speech is continually directed to the bad side. Children may be confused initially by a CROS hearing aid; a supervised trial should precede a firm recommendation.

The other major member of the CROS family is the *BICROS,* or *bilateral routing of signals.* In this arrangement, although there again must be one functional and one nonfunctional ear, the functional ("good") ear can use and benefit from amplification. As in the CROS arrangement, a microphone is placed in a BTE case behind the "bad" ear, and the signals again are directed to the better ear by a wire going around the back of the neck or by a radio wave. The BICROS set up, however, places a complete hearing aid on the better ear as well. Thus, although two microphones detect acoustic signals, one behind each ear, the sound they detect is transmitted to just the one better ear.

In a BICROS hearing aid, the signals usually terminate in a closed mold, to avoid producing feedback when the sound escaping from this ear is picked by the microphone and reamplified. In some instances, however, when the good ear exhibits a mild or moderate high-frequency hearing loss, the child can use a vented or a nonoccluding earmold (which permits the amplified low-frequency sounds to escape from the mold). The basic advantage of the BICROS is the same as with the traditional CROS hearing aid—receiving in the good ear speech directed to either side of the head.

One of the major advantages of all ear-level hearing aids over body aids is the greater convenience in using *binaural amplification*. Clearly, as supported overwhelmingly by the evidence (see Ross, 1980, for a review), binaural amplification presents the method of choice for *most* hearing-impaired children. However, some children, but mainly their parents, put up a great deal of resistance to "wearing another one of those things." It is as if they will be considered, and consider themselves, doubly handicapped because they wear two hearing aids. For some parents the cost of two hearing aids may be prohibitive, but a number of state and private agencies will assist in their purchase.

Other children may be poor audiological candidates for binaural amplification on the basis of a very wide disparity in hearing acuity or speech discrimination scores between the ears. One should not, however, rule out a priori a recommendation for binaural amplification in such cases. Some children with wide assymetry between the ears can synthesize and benefit from the different auditory sensations arriving from the two ears. This kind of determination cannot be made during the short, routine audiological clinic visits. It takes the close observation of parents, teachers, and clinicians over a period of time, considering both speech production as well as reception, to determine the benefits of binaural hearing aids, particularly for older children with no prior experience using binaurally amplified sound.

Some children's apparent audiological suitability for binaural amplification is not borne out even after an extensive trial, which may reflect the effects of binaural sensory deprivation (our personal conviction for the majority of such cases). This suggestion comes not just on the basis of clinical experience and intuition, but from the results of controlled animal research that clearly demonstrates functional and structural binaural abnormalities after a period of monaural deprivation (Silverman & Clopton, 1977; Clopton & Silverman, 1977; Evans, Webster, & Cullen, 1983; Webster, 1983).

For the vast majority of hearing-impaired children, binaural hearing aids improve the ability to comprehend speech in both quiet and noisy environments, make comprehending speech under difficult listening conditions less fatiguing, improve the ability to localize the source of speech (very important in classroom discussions), and allow them to hear and respond to speech directed to either ear. A bonus consideration is the fact that a binaural speech signal can produce the same loudness sensation as a monaural signal with 6 dB less sound pressure level. That is, a 100 dB binaural sound would be perceived as loud as a 106 dB monaural signal. If one is concerned with the possible deleterious effects of high sound pressures on the impaired ear, this 6 dB reduction in the required output can offer additional protection for a child. Binaural amplification should be the initial fitting of choice for all children unless some definite contraindications arise. Only when functioning with two aided ears becomes clearly worse than, not just equal to, functioning with one ear should a child revert to monaural amplification.

Cochlear Implants

In recent years, a great deal of interest has turned to cochlear implants. Although relatively few children have received such systems, it presents an exciting research area. As a matter of fact, it seems sometimes that more articles appear about cochlear implants than there are people wearing them. However, the interest in implants does have implications for children who wear conventional hearing aids; this interest has stimulated more refined speech perception techniques and more rigorously planned habilitative procedures.

Cochlear implants are not hearing aids. They do not amplify sound and deliver it to the ears of a hearing-impaired person. Rather, they convert sound to an electrical current, then transmit it into the inner ear. These devices help those who cannot benefit at all or only minimally from a hearing aid. The best candidates for cochlear implants have experienced adventitious hearing losses, although some cases have been persons with congenital losses as well. Because the implant delivers an electrical current into the inner ear, the prospective recipient must possess intact and functional eighth-nerve fibers to detect this current.

A cochlear implant consists of two main parts, a surgically implanted internal portion and an external device worn on the body. The internal part consists of a receiver and a wire electrode. The receiver is implanted in the mastoid process behind the pinna, and the electrode passes through the middle ear and into the inner ear. The operation to insert the receiver and the electrode is not considered dangerous.

The external part of the implant consists of a microphone (located near the ear), a signal processor (worn on the body), and a stimulator, which fits over the receiver and stays in place through a magnetic connection. There are two basic types of cochlear implants, single and multichannel systems. At present a developing professional consensus believes that the multichannel system offers more potential advantages. It should be noted, however, that "successes" and "failures" occur with both types of systems.

In either implant system, sound is detected by the microphone, sent to the signal processor on the body via a wire cord, and then delivered to the transmitter on the surface of the mastoid. This transmitter conveys the processed signal to the embedded receiver, which then passes it on to the electrode in the inner ear. In the most common multichannel implant, 22 active electrodes rest in the inner ear, and the processor is individually tuned to provide the most salient signal in all 22 channels. This processor, a sophisticated minicomputer, analyzes incoming sounds and then extracts and codes changes in the fundamental frequency of a person's voice and in low and high frequency concentrations of energy (corresponding to the first and second formant). These formants are transmitted rapidly and sequentially to different locations on the inner ear's electrode array that correspond to the normal maximal stimulation point for the first and second formants.

For all types of cochlear implants, results have varied from little improvement to a surprising degree of open-set word recognition. Most recipients find that their speechreading skills improve with the addition of the auditory sensations the implant provides. Further, a few subjects (mainly persons with adventitious hearing losses) have demonstrated an ability to converse on the telephone, albeit with some difficulty, and to engage in relatively effortless face-to-face conversation. At the time of this writing, relatively few children have worn the multichannel implant for more than a few years, but results for some appear encouraging. One of the present authors is directly involved in a habilitative program with implanted children, seeing auditory skill development results that would not have been predicted several years ago.

Electroacoustic Characteristics

In the United States, the procedures and measurement conditions for determining the electroacoustic characteristics of hearing aids come from the American National Standards Institute (ANSI; 1982). The following sections will abstract from this large body of data the most pertinent information for the prospective teacher/clinician. It should be noted that ANSI specifications are designed to describe the performance of hearing aids under standard measuring conditions, and not how they actually function on human beings. More detailed information on the ANSI specifications and hearing aids in general appears in several recent textbooks (Hodgson, 1986; Pollack, 1988; Skinner, 1988).

The *gain* of a hearing aid/FM system is the difference between the input sound levels at the microphone and the output levels emanating from the output transducer (the hearing aid receiver). ANSI specifications require that gain be described in two ways. In the first, the gain/volume control is turned to the full-on position and input sounds of 60 dB SPL (for aids without an automatic gain control) are delivered to the microphone. The 60 dB are subtracted from the average of the amplified output at 1000, 1600, and 2500 Hz to give the average full-on gain. Thus if the output at these three frequencies was 100, 105, and 110 dB SPL, respectively, the individual gains would be 40, 45, and 50 dB, while the average gain would be 45 dB.

In the second method, using the same 60 dB input, the gain/volume control is adjusted until the output average at the same three frequencies is 17 dB below the maximum sound pressure output of the hearing aid. Called the reference test gain (RTG) position, this becomes the gain setting used when evaluating the distortion and frequency response characteristics of a hearing aid. For example, if the maximum possible output of a hearing aid averages 132 dB SPL, then the output at the reference test gain position should average 115 dB, or a reference test gain of 55 dB (115 dB minus 60 dB input). This setting is considered the standardized replication of the average gain setting that a person will or should use. (One would not want to wear a hearing aid with the gain full-on because of the likelihood of increased distortion at that setting and the lack of any gain reserve for listening to soft speech.)

Statements regarding the gain of a hearing aid without specifying which one is being discussed can be confusing, because one method describes the maximum gain while the other replicates an optimal "use" setting. It is also possible to refer to the *actual use* gain setting of a hearing aid, which may differ from both ANSI methods of determining and describing gain.

One should not assume that the gain of a hearing aid at a particular frequency should resemble a person's hearing loss. For example, if a child has 60 dB hearing loss, it may seem logical to amplify speech by 60 dB and thereby fully compensate for the hearing loss. Unfortunately, however, this is not how the ear operates. With a gain of 60 dB and an input of 70 dB SPL, the hearing aid would produce an output signal of 130 dB SPL (see discussion of "output" for certain qualifications), just about the limit of human tolerance for intense sounds. People with hearing losses cannot necessarily tolerate more intense sounds than those with normal hearing.

As the hearing loss increases, the dynamic range, the difference between threshold and maximum tolerable sounds, is reduced. The so-called 50% law for estimating gain states that an individual's gain requirement is approximately one half the degree of the hearing loss; that is, a

60 dB hearing loss requires not 60 dB gain but about 30 dB gain. The required gain also is usually a frequency-dependent function, with the gain required at each frequency adjusted to the degree of hearing loss at that point. For children with milder losses, it is desirable to provide less gain than one half of the hearing loss; for those with severe and profound hearing losses, it is necessary to provide somewhat more gain than this percentage. The overriding principle, which shall be discussed more fully later, seeks to ensure that the average speech signal is sufficiently, but not overly, audible at each frequency.

The electroacoustic dimension of *output* is often confused with gain. Output refers instead to the intensity level of the signal emitted by the hearing aid. In the preceding example, an input signal of 70 dB SPL and a gain of 60 dB resulted in an output of 130 dB SPL—the sound pressure delivered to the ear of a hearing-impaired person wearing a hearing aid.

The SSPL-90, which stands for the saturation sound pressure level at a 90 dB input, is the intensity level at which no further increase in output is possible, regardless of the input or gain level. One measures the SSPL-90 by exposing a hearing aid, set on the full-on gain position, to a 90 dB SPL input across frequency (from 200 to 5000 HZ at a minimum). The outputs at the frequencies 1000, 1600, and 2500 Hz are averaged and termed the SSPL-90 of the hearing aid.

The maximum or peak SSPL-90 is the highest output occurring at any of the frequencies measured. The average SSPL-90 can be significantly less than the peak SSPL-90 in instances where the output curve varies widely with frequency. For example, some hearing aids or FM systems may produce a peak SSPL-90 10 or more dB higher than the average SSPL-90. The SSPL-90 can be appropriate but the aid itself unsatisfactory because of a high peak SSPL-90. Teachers and clinicians should know both of these figures for the hearing aids and auditory trainers fitted to their students. Any concern that the output of an amplification device is too high for a child should prompt an immediate referral to an audiologist.

If the SSPL-90 of a hearing aid is 130 dB SPL, and the gain is set at 60 dB at that frequency, then an input of 70 dB results in an output of 130 dB SPL. However, keeping the gain at 60 dB and increasing the input to 80 dB does *not* produce an output of 140 dB SPL. The hearing aid cannot exceed its own output design limitations, in this example 130 dB SPL. This concept is conveyed by the term *saturation*. When a towel becomes saturated with water, it cannot absorb any more no matter how much longer it soaks. Similarly for the SSPL-90; once this point is reached, the aid becomes "saturated" and cannot deliver sounds of a higher intensity level.

An excessively high SSPL-90 very commonly will cause some hearing-impaired persons to reject amplification. Satisfactory hearing aid usage cannot occur if the SSPL-90 exceeds a person's uncomfortable loudness level (UCL). For example, if a child's UCL is 110 dB SPL and the SSPL-90 of his hearing aid is 125 dB SPL, he could tolerate inputs of 70 dB SPL if the gain of the aid were 40 dB (output = 70 dB + 40 dB, or 110 dB), but any inputs greater than this would produce uncomfortable, and perhaps painful, loudness sensations. Sounds of doors slamming, excessively loud speech, playground activities, cafeteria babble, dishes clattering, heavy traffic—all may produce inputs greater than 70 dB SPL and therefore would cause problems.

If this child decides to reduce the gain to keep the resulting outputs from exceeding his UCL, he might find he cannot understand speech being delivered at 60–70 dB SPL. So he turns the gain back up, but then when he encounters intense inputs again, he reduces the gain to avoid uncomfortable loudness sensations. A few times like this and the gain either stays reduced or the hearing aid stays out of the ear. The solution for this child is to keep the gain at the required level but reduce the SSPL-90 to 110 dB SPL.

Output is the dimension of hearing aid performance often implicated regarding the possible effect of high sound level on a person's residual hearing. The question is often asked, if the SSPL-90 of a hearing aid is set too high, can this sound produce further decrements in hearing acuity? The outputs of hearing aids and auditory trainers can far exceed the sound pressure levels that can produce temporary or permanent threshold shifts for normal-hearing people. Insofar as hearing-impaired children are concerned, there are some grounds for caution but not alarm (see Rintelman & Bess, 1988, for a recent review, and comments by Ross & Seewald, 1988, pp. 209–210).

A number of documented case reports have shown further deterioration of hearing acuity unambiguously related to hearing aid usage. However, the most recent *group* studies examining such a possibility of permanent threshold shifts have not revealed any further average decrement of hearing thresholds. The reports of individual cases cannot be ignored but should be put in perspective. Because high SPLs may relate to threshold shifts, no one should be fitted with hearing aids having higher than necessary SSPL-90s. Hearing aid outputs in excess of 132 dB SPL should be recommended only for those with the most severe hearing losses.

Although no professional would favor taking unnecessary risks with a hearing-impaired child's residual hearing, one also cannot apply an exaggerated concern that deprives these children of usable amplified speech sensation levels when they need it most. In response to fears of overamplification, one sees many children now whose SSPL-90s appear unnecessarily low. Children's residual hearing does them no good at frequencies where the amplified speech spectrum falls below their thresholds. During their early years in particular, these children have to *hear*. Without hearing there is no natural development of speech and language skills.

An active audiology management program provides the best of both. Children can be fitted with hearing aids that provide a suitable pattern of audible amplified speech, and professionals can monitor their hearing thresholds frequently to detect possible instances of shifts. The thresholds for the great majority of children are going to be stable. For those in whom bilateral shifts seem to occur (assuming binaural amplification), remedial measures can be taken. Is a medical condition responsible for the shift? This should be ruled out. Is the SSPL-90 set too high? This can be reduced, and the child's behavior monitored to ensure that levels are not too low. What happens when one aid is withdrawn? Is there a recovery of hearing thresholds in that ear? What should not be done is to deprive children of amplified sound, with all its implications on their communication skills, academic performance, and behavioral adjustment.

The *frequency response* of an acoustic device expresses its relative gain across frequency. The hearing aid is exposed to a range of frequencies from at least 200 to 5000 Hz, which may be extended if the hearing can respond at lower and higher frequencies. The hearing aid is set at the reference test gain (RTG) position, and a constant input signal of 60 dB SPL is directed to its microphone. Because few, if any, hearing aids or FM systems amplify such inputs to exactly the same degree at all frequencies, the resulting output curve demonstrates different degrees of gain at the different frequencies and thus displays the *relative* gain of the hearing aid across frequency. A typical frequency response is shown in Figure 8.6.

A so-called "flat curve" in a hearing aid or FM system occurs when there is a an equal amount of gain at all frequencies; in reality this is not very "flat" for all wearable amplification devices. Ironically, even the cheapest stereo receiver has flatter, and more flexible, frequency responses than the most expensive hearing aid. A high-frequency response is one that amplifies the high frequencies more than the low frequencies. Just about all hearing aids and FM systems include controls to modify the frequency response; one can, for example, emphasize the low frequencies relative to the highs (occurring only rarely, when the person exhibits a rising threshold configuration) or the high frequencies relative to the lows (a more common occurrence).

Various degrees of selective amplification are possible. As with the gain, a temptation arises to compensate for the hearing loss by matching the frequency response to the hearing loss configuration. In this approach, the hearing aid gain at the different frequencies would be set equal to the degree of hearing loss at the same frequencies. Both problems and merit attend to this approach. The preponderance of recent evidence supports the advantages of a modified form of "selective amplification" (i.e., amplifying certain frequencies more than others). Precise selective amplification, while perhaps feasible technically, is not advisable because of the way

FIGURE 8.6 Typical frequency response of an acoustic device.

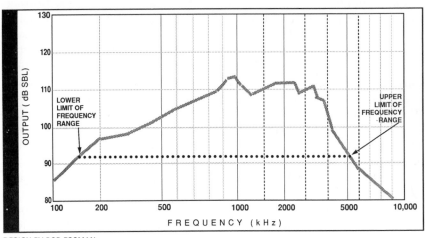

DESIGN BY BOB ESSMAN

the ear operates. At relatively low suprathreshold sensation levels, the *loudness* sensations produced by most impaired ears resembles those occurring in a normal ear. This phenomenon, called *recruitment*, offers one reason why precise selective amplification is undesirable.

The frequency response requirements at suprathreshold listening levels, therefore, cannot equal the threshold configuration but can, in large part, be based on them. For hearing-impaired persons who exhibit a gradually sloping threshold curve (a high-frequency hearing loss), there is merit in generally duplicating the threshold configuration with the frequency response, but not to the degree of loss at each frequency; that is, one should provide the person with sufficient amplification at each frequency to produce an *aided* threshold curve that parallels, but does not equal, the normal *unaided* thresholds. Thus the person with a high-frequency loss would receive relatively more amplification at the high frequencies than at the low ones (Pascoe, 1975). For those with more extreme threshold slopes, aided audibility at the higher frequencies most closely relates to speech perception. (The most sophisticated and comprehensive treatment of this and related issues is presented in Skinner, 1988.)

The concept of *aided audibility* of a speech signal input forms the overriding principle by which the suitability of a frequency response should be judged. Maximizing the audibility of a speech signal, combined with providing an optimal speech-to-noise ratio, will ensure that a child can receive the most, and most salient, information consistent with his or her hearing loss. The concept applies regardless of slope and degree. The gain and frequency response of an amplification device should optimize the important speech acoustic information that a child can receive, regardless of the type and degree of hearing loss. The child must *hear* as much of the full range of speech sounds as possible in order to use audition fully for the development and recognition of speech and language.

It is important to realize, however, that one cannot translate the frequency response specifications published by a manufacturer to the actual sound pressures occurring in the ear canal of a specific child. The manufacturers follow ANSI standards, as they should, in making acoustic measurements of their instruments, and they employ a 2 cc coupler as a real ear simulator. As discussed in chapter 4, though, real ears, particularly children's ears, vary to some degree or other from this "simulated" real ear. The difference between the cavity dimensions of an actual ear and that of the standard simulator explains why the frequency response of a hearing aid is measured while actually being worn by a child. This *functional* response is defined as the difference between the aided and the unaided sound-field threshold.

Figure 8.7 provides an example of the wide variations from the coupler-measured frequency response occurring in five normal ears (Dalsgaard & Jensen, 1976). The solid line shows the results obtained in a 2 cc coupler, while the shaded area gives the real-ear variations. This figure shows how one cannot predict the frequency response of a hearing aid on a child simply by looking at the manufacturer's specifications. Real ears present just too many variations.

Hearing aids and FM systems do not amplify extremely low and high frequencies; the *frequency range*, therefore, refers to that band of frequencies that *is* effectively amplified by the instrument. In the 1982 ANSI method of determining frequency range, outputs at 1000, 1600, and 2500 Hz on the basic frequency response curve are averaged, then a horizontal line is drawn on the chart 20 dB below this average figure. The points where this line intersects the upper and lower frequencies on the frequency response curve define the frequency range.

A basic frequency response curve is displayed in Figure 8.6. The outputs at 1000, 1600, and 2500 Hz are 114, 110, and 109 dB, respectively, for an average of 111 dB. The horizontal line drawn 20 dB below this point falls at 91 dB. As one can see, this line intersects the lower part of the curve at about 150 Hz and the upper portion at about 5200 Hz. These two numbers define the effective frequency range of the instrument.

The frequency range presents an extremely important, but frequently underestimated, dimension of hearing aid performance, particularly as it applies to congenitally hearing-impaired children. One can best appreciate its significance by relating it to the acoustics of speech signals, the stimuli

FIGURE 8.7   Difference between the 2 cc coupler response of a hearing aid and the performance of the same aid (measured with a probe microphone in the ear) on five persons (solid line = coupler response; shaded area = individual real-ear variations). From "Measurement of the Insertion Gain of Hearing Aids" by S. C. Dalsgaard and O. D. Jensen, 1976, *Journal of Audiological Technology, 15,* p. 170. Copyright 1976 by Median-Verlag. Reprinted by permission.

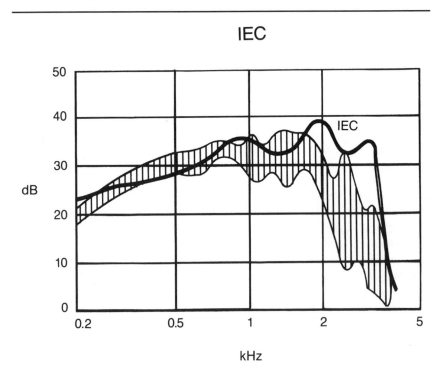

of most interest in amplification efforts for children. As noted previously, vowels are generally of lower frequency and higher intensity than consonants, with the voiceless consonants showing the highest frequencies and some of the weakest intensities of any speech sound.

Consider, for example, the acoustics of the phoneme /s/ as shown in Table 8.3. Its major energy concentrates between about 3500 and 8500 Hz, which means that any hearing aid with an *upper* frequency range of 3500 Hz or less will not amplify this phoneme, as its *lowest* frequency is also 3500 Hz. As pointed out earlier, this particular phoneme has not only great phonological significance, considering how often it appears in our spoken language, but it also carries the greatest morphological load of any in the language. It is also particularly difficult for hearing-impaired children to produce, especially in blends. The best ally for attempting to "teach" hearing-impaired children speech and language resides in their own natural abilities. When a child has sufficient residual hearing to learn naturally the full linguistic implications of /s/, but his or her amplification system precludes its perception, this reduces not only the effectiveness of therapeutic endeavors, but it sets unnatural limits on the child's linguistic development.

Time and time again, as one observes children's aided thresholds and relates them to unaided thresholds and the spectrum of speech, it is apparent that many potentially perceptible (and technologically possible) high frequencies have been excluded from the child's awareness. The proper hearing aid coupled with an appropriate earmold (see below) currently will permit aided audibility for most children to at least 4000 Hz, and possibly 6000 Hz for those with less severe hearing losses. Furthermore, the development of new hearing aids and transducers suggests even greater possibilities to come. The limitations of the future will not be the physical limitations of hearing aids, but the goals set by clinicians.

The low frequency range is also important, even if less so with respect to transmitting the intelligibility of speech. Just about all hearing-impaired people with any residual hearing at all can hear low-frequency sounds. If they can hear the high frequencies as well, then this should be reflected in the frequency range of the hearing aids fitted to them. If, however, their residual hearing is concentrated only in the low frequencies, then special concern becomes necessary to ensure that the low frequency range of the hearing aids extends past their residual hearing.

For example, if a child has a left-corner audiogram with no auditory responses past 500 Hz, then a hearing aid with a lower frequency range limit of 500 Hz or higher will not provide audible sound to this child. That is, the *lower* limits of the frequency range fall *above* the child's hearing range. Is this exclusion of sound relevant, considering how little intelligibility information is contained in the low frequencies? Consider the following:

1. Suprasegmental speech information can be conveyed by the low frequencies (intonation, stress, duration, etc., in speech, syllabification, etc.). The entire rhythmic pattern of speech, in other words, is perceptible if the low frequencies are audible.

2. The first formant of most vowels will be audible in the low frequencies, as will possibly some portion of the second formants of the back vowels.

3. The difference between voiced and voiceless cognates should be discernible, if not by the voicing contrasts then by the timing differences in the onset of voicing (the VOT, or voice onset time).

4. At low frequencies the nasal resonance can be perceived for all nasal sounds, which helps distinguish between the /m/ and other bilabial phonemes, and the /n/ and other lingua-aveolar sounds.

5. All of the above applies not only to the speech of others, but to self-monitoring.

6. If the manner of articulation is conveyed and can be perceived with just low frequency hearing, this coupled with visual information about place of articulation enhances bisensory reception of speech, which is superior to that possible only through lip-reading.

In short, concern about the upper and lower limits of the frequency range has direct clinical/educational significance. Fortunately, aided audiograms will display what a hearing aid provides. One should not be satisfied with less than is possible.

Earmolds traditionally have been considered at best just a conduit for delivering amplified sound from a hearing aid to the ear canal, and at worst simply a pain in the ear. However, in addition to both of these possibilities, earmolds also must be recognized as an integral component of the acoustical chain, beginning with the hearing aid microphone and ending at the eardrum. Importantly, some acoustical effects become possible by modifying an earmold's physical dimensions or structure.

The simplest kind of earmold modification, referred to previously with regard to CROS hearing aids, is to use no earmold at all and simply lead a section of tubing from the hearing aid down into the ear canal. Sometimes a frame fitting around the periphery of the outer ear can anchor the tube in place. The acoustic effects of such an "open ear" condition, compared to that of a closed earmold, result in a severe reduction in the amplified frequency response below 1000 Hz. With an open ear, these low frequencies find the path out of the ear offers less resistance than is presented by the eardrum. At the same time, the tubing offers no blockage to sounds entering the ear canal naturally. The unblocked ear canal also permits the natural amplification of sound that occurs ordinarily in human ears. This increase in energy occurs because the normal ear canal is "tuned" to the frequencies from about 2000 to 5000 Hz and produces a resonation effect of about 15–20 dB at these frequencies.

Venting an earmold is a frequent audiological practice. In the most common type of vent, a channel is drilled parallel to the sound bore through which sound is delivered to the ear. This parallel vent thus permits a direct air connection between the external atmosphere and the cavity between the tip of the earmold and eardrum.

Figure 8.8 presents an example of a parallel vent through an earmold. The diameter of the vent basically determines its acoustical effect. The vent functions to reduce the low-frequency response of a hearing aid (i.e., to provide less amplification in the low frequencies). The larger the diameter

FIGURE 8.8   Parallel vent through an earmold.

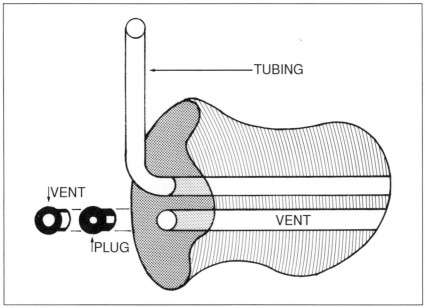

DESIGN BY BOB ESSMAN

of the vent, the greater its effects in reducing the low frequencies. The acoustical effect of the largest vents approximates that of an "open" or tubing earmold. A very small vent will produce very little acoustical change, but it may serve to equalize the air pressure in the ear canal to that of the atmosphere and thus relieve the "stuffy" feeling complained of by many hearing aid users.

Vent size can be used to fine-tune the overall response of a hearing aid, as the size a child requires may change depending on a quiet or noisy environment. Because too large a vent may produce feedback at desired gain levels, an SAV (select a vent) insert is recommended, which seats in the outside face of the earmold (see Figure 8.8). Various SAV sizes either open or shut the vent.

The diameter and length of the sound bore also can be varied to change the response of a hearing aid. When the diameter of the sound bore narrows and its length increases, this enhances the low-frequency response of the entire electroacoustic system (hearing aid/earmold combination), lowering the frequency range and increasing the overall sound pressure level in the ear canal. When the diameter of the sound bore increases and the length shortens, one sees a general shifting of the fre-

FIGURE 8.9   "Horn" or "step bore" earmold.

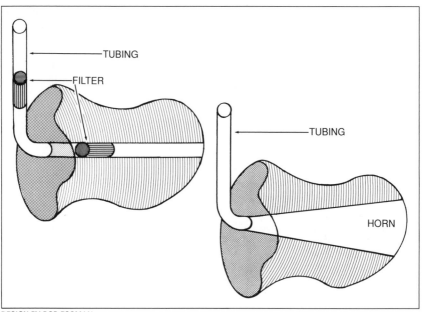

TUBING

FILTER

TUBING

HORN

DESIGN BY BOB ESSMAN

quency response toward the high frequencies. The interactions among these modifications can be quite complicated, as many values of sound bore diameter and length can be selected. Some of these effects also work in opposition to one another, as when an earmold is short, but the sound bore diameter is large.

The difficulty in predicting the acoustic interactions of these and other modifications (e.g., vents, "horn bores") lends further support to the practice of measuring the aided response of hearing aids in a sound field. Many clinical centers now also routinely measure the aided output of hearing aids with a probe-tube microphone device. Both of these measurement conditions reflect the influence of all the electroacoustic factors that can modify the response of hearing aids *when worn by the child.*

A final earmold modification, the "horn" or "step bore," relates only to BTE hearing aids. Here the cross-sectional diameter of the entire tone hook/tubing/earmold combination progressively enlarges from the hearing aid to the ear canal (see Figure 8.9). The diameter as well as the nature of the progression can be altered to produce specific kinds of desirable acoustical effects. Horn bores can be designed to emphasize the important frequency band from 2000 to 5000 Hz, and thus replace the natural resonation lost when an earmold is inserted in the ear canal (the so-called "insertion loss"). Some horn bores permit the upper frequency range of a hearing aid to extend to 6000 or 7000 Hz (depending, of course, on whether the hearing aid itself can deliver these high frequencies). At the present time, these high frequencies can be realized only with moderate-power hearing aids. Taken in conjunction with an acoustic filter placed in the tone hook itself, which depresses unwanted peaks in the frequency response curve, it is possible to deliver to the eardrum a smooth, wide-band frequency response of varying desirable slopes of amplification (Killion, 1980).

Through the knowledgeable exploitation of earmold acoustics, one can alter the real-ear response of a hearing aid in a variety of ways, beyond those adjustments included in the hearing aid itself and those touched on in this discussion. The earmold has long since graduated from "necessary evil" status to a tool with which to alter the amplified sound pattern as well as couple the aid to the ear. Clinician can no longer consider the earmold an extraneous event when fitting a hearing aid. If the changes it can produce in the response of a hearing aid are not considered, they are not likely to be entirely positive. School personnel need to be aware of this potential impact, both positive and negative, as they interact with audiologists. An informed consumer will likely be a much more satisfied one (to the benefit of the children who are served).

9

Auditory Management Practices

Speech acoustics, electroacoustics, and classroom acoustics interact with a child's hearing loss to attain the overall goal of auditory management efforts: aided residual hearing. Within the range set by the thresholds of hearing across frequency and the child's uncomfortable loudness level (UCL), the audiologist chooses a maximum desired amplification output (SSPL-90) with the intention of making speech as audible as possible. *Audibility, the detection of the acoustic energy of speech, is the crucial foundation of auditory management.* If speech cannot be heard, spoken language acquisition will be compromised.

PLOTTING AIDED RESIDUAL HEARING

Unaided and Aided Thresholds

Currently, the simplest way to display the aided sensation levels of speech involves plotting the child's unaided and aided sound-field audiogram. As described previously, the difference between the two types of thresholds

FIGURE 9.1   Unaided and aided sound-field audiogram: across-frequency hearing loss (S = unaided; A = aided).

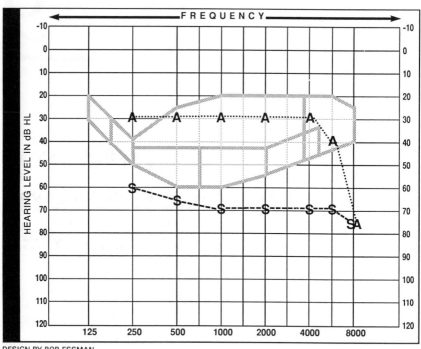

DESIGN BY BOB ESSMAN

represents the functional gain of the amplification. The speech spectrum then can be overlaid on the aided thresholds in order to visualize aided sensation levels for the various speech sounds.

In Figure 9.1, the unaided thresholds of a child with a hearing loss of approximately 70 dB HL across frequency are plotted on an audiogram that also includes an overall display of speech acoustics. As one can see, the energy in the speech signal falls below the unaided thresholds, indicating that conversational level speech is inaudible to this child without amplification. The subsequent aided audiogram of the same child (also in Figure 9.1) shows that her hearing aids provide a functional gain of approximately 40 dB (70 dB minus 30 dB). As can be noted, most of the energy of the speech spectrum now falls above the aided thresholds, indicating that the same input level of speech now is audible when this child uses her amplification.

The degree to which the speech signal surpasses the aided thresholds defines the aided sensation levels (which is a more precise way of describing aided residual hearing or the audibility of a speech signal). In the example just given, only the weakest portions of some consonants would not be heard because the energy was below the aided thresholds. This example shows a child who is able to detect some of the energy in the sibilants through 6000 Hz. Note, however, that there is still some speech energy that is not normally available to her; rarely can a hearing aid *completely* compensate for a hearing loss. Still, with this much aided residual hearing, no other handicapping conditions, and effective auditory management, the prognosis for appropriate performance in all areas would be quite good. Acquisition of language, social, and academic skills will not happen automatically, however; language development entails a gradual unfolding, not a sudden revelation. All that one assures by providing appropriate amplification is the necessary acoustic raw material. The rest of the management process still lies ahead.

The unaided and aided sound-field audiogram shown in Figure 9.2 depicts a child with a high-frequency hearing loss. Without hearing aids, he can receive all of the speech signal below 500 Hz, half around 1000 Hz, and none above 2000 Hz. In daily listening situations, this child presents a very perplexing picture. Clearly he hears. As a matter of fact, below 500 Hz his hearing acuity falls within the normal range. At 4000 Hz and above, however, he is profoundly hearing-impaired. Children with this hearing loss configuration, because they can "hear" speech at normal conversational levels, are sometimes not identified until quite late. Although they can perceive the low frequencies of speech, their inability to hear the high frequencies hinders their development and understanding of language.

Viewing the aided audiogram for this same child, it is apparent that with amplification he can detect all of the speech energy at 1000 Hz, the formants of all the vowels, much of the consonant information at 2000 Hz, but only a trifle of the lower portion of the high-frequency sibilants. An important goal of amplification would be to provide enough of the higher frequencies so that he could perceive the /s/ phoneme unambiguously, but this is precluded by the degree of his hearing loss at the very high frequencies.

If the child whose audiogram is displayed in Figure 9.2 has been amplified relatively late in life, at first he may find this pattern of aided residual hearing uncomfortable. Having no previous exposure to high-frequency speech sounds, not yet able to associate the acoustic information to its linguistic counterpart, and perhaps unable to integrate the new signals with his old familiar auditory sensations, he may reject the hearing aid. For a while, with this pattern of amplification, he may show little improvement in the ability to perceive certain sounds. This child requires an auditory training program that integrates hearing aid use with development of auditory perceptual skills. Such a program could increase the

FIGURE 9.2 Unaided and aided sound-field audiogram: high-frequency hearing loss (S = unaided; A = aided).

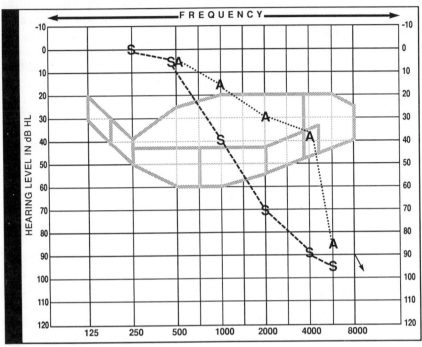

DESIGN BY BOB ESSMAN

child's chances of being able to use the new pattern of auditory sensation to enhance his overall speech perception and auditory learning. One way to accomplish this involves slowly increasing the high-frequency response of his hearing aid until it reaches the predetermined goal. Perhaps this child will never be able to effectively exploit the high frequencies of speech, but considering the potential value of the additional acoustic information, the attempt must be made.

A third example (Figure 9.3) presents the unaided and aided audiogram of a child with a profound hearing loss. As the unaided audiogram illustrates, without amplification she could not detect even loud speech at close distances. With hearing aids whose electroacoustic parameters are set to provide the displayed aided threshold curve, this child can pick up fundamental frequency information, nasal resonances, first formants of all the vowels, and a bit of consonant and low second formant information. As the rhythm of speech is conveyed mainly by the low frequencies, she

FIGURE 9.3 Unaided and aided sound-field audiogram: profound hearing loss (S = unaided; A = aided).

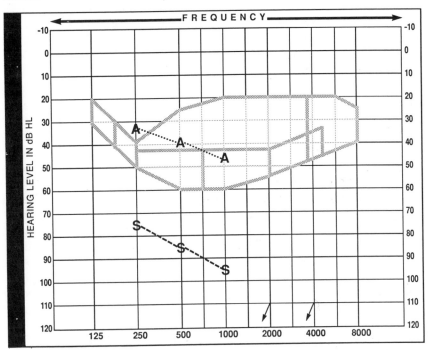

DESIGN BY BOB ESSMAN

therefore should be able to detect (and self-monitor) changes in intonation, stress, and timing. This much acoustic information can be used to help develop acceptable speech and voice quality; in addition, combined with the visual cues of speechreading, it will contribute greatly to the child's speech perception.

When interpreted with some knowledge of speech acoustics and the goal of maximizing audibility for as wide a band of speech as possible, aided audiograms obviously can provide valuable information. The potential audibility of the various speech sounds can be observed, as can irregularities in the frequency response of a hearing aid when the low or medium frequencies are amplified too much in reference to the higher frequencies. Such an amplification pattern may actually interfere with the perception of high-frequency sounds because of masking effects within the cochlea.

A note of caution is important, though, on the use of aided audiograms. A temptation exists to use this graphic presentation of aided and unaided thresholds to demonstrate how "normal" a child's hearing has become with amplification. The professional must take care to distinguish between the degree of benefit afforded by hearing aids and the erroneous idea that aided thresholds are equivalent to an unaided hearing loss of the same degree; the aided condition exposes the ear to a much higher sound pressure level than when there is no amplification.

Consider the example presented in Figure 9.1. At 1000 Hz, the unaided threshold is 70 dB and the aided threshold is 30 dB. The functional gain, therefore, is 40 dB. With an average speech input of 45 dB HL, the aided ear actually would be exposed to a sound level of 85 dB HL (45 dB input + 40 dB gain = 85 dB). Of course, only 15 dB of this is audible because the child has a hearing loss of 70 dB; however, the actual intensity level reaching the cochlea is not 15 dB, but 85 dB. For a child with a hearing loss of 30 dB, a speech signal of 45 dB also would fall just 15 dB above his or her threshold. However, the actual sound energy reaching the cochlea would be 45 dB and not 85 dB as in the previous example. This distinction is important because the ear, particularly a damaged one, does not function the same at high intensity levels as a normal ear would at lower intensity levels. These high levels decrease the frequency and temporal resolution capacities of the cochlea, and thus distort speech sounds. Therefore, even when speech sounds presented to different ears have equal sensation levels, the actual intensity level received by the more impaired ear is higher and will sound qualitatively different due to distortion within the cochlea.

The preceding explanation was not meant to convey any reservations about using aided audiograms to display the benefits of hearing aids. Even if the actual sound pressure reaching a child's cochlea is very high (unavoidable in children with severe hearing losses) and produces various distortions, one still must provide the most effective pattern of audibility possible. Fortunately, the speech signal is a redundant source of acoustic (and linguistic) information, and the human brain possesses an incredible capacity to extract meaning from even reduced and distorted acoustic messages. The cues a hearing-impaired child learns to depend on may differ from those used by a normal-hearing child, but they can and do serve the purpose of developing, and engaging in, the aural communication process.

Phoneme Error Analysis

In order to evaluate the specific speech sounds available with amplification, the examiner can employ the method of phoneme error analysis briefly presented in chapter 4. Plotting speech acoustic information on an aided audiogram is again the method of choice, but in this case, the speech information will be that specific to the predicted phoneme errors that a child makes (Maxon, 1982).

The PB-K lists (or other appropriate word lists) are presented to the child at a normal conversational level with no visual cues. The examiner records the exact spoken response of the child (who has been instructed to repeat exactly what was heard) to each given stimulus. The issue of percent correct responses is not germane to this method of assessment because only the phoneme errors are to be analyzed. Therefore, if the stimulus word was *please* and the child responded "plead," only the /d/ for /z/ substitution would be considered in the analysis. In this example, the fact that the child perceived the voicing component and misperceived the manner of articulation is important, both in planning auditory training and in verifying the appropriateness of the amplification pattern.

The phoneme error analysis is accomplished by deriving the acoustic information for the stimulus and the response (as taken from Table 8.4) and plotting both on the aided audiogram. If the child depicted in Figure 9.4 made the /d/ for /z/ error, one can see that, when the energy for /d/ is displayed as the cross-hatched rectangles and the energy for /z/ as the solid rectangles, the low-frequency bands (200–300 Hz) for both phonemes overlap but the high-frequency ones do not. Because this child's aided residual hearing does not allow high-frequency energy to be audible while at least part of the low-frequency information is, the error that maintains voicing is considered acceptable.

If this same child had better high-frequency hearing and therefore was able to achieve better aided residual hearing in the high frequencies, then one would not consider the error acceptable. If the aided audiogram indicated that the important acoustic components of the stimulus (/z/, this example) were indeed audible, then the need for an auditory training program to exploit the availability of hearing would be indicated. As will be discussed in chapter 11, such training should be an integral part of the overall management program and should include the use and recognition of syntactic, phonological, and morphological rules.

Sound Pressure Levels

As noted earlier, plotting residual hearing with a sound pressure level (SPL) reference can prove useful. For the professional who makes reference to manufacturers' specifications, and/or the graphs resulting from electroacoustic analysis or a probe-tube microphone, familiarity with SPL plotting may be desirable. These measures given in SPL will make the most

FIGURE 9.4   Example of plotting speech perception errors on an aided audiogram.

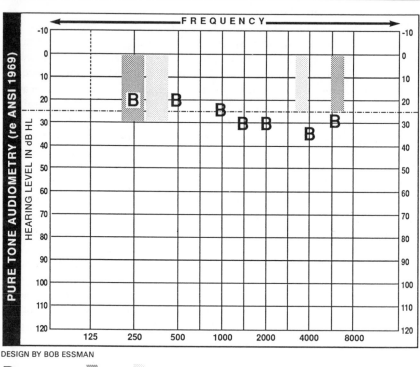

DESIGN BY BOB ESSMAN

B binaural aided   [▓] = /z/   [░] = /d/

"please" - response - "plead"

sense when plotted in conjunction with the other dimensions of interest: unaided thresholds, speech spectrum, aided speech spectrum output, and desired sensational levels.

In direct contrast to the HTL audiogram, an SPL chart depicts increasing intensity as rising from the bottom of the ordinate. Therefore, poorer hearing is shown at the top of an SPL graph. The normal thresholds shown at the bottom of Figure 9.5 represent the average of the monaural, unaided sound-field thresholds that normal-hearing listeners would produce (Morgan, Dirks, & Bower, 1979). As one can see, the normal thresholds in SPL terms are poorest at the low frequencies and best at the mid-frequencies (they are also poor at the very high frequencies, beyond 8000 Hz, but this is

FIGURE 9.5 Example of an SPL graph.

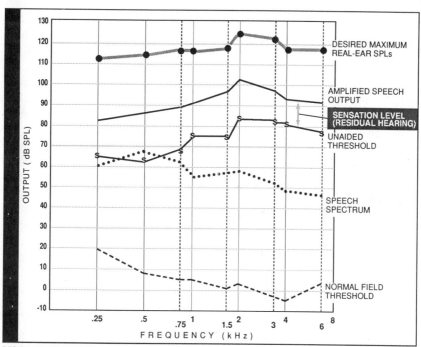

DESIGN BY BOB ESSMAN

not apparent on an audiogram). This indicates that the SPL of low-frequency sounds must be higher than mid-frequency sound in order to be perceived.

In this figure, hearing loss is represented as the difference between the normal field thresholds and the curve labeled "unaided threshold." In order to convert from SPL to HL, the curve labeled "normal field threshold" would become the base. Therefore, if these same results were plotted on an audiogram, the hearing loss at 250 Hz would be 45 dB HL (or the difference between 20 dB SPL, the normal threshold at this frequency, and 65 dB SPL, the measured threshold for the hearing-impaired child in this example). The average speech spectrum portrayed on the graph comes from a newly developed hearing aid selection procedure (Seewald, Ross, & Stelmachowicz, 1987; Ross & Seewald, 1988). The peaks of speech are 12 dB above and the troughs 18 dB below this average, or a speech range of 30 dB across frequency.

As with the plotting of aided residual hearing on an audiogram, one can determine the audibility of speech with this method. Note that in Figure 9.5 the unaided thresholds overlap only slightly at 500 Hz with the average speech spectrum. That is, the speech spectrum exceeds the threshold of hearing only slightly at this one frequency region. This child can barely detect the presence of conversational speech without amplification. The curve labeled "desired maximum real-ear SPLs" shows the maximum SPL that the child can comfortably or safely tolerate. In actual practice, whether this figure could be exceeded can be determined with a probe-microphone (Seewald et al., 1987). The curve marked "amplified speech output" becomes the one of most relevance at this point.

This latter curve depicts how an average speech spectrum would be amplified by the hearing aid and shows the actual SPL existing in the child's ear canal. The functional gain, the difference between aided and unaided sound-field thresholds, is adjusted to amplify the input speech spectrum to the desired aided output. At 250 Hz, the child needs about 22 dB functional gain; at 2000 Hz, about 44 dB. The difference between the unaided sound-field thresholds and the amplified speech output is the sensation level (or the actual amplified residual hearing). Plotting results in this fashion helps demonstrate that a hearing aid normally amplifies suprathreshold speech signals and delivers the product at even higher intensities into the ear. The conventional aided audiogram, on the other hand, displays the *softest* sounds detectible while wearing a hearing aid. Both methods are valuable, and provide complementary information.

The aided sensation level (the amount of residual hearing) depicts the amplified audibility of the speech spectrum. Audiologists must ensure that this dimension is appropriate across the entire frequency range, thereby providing audible access to the various speech sounds. With an SPL scale, the aided sensation level can be visualized as it relates to the unaided thresholds, the maximum permissible sound output, the speech spectrum, and the ambient room noise. In the Figure 9.5 example, one can see that the child is being provided with an excellent speech sensation level right through 6000 Hz. Inadequate electroacoustic responses are also readily visible, as when a hearing aid does not provide either sufficient audibility at the high frequencies (for children with residual hearing through 4000 and 6000 Hz) or enough low frequency amplification (for children with left-corner audiograms).

Regardless of how aided residual hearing is depicted, whether on a HTL or SPL scale, it is critical that it *be* provided. The first, and prerequisite, step in a comprehensive management program is ensuring that a hearing-impaired child receives the best possible auditory signal consistent with his or her hearing loss.

WIRELESS FM SYSTEMS

The single most important determiner of speech perception through amplification is the relationship between the intensity levels of the speaker's voice and the background noise. The signal-to-noise ratio (S/N) at the microphone of the amplification system can have significant effects on how well a child can discriminate among the various speech sounds and, therefore, correctly perceive and comprehend the speech signal. If the speech signal is buried in the noise and cannot be separated, nothing will make that signal intelligible. The greater the intensity of the speech signal with respect to the intensity of the noise (i.e., the higher the S/N), the more intelligible the speech signal will become. Moreover, optimal verbal language development will not occur if speech perception is not optimized. As discussed earlier, the intelligibility of speech sounds varies according to phoneme, with more intensity needed for perception of consonants than vowels. The signal-to-noise ratio that yields the highest speech discrimination score for hearing-impaired adults lies between 25 and 30 dB.

When considering Figure 8.5 (effects of distance on audibility) in the preceding chapter, one can see that the only way a hearing-impaired child could be expected to achieve optimal speech discrimination scores, at all times, in a typical classroom (where the teacher speaks at a normal conversational level—65 dB SPL—and the ambient noise level averages 60 dB SPL), is to have the teacher within 4 inches of the child's hearing aid microphone. Such a demand is hardly realistic; therefore, to maintain an optimal listening condition, one must use an amplification system that (a) will bridge the distance between the teacher and the child and (b) will afford mobility to both. Such a device is commonly referred to as a *wireless FM system* (or FM auditory trainer). The main purpose and major attribute of an FM system is to enhance the signal-to-noise ratio and thus help create the acoustic conditions for maximizing speech perception. The wireless FM system is used in regular classrooms because it is the only device currently available that will readily provide this advantage in such settings.

The effect of improved listening conditions on speech discrimination for hearing-impaired children becomes clear in Table 9.1 which displays results from Ross, Giolas, and Carver (1973). These 11 hard-of-hearing children had hearing losses that ranged from mild to profound, with configurations ranging from flat to sharply sloping. Their speech discrimination scores were measured in an ordinary classroom, at a distance between 8 and 14 feet from the talker. Scores were obtained with their own personal hearing aids (or without for those who did not use amplification) and with an FM system. The differences between conditions always demonstrated a better score with the FM system. For three of the subjects, optimal scores were quite poor. Significantly positive improvement was seen for at least

TABLE 9.1 Word Discrimination Scores Obtained Using a Wireless FM System vs. Normal Amplification

Subject	FM System	Normal Amplification*	Difference Score
1	48%	20% (M)	28%
2	98%	52% (M)	46%
3	24%	12% (M)	12%
4	68%	16% (M)	52%
5	22%	8% (B)	14%
6	58%	36% (N)	22%
7	50%	30% (B)	20%
8	24%	4% (B)	20%
9	52%	16% (B)	36%
10	98%	22% (B)	76%
11	96%	26% (N)	70%
Mean	58%	22%	36%

*M = monaural; B = binaural; N = none

two others (#10 and #11), who showed increases of 70% or better (Ross, Giolas, & Carver, 1973). Many of the children doubled, even tripled their scores under the FM condition. These results demonstrate an improved ability to use residual hearing for all subjects that can be attributed to the improved S/N produced by an FM system.

It is difficult to think of any other management technique for hearing-impaired children that results in such impressive immediate benefits. In general, a wireless FM system consists of a microphone/transmitter (used by the speaker/teacher) and a radio frequency receiver/hearing aid (used by the listener/child). A variety of available styles exist, from traditional self-contained units to those that incorporate the child's personal hearing aids.

Traditional Units

In the traditional set-up, the teacher wears the transmitter/microphone either around his or her neck or clipped to a lapel. Either arrangement ensures the constant distance from the speaker's mouth that produces the favorable S/N. The microphone/transmitter allows for the signal to be broadcast on a radio frequency (frequency modulated—FM) with an equal distribution of signal strength within the confines of a given area. There-fore, each FM transmitter is tuned to a specific carrier-wave frequency. Typically even in large classrooms and lecture halls a listener can receive a clear signal at any place in the room.

The student receiver for each system is tuned to receive the carrier frequency of its companion microphone/transmitter. In order to facilitate several hearing-impaired children in one room, more than one receiver can be tuned to the same transmitting frequency, thereby requiring only one microphone. Conversely, if one child must move around to several differ-ent rooms in which other children also use FMs, then the receiver fre-quency can be changed, typically by flipping a switch or changing a small component module, depending on the manufacturer.

In addition to receiving the transmitted signal from the teacher's microphone, the child's unit has environmental microphones. When func-tioning, they can serve as hearing aids when FM transmission is not appro-priate or provide other auditory signals in conjunction with the FM transmission. These microphones enable children to monitor their own speech, to hear the other children, and to hear any other sounds in the classroom. The gain, output, and frequency response characteristics of the child's unit can and should be set appropriately for the individual child's hearing loss. As these units are binaural (i.e., they have two separate environmental microphones and transducers), one can set each channel (right and left) individually. (Chapter 8 presents more specific information about the electroacoustic characteristics of amplification systems.) The output levels of the FM signal (from the teacher's microphone) and the environmental microphones are adjusted to permit the teacher's transmis-sion to dominate.

The child's part of the traditional unit typically is worn mounted on the chest, with cords and snap-on (button) transducers coupling to the child's ears via earmolds. Younger children usually consider this arrange-ment quite acceptable; however, the advent of adolescence may result in unhappiness with this configuration. The traditional unit also can be arranged to be worn at the waist by using longer cords. The major problem with this particular set-up occurs when the child sits at his or her desk, decreasing the signal received by the environmental microphones.

Figures 9.6 and 9.7 illustrate two representative makes of currently available traditional FM systems.

Personal Systems

Personal FM units were developed to accommodate some of the cosmetic and convenience preferences of older hearing-impaired children and

FIGURE 9.6 Traditional FM system models. Photograph courtesy of Telex Communications, Inc.

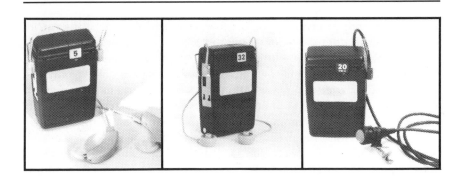

adults (who have begun using them in large group/lecture situations). Although there are several different ways in which the unit can be coupled to the child's ears, certain commonalties exist among the different configurations.

The microphone/transmitter functions here in the same way as described for the traditional unit. Worn by the speaker/teacher (either hung around the neck or clipped to the clothing), the microphone allows for a close, constant distance from the speaker's mouth, thereby maintaining a positive S/N. Some makes and models can use the same transmitter with either traditional or personal FM receivers. In cases where two children have different needs, traditional and personal units can operate in the same classroom.

The major difference between traditional and personal units pertains to the coupling of the child's receiver. The personal FM receiver accepts the carrier frequency of the transmitter, but the signal is amplified and electroacoustically modified by the child's hearing aids rather than the unit itself. Therefore, there are no snap-on transducers used for the coupling to the earmolds. In typical use the hearing aids provide the environmental signal. The child's receiver delivers the FM signal to the hearing aids in several ways; the two most common methods of coupling to the hearing aids are (a) induction loop to a telecoil and (b) direct audio input.

The first system, *induction loop* (teleloop), makes use of the hearing aid's telecoil (governed by the telephone or "T" switch). When set to "T," a hearing aid will deactivate the regular microphone to allow receiving an electromagnetic field from a telephone. To use this telecoil with an FM system, the child must use an induction loop powered by the FM receiver and worn around the neck. The FM signal received is delivered to this loop,

FIGURE 9.7 Traditional FM systems in use. Photograph courtesy of Phonic Ear, Inc.

which in turn sets up a relatively small magnetic field. When a hearing aid is set to "T" and placed within this magnetic field, the signal will be picked up by the telecoil, processed by the hearing aid, and delivered to the child's ear via the earmold. An example of a loop system can be seen in Figure 9.8. The appeal of this configuration comes from no direct connection (i.e., wires) from the receiver to the hearing aids, making it considerably less conspicuous than the chest-mounted models.

In order to pick up environmental sounds as well as the FM signal, the hearing aid must have a microphone/telephone (M/T) switch that allows for both the regular hearing aid microphone and the telecoil to function at the same time. If the hearing aid does not have this capability, the child will receive only the FM signal. For children who have hearing aids without M/T switches, one can purchase FM receivers that incorporate environmental microphones. In either case, the positive S/N advantage of the FM system can and should be maintained.

Unfortunately, the loop models have disadvantages that also must be considered. Because the loop sets up a rather small magnetic field, the strength of the signal received by the hearing aid is affected by its prox-

FIGURE 9.8 FM system with loop. Photograph courtesy of Earmark, Inc.

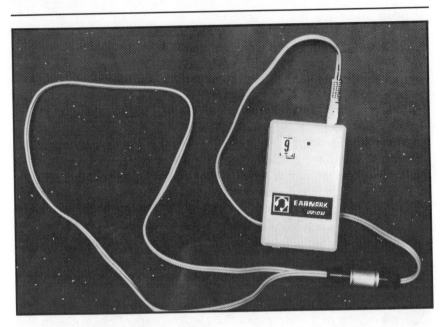

imity to the loop. Hawkins and Van Tassell (1982) demonstrated that normal head movements can produce significant changes in the strength of the signal received. Other concerns about the loop relate to the electroacoustic characteristics of the hearing aid telecoil. Originally developed only for telephone listening, the coil was not designed to provide as high a fidelity signal as the hearing aid microphone. Knowing the characteristics of the telecoil, one can determine the appropriateness of the speech signal quality it presents to the child.

When a school system considers purchasing an FM unit with a loop, the child's clinical audiologist must become an integral part of the decision-making process because the child's personal hearing aids will become part of the classroom amplification. If new hearing aids are to be purchased, the audiologist will want to consider (a) the availability of an M/T rather than just a T switch, and (b) the electroacoustic characteristics of the telecoil as well as the hearing aid microphone.

The second most common type of coupling for the personal FM system is *direct audio input.* In this unit the child's receiver delivers the FM signal to the hearing aid via a cord and direct electrical coupling. That coupling is accomplished with either plugs that slip into the hearing aid or a "boot" (or "shoe") that accommodates surface contacts on the hearing aid. The boot selected must fit with both the specific FM system and the child's specific hearing aids. Table 9.2 displays the boots that accommodate particular hearing aids.

Typically, environmental sounds picked up through the hearing aid microphones are not affected by the direct audio input coupling. The presumed advantage of this coupling method was that the electroacoustic characteristics of the hearing aids are responsible for shaping the FM signal delivered to the child's ear. Because of the typically more rigorous selection procedure for personal hearing aids, it was assumed that the child would have a better fit with direct audio input than any other type of FM. Recent research, however, has indicated that direct audio input signals may not be as consistent with the hearing aid microphone specifications as was originally assumed (Hawkins & Schum, 1985). Some preliminary research has indicated that changing settings on the FM unit will not result in the expected changes in the signal delivered to the ear (Lemay & Maxon, 1991).

As with the loop, the clinical audiologist must be directly involved in the decision-making process for the direct audio input unit. The specific hearing aids needed, as well as the boot/shoe and the settings of all the components, must be determined carefully. In fact, an audiologist should become directly involved at various points in the selection, purchase, and implementation of FM amplification systems, regardless of the model. Although FM systems have been used in classrooms for almost 20 years, the role of the clinical audiologist has remained quite small (Maxon, Brackett, & van den Berg, in press). Figure 9.9 illustrates an example of a direct audio input unit.

Recommended Features

The following discussion comprises a list of some important features found in current wireless FM systems. Not all of them are incorporated in every manufacturer's unit, and not all are equally desirable. Further, the order in which they appear indicates no relative importance:

1. *Electroacoustic characteristics.* All traditional FM systems incorporate controls for modifying the frequency response and the output of the receiver unit. This is an essential provision, permitting variations in the electroacoustic characteristics to suit individual requirements. The modifications are such that one can reduce the output to accommodate the mildest hearing loss, and adjust the frequency responses to suit most hearing loss configurations. Binaural units permit setting each channel separately for the child who does not have the same hearing loss in both

TABLE 9.2 Direct Audio Input (DAI) Interface for Various FM Systems

Audio Equipment (ATE)	Selection of Cord		Plug Type	Selection of Audio Shoe			
	Monaural Cord	Binaural Cord		E25,27, 28,30,31	E34	E35,37, 38,39	E40,42, 44
Phonic Ear 461 & Telex except AAR-1, AAR10	DT30	Two DT30 or DTT30	3-pin	AP12	AP342	AP22	AP402
Phonic Ear except 461	HT30	HTT30	2-pin	AP12	AP342	AP22	AP402
Comtek, Williams Sound, & Telex AAR1, AAR10	JT30	JTT30	Mini 3.5mm mono plug	AP12	AP342	AP22	AP402
"Walkman" type Stereo/Tape Player	OT35	OTT30	Mini 3.5mm stereo plug	AP12	AP342	AP22	AP402
External Microphone Oticon MIC 30	TT70" TT17"	TTT70"	3-pin polarized Euro-plug	AP10 AP11	AP341	AP21	AP401

Switch Sequences

E25, 27, 30, 31, 42	E28	E40	E35, 37	E38, 39
M = M+DAI	M = M+DAI	M = M+DAI	M = M	M = M
T = T	MT = MT	T = T	T = DAI	MT = M+DAI
O = O	T = T	NS = NS	O = O	T = DAI
	O = O			O = O

Key: DAI = direct audio input; M = internal microphone; NS = noise suppressor; O = off; T = telephone pick-up

FIGURE 9.9 FM system with direct audio input. Photograph courtesy of Telex Communications, Inc.

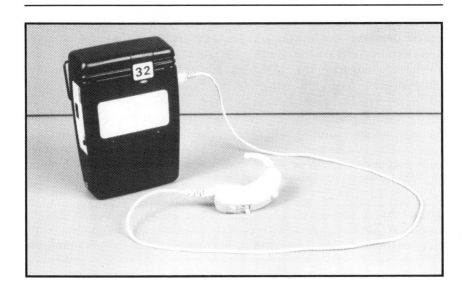

ears. In the personal FM system, the hearing aids determine the electroacoustic characteristics. As indicated previously, the hearing aids function as they ordinarily would, plus process the FM transmitted signal.

2. *Binaural environmental microphones.* Traditional FM units should include binaural environmental microphones. Although not an issue when the focus is on the teacher's speech, this feature may become desirable during periods such as lunch. At such times, the child's unit functions like a hearing aid and, in most cases, should be binaural.

3. *Auxiliary input.* It is sometimes advantageous to use the teacher's microphone for auxiliary input, such as from a tape recorder, a movie projector, or a television monitor. Simply placing the microphone next to the speaker on such equipment does not work satisfactorily because these devices often emit noise while they operate. An auxiliary input permits a direct electrical connection between the FM microphone/transmitter and the sound source. Some FM microphone/transmitters include an optional talkover circuit to enable the teacher to override the auxiliary input for instructional purposes. Some systems also permit making a direct electrical connection with an auxiliary input to the child's FM receiver. Problems may arise when using the auxiliary input if the sound source cannot accommodate both an auxiliary output and an external speaker. That is, the use

of the auxiliary circuit may deactivate the external speaker of the source, and the only one to hear the sound would be the hearing-impaired child.

4. *Environmental microphones on personal FM systems.* The receiver should include an environmental microphone option so that the child can use the unit when the hearing aids are not functioning. The problem with units that incorporate the child's personal hearing aids is that when the aids break, they leave the child without any form of amplification. This possibility thus suggests keeping a set of cords and snap-on transducers, as well as snap-on earmolds, at hand for when the aids break down.

5. *Problem indicator lights.* Many FM systems include a light on both the microphone/transmitter and the receiver that indicates when the battery is losing its charge, is low, or is dead. Younger children in particular frequently do not know, or will not say, when they no longer can hear the teacher through the FM microphone/transmitter, the environmental microphones, or both. This feature offers a convenient visual check on the battery throughout the entire day. In addition, some manufacturers provide a "No FM" light, meaning no FM transmission is being received. This is an efficient way to determine if the transmitter is turned on and/or functioning.

6. *Listening condition controls.* FM systems may include a switch on the receiver unit to permit the child to receive just the teacher transmission, just the environmental signals, or both at the same time. Typically, the unit functions in a "both" condition, but in situations such as lunch, the transmitter should not be operating. In rare cases, for example during industrial arts classes, the environmental microphones also may need to be turned off.

7. *Batteries.* All FM systems include rechargeable batteries; a few, however, also will operate on a 9-volt battery. This is a useful option in an emergency, such as when the charger itself is not working.

8. *Carrier frequencies.* Some FM instruments permit the selection of one or two carrier wave frequencies on both the transmitter and the receiver. The U.S. Federal Communications Commission (FCC) has set aside specific frequency bands on which these signals may be transmitted. Schools can employ 32 narrow-band frequencies without crossover from other units or transmitting devices. This arrangement prevents possible interference from nearby transmitters (CB radios, paging systems, etc.) operating on the same frequency. The way in which a specific FM manufacturer designates which carrier band is being used varies. Table 9.3 shows how four major companies code their transmitter frequencies (Lynch & Ross, 1988). Having the capability to switch from one carrier frequency to another can be useful in any school where more than one hearing-impaired child is enrolled. The major advantage of this provision, however, would be realized in programs educating large numbers of these children. An

TABLE 9.3 Conversion Table of 32 Narrow-Band FM Frequencies

Number*	Color Code*	Frequency (MHz)	Number	Color Code	Frequency (MHz)
1	Red/Gray	72.025	17	Green/Brown	72.825
2	Brown/Gray	72.075	18	Black/Gray	72.875
3	Red/Brown	72.125	19	Green/Red	79.925
4	Brown/Red	72.175	20	Black/Red	79.975
5	Orange/Brown	72.225	21	Black/Orange	75.425
6	Brown/Orange	72.275	22	Green/Yellow	75.475
7	Yellow/Brown	72.325	23	Black/Yellow	75.525
8	Brown/Yellow	72.375	24	Green/Blue	75.575
9	Yellow/Gray	72.425	25	Black/Green	75.625
10	Brown/Green	72.475	26	Green/Pink	75.675
11	Yellow/Pink	72.525	27	Black/Blue	75.725
12	Brown/Blue	72.575	28	Green/Black	75.775
13	Yellow/White	72.625	29	Black/Pink	75.825
14	Brown/Pink	72.675	30	Pink/Gray	75.875
15	Green/Gray	72.725	31	Black/White	75.925
16	Brown/White	72.775	32	Pink/Yellow	75.975

*Numbered frequencies for ComTek, Earmark, and Telex, and color codes for Phonic Ear

"assembly" frequency can be common to all the children and used for large-group communication.

Selection of an FM System

All hearing-impaired children enrolled in regular schools are potential candidates for a wireless FM system. When determining the urgency of the need and the degree to which a specific child can benefit, one must consider the classroom in which the child functions, the educational practices in the school, and the organization of the school day. If the school follows the classical tradition, that is, the teacher lecturing from the front and the children sitting in rows, an FM system can easily be very effective. The optimal listening condition created will allow the hearing-impaired child to hear the teacher and, therefore, have equal access to verbally presented material.

Very few schools adhere completely to this rigid kind of classroom format, however. Most display a mix of instructional models, including formal lectures, class discussion, small group instruction, and seatwork or other individual activities during which the teacher circulates and interacts individually with the children. Preschool and kindergarten classrooms are the least likely to implement a great deal of formal lecture style. Therefore, the effectiveness of an FM system must be carefully evaluated and demonstrated in those settings. Observation in the prospective setting allows the case manager to quantify the amount of time during the day that a need arises for a teacher-worn microphone. If that time proves very minimal, then one must weigh the demands of using the microphone versus the actual need for it. In classes where an FM system is necessary, the willingness of the classroom teacher to learn microphone technique is essential and must be supported with sufficient instruction and consultative services.

The hearing-impaired child always benefits from an enhanced speech signal, whether as part of a group or individually. The FM advantage, of course, would be least during individual instruction, with the teacher close to the child. In those circumstances the distance between the teacher and the child's hearing aid microphone decreases, thereby maximizing hearing aid reception. However, even at such times the teacher generally would not or could not be speaking within 6 inches of the hearing aid microphone, so the FM advantage would carry over.

Because high ambient noise levels supply one of the main reasons for using an FM system, it may be beneficial to make sound level measurements with a sound level meter. Although the school system probably would not have such equipment, an audiologist could be brought in to measure the intensity of the background noise in different classrooms, hallways, and so forth.

Experience on the previously cited UConn Mainstream Project and other classroom observations since then has demonstrated that most hearing-impaired children in public school settings, regardless of degree of hearing loss, classroom environment, age, or type of instruction, will receive benefit from the *proper* use of an FM system. The key to success is flexibility on the part of the classroom teacher and other personnel working with the child. In evaluating such an implementation one should look for the conditions that demonstrate the child's need for an FM system rather than those that argue against it. The recommendations for an FM system should result from consultations among the case manager, speech-language pathologist and/or teacher of the hearing-impaired, audiologist, classroom teacher, parent(s), and child. The following steps detail how to demonstrate a specific child's need for an FM system:

1. Obtain a loaner FM for 1 month. The school will have to provide the appropriate earmolds for the trial.

2. Use the PB-K lists to obtain percent-correct scores (auditory only) with the child using personal hearing aids and then the FM system for the following conditions:

> a. quiet—close to the child (3 feet)
> b. quiet—far from the child (10 feet)
> c. noisy—close to the child
> d. noisy—far from the child

3. Administer an oral paragraph comprehension task under the same amplification and listening conditions given in #2.

4. Provide teachers and school administrators with an audio- or videotaped presentation of the way speech sounds when processed through hearing aids and FM systems in different listening conditions. (These tapes are available through the Department of Communication Sciences at the University of Connecticut.)

5. Keep logs according to the following protocol for 1 month prior to receiving the FM, for the month of the trial, and for 1 month after finishing the trial:

a. The classroom teacher should keep a log of various situations in which the child has difficulty: group discussions, background noise, one-to-one discussions, lectures, other children giving presentations, audiovisual presentations, and so forth.

b. Other school personnel should report any listening problems to the child's case manager, who keeps a log about physical education, music, art, recess, lunch, and so on.

c. School personnel should notify the case manager about any difficulty they have handling the FM system.

d. The case manager should elicit information from the child and log his or her feelings about using the FM, having listening difficulties, and so forth.

e. Any questions or concerns should be directed to the case manager.

Employing these guidelines reduces many of the concerns expressed by school personnel, including the administrators who must justify the allocation of funds to one child. In addition to the preceding, often a letter from the child's audiologist can help, explaining the reasons for introducing the FM system even though the child wears personal hearing aids. (A sample of such a letter can be found in Appendix A.)

Management of FM Systems

Once an FM recommendation has been made and the unit has been acquired for the child, the task becomes ensuring correct use. Five examples appear in Figure 9.10 of typical and difficult listening conditions for a child functioning in a classroom when using hearing aids. A "traditional" instructional situation is depicted in example A. The teacher is talking, the children are generating the usual amount of classroom noise, and the child with the hearing aids (X) is receiving a speech signal that is, at best, slightly louder than the background noise (S/N = +5 dB) because of the distance from the teacher and the amount of noise. Example B presents a more difficult situation. The teacher asks a child (1) a question, but the hearing-impaired child (X) does not hear the answer because of the distance from 1 and the ambient room noise. In example C a videotape is being shown, but the hearing-impaired child (X) is sitting too far from the TV monitor to receive a strong signal. In example D, the teacher in this preschool class is conducting "group" around the table, with the rest of the class in free play. The hearing-impaired child (X) is having difficulty hearing the questions, answers, and group discussion because of the noise the other children are making. Example E shows the hearing-impaired child watching a play in the "multipurpose room" (a large area that can be arranged to serve as a gymnasium, cafeteria, or auditorium at different times). The poor acoustics and the child's distance from the stage makes speech reception difficult.

All of these examples demonstrate that although the child's hearing aids are appropriate, their full benefit is compromised in less than optimal listening conditions. Whenever room noise, child noise, or distance from the talker adversely affect the S/N, hearing aids will not provide the speech signal at necessary loudness levels.

FIGURE 9.10 Difficult listening conditions when using a hearing aid.

A

Teacher is talking. Child **X** is using a hearing aid. Due to the distance from the teacher and general classroom noise, there is a less than optimal signal-to-noise ratio. Child **X** is unable to hear the Teacher's speech.

SOLUTION: The Teacher should use an FM system.

B

Teacher asks child **1** a question. Child **1** responds. Child **X** is using a hearing aid and cannot easily hear child **1** because of the distance and general classroom noise.

SOLUTION: The Teacher should use an FM system and repeat the answer given by child **1** to child **X**.

C

A videotape is being shown to the class. Child **X** is using hearing aids, but the distance from the monitor makes it difficult for the child to hear well.

SOLUTION: Use an FM system with a jack connecting the auxiliary input on the FM system's microphone/transmitter directly to the VCR allowing child **X** to hear without interference.

FIGURE 9.10 (Continued)

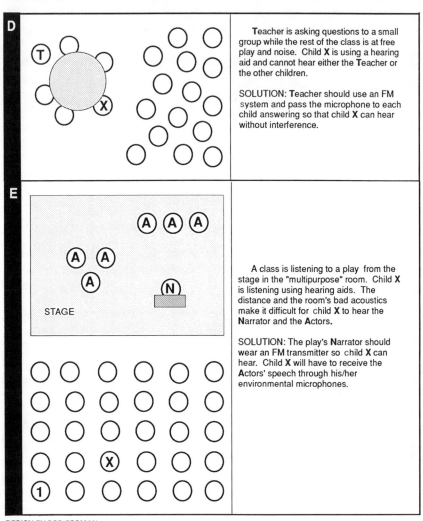

D

Teacher is asking questions to a small group while the rest of the class is at free play and noise. Child **X** is using a hearing aid and cannot hear either the Teacher or the other children.

SOLUTION: Teacher should use an FM system and pass the microphone to each child answering so that child **X** can hear without interference.

E

STAGE

A class is listening to a play from the stage in the "multipurpose" room. Child **X** is listening using hearing aids. The distance and the room's bad acoustics make it difficult for child **X** to hear the Narrator and the Actors.

SOLUTION: The play's Narrator should wear an FM transmitter so child **X** can hear. Child **X** will have to receive the Actors' speech through his/her environmental microphones.

DESIGN BY BOB ESSMAN

Through the scenarios portrayed in Figure 9.11, examples of incorrect FM use are illustrated. Some ways to overcome the problems also are provided for each. In example A the teacher has the FM microphone/transmitter turned on, so that the hearing-impaired child (X) is receiving a signal from the transmitter and the environmental microphones. The teacher calls on several normal-hearing children to read and then asks a question of the class. A student (1) answers the question, but in a very soft voice. The teacher says "correct" and asks X to repeat the answer, which he cannot do because he has not heard what 1 said.

There are several solutions here. The teacher, using the FM transmitter, can repeat the answer given by 1 to ensure that X has heard it. An alternative possibility would be to pass the FM microphone/transmitter to the children doing the reading and then to those answering the questions. The logistics of this situation may preclude its practicality in a large class, but it may work in a small group. Another technique would have the teacher use the name of the child answering the question so that X could direct his attention to the speaker.

Example B shows the FM unit again being used in a "both" condition (the child [X] is receiving signals from both the transmitter and the environmental microphones). The teacher is conducting a reading group and asks X to continue reading after one of the other children (1) has finished. X is unable to do so because he could not hear 1 well enough to follow.

The solution to example B relates to the size of the group using the FM system. This small-group situation creates an environment in which the teacher can pass the FM microphone to each of the children in the group as they read. Other situations conducive to this use of the transmitter include student reports and "show and tell."

Examples C, D, E, and F present variations on the same theme. All share in common the fact that the teacher (T) is transmitting an FM signal during periods when the hearing-impaired child (X) should not hear her. In examples C and D, T's speech will interfere with X's ability to converse with her classmates. In example E the hearing-impaired child (X) is listening to a private conversation. When the teacher is using an FM microphone, the hearing-impaired child receives his or her speech at a favorable intensity regardless of where they are both situated in the room. In most classroom listening situations this is the real advantage of the system, but when the teacher forgets to shut off the FM microphone, the unit may become a source of interference or embarrassment.

Example F shows that an FM system may be necessary in a physical education class but must be used carefully. The teacher (T) appropriately used the microphone to give directions for a relay race but did not turn it

FIGURE 9.11 Appropriate and inappropriate use of an FM system in the classroom.

A ⓣ ◯ ◯ ② ◯ ◯ ◯ ◯ ③ ◯ ◯ ◯ ◯ ◯ ◯ ◯ ◯ Ⓧ ◯ ◯ ① ◯ ◯ ◯ ◯	Teacher is using microphone/ transmitter. Child **X** is receiving both FM and environmental signals. Teacher asks child **2** to read and child **3** is asked to read next. Teacher asks a question about the reading. Child **1** answers the question softly so that **X** cannot hear. Teacher says "correct." **X** is asked the question and still does not know the answer. SOLUTION: Teacher should use an FM system and repeat child **1**'s answer to make sure that **X** was able to hear it.
B ⓣ ① ◯ ◯ Ⓧ	Teacher is wearing an FM microphone/ transmitter. Child **X** is receiving both FM and environmental signals. Teacher, conducting a reading group, asks child **1** to read out loud. Child **X** is asked to continue where child **1** has left off and starts at the wrong spot. SOLUTION: Teacher should pass the FM microphone around to each child who is asked to read.
C ⓣ with table and seated children ◯ Ⓧ ◯ ◯ ◯ ◯ ◯ ◯ ◯ ◯ ◯ ◯	Teacher is wearing an FM microphone/ transmitter. Child **X** is receiving both FM and environmental signals. Teacher, conducting a reading group. Child **X** is doing seat work. SOLUTION: Teacher should shut off the FM microphone/transmitter or child **X** should shut off the receiver. One or both of these units have on-off switches.

FIGURE 9.11 (Continued)

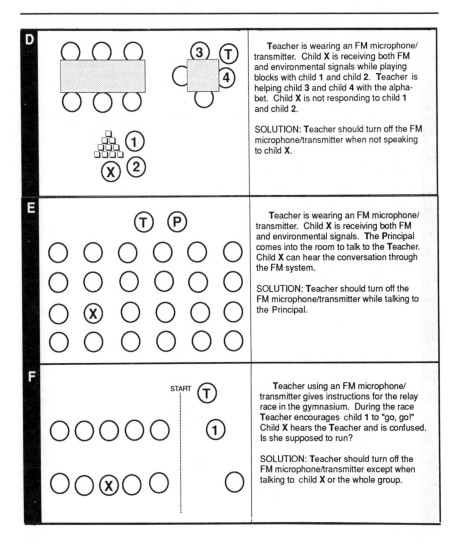

D

Teacher is wearing an FM microphone/transmitter. Child **X** is receiving both FM and environmental signals while playing blocks with child **1** and child **2**. Teacher is helping child **3** and child **4** with the alphabet. Child **X** is not responding to child **1** and child **2**.

SOLUTION: Teacher should turn off the FM microphone/transmitter when not speaking to child **X**.

E

Teacher is wearing an FM microphone/transmitter. Child **X** is receiving both FM and environmental signals. The Principal comes into the room to talk to the Teacher. Child **X** can hear the conversation through the FM system.

SOLUTION: Teacher should turn off the FM microphone/transmitter while talking to the Principal.

F

Teacher using an FM microphone/transmitter gives instructions for the relay race in the gymnasium. During the race Teacher encourages child **1** to "go, go!" Child **X** hears the Teacher and is confused. Is she supposed to run?

SOLUTION: Teacher should turn off the FM microphone/transmitter except when talking to child **X** or the whole group.

FIGURE 9.11 (Continued)

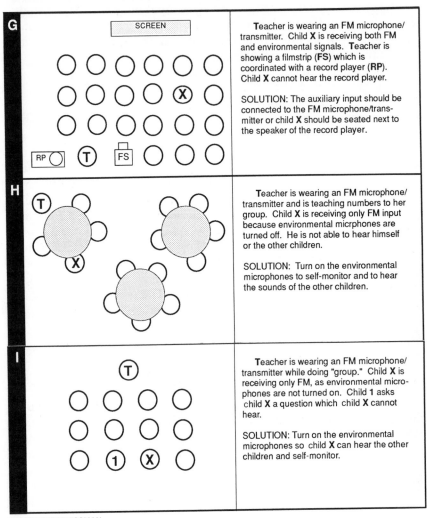

G Teacher is wearing an FM microphone/transmitter. Child **X** is receiving both FM and environmental signals. Teacher is showing a filmstrip (**FS**) which is coordinated with a record player (**RP**). Child **X** cannot hear the record player.

SOLUTION: The auxiliary input should be connected to the FM microphone/transmitter or child **X** should be seated next to the speaker of the record player.

H Teacher is wearing an FM microphone/transmitter and is teaching numbers to her group. Child **X** is receiving only FM input because environmental micrphones are turned off. He is not able to hear himself or the other children.

SOLUTION: Turn on the environmental microphones to self-monitor and to hear the sounds of the other children.

I Teacher is wearing an FM microphone/transmitter while doing "group." Child **X** is receiving only FM, as environmental microphones are not turned on. Child 1 asks child **X** a question which child **X** cannot hear.

SOLUTION: Turn on the environmental microphones so child **X** can hear the other children and self-monitor.

DESIGN BY BOB ESSMAN

off once the race started. Thus his encouragement ("go, go") to one of the runners (1) confuses the hearing-impaired child (X).

Example G shows when the auxiliary input on either the transmitter or receiver should be used. Both the FM microphone and the environmental microphones in this example are too far from the record player to receive an acceptable acoustic signal.

Examples H and I demonstrate the inappropriateness of using only the transmitter and not the environmental microphones. Sometimes the environmental microphones should be deactivated. One such example, offered previously, involves industrial arts class, when activities generate very loud sounds and little peer-peer discussion ensues. (In the event of an emergency the teacher can get the hearing-impaired child's attention through the transmitter.) On very few occasions is such a configuration appropriate, however, because in that condition the child hears *only* what emits from the transmitter and not from other children or him or herself.

These examples illustrate the major principle underlying the teacher's use of an FM system; that is, the microphone should be functioning when the teacher intends to talk to a hearing-impaired child, either as a member of a group or individually. As soon as his or her speech is directed to someone other than that child, the FM microphone/transmitter should be shut off. Teachers simply forget to do this. The older hearing-impaired child thus must take some responsibility and indicate when inappropriate speech sounds are being received.

As indicated in several of the examples, one should encourage not only teachers to use the microphone but the hearing-impaired child's classmates as well. Normal-hearing peers find it not only feasible but often enjoyable to use the FM microphone when they present information. Such practice with the equipment also helps to eradicate some of the mystique of the FM system. Although a great deal of emphasis is placed on the transmitter, care must be taken to use the environmental microphones properly as well. As stated earlier, only rarely should the child turn off the environmental microphones; they are crucial for hearing peers, oneself, room sounds, and so forth. Although the point of the FM is to improve the listening situation by increasing the signal-to-noise ratio, that should not be done at the expense of all other sounds.

Finally, as with hearing aids, the FM system will do no good if not functioning properly. The unit should be charged at the end of every school day, and troubleshooting should be conducted every morning.

Troubleshooting Amplification

The continued operation and optimum performance of a hearing aid or wireless FM system never can be taken for granted. These instruments, particularly as used by children, perfectly exemplify Murphy's Law: anything that can go wrong will go wrong.

Even when the hearing-impaired child receives the most effective amplification of the speech signal possible and is listening in an optimum acoustic environment, a dead battery, a poorly fitting or blocked earmold, or a broken wire or antenna can undo all the advantages. If the auditory signal the child receives is distorted, intermittent, frequently absent, or intrusive, he or she cannot function at full potential and likely will develop negative attitudes toward amplification use. Moreover, if the classroom teacher is unaware of the malfunction, he or she may assume that observable differences in behavior stem from other problems when in fact the amplification condition is at fault.

Although troubleshooting is the primary responsibility of a designated school professional, beginning no later than about second grade hearing-impaired children should be responsible for some important aspects of caring for their personal hearing aids. They should be taught to use a battery tester and insert new batteries, examine the state of their earmolds and tubing, and alert the teacher to any gross changes in the amplified signal. The child's report can be incorporated into the daily routine. By comparing the child's report to that of the adult examiner, the child will begin to develop better skills in this area.

Those children who participate in troubleshooting their own amplification will be more likely to accept themselves and their hearing status than those who have not assumed this personal responsibility. For the former group of children, the sound provided by amplification is incorporated into their experience of the sensory world and taken for granted. The opposite of this occurs for children who are not even aware when their hearing aids are inoperable or malfunctioning. For these children, amplified sound is either irrelevant or insufficiently useful to outweigh the perceived disadvantages of wearing hearing aids or FM systems. To avoid the latter, professionals and parents must ensure in a child's early years that the hearing aids and FM systems work well at all times.

The expectation that children should be ultimately responsible for their own amplification systems does not relieve parents and professionals of their role in troubleshooting for three major reasons. First, very young children cannot be expected to perform this function; second, checking out an FM system depends on employing a second person to evaluate the microphone/transmitter worn by parents and teachers; and third, the stakes in ensuring and sustaining appropriate amplification run too high not to to verify the correct operation of all amplification systems at all times. Troubleshooting should occur on a daily basis, using the following protocol as a guide:

1. *Equipment needed:*

a. *Battery tester.* The preferred battery tester is calibrated in volts, not just "good" or "bad." If the system uses (or can use) 9-volt batteries, the tester must accommodate them as well.

b. *Listening stethoscope.* This tool allows the normal-hearing listener to couple the amplification to his or her ears. For listening through the earmold or tone hook of ear-level instruments, the tubing attached to the stethoscope works well. To listen to snap-on (button) transducers, the tubing can be removed and the transducer snapped directly to the stethoscope's earpieces.

c. *Personal earmold.* The examiner may choose to have a personal earmold fabricated for troubleshooting purposes or he or she can make use of a "stock earmold" (with a snap-on ring and an adapter for the ear-level fittings). A local audiologist can provide information about purchasing an earmold.

d. *Earmold cleaner.* Either earmold antiseptic or warm water and a mild soap serve equally well to clean earmolds. Pipe cleaners, toothpicks, or an air syringe can help remove wax from a clogged earmold.

e. *Extra batteries, cords, and transducers.* Supplies should be available for quick replacement of inoperable parts. The child's family should provide batteries or other parts for personal hearing aids, but extra FM parts come from the school system.

2. *Personal hearing aids:*

a. *Visual inspection:*

(1) *Case.* Look at the case for dents or other disfigurements. Although such physical damage by itself does not always mean electroacoustic problems, it may well be associated with a malfunctioning instrument. Examine the battery compartment for corrosion and improper battery contact. Occasionally battery terminals are bent, corroded, or missing, resulting in an inadequate electrical connection.

(2) *Controls.* If the hearing aid includes a telephone coil ("T" switch), deactivate it at the time of the listening inspection; otherwise, the hearing aid microphone will not function. Verify the correct positioning of all external controls, such as for tone and output, per the specific settings provided by the audiologist. (Keep all such pertinent information—obtained from the audiological report—on an index card.)

(3) *Tone hook.* The tone hook of ear level hearing aids connects to the earmold tubing. Examine it for cracks and for a secure connection at the hearing aid and at the earmold tubing. If the tone hook screws onto the hearing aid case, rotation should not be continuous; if it is, the threads may be stripped and the tone hook may need replacing.

(4) *Connecting cords.* Body aids have cords that connect the transducer to the hearing aid case. CROS hearing aids may have a cord that connects the microphone pick-up to the receiver. Hearing aids with bone

conduction transducers also will have cords that connect the body of the aid to the transducer. In all cases, examine the cords for stripped insulation, which makes a short circuit or broken connection very likely. The prongs on both ends of the cord must all be intact, fit snugly into the outlets, and be fully insertable.

(5) *Transducers.* A frequent cause of malfunction in body hearing aids (including self-contained FM receivers) is damage to the transducer. The same is true of the bone conduction transducer. Look carefully for cracks or dents.

(6) *Earmolds.* Ensure that the surface of the earmold is clean; if not, it can abrade the ear, producing discomfort. Inspect the sound bore for any wax clogging it; wax-occluded earmolds are often mistaken for hearing aid malfunction. Clean the earmolds if necessary with a mild soap and warm water. Examine the earmold tubing on ear-level hearing aids for cracks, crimping, and inflexibility. Any minor tubing problems can be remedied by the child's audiologist. Be aware of any earmold modifications so as to avoid closing up a vent or removing a filter that looks like a piece of lint. (Note any modifications on the file card that lists the child's amplification settings.)

b. *Battery check.* Prior to the listening inspection, test the batteries to be sure they produce the appropriate voltage reading. If low, replace the batteries immediately.

c. *Earmold insertion.* Observe the child when he or she inserts the earmold into his or her ear to ensure that it is fully seated in the concha and that there is no feedback or discomfort. If the child complains of discomfort, inspect the ear for lacerations and discolorations.

d. *Listening inspection.* Use either the hearing aid stethoscope or the personal earmold to conduct the listening inspection. Changes in amplified sound since the last inspection may take the form of distortion, noise, intermittent signals, or inadequate amplification. If possible, listen to the hearing aid at the volume level the child uses, as distortion and other undesirable effects may occur only at high sound levels. This is not recommended for high-gain hearing aids that produce sound levels that may be extremely uncomfortable or painful to a normal-hearing listener. In such instances, only listen at tolerable volume levels. Routine electroacoustic analyses as described in chapter 4 will detect any serious problems.

(1) *Volume.* In rotating the volume control from the off position, the signal should get gradually louder and not jump to maximum amplification with only a slight turn. This check of linearity does require some manipulation of volume to levels that may be slightly uncomfortable, but it should not last for more than a few seconds. During this check also listen for static or other noise that occurs when the volume control is moved.

(2) *Cords.* Manipulate the hearing aid cords to determine if doing so causes changes in the sound amplification. If inserting the cords into the input jacks produces an intermittent signal or static, replace the cords.

(3) *Sound quality.* The sound quality should be clear and nondistorted. Although the tone settings may make the sound "tinny" or "low pitched," those sounds should be consistent with the appropriate settings of the hearing aid and should not represent a change from that heard at previous listening checks.

(4) *Earmold.* Although visually inspected previously, also listen to the child's amplification through the earmold to be sure it is not clogged.

3. *Traditional (self-contained) FM systems:*

a. *Visual inspection.* Follow the guidelines presented under "personal hearing aids." Take care to check both the receiver and the transmitter as follows:

(1) *Receiver (child's unit).* Inspect both right and left channels when checking the cords, transducers, earmolds, and settings.

(2) *Transmitter (teacher's microphone).* Check the antenna for cracks and breaks that will interfere with the signal transmission. If a lapel microphone is part of the transmitter, examine its cord and connections in the same manner as the transducer cords. If auxiliary input is available, note that the lapel microphone is plugged into the proper outlet and that the transmitter is set correctly to microphone and not auxiliary control.

(3) *Batteries.* Check the battery compartments on both the receiver and transmitter for loose contacts and broken wires.

b. *Listening inspection:*

(1) *Receiver.* As with body hearing aids, check the cords and transducers for any interference with the conduction and/or quality of the sound when they are manipulated (turn off the FM transmitter before trying to determine if the environmental microphones are functioning properly). Confirm the linearity of the volume control, the amplification level, and the quality of the signal. All these steps pertain to both the right and left channels of the unit. For FM systems with an ear-level microphone option on the child's receiver, deactivate the environmental microphones on the unit itself before the listening check.

(2) *Transmitter.* The FM transmitter can only be checked in conjunction with the FM receiver, which requires a second person to speak into the microphone while the examiner listens at a distance. Listen with FM-only reception (turning off the environmental microphones on the child's unit) and with both the FM and environmental microphones activated. The signal arriving at the FM microphone should be louder than the signals arriving at the environmental microphones. For this listening con-

dition, the helper should speak into the transmitter from about 10 feet away while the examiner simultaneously speaks into the environmental microphones, thus simulating a real-life situation. As with the environmental microphones, listen to each channel (right and left) separately.

4. *Personal FM systems.* For personal FM systems, check the hearing aids that couple the FM receiver to the child's ears first. This ensures that any problems noted can be attributed to the appropriate part of the system.

   a. *Visual inspection.* The visual inspections described previously apply here, with specific attention paid to the following:

   (1) direct audio-input cords
   (2) direct audio-input shoe/boot
   (3) induction (neck) loop for telecoil reception
   (4) telephone switch on the hearing aid

   b. *Listening inspection.* Although the listening conditions described for traditional FM systems carry over here, note that troubleshooting with these modified couplings can be quite confusing and the results misleading. Pay particular attention to the following:

   (1) When listening via a loop coupling, wear the loop and hold the hearing aid at ear level to determine whether the child receives a strong enough signal in typical listening positions. Move the hearing aid around to check for changes in the strength and quality of the signal with head movement.

   (2) With direct audio-input coupling, examine each boot/shoe and cord individually to rule out interfence related to the connection.

   With both couplings, be sure to deactivate the hearing aid microphones when listening to FM-only transmission. As this is more easily accomplished with some configurations than with others, contact the child's audiologist with any questions about how best to accomplish this. The primary cause of problems with direct audio input is a malfunctioning FM transmitter going undetected during ill-conducted troubleshooting. If the hearing aid microphones are not deactivated and no attempt ensues to listen to the FM signal alone, the signals the examiner hears could come from the hearing aids or the FM microphone. If not separated out, the malfunction will go undetected and the purpose of using an FM system will be defeated.

   c. *Batteries.* Most personal systems have rechargeable batteries that should charge overnight. Batteries that show problems holding a charge should be replaced by the manufacturer. In some newer units, a 9-volt battery can replace the nickel cadmium type.

Implementing a Troubleshooting Program

The IEP should clearly designate the person who is to conduct the daily troubleshooting. In some settings the school nurse takes this responsibility, while others call on the speech-language pathologist or the teacher of the hearing-impaired. In schools with a staff audiologist, he or she performs the troubleshooting. The individual's title is not important, but rather that he or she is on-site daily and has a secure area in which to keep all of the equipment. This person must have received training in the "art" of troubleshooting, be familiar with amplification in general and that specific to the child, and be able to make minor repairs. If the daily examiner is other than the child's case manager, any questions that arise concerning the troubleshooting procedures or how to remediate any problems noted should be directed to a professional who can resolve them.

In order to ensure that the hearing aids and FM systems are set properly for the child, the designated troubleshooter should keep a file of all pertinent information. The child's audiological report should contain the necessary data. If not, the audiologist who recommended the settings should be contacted. When settings are changed from those originally reported, the audiologist should inform school personnel so that no confusion results. Any time an FM system is returned from repair, the troubleshooter should check the settings carefully against those on file to confirm they are correct. The following list notes some of the significant items to keep on file at school:

1. electroacoustic settings of the hearing aid and FM system, including frequency response (tone, AGRAM), SSPL-90 (output, MPO), output limiting (PC, AGC), and volume control setting

2. other specific settings for the FM system, including FM-to-environmental-microphone ratio, BTE vs. internal microphones, and M/T vs. T switch for use with induction loops

3. type of earmolds, including any modifications (e.g., venting, filters, flared bore, short bore)

4. batteries used, according to number (e.g., #675)

5. specific boots/shoes and cords for coupling an FM through direct audio input (any mismatch can completely alter the output of the amplification)

As stated previously, troubleshooting should take place on a daily basis, preferably at the start of the school day. As the child must be able to report to the troubleshooter/case manager any time the amplification begins to malfunction, a particular site should be designated at which troubleshooting is conducted. This may be the health office, the speech-language pathologist's office, a resource room, or any other place that allows for a certain degree of privacy and security. Typically a child will change from personal hearing aids to classroom amplification at the beginning of the day. The child may feel more comfortable leaving his or her personal amplification at the troubleshooting site; therefore, the area should not be readily accessible to other children. The FM also should be kept there when not in use. The troubleshooter remains responsible for ensuring that the FM system is charged on the weekends and during school vacations as well as overnight. This job may be given to older children in the continued effort to make them responsible for their amplification. School maintenance personnel should be informed that the unit is not to be unplugged.

Should problems arise that the troubleshooter cannot readily resolve, a specific procedure must exist for reporting this. For example, if the issue involves the child's personal amplification, the parents should be notified so that they can have the hearing aids repaired and arrange for loaners. If the school amplification needs repair, the manufacturer's repair service should be contacted and the FM system sent to them quickly. In some areas it may be possible to arrange for a loaner FM system during the repair period. As noted previously in the troubleshooting protocol, after any repairs the settings should be checked.

At the end of the school year, FM systems should be sent to the manufacturer for an "overhaul." Systems with rechargeable batteries should have them replaced at this time. Many problems can be greatly reduced if the classroom amplification is set properly and functioning well at the start of the school year.

FM SOUND-FIELD AMPLIFICATION

The past several years have seen an innovative use of FM systems developing (Sarff, 1981; Sarff, Ray, & Bagwell, 1981; Ray, 1989). Basically this application involves transmitting the teacher's voice to an integrated FM receiver/loudspeaker system via the FM microphone. Several loudspeakers ensure an equal distribution of the teacher's speech energy throughout the classroom, with a goal of delivering his or her voice at approximately 10 dB above the existing ambient room noise. Conceptually the same as a public address system, it differs significantly in that teacher mobility is preserved through the wireless FM microphone/transmitter. The accumulating body of research and educational experience with this system indicates great benefit to children with minimal hearing losses and learning disabilities; additionally, teachers who use the system perceive it as beneficial (Gilman & Danzer, 1989; Flexer, 1989).

Two basic rationales underlie the employment of an FM sound-field system. One maintains that the acoustical conditions existing in the average classroom affect not just the children with moderate or greater hearing losses but also those with mild and minimal hearing losses as well as those with normal hearing (Boney & Bess, 1984; Klee, Kenworthy, Riggs, & Bess, 1984). That children must hear the speech signal clearly in order to learn the material may seem an obvious contention, but in practice it is often overlooked.

The second rationale for sound-field FM use derives from the fact that a large percentage of children in regular education classrooms have minimal and/or fluctuating hearing losses, and this condition has educational significance. As reviewed previously, Sarff (1981) demonstrated that, using rigid audiometric fail criteria (not hearing a 10 dB HL signal at 6 out of 10 test frequencies), 33% of the children tested failed. Moreover, 57% of those who failed exhibited an academic deficit to some degree. These are very high percentages, and one perhaps would doubt their validity if other studies using similar criteria had not corroborated these results (Bess, 1986; Gilman & Danzer, 1989). The amplified teacher's voice emanating from the loudspeakers helps reduce the impact of the hearing loss for these children.

Employing sound-field FM systems will provide good listening conditions for the hearing-impaired children most often overlooked: those with minimal and fluctuating conductive hearing losses who often can "get by" because they certainly can hear. When compared to others with mild to profound sensorineural hearing impairment, these children appear to function much more easily. Because they typically do not have personal amplification, the need for classroom amplification is not even considered; it is assumed they do not need it. Research with sound-field FM systems has demonstrated the inaccuracy of this assumption.

The initial study evaluating the efficacy of FM sound-field classroom amplification (Sarff, 1981) considered two groups of children with minimal hearing losses. Both groups met the study's criteria for learning disability, wherein the children demonstrated average intellectual potential and achievement test scores below the average. Group A subjects received approximately 1 hour a day of special help and were not placed in an amplified classroom. The others (Group B) received no special help but were placed in a classroom with FM sound-field amplification. The teachers in these classrooms did not know the identity of the children in the study. During the first year, Group B children showed greater improvement in reading skills and language arts than did the members of Group A. Moreover, this group difference was sustained during the 3-year course of the study. The children receiving extra tutoring never achieved the performance level of the group placed in the amplified classroom.

Reports from those who currently use sound-field FM systems are overwhelmingly favorable. According to teacher ratings (Gilman & Danzer, 1989), use of the systems improves attentiveness and reduces voice fatigue (not an insignificant factor for teachers simply exhausted after a full day of talking loudly). Fully 50% of the schools that adopted the sound-field FM system chose to expand its use to other classrooms because the advantages were so immediate and apparent. As with individual wireless FM systems, multiple use is possible with the provision of different carrier FM frequencies. One small rural county in Ohio has 47 units in place and is acquiring more each year (Flexer, 1989).

In spite of the fact that these sound-field systems have existed for over 10 years, and despite the published reports attesting to their effectiveness, use throughout the country is still relatively rare. The history of their adoption is following the same slow course seen with individual wireless FM auditory systems, although the evidence of the effectiveness of both devices is clear and unambiguous: the better children can hear, the (significantly) better they do academically.

10

Communication Management Principles

In order to understand the impact of a hearing loss on the development of spoken language, one must take into account the origin of the communication problem. Language learning occurs within an interactive framework, with parental speech providing the raw material from which the rule-governed system derives. Normal-hearing children require the following elements as they learn language:

$$\boxed{\text{Audible Speech}} + \boxed{\text{Repeated Exposure}} + \boxed{\text{Meaningful Contexts}} = \boxed{\begin{array}{l}\text{Language}\\\text{Learning}\end{array}}$$

Hearing-impaired children should be approached as if they possess an intact language system ready to be activated, as in normal-hearing children, by audible speech. This approach assumes the child would have little difficulty learning language if the missing ingredient—hearing—were supplied. To do this the audiologist carefully selects amplification that places the suprasegmental and segmental aspects of speech within the child's aided residual hearing. Whatever aspects of the speech signal fall outside this region can be supplemented through visual means.

The process of making speech audible to children would be easy if amplification was the only consideration. But the child must function in an environment in which background noise and proximity to the speaker can markedly affect speech reception. Because no teacher or audiologist can totally control these environmental factors or restore hearing to normal with even the best amplification, the equation is uneven, with the audibility of the speech signal compromised. Therefore it becomes essential to strengthen the other prerequisites if language learning is to result.

Repeated exposure to language occurs as parents reiterate words, phrases, and sentences in similar situations over time. Adults repeatedly label the objects in a baby's environment ("Here's your bottle") and comment on frequently occurring events ("Your diaper's wet"). The first words take many repetitions before children discern their meaning. The process gains speed as a child uses old words to learn new vocabulary, until finally learning can occur after a single presentation.

Because hearing-impaired children do not overhear the comments and conversations of others, their exposure to speech automatically is reduced. To compensate for this variable and reduced audibility, their caregivers must be conscious of increasing the quantity of their input. As they cannot assume that these children will automatically learn the meanings of words, phrases, and sentences, they must purposefully introduce, use, and reinforce language as it logically occurs in daily routines.

Most children, hearing-impaired or otherwise, lead lives rich in the contexts necessary for learning language. Their daily routines, school activities, and social interactions provide the framework to which the words, phrases, and sentences can become attached. However, when the other parts of the equation are absent or weak, the meaningful context becomes just another circumstance or activity.

SOCIAL AND ACADEMIC COMMUNICATION

The need to emphasize either social or academic communication changes somewhat with chronological age. In the preschool years, the social aspects of communication predominate, as the goal of early childhood education is preparation for social interactions within a group. Once the hearing-impaired student reaches school age, the balance between social requirements and academic necessities equals out. While the academic demands in a mainstream educational setting seem obvious, it is unrealistic to envision the child as merely an academic being. Many situations in the educational environment call on children to interact with each other in large or small groups, during class activities or nonacademic routines. As students mature into young adults and begin to consider their employment possibilities, academic communication decreases in importance as social interaction ascends.

Together the social and academic communication demands of the educational environment should tailor the focus of the communication management program:

Social Interaction	*Academic Interaction*
Speech intelligibility	Content vocabulary
Conversational rules	Formality of written language
Situational context	Language of instructions
Appropriate topics	Teacher-selected topics

Being aware of the social interactive components of communication comprises only part of the skill "package" the student must acquire to be successful in the mainstream educational setting (Brackett, 1990). It is within the demands of the academic environment that hearing-impaired students demonstrate the inadequacies of their language. Each deficit area revealed in the evaluation must be viewed as it affects the student's functioning in these contexts. This huge task faces speech-language pathologists as they design effective intervention for hearing-impaired students in mainstreamed settings.

GENERAL PRINCIPLES OF COMMUNICATION MANAGEMENT

Regardless of the deficit areas to be addressed in the remedial sessions and the classroom management program, the following general management principles apply in both areas:

1. Selection
   a. relevance
   b. rapid success potential
   c. developmental appropriateness
2. Therapy Techniques
   a. pick stimuli that occur frequently during routine activities
   b. train using multiple cues
   c. use old information to learn new
3. Practice
   a. in therapy setting
   b. in classroom setting
   c. in social interactions with family and friends

4. Generalization
   a. decrease external control
   b. increase self-monitoring

Selecting Targets

A fundamental component of communication management requires selecting targets that will have the greatest and most immediate impact on function. Initially this approach is easy to implement because these children exhibit so many problem areas. As the child's communication skills improve to a functional level (i.e., the message that was intended was the one that was received), it becomes more difficult to convince the child and sometimes the family that intensive effort remains necessary. Very often at this point progress slows down, resulting in an unfinished, unrefined outcome to the therapy process. By starting early, it is possible to reach the refinement level at a point in the age continuum that the child is still willing to work.

By selecting targets within the student's developmental grasp, advancement becomes rather effortless from one stage to the next. When targeting correction of inappropriate phonemes, vocabulary, or syntactic forms, progress may be minimal until the student is developmentally ready or has acquired the prerequisite skills to move to a more advanced level. Following this advice requires knowledge of the simultaneous development of the phonologic, semantic/syntactic, and pragmatic systems. For instance, when the child's MLU begins to increase, it is appropriate to target the early developing morphemes and the phonemes required to formulate them. When the optimal developmental timeframe is disrupted (e.g., MLU = 7+ with no morphological endings present), it is much more difficult to attain mastery within a short time period.

Therapy Techniques

The same therapy techniques applied to hearing students with speech-language deficits can be utilized with mainstreamed children as long as one takes into account the audibility of the stimuli. The speech-language pathologist must become adept at identifying familiar routines that inherently involve words and phrases containing the selected target (e.g., "<u>mommy</u>"; Je<u>ss</u>ie"; "<u>st</u>op it"; "I <u>c</u>an't"). Then on each occasion that the routine occurs, the child will have an opportunity to practice correct productions.

The relevance of the target to more than one area of function may determine how quickly the skill is learned, generalized, and automatized. For example, carryover occurs more quickly if the /s/ phoneme can be simultaneously trained and reinforced as the marker for plurality, possession, and verb tense. Further, using old, familiar information to assist in learning new words, sounds, or phrases provides associative context. For example, if /ch/ is the target, then using the child's correct production of its component parts /t/ and /sh/ can speed up the initial learning process; if *biped* is the vocabulary item, then assisting the student in recalling other words with the same root (e.g., *pedestrian, pedal*) and applying the root to the new word becomes a useful teaching and reinforcement strategy.

Practice

To accelerate the rate of new skills acquisition, practice must occur in the therapy setting, in the classroom, and in the home. Practice can be the most difficult goal to implement in communication management because the therapist has little control outside the therapy setting.

After the child has learned a skill through a structured task during therapy, practice with the therapist should take on a more natural approach in obligating the child to use the newly learned item. This one-to-one setting allows for only minimally loosening the external controls. The mere presence of the therapist can act as a reminder to use the new skill.

In educational settings, although having the teacher assist in monitoring correct productions would be ideal, classroom practice can be difficult to arrange due to the large number of children the teacher oversees. One way to facilitate carryover into the classroom is to target during remedial sessions the content words that will come up in classroom lessons. When the child then confronts these words in classroom discussion, it should trigger a memory for production characteristics or meaning. In order to implement this procedure, the speech-language pathologist needs to obtain lists of upcoming academic vocabulary from the child's classroom teacher. It may be possible (and easier) to obtain the teacher's support in specific contexts, such as requiring correct speech during oral reading or encouraging longer utterances when answering content questions in small reading groups.

Practice in social settings begins with the immediate family, eventually branching out to include peers. Family commitment and expectation play an enormous role in the amount of improvement a child can ultimately attain. As parents have the child's interests in mind, they should be willing to spend time facilitating practice in a naturalistic environment. Enlisting parental assistance is effective as long as one makes the parameters for evaluating the accuracy of responses explicit. Each social/interactive encounter that affords the child an opportunity to practice the targets correctly means more rapid acquisition of the skill and knowledge of when to use it.

The hearing-impaired child can practice correct productions during peer interactions as long as the target has been practiced and mastered within frequently occurring social phrases ("Do you want to play?") or routines (greetings and departures). Then when the phrases or routines occur, the student can easily recall the correct productions. As soon as the child begins to self-monitor his or her own productions, then merely producing the target correctly will be reinforcing and will encourage further correct productions.

Generalization

Carryover or generalization of targets to the spontaneous level becomes most likely when the skills can be transferred to meaningful contexts within the educational or social setting. Carryover occurs gradually as the child begins to "internalize" the correct sound of the form; that is, he or she recognizes when the target "sounds" correct. Assimilating the newly learned forms into automatic use represents the most time-consuming aspect of the hearing-impaired student's remedial program. This gradual process begins when the child has mastered the target in structured tasks. Then, through a gradual lessening of external control, he or she learns to self-monitor speech productions and correct any errors that arise. Frequently, however, the professional inadvertently lengthens this process by providing a model to imitate during correction instead of making the child depend on his or her own analytic skills. By eliminating the self-analysis stage, mastery becomes postponed or elusive. The following diagram illustrates this point:

(A)

CORRECT   CORRECT
↑   ↑
PRODUCE → (external analysis) → MODEL → (self-analysis) → MASTERY
↓   ↓
INCORRECT   INCORRECT

(B)

CORRECT
↑
PRODUCE → (self-analysis) → MASTERY
↓
INCORRECT

To avoid this pitfall, the professional should stop providing the model and instead substitute a generic "What?" This signals to the child that the listener has not understood some aspect of the message and puts the responsibility back on him or her to fix it. Through self-analysis the child should be able to decide which aspect of the message was incorrect—grammar, syntax, phonology—and provide a clarification that incorporates the correction.

11

Communication Management Practices

From a case management perspective, hearing-impaired children have a distinct advantage over normal-hearing children with speech and language problems. First is the clear-cut reason for the hearing-impaired child's problems. Understanding the precise origin of a child's difficulties certainly makes planning a therapeutic program a less chancy affair. Secondly, the hearing-impaired child's presumed biological capacity for learning speech and language offers the greatest natural therapy ally.

The hearing-impaired student typically exhibits deficits in the following communicative areas: speech reception, speech production/intelligibility, vocabulary, syntax/morphology, and language usage. Just as they are all interwoven in the child's utterances, so in remediation it is difficult to isolate particular skills. The speech-language pathologist must address each of these areas in providing remedial services. Further, in addition to direct remediation of the deficit areas, he or she is responsible for facilitating classroom communication, by regularly observing the students as they participate in the classroom and by suggesting alternative ways of making classroom conversation accessible to them. Each deficit area thus must be considered vis-à-vis remedial activities and classroom suggestions.

SPEECH RECEPTION

Remediation Consideration and Activities

As the communication problems of hearing-impaired children stem directly from the hearing loss, it is logical first to address optimizing speech reception. In planning speech reception programs for mainstreamed hearing-impaired students (who, by definition, function with an impaired auditory system), educators often ignore listening-related issues and concentrate instead on visual enhancements. A more effective approach, however, to improving speech perception incorporates the full use of a child's residual hearing. This combined with speechreading cues results in better speech recognition scores than would be obtained by employing the modalities singly.

An auditory management program can be employed for any student with a hearing loss, regardless of the degree or configuration. Contrary to popular thought, not only the students who depend on their hearing but also those who use it to supplement visually acquired information require thoughtful attention to the auditory aspects of speech reception.

To utilize an approach that emphasizes audition, the amplification system worn by the student must provide an optimal auditory signal (i.e., afford full accessibility to speech given the particular degree and configuration of the hearing loss). Amplification that makes speech audible at normal conversational levels (45 dB HL or better) is desirable if one intends to help the student use all available acoustic cues.

Given appropriate amplification, designing an amplification monitoring plan that includes daily troubleshooting follows (see chapter 9). Next, in-service programs (chapter 13) should be scheduled for the classroom teacher, to demonstrate the appropriate use of both classroom amplification (FM units) and personal hearing aids and to ensure that interfering factors such as background noise and distance from the primary speaker are considered. Classroom observation makes it possible to examine the potential noise sources and perhaps counteract their effects with sound-absorbing materials. By also viewing actual classroom routines and interactions, one can note the teacher's use of the FM microphone and suggest necessary modifications. To "demystify" the FM unit or hearing aids, the hearing impairment specialist can provide an informational, hands-on workshop for the child's normal-hearing classmates. Often when other children understand how these amplification systems function, they ignore their presence on the hearing-impaired child. In addition to these general auditory management considerations (listed on the IEP), one must address specific speech reception goals and objectives that pertain to the child's functioning in remedial and classroom settings (see Table 11.1).

TABLE 11.1 Remedial and Classroom Objectives for Speech Reception Improvement

Speech/Language Therapy (objectives for child)	Classroom Communication Management (objectives for teacher)
Resolve perceptual errors through minimal pair contrasts	Gain student's attention
	Repeat answers to questions
Introduce or reinforce new sounds, words, or grammar (listen only)	Direct classroom discussion by naming participants
Increase dependence on audition for speech reception	Use visual demonstration
Self-monitoring speech skills	Write key words on board
Practice under negative listening conditions (background noise, distance, no context)	Avoid turning back to student
	Alternate speaking and demonstrating
Increase knowledge of maintenance and repair of amplification	Ensure that teacher's face is fully visible, well-lighted away from glare
	Seat student away from obvious noise sources

Note. From "Communication Management of the Mainstream Hearing-Impaired Student" by D. Brackett in *Hearing-Impaired Children in the Mainstream* (M. Ross, Ed.), 1990, Parkton, MD: York Press. Copyright 1990 by York Press. Reprinted by permission.

Coping as they have with reduced auditory input for their entire lives, hearing-impaired children often evolve strategies for speech perception that unduly deemphasize auditory dependency. The intention of enhancing speech perception is not to restrict visually acquired information, but rather to increase the child's auditory capacity and thereby enhance the total perceptual process. Many students have learned to depend heavily on a consistent, though inadequate, visual system for language comprehension rather than an inconsistent *and* inadequate auditory system.

For children who need encouragement and practice to increase their confidence and dependence on the auditory perception of speech, training begins by increasing the facility with which they deal with auditory messages. One can step up the child's awareness of the amount of information available through hearing by gradually increasing the amount of familiar material the student is required to receive without visual cues. By incorporating listening activities into all aspects of communication management, listening becomes the vehicle by which children are exposed initially to the speech/language targets and by which they monitor their own productions.

Students should be able to determine, through hearing alone, one of several familiar words presented in a closed set in which all the members of the set are known. To ensure familiarity with the words and task, the professional should initially present the activity full face. So this activity does not become a useless task, the familiar words can be placed in a meaningful scenario, giving the student a logical use for the skill:

One Syllable	*Two Syllables*	*Three Syllables*
boy	toothbrush	grandfather
comb	jacket	umbrella
sock		
shoe		

Nonfunctional task: Place eight picture cards of familiar items and people, differing according to designated parameters (in this case syllable number), on the table in front of the child. Ask the child to point to the picture that corresponds to the word presented without speech-reading clues: "Give me . . . grandfather."

Functional task: Ask the child to place objects in a suitcase for two familiar characters who are going on a trip. Present without visual clues the name of the person whose suitcase is being filled and the object being placed in the suitcase: "Grandfather wants the sock in his suitcase."

As the child becomes facile at identifying these familiar words (which vary widely in their phonetic components), the words selected should contain less distinctive contrasts. Further, as confidence grows in the ability to recognize words through hearing, the number of words to be recognized in the utterance can be increased. By changing the color (red, purple, orange), size (big, little), action (running, walking), person (boy, girl), and location (on the street, on the floor), one can increase the complexity of the task dramatically. Even though these words are presented within a sentence framework, it is impossible to apply linguistic knowledge to predict which words were used:

	GIRL		LITTLE	RED		WALKING		STREET
The		with the		PURPLE	hat was		on the	
	BOY		BIG	ORANGE		RUNNING		FLOOR

TABLE 11.2 Easy to Difficult Sentence-Level Material

Easy	Difficult
Clued ("It's about camping."): "I took a sleeping bag with me."	Unclued: "I took a sleeping bag with me."
Simple structure: "I walked down the street."	Complex structure: "The boy the man drove to school got out of the car."
Related sentences: 1. "We went camping in the summer." 2. "I slept in a tent."	Unrelated sentences: 1. "I walked down the street." 2. "My TV set is broken."

Hearing-impaired children need to understand the strategies they can and do employ to comprehend a message despite missing many of its component parts. While the foregoing activities focus on the ability to recognize words, one also can help the child infer meaning from phrases or sentences without perceiving all their acoustic/phonetic or linguistic constituents. Sentences can increase from easy (E) to difficult (D) based on the number of topic clues available, the complexity of the language, and the interrelationships among sentences (see Table 11.2). The easy utterances facilitate prediction based on factors other than the acoustic events of the sentences themselves. Topic clues and linguistic context all help the listener infer meaning. Techniques such as repeating the sentence a second time give students enough added information to guess at the rest of the words in the sentence.

Suggested listening activities include *cloze procedures* and *speech tracking*. With cloze procedures, the therapist places a script with every third, fourth, or fifth word deleted in front of the child and plays a recording of the full script. The child must use a combination of acoustic and linguistic information to fill in the missing words. In speech tracking the therapist asks the student to repeat all the words he or she perceives of each sentence in a paragraph read aloud. When errors occur, the therapist repeats the sentence and the child is given another chance at the task. Specific strategies then are employed that systematically increase the number of acoustic and/or linguistic cues given to the listener until correct perception results, after which the speaker repeats the stimulus under the original conditions. The list of cues generated by Ying (1990) can be employed vertically or horizontally, depending on the student's linguistic competence. If one knows the child can handle the language level in the sentence, then the acoustic modifications are applied hierarchically. Conversely, if the errors appear more related to insufficient knowledge of the utterance's semantic or syntactic structure, then the linguistic modifications are applied initially (see Figure 11.1).

Resolving perceptual errors relies on the premise that audible speech leads to the development of accurate speech perception. Therefore, the child should be able to identify those phonemes whose acoustic energy falls within the range of aided residual hearing. By selecting errors with the potential to change, one can design remedial activities that highlight the cues to which the child should attend.

The starting point for this procedure derives from the results of the speech perception testing completed during the evaluation phase. If the student's performance indicates that he or she has difficulty with vowel discriminations, then the words selected to compare and contrast should incorporate vowel differences. The pairs initially consist of one of the errors contrasted with a phoneme having little in common with it, giving the child an opportunity to successfully identify the original phoneme (Table 11.3). Gradually the pair of sounds begins to share more of the same acoustic characteristics, making identification of the correct phoneme from the error phoneme more difficult.

A close relationship exists between the abilities to produce and perceive specific phonemes. The common belief is that perception precedes production; that is, the child must first be able to perceive the features of the phonemes before he or she can attain production. The opposite, however, also is true: Learning how to produce a phoneme can facilitate one's perception of the sound. These two approaches to perception and production closely intertwine. Although children must have access to the frequency-specific features of speech, it is the act of producing the sound correctly that provides them with a model against which to compare future productions.

Repeat-back responses can provide an accurate view of the child's perceptual abilities as long as one takes habitual articulation errors into account. When the reason for the presence of articulation errors is considered, then the errors the child presents should be the result of what he or she is hearing. For children just learning the sound system, their repeat-back response reveal which features of the speech signal have developed at the time of sampling. For example, given an auditory-only presentation of /sh/, the child who produces /h/ demonstrates that he or she perceives the aspects of *voicing* and *manner* (fricative). As he or she then becomes cognizant of the *place* feature, examples of /sh/ should emerge in spontaneous utterances.

In older children, one can ascertain which features of the speech signal have been perceived auditorily by examining the repeat-back responses.

FIGURE 11.1 Acoustic and linguistic modifications to assist in speech reception.

Acoustic	Linguistic
Initial presentation (listen alone)	Repetition of target form with expansion cues (providing old/familiar vocabulary or concepts)
Exact repetition	
Repetition with stress on key word	
	Repetition of error, immediately followed by targeted form
	Repetition with descriptor or function clues
Repetition of error response with question intonation, signaling the need for repair or lack of understanding	
Provide indirect model (giving several examples of target form)	
Partial presentation (combined look and listen with only key words presented listen alone)	Provide full-face topic clue and permit child to anticipate what might be said (then repeat target listen alone)
Partial presentation (same as above) with key error phonemes prolonged or exaggerated	
Direct attention to error by requesting to "listen for" given type of information	
Provide look and listen repetition	Provide an auditory choice of two different alternatives (i.e., target form contrasted with contrast that could not semantically fit within given context)
Same as above with accompanying sign or cued speech cues	
Same as above with accompanying symbolic gestural cues	
Definitive gestural cue (i.e., pointing directly to object) while presenting only key words	
	Same as above except model is presented look and listen
Gestural cue without speech	

TABLE 11.3 Training Stimuli That Gradually Increase Shared Distinctive Features

Error	Training Contrasts	Stimuli	# of Common Features
/Eh/ for /I/	1. /Ih/ with /ah/ or /uh/	hit/hot pit/putt	0
	2. /Ih/ with /ae/	pick/pack sip/sap	1 (high)
	3. /Ih/ with /Eh/	sit/set mitt/met	2 (high-front)
/k/ for /t/	1. /t/ with /m/	top/mop	0
	2. /t/ with /sh/	mat/mash	1 (voice)
	3. /t/ with /k/	sit/sick tee/key	2 voice-manner)

Any habitual errors that occur when the student imitates the stimuli with full auditory and visual input should be eliminated in the error analysis. The following diagram illustrates this process:

Stimulus		Response		Analysis
"pat" unvoiced plosive Lingua-Alveolar	→	"pack" unvoiced plosive Linguapalatal	→	PLACE of articulation is incorrect

Many of these phonemic errors appear to disappear when the words are placed in a context. However, what really happens is that the child uses linguistic information to predict the correct response rather than relying on perceiving each feature of the acoustic signal. Only when the word is taken out of this global task can one view the exact nature of the child's perception.

By using a combination of global tasks (which require discerning meaning) and analytic tasks (which contrast minimal pairs), children can refine their listening skills at the phoneme level as well as in connected discourse. It is possible to present these simultaneously as long as one gives care to the language used. If analytic work is expected, then the contrasting pairs must be linguistically interchangeable in the utterance. To facilitate the rapid acquisition of these perceptual skills, each task must be phonetically loaded with the error features that constitute the focus of the training. Selecting names for characters offers an easy way to implement this approach:

(k/t)*Mac Matt* or (M/N)*Matt Nat*
Matt
      went down the street
Mac

While the child is applying global strategies for understanding the story or scenario, he or she also must apply phonetic analysis to determine which character is being talked about.

Classroom Management

The decision to place a student in a mainstreamed setting assumes that he or she will have access to the rich auditory-verbal environment of the regular classroom. In order to realize the potential of this environment, one must ensure that the child has auditory and visual access to the speech of teachers and classmates. Modifications previously described in classroom set up, routine, and presentation can enhance the student's access to sound. Seating the student away from any obvious noise source and in a place where the teacher's face is well lit without glare sets the stage for optimum reception. Gaining the student's visual and auditory attention before speaking by calling his or her name prepares the child to receive speech.

Teachers should avoid certain patterns of presentation that eliminate one of the input modalities. For example, when one writes on the board and talks simultaneously, this reduces both visual (speechreading) and auditory information because the speech is directed at the board. The acoustic energy dissipates before it can reach the hearing-impaired child (unless an FM microphone is used). Without access to both visual and auditory input, the student must rely on the words written on the board to compensate (inadequately) for the missing information. Also, when students change their focus from the teacher's face to the picture, map, or science experiment, they must rely solely on the auditory modality for speech reception.

In classes such as home economics, shop, or physical education (which generate noise by the nature of the activity), the student relies primarily on visual input (speechreading, demonstration, outlines, and gesture) to receive speech. Visual support for the classroom content is best achieved by preparing outlines, highlighting key words on the board, or designating shifts in topic through written clues.

Classroom discussions present a particularly difficult but common learning format in the regular classroom. Here the hearing-impaired student no longer monitors just what the teacher says, but also must follow the content of all the participants. Due to the varying distances of speakers and the rapid transmission of information from changing locations, discussion groups present a nightmare for the hearing-impaired listener.

To help ameliorate this situation, the teacher can designate by name the next speaker in the discussion, thus effectively giving the hearing-impaired student sufficient time to connect visually with the speaker. In the upper grades, it is often possible to rearrange desks into a "U" or a circle, which allows maximum visibility of all discussants. In the younger grades, allowing the hearing-impaired students to change seats to the far right or far left allows them visual access to the entire room when turning slightly in their chairs. Smaller discussion classes can pass the FM microphone to the next speaker, which slows the pace of the discussion and visually and auditorily designates the speaker. (The latter has been especially effective in college seminars or honors classes, but unfortunately most discussions are rarely that controlled.) Finally, the teacher can reiterate pertinent points of the discussion either standing near the hearing-impaired student or by talking into the FM microphone.

All the above modifications require minimal disruption in the regular classroom routine. They actually represent aspects of teaching encouraged in teacher training programs because they enhance the classroom presentation for all students.

SPEECH PRODUCTION

Remediation Considerations and Activities

As stated previously, speech perception and speech production skills closely intertwine. The reason that any speech production errors exist relates directly to the longstanding nature of the hearing loss. That is, during the period in which the phoneme system was being organized auditorily (0 to 12 months), the child could not access some or all of the acoustic energy necessary to form the decisions. Under these conditions, when words are first learned, the sounds used to express them are incorrectly produced, learned, and habituated. When such a child then uses amplification, he or she must redefine these old phoneme categories according to the amplified sound coming in. Given the poor fidelity of most hearing aids, particularly in the high frequencies, it is not surprising that many students cannot resolve their perceptual errors even with amplification. In children who gradually lose their hearing or have a sudden onset loss after the prime language learning years, a deterioration in speech stems from the disrupted auditory feedback loop.

In either case, speech remediation is indicated and consists of two components: refinement of the phoneme system and improvement of speech intelligibility following communicative breakdown. Table 11.4 lists remedial and classroom objectives for improving speech production.

The first step in refining phoneme production entails determining if the student can produce the phoneme correctly following a visual and auditory model. Most habitual errors will fall in this category. Next a period of generalization activities should be designed to assist the child in habituating the production. During these activities, the visual aspects of the model should fade gradually until all correction occurs by listening alone, so the student begins to compare his or her own production with the auditory version of the model.

When correct production cannot be achieved through the imitation of a model, then the therapist should employ added visual, gestural, tactile, and written methods to establish the production in isolation or at the syllable level. Once established, the activities for generalizing the skill are the same as those described below.

While practice using the newly acquired phoneme in multiple contexts is important, it is equally critical to reduce the amount of cueing/modeling, letting children rely on their ability to self-monitor. Cueing progresses through the following hierarchical stages, from a direct model to eventual self-monitoring:

Self-monitoring

Timed period of correct production

Written feedback (plus or minus during ongoing discourse)

Facial expression

General feedback (child must figure out error)

Feedback on the error word signaled by a *wh*-word ("Your mother did *what?*")

Error model

Exact model

Quick progression through these stages is important if a child is to achieve self-monitoring rapidly. Each new stage represents more responsibility on the child's part for self-monitoring the quality of speech.

TABLE 11.4 Remedial and Classroom Objectives for Speech Production Improvement

Speech/Language Therapy (objectives for child)	Classroom Communication Management (objectives for teacher)
Practice recognizing own errors	Ask student to write unintelligible answer
Accept responsibility for making oneself understood	Ask for repetition of a misunderstood word
Give back more precise speech following request for clarification	Give student a limited number of choices from which to pick answer
Refine phoneme production; facilitate carryover into spontaneous speech	Repeat that part of student's statement that is understood
Gradually reduce external feedback	

Note. From "Communication Management of the Mainstream Hearing-Impaired Student" by D. Brackett in *Hearing-Impaired Children in the Mainstream* (M. Ross, Ed.), 1990, Parkton, MD: York Press. Copyright 1990 by York Press. Reprinted by permission.

Hearing-impaired students experience many instances in which their intended message fails because the listener cannot understand what they have said. Although language structure and vocabulary play some role, speech intelligibility primarily and most dramatically affects message reception. Obviously, the closer the utterance conforms to correct English and syntax the easier it is to decode, but the words must be intelligible.

Recognizing that a listener is requesting clarification becomes an important skill for the hearing-impaired student. In most cases listeners provide some feedback to signal that they did not understand all or part of the utterance. Hearing-impaired students often interpret the breakdown to occur in the loudness of the utterance, where they experience the most trouble in the role of listener. However, the normal-hearing listener usually signals breakdown when intelligibility interferes with decoding. In response to these signals, the student is expected to provide a more precisely articulated version of the utterance, not a louder one. If after restating the breakdown continues, the student may have to paraphrase or supply a different word.

Classroom Management

While the child is refining his or her speech, the teacher must manage the process within the classroom. As so many of the transactions that occur in the classroom are spoken, the teacher has many opportunities to experience the student's speech intelligibility. Even though he or she can produce most sounds correctly within the therapy setting, the student probably will not use these optimum skills consistently, resorting instead to habitual patterns. The result of this "backsliding" is that the teacher may have difficulty understanding the child's message. Although ideally these occurrences are few and resolved without embarrassment, occasionally one of the partners, either teacher or student, will become frustrated over the inability to transmit or receive the message.

In order to facilitate classroom communication, the teacher will require strategies for handling communication breakdown. When utterances are misunderstood, he or she can request a direct repetition or can repeat back the part that was understood, thus providing an obvious clue to the nature of the breakdown (e.g., "Columbus sailed where?"). The student has an opportunity to repair the utterance by concentrating on the word or words that were misunderstood. When requests for clarification do not resolve the breakdown, the teacher may need to provide a limited number of choices from which the student can select the answer (e.g., "Is it XX or YY?"). Further clarification can be sought by having the student write down the answer, even though the orderly flow of conversation is disrupted.

Consider students who never raise their hand in response to questions posed to the entire class. In all likelihood they can understand at least some of the teacher's questions. Their lack of participation may be due to embarrassment about the quality of their speech. Many hearing-impaired children are quite aware that their speech is "different." Having experienced the stares of people in public places, they may not want to expose themselves to the potential ridicule of their peers. Teachers can encourage such students to increase their classroom participation by setting up the communication interaction so all parties know what is being said. Oral reading sessions, in which all the other students read along silently, offers a situation in which the spoken material can easily be followed by everyone. Success in such structured exercises should lead the hearing-impaired student to more confidence in less controlled situations. Care should be taken to only gradually reduce the amount of shared knowledge between the hearing-impaired speaker and the listeners.

VOCABULARY

Remediation Considerations and Activities

Language therapy should be based on the following premises:

1. While trying to arrange linguistic contexts to foster the induction of a morphological rule or syntactic structure, one should use only highly familiar vocabulary.

2. While teaching new vocabulary, the linguistic context should contain only those syntactic/morphological structures that reside in the child's automatic repertoire.

Most hearing-impaired children manifest some limitations in their vocabulary development. For normal-hearing children, vocabulary growth proceeds almost effortlessly, as does grammatical development. As their caregivers continually label objects and occurrences in the environment, children learn many new lexical items through ongoing auditory exposure to language. A normal-hearing child can tune in to, even "overhear," language spoken anywhere in his or her auditory field. Much of this vocabulary acquisition proceeds unconsciously, as a kind of auditory osmosis associated with the pertinent nonlinguistic experiences. Although vocabulary growth normally continues throughout an individual's life, not so with syntactic development, which shows few changes (particularly in oral communication) after the elementary years.

For the hearing-impaired child, a restricted lexicon may prove more injurious to the ultimate ability to communicate effectively than any grammatical deficiencies. Words are learned best when specifically directed to the child in the proper motivating and acoustic circumstances. For example, when the hearing-impaired child crowds around an ice cream truck with a group of children asking for exotic flavors, he or she may not hear (because of street noise and multiple talkers) this rich input and thus cannot associate their requests with a specific flavor. When the time for stating a choice arrives, that child may be restricted to "white" (for vanilla) or "brown" (for chocolate), or even to pointing at a picture.

Normal-hearing children ordinarily can figure out the meaning of new words from their linguistic context; for many hearing-impaired children, the linguistic context may be as unfamiliar as the new word. Academic subjects such as reading, social studies, and science rapidly expose schoolchildren to new vocabulary. Getting the meaning of a new word, retaining it, and making it automatic presents a difficult task under the best of circumstances. The meager linguistic resources of many hearing-impaired children preclude effectively using linguistic context to gain comprehension of new school words. These vocabulary deficiencies also extend to everyday words, ones the child should know when he or she enters school.

TABLE 11.5 Remedial and Classroom Objectives for Vocabulary Improvement

Speech/Language Therapy (objectives for child)	Classroom Communication Management (objectives for teacher)
Learn vocabulary from content material in classroom	Write important words on board
	Define words by using in a sentence
Review old words at regular intervals	
Know "sound" of new words, not just visual appearance	Give list of vocabulary to support staff
Enlist parental support and reinforcement	Select vocabulary from academic material in the lessons
Expand language with multiple meanings, synonyms, antonyms, and idioms	Ensure that directions are understood
	Encourage child to give specific answers
Use high-interest words from board games, sports, or hobbies	
Use old words to learn new "instruction" words	

Note. From "Communication Management of the Mainstream Hearing-Impaired Student" by D. Brackett in *Hearing-Impaired Children in the Mainstream* (M. Ross, Ed.), 1990, Parkton, MD: York Press. Copyright 1990 by York Press. Reprinted by permission.

This problem occurs primarily because of exposure limitations. In order to facilitate the communication process, normal-hearing adults and children often modify their linguistic input to hearing-impaired children based on their perception of the child's level of function, which restricts the crucial linguistic exposures necessary for the acquisition of vocabulary. Parents in particular often will continue to use a simplified lexicon to assure transmitting their message accurately. While the intent is positive, the results may well be negative in terms of the child's vocabulary growth. Table 11.5 lists remedial and classroom objectives designed to improve the child's vocabulary.

In attempting to expand functional vocabulary, a number of general principles apply and must be considered. When purporting a naturalistic approach, one must permit the child's cognitive and maturation levels, interests, needs, and motivations to direct which procedures are adopted and the specific vocabulary targeted. Beyond this, society, through the child's community and school, has evolved expectations for vocabulary performance that also must guide the selection of specific therapy goals. With all these possibilities, an astute clinician can determine the words that will make the most difference in academic performance and social interaction as well as those that can best serve the child's own interests and needs.

In learning any new word, repetition, redundancy, rephrasing, and associations are necessary. One cannot expect children with spotty linguistic backgrounds to fully comprehend, retain, and utilize new words after only one or two exposures. The child must have repeated exposures to the words in different meaningful contexts and be given many obligatory contexts in which to use the targets. This phenomenon can be confusing to the beginning professional who, after introducing a year's worth of vocabulary in weekly sessions, realizes during year-end testing that the student's recognition rate for the words is low. Short-term recitation does not supplant the practice and repetition essential to placing words in long-term storage.

When possible, vocabulary should be taught in a way that actively involves the child in using the object, carrying out the action, or demonstrating the feeling or adjective. Carryover becomes much more rapid when children must act on a request or come up with the word on their own. At a later stage, when learning abstract vocabulary, words may have to be used to define other words, but even then situations that give a context can be devised to illustrate the meaning of the word.

For the school-age hearing-impaired child, new words must be presented orally first and then graphically to provide support. This is particularly important when the written form of the word does not reflect standard pronunciation. Confusion can arise, for example, when the child hears the words *doubt, ghost, thought,* and *recipe* spoken after having studied the written form first for a spelling test. This written-spoken confusion is exacerbated when students have a faulty sound-symbol system that causes them to say words incorrectly to themselves. For example, if the student has mentally pronounced the word *donate* as "do-nat-ee" after encountering it in print, he or she will have difficulty recognizing the word when it is spoken. As reading provides an important means of learning vocabulary and should be encouraged, only through an increased awareness can professionals and parents address this discrepancy. Oral reading and astute listening during conversation also help the recognition process.

The ultimate goal of vocabulary remediation is to reach a point where the child's linguistic development allows him or her to use printed material as a major avenue for vocabulary acquisition. The child should not be asked to recite the definition of a new word, but instead should be able to employ it correctly in a sentence. Repetition and review must permeate every lesson, much more than with normal-hearing children, simply because the hearing-impaired child's previous auditory exposure to the new words is apt to be minimal.

The speech-language pathologist should consult with all the student's teachers and secure from them a list of words that all children in the class are expected to know. These can relate to past lessons or activities, or simply to the school situation (e.g., *recess, erase, PA, secretary,* etc.). One cannot assume that the hearing-impaired child understands the use of words specific to the school situation unless he or she can explicitly demonstrate it. In addition, one should query the child's teachers regarding their observations of words the child seems not to understand. All "special" teachers should be asked to compile a vocabulary list specific to their specialty, such as *easel, canvas,* and *kiln* for the art teacher and *stacks, encyclopedia,* and *directory* for the librarian. This is the lexicon mastered by hearing classmates, which the hearing-impaired student also must understand and use if he or she expects to participate on equal footing.

The speech-language pathologist determines mastery of a particular word by having the student use it in a sentence or carry out a directive containing the word. This method of checking word knowledge is useful regardless of the approach to word selection. For example, after a chapter on light, the teacher may select the following words for emphasis, which the child can be asked to use in a fill-in-the-blank exercise:

photons	concave	spectrum
opaque	convex	prism
transparent	mirage	lenses
translucent	refraction	retina

Another beneficial activity has the child read material from the current or upcoming curriculum and underline any word that he or she does not fully comprehend. The speech-language pathologist then goes through the same material and underlines those additional words the child may have difficulty with. Subject areas such as social studies and science, which cover a lot of vocabulary in a short time, should be prime targets for this approach. It is good practice to include some words the child does understand and can, when asked, use in a sentence. These children know they have problems; once in a while some positive reinforcement can boost their self-image and improve their motivation.

The speech-language pathologist should extract the vocabulary dealing with instructions from the child's seatwork, workbooks, and tests. Often this language is more complex than the tasks themselves. The student's failure to perform during these tasks may relate more to difficulty in comprehending the directions (*underline, circle, match, connect, fill-in, complete*) than to the tasks themselves. The following lists of direction vocabulary from two reading workbooks could serve as vocabulary goals:

study	pattern	rewrite	work up	add
trace	sentence	in order	that fit	grow
copy	finish	tell	story	another
compare	scrambled	missing	work across	
underline	phrase	opposite	alike	
belong	blank	space	right	
group	fill	spell	check	
correct	rhymes	correctly	first	
complete	list	below	column	

The most motivating vocabulary derives from that which the student selects. As children discuss their hobbies, interests, and activities, instances of word finding and overly general word use (when a specific vocabulary item was intended) will occur. The child taking driver's education might select the following vocabulary:

Part of Car	*Action*
steering wheel	speeding
gear shift	overheat
speedometer	shifting
windshield wipers	steering
seat belts	backing up
clutch	forward
brake	reverse
engine	fill up
battery	tune up
radiator	parallel park
blinker	check oil

Many children enjoy playing games in and out of school and are avid sports fans. The vocabulary associated with the rules of the games and the accomplishments of various teams and players offers a unique opportunity to capture the interest of a child in learning vocabulary. Further, although the child may know the reasons for certain events and the scoring rules, he or she may not know the associated verbal labels—*foul, penalty, offside, huddle, block, intercept, end.* For children to compete on equal footing with their sports-discussing peers, they must learn the special vocabulary of each game. More immediately, they must understand the rules of the games played in the school yard and in the neighborhood. Teaching the meaning of this highly specialized vocabulary may result in improved self-image and social adjustment, which relates directly to the ability to successfully interact with peers. The following vocabulary concerns playing and enjoying baseball:

home	right field	slide
home base	left field	bunt
first	foul line	out
first base	pitcher	strike
play first	catcher	ball
shortstop	pop fly	home run
safe	fly ball	homer
outfield	tag	

Board games also can be used to enhance vocabulary; some are actually designed with this in mind. The variety of board games currently available enable the clinician to concentrate on many different facets of a child's difficulties. Some include sorting words according to categories, such as transportation, occupations, food, and appliances; others employ problem-solving activities, make use of verbal analogies and reasoning, and require inferential reasoning. It is also possible to devise simple board games using whatever category of lexical items is pertinent, such as coins *(penny, nickel, dime)* or sports events *(tennis, javelin)*. Properly used, these resources permit the speech-language pathologist to supply germane vocabulary to a child in a relevant context during periods of high motivation. The general vocabulary needed for a board game includes the following:

spin	win	dice
spinner	roll	tie
turn	jump over	go past go
man	king	pay the bank
forward	move	cut
back	shuffle	wind
lose	card	

During conversational exchanges with a child, the speech-language pathologist should note which words are used incorrectly or with an unintended nuance, and those that are labeled with a nonspecific indefinite pronoun or adjective *(that, this, thing)*. Typically, one may consider that children using such forms as demonstratives or indefinite pronouns demonstrate sophisticated mastery of the language. For hearing-impaired children, however, this may not be true. They tend to use such words as *that, this, these, those,* and *it* when they cannot recall the label due to vocabulary limitations.

By offering children proper labels when they use nonspecific terms or employ such strategies as "you know," they are supplied with the pertinent word at a psychologically appropriate time. During the next few utterances, the therapist should engineer a context that obliges the child to use the new item presented. Motivation is maximum, and the new word thus can be spoken immediately in a relevant communicative context.

Prepared vocabulary lists can augment the therapist's efforts. The one developed by Ling and Ling (1977), for example, contains 2,000 words used by normal-hearing children arranged according to frequency of use. Lists of word relationships (synonyms, antonyms, multiple meanings) also can serve as a jumping off point for a vocabulary program. Hearing-impaired children often employ words in a very narrow or specific sense, unaware that the same word in a different linguistic context can have a different meaning. The word *hot*, for example, can refer to heat, anger, excitement, proximity, theft, zealousness, or lust. Children who use this word only to convey the concept of excessive temperature have cut themselves off from a great deal of human communication.

Hearing-impaired children need a great deal of exposure and practice with idiomatic expressions if they are to be "with it" in conversation with their peers. As with metaphorical expressions, it is useless to literally decode the individual words to try to arrive at the intended meaning; one must learn through structured exposure in context. Phrases like "under the weather," "pain in the neck," and "chip on your shoulder" require such a context. Slang words such as "awesome," "excellent," or "gross" are not likely to be used by the adults in the child's world and may not have been heard often enough or clearly enough from their peers to be understood.

The latest craze, though seemingly unworthy of study, could lead to stimulating discussions that include interesting vocabulary words and grammatical constructions. For example, the 1990 "craze" of the Teenage Mutant Ninja Turtles encompasses unusual adjectives *(lean, slimy)*, humorous absurdities (jam and jellybean pizza), abstract concepts ("lean, green machine" describing the turtle body), and highly colorful vocabulary *(mutagen, ooze, master, sewer)*. In the 1970s "Wacky Stickers" were popular with 7-to-12-year-old children. Each sticker resembled a well-known product in color, shape, and design, but was labeled with an absurd sound-alike that applied a derogatory meaning to the product. For example, "Life" cereal was labeled "Lice" with corresponding insects drawn on the package; "Bold" detergent carried the name "Bald." These semantic absurdities provide the raw material for vocabulary expansion.

Words with multiple, frequently nonliteral meanings (e.g., *run*) also give these children a great deal of difficulty. They need to experience as much as possible the situations and varied contexts requiring the use of these different meanings ("running" for president; a "running" nose). Normal-hearing elementary schoolchildren have an obsession for riddles and jokes (Why is a room full of married people like an empty room? Because there is not a single person in it.) A typical feature of riddles is the multiple meaning that adds an absurd element.

In short, arriving at specific vocabulary targets for hearing-impaired children may seem on the surface a simple task, but one made much more complex by the all-encompassing nature of the problem. With so many gaps present, establishing priorities becomes critical. Each hearing-impaired child will demonstrate different capabilities and deficits, making it difficult to recommend a specific sequence of vocabulary goals. Vocabulary intervention is most effective when the child is motivated; therefore, the child's interests and needs must be explored. Beyond this, however, the focus should stay on the vocabulary items that can make the greatest difference in performance; that is, those words the world (school, home, and community) expects the child to know.

Classroom Management

Managing the vocabulary-deficient student in the regular classroom presents a challenge for the educator. When students enter the learning environment with delays of 6 months or more relative to peers, the potential arises for disruption in understanding and using written and spoken language. For these students, all language-based subjects become problematic. When reading is a component of the activity, the hearing-impaired student has difficulty competing on an equal basis because his or her reading comprehension is compromised much the same as the understanding of spoken language.

Careful preparation for lessons can become the best approach to managing this vocabulary lag. The classroom teacher and the academic support personnel need to closely coordinate a vocabulary acquisition program based on the lexicon required for the subject matter. The classroom teacher must identify the words stressed in the lessons, used on the spelling tests, or explained during class and transmit this information to support personnel. In the week preceding the planned use of the words, the support staff can introduce, familiarize, and reinforce the new vocabulary in a variety of activities and formats. Then when the child hears or sees the words during the actual lesson, he or she will understand the content more easily. In the weeks following the lesson, support personnel should keep the words "alive" through related activities.

In addition to assisting in the vocabulary learning process, the teacher can facilitate the transmission of information by using demonstration or other visual aids to support the verbal component. The student then can combine the familiar words with the visual support to glean the meaning of the utterance. For example, when giving instructions for a paper-and-pencil task, the teacher can simultaneously point to pertinent parts of the worksheet while presenting the information. Instructions can be paraphrased when the teacher checks that the class has understood the task. For example,

> *First presentation* (unmodified): "Read the incomplete sentences at the left below. Then read the lettered phrases at the right. In each blank, write the letter of the phrase that correctly completes that sentence. All the phrases will not be used."

> *Second presentation* (modified): "You have a sentence here [points] that has no ending. In the right column [points] you pick the best ending for this sentence. Two of them you will not use."

As spelling words are assigned, the teacher can insist that the meaning is learned as part of the spelling routine and used during the end of the unit test. As students learn vocabulary as part of a geography class, for instance, the teacher can insist that they not only memorize the meanings of words such as *tundra, fault, continental drift,* and *polar* but also be able to use the words in a meaningful sentence. The classroom brims with opportunities for expanding and broadening the vocabulary skills of these students. It is important for teachers to realize the important role they play in providing the meaningful context in which words are learned.

For students whose deficient vocabulary interferes with their ability to answer questions with the necessary specificity, the teacher can encourage less reliance on general, nonspecific designators (e.g., *this, that, thing, it*) and minimally provide a description of the object, person, action, or feeling being discussed. Once the descriptor is thrown into the discussion, the teacher can seize the opportunity to apply the specific label that was missing. Again the intent to communicate the information and the meaningful context are present, both necessary for lexical acquisition to occur.

SYNTAX/MORPHOLOGY

Remediation Considerations and Activities

The spoken syntax used by hearing-impaired children often appears superficially adequate, unlike that of deaf children. In face-to-face conversational interactions, hearing-impaired children can select any one of a number of potentially suitable linguistic structures to express a message. It is logical to assume that students will choose those forms with which they have had the most familiarity and success in the past. To facilitate accurate understanding of conversation, these children can access the normal linguistic redundancy of spoken language and situational context. In addition, during social conversation it is acceptable for participants to use syntactically unorthodox ways of transmitting the message, such as sentence fragments, gestural indicators, and run-on sentences; therefore, any minor inadequacies in the conversation of hearing-impaired students easily can be overlooked by peers, teachers, and service providers.

Syntactic problems become much more evident in the child's school performance where accuracy and formality supersede familiarity and efficiency. Although these deficits may not be readily obvious during social interaction, areas of misunderstanding or misuse readily come to light with sophisticated evaluation techniques or sampling procedures. Any morpho/ syntactic inadequacies in spoken language will be reflected in the language-based skills of reading and writing. Because of the ultimate impact on academic performance, service personnel must not only attend to those children showing clear deviations but also to those for whom the use of simplified grammar and syntax does not seriously interfere with their spoken communication. Table 11.6 suggests remedial and classroom objectives for morpho/syntactic improvement.

Early intervention plays a pivotal role, exposing young hearing-impaired children to age-appropriate morpho/syntactic structures at an optimal point in their development. A child more easily learns specific forms when they cognitively match his or her communicative intent. For example, normal-hearing toddlers begin to use word combinations to express relationships that are newly apparent to them. It is more difficult to assist older hearing-impaired children in utilizing the same variety of word combinations when cognitively they have far more complex interrelationships to express.

Additionally, adults begin to feel the effects of the linguistic age–chronological age mismatch and adjust their input to the child accordingly. When linguistic level matches what is typically expected from a child of a particular size or age, there is a better chance that the parent will respond with appropriately adapted input. Problems occur when the child's physical appearance, interests, and age conflict with language competence, resulting in adult uncertainty regarding which cues to attend to when determining input level. For example, the parent of a young child who misbehaves is much less likely to explain cause and effect with the clauses "If . . . , then . . ." or "When . . . , you will . . ." than the parent of a schoolchild. Yet the older hearing-impaired student may not have the language facility necessary to comprehend this age-appropriate, syntactically complex explanation, requiring instead the simplified version typically presented to a much younger child. Boothroyd (1982) describes this mismatch as developmental asynchrony, which can be avoided only by direct, intensive, early intervention.

A clear relationship exists between the syntactic problems of hearing-impaired children and the configuration and extent of a hearing loss. First,

TABLE 11.6 Remedial and Classroom Objectives for Morphological/
Syntactic Improvement

Speech/Language Therapy (objectives for child)	Classroom Communication Management (objectives for teacher)
Expand simple forms	Check comprehension of lecture and instruction
Self-monitor morphological endings	Paraphrase into simpler form
Recognize obligatory context and respond accordingly	Write assignments on board
Produce audible morphological endings	Give different grade for content and grammar
Increase flexible use of grammatical forms	

Note. From "Communication Management of the Mainstream Hearing-Impaired Student" by D. Brackett in *Hearing-Impaired Children in the Mainstream* (M. Ross, Ed.), 1990, Parkton, MD: York Press. Copyright 1990 by York Press. Reprinted by permission.

morphological endings are difficult to hear due their high-frequency nature and unstressed use in context. Therefore, when students monitor their own productions, they cannot determine if these morphological elements are present. Additionally, when the same elements occur in the speech of others, hearing-impaired students may not notice their presence, thus missing the obligatory linguistic context in these situations. Due to their lack of audibility, students have a limited opportunity to hear these morphological elements in meaningful contexts.

Based on the knowledge of when these problems exist, the therapist can devise remedial programs that will increase exposure in meaningful contexts. A key element is to linguistically load the interaction with many correct examples of the forms or structures in use. For example, one can read a story in past tense rather than present, or read it in present tense and have the child retell it in past. This especially good approach puts the child's utterance in a stressed obligatory context. He or she learns not only how to generate the form but when to use it. A naturally occurring external cue (past tense ending of the story or adult query) signals the student to use a particular form (past tense) in this context. Therefore, if learning the form is always paired with the context in which to use it, then the two will logically emerge together. Examples of additional activities follow:

1. Adapt a story to include *after* and *before* by putting two events together.

Original:

Mary was skipping down the street.

She saw her friend Jo duck into the store.

Mary tiptoed up to the store window and peaked inside.

There was Jo, buying the toy that Mary wanted for her birthday.

Adaptation:

Before Mary saw Jo, she was just skipping down the street.

After Mary saw Jo duck into the store, she tiptoed up to look in the store window.

2. Role play, using syntactic structures that are critical to the dialogue.

It is important to distinguish between those children who do not know the meaning of the morphological ending and those who know the meaning but omit the ending for acoustic reasons. Although the communicative behavior appears the same, the underlying reasons are different, leading to different management approaches (See Table 11.7).

Morphological endings ordinarily go unstressed in conversation; that is, they have weaker intensity than the words to which they are attached (e.g., the past tense /ed/). A hearing-impaired child has difficulty detecting the acoustic correlate of the suffix and therefore cannot learn its meaning easily. In addition, many function words, verb forms, and contractions are similarly unstressed in speech. In utterances such as "Where's he going?", "He's walked home," "Let's go in there," "He's got the boat"/"He's got a boat"/"He's got some boats," and "The teacher's in the room"/"the teacher's room," a hearing-impaired child has difficulty hearing the contracted and assimilated forms of the verbs, articles, and function words.

An additional complication for many hearing-impaired children is the high-frequency composition of many of these elements, which makes them much harder to detect. Because of this the hearing-impaired child will find it difficult to induce the correct grammatical rules from conversational samples and learn to employ them appropriately. Some of these elements are also very hard to speechread, such as the article *a*, the preposition *in*, and the /s/ and the /t/ endings, particularly in a high-front vowel environment where the lip opening is minimal.

Not only do these children have difficulty detecting specific linguistic elements, but they are in general exposed to a reduced complexity and quantity of relevant language input. The people in their environment commonly simplify their speech, emphasizing what the children can understand easily. Students thus will achieve a level of communicative competence just

TABLE 11.7 Alternative Reasons Behind Similar
Communicative Behaviors

Behavior	Reason	Management Suggestions
No use of plural /s/: "I saw two cat"	Does not know plural rule (LINGUISTIC)	Teach plural rule by example
No use of plural /s/: "I saw two cat"	Knows plural rule but consistently omits final /s/ because it is hard to hear (ACOUSTIC)	Discriminate plural vs. singular Produce plural vs. singular

adequate for talking to peers, teachers, and parents who can understand them. Being content with the fact that the child communicates results in an air of acceptance that in turn reduces exposure to new forms and encourages the child to remain at a lower level of syntactic performance.

A prime example of this exposure concept can be observed in the trouble hearing-impaired children experience trying to learn passive constructions. Conversation generally takes place in the active rather than passive voice because of English conversational constraints. Due to this lack of meaningful exposure to passive voice, therefore, the hearing-impaired child does not become fluent in its use. If the opposite were true, that conversation normally transpired in the passive voice ("The boy was bitten by the dog" rather than "The dog bit the boy"), the active construction would give hearing-impaired children the difficulty. The main focus of the therapeutic approach, therefore, should be *structured exposure to developmentally appropriate targets.*

The latter does not suggest that children be bombarded with conversation. To deduce the linguistic rules of a language, the enriched exposure children receive must be relevant to the nonlinguistic events they experience. Furthermore, such exposure must occur when children are developmentally ready and motivated to receive it.

Explaining a syntactic rule to a child does not teach the rule. In deciding how to denote past tense, people do not recite to themselves, "When the last sound in a word is voiced, a /d/ is added; if the last sound is unvoiced, /t/ is used, except when the last sound in the word is a /t/ or /d/

and the /ed/ ending is added"; they deduce the rule from their auditory/ linguistic experiences and judge its application in different situations by how it sounds. Until children have worked out the relationships between nonlinguistic and linguistic events or know what it is they want to communicate and the necessary linguistic forms to do so, the generalization or carryover to nontherapeutic situations will be minimal. The following example shows how an adult can expose the child to correct linguistic forms during the course of an ordinary conversation:

Child	*Adult*
"Where going?"	"I don't know. Do you know? Where *is* she going?"
"Yeh."	"She's going to get some soda. Where *is* he going?"
"He's going outside."	"Oh, he *is going* outside. *I'm going* outside, too. Where *are* you going?"
"I'm going outside, too."	"Let's go."

The creative clinician will find ample opportunities to contrive relevant experiences that facilitate learning specific linguistic rules. For example, if a child has difficulty comprehending or using one sentence embedded into another, offer a stimulus such as "The boy who was chasing the dog fell down" and ask the child to select from an array of pictures (a boy chasing a dog that falls, a dog chasing a boy who falls, and a boy and a dog both falling, etc.) the correct depiction of the event. After being exposed to a number of these tasks and responding correctly, the student can be asked to generate similar sentences when given a similar scenario. The goal is to expose the student to many relevant examples of the problematic linguistic structures and obligate him or her to utilize the form in their response. The child's response in the obligatory context gives a clue as to his or her ability to form and use the morpho/syntactic elements. The following diagram further illustrates this point:

EXPOSE	→ OBLIGATE	→ CHILD RESPONDS	→ ANALYZE RESPONSE
He went	"Tell *Tom*	"He come."	Incorrect tense formulation
He saw	what the	"He see."	Incorrect obligatory use
He chewed	boy *did.*"		
He sat		"He camed."	Incorrect tense formulation
		"He sawed."	Correct obligatory use
		"He went."	Correct tense formulation
		"He saw."	Correct obligatory use

In order for children to learn any syntactic construction that causes difficulty, they require repeated exposures to the construction in a meaningful situation. In the early stages of therapy, the clinician must increase the saliency of the input by exaggerating the stress, intonation, or duration with which specific linguistic constructions are expressed. The rate of input can be slowed to give the child a better opportunity to process the presence of the hard-to-perceive elements. The task is to encourage monitoring of spoken messages.

The type of language that students meet in reading differs from that used in oral communication. Therapeutic activities initially should stress auditory language development and then include written lessons based on progress in the latter. When the child can use the context of a reading lesson to deduce the meaning and usage of unknown forms, then reading assignments begin to play a major role in learning syntax.

Classroom Management

The greatest impact of delayed morpho/syntactic development is apparent in subject areas that require written-language responses. As hearing-impaired students record their thoughts on paper, they frequently eliminate verb endings, demonstrate poor noun-verb agreement, and utilize simplified syntax. Even when these forms emerge in their spoken language, they may find it hard to translate this spoken-language knowledge to written forms. As creative writing and essay questions make up part of every child's school experience, the classroom teacher must decide how to grade and correct the child's morpho/syntactic errors. If the focus of the lesson is to learn written language skills, then taking points off for such errors is appropriate. However, if written language is the vehicle by which the child expresses knowledge about content, then the grade should reflect the information learned by the student. An additional grade can be given for the accuracy of the child's grammar. To facilitate the conversion of spoken to written language, the teacher can encourage students to proof-read the written response aloud so they can hear the inaccuracies and modify the response accordingly.

Morpho/syntactic inadequacies are less apparent as students express themselves orally because the listener often unconsciously fills in the missing elements. As most students in mainstream settings can formulate an understandable message and relay it to adults and peers, the accuracy of the linguistic structure becomes less of an obstacle and in many cases is ignored. However, as students attempt to understand the overwhelmingly complex language used in classroom instruction, their delayed morpho/syntactic skills interfere with the successful transmission of the academic material. These students may not understand the subtle differences among subordinate conjunctions used in complex sentences (*after, although, as, whether, while, before*) and therefore not fully comprehend the intended meaning. Over time, these missed nuances and altered meanings lay down a foundation of misinformation and inadequate concepts.

Consider the following, presented verbatim by a 10th-grade teacher giving instructions to his class (in which a hearing-impaired child was enrolled) about the cancellation of a quiz and the scheduling of a test:

> We definitely will not have the quiz Monday. That's for sure. I want to finish what we're doing here today and I want to start the narrative. O.K. Reading that along with the oral questions based on the narrative. And we have one more listening exercise to do—comprehension in the workbook. After we finish this and we have the test, I'll review the chapter. Remember the bargain I made with you. Right. This test can count as two tests so I want to make sure that you are prepared for it. If not, some of you are going to bite the dust this semester.

Ten different information units are contained in this nine-sentence paragraph. It is easy to see how these syntactically complex instructions could cause confusion for a child with reduced language skills, even to the extent that essential information is missed.

To avoid this situation, the classroom teacher can check the students' understanding of a particularly complex concept by having them paraphrase the content. A yes/no question such as "Do you understand?" typically will produce an affirmative response, while a more probing *wh*-question should yield information one can assess for its appropriateness. Though this comprehension checking is ideal in terms of learning, it is awkward socially to single out the hearing-impaired student for this added attention. To avoid the stigma, the teacher can quickly tap many students regarding this concept, only one of which is the hearing-impaired child.

To further reduce chances of a misunderstanding, assignments should be written on the board and copied by the students. Then assignments not handed in or wrong assignments completed can be attributed to poor study habits, lack of interest, or inadequate organization rather than to comprehension errors.

LANGUAGE USAGE

Remediation Considerations and Activities

Learning to use language means learning to make inferences about the differences in social and contextual situations and then how to code these differences with unique linguistic forms. Ordinarily children learn the proper use of a linguistic form as it occurs spontaneously in the speech around them. Such expectations do not hold for hearing-impaired children, however; their exposures are insufficiently audible, diversified, or frequent to permit unconsciously deducing the rules of language usage. They may not know the proper linguistic form to request, state, invite, threaten, or cajole, or how to modify the expressions in different situations for listeners with different degrees of prior knowledge. Objectives for improving these skills both in therapy and in the classroom appear in Table 11.8.

An effective procedure for enhancing and facilitating language usage is to arrange role-playing activities, with the clinician periodically switching roles with the child so as to generate correct usage models for him or her. By simulating actual situations, the student can practice the modifications required for the effective transmission of information. For example, the student has lost a library book. He tells (a) a friend, (b) a parent, and (c) the librarian. For each situation the child needs to adapt the tone of voice, the intent (convince, negate), and the actual language used as interaction occurs regarding the topic of the lost book. To the friend, the student may try to lessen the severity of the problem by calling it a "dumb book" and indicating a "Who cares?" attitude. During interaction with the parent, the student's belligerence may be apparent as he states his innocence. When telling the librarian, the student should be apologetic and suggest a method of "payback" to compensate for losing the book.

Specific practice in the subskills inherent in such a task may be necessary to call the child's attention to the salient point. To become flexible in using language to express intent, for example, the student could try the following exercises:

1. Ask for an object in several different ways:
   "I want the _____."
   "Would it be possible for me to have _____?"
   "Can I have _____?"
   "I can't have _____, can I?"
   "Do you think I could have _____?"
2. Direct another child to get off their chair:
   "Stand up."
   "It's time to stand up."
   "Please stand up."
   "Who wants to stand up?"
   "Can you get out of my chair, please?"
3. Negate a request:
   "No way!"
   "I won't do it."
   "Not on your life!"

TABLE 11.8 Remedial and Classroom Objectives
for Pragmatic Improvement

Speech/Language Therapy (objectives for child)	Classroom Communication Management (objectives for teacher)
Learn rules of conversational appropriateness	Explain "teacher talk" style at beginning of the year
Adapt speech to the listener	Insist that student maintains topic
Learn a variety of ways to ask, state, direct	Require child to assume responsibility for making him/herself understood
Learn colloquialisms and slang	
Adhere to obligatory contexts	Insist on adherence to noninterruption rules

Note. From "Communication Management of the Mainstream Hearing-Impaired Student" by D. Brackett in *Hearing-Impaired Children in the Mainstream* (M. Ross, Ed.), 1990, Parkton, MD: York Press. Copyright 1990 by York Press. Reprinted by permission.

"Maybe I'll do it later."
"I don't want to do it."
"Not now."

Additional practice may be required to learn strategies for encoding the emotional coloration of an utterance—fear, sarcasm, pleasure, politeness, negativism, ingratiation, or boasting. As students gain control over these skills, they should be able to vary them at will. The next step involves learning when to use these emotional variations, which implies an understanding of community mores on respect and authority. For example, children typically afford adults respect in their interactions; adults address certain other adults respectfully or reverentially because of their status or profession. The hearing-impaired student may have acquired some knowledge of the "power" hierarchy through life experiences but could remain unaware of the communication modifications that reflect these status differences.

Hearing-impaired children usually need further practice in assessing the listener's knowledge of a discussion topic. In normal conversation the speaker takes a quick assessment of the listener's potential for understanding and makes the first adjustment in the language used. As the listener indicates understanding, the speaker can further adapt by eliminating unnecessary descriptors or adding further explanations as necessary. For example, to a knowledgeable listener one might say, "Mary, as she was driving to the mall, had a car accident." To someone unfamiliar, one would adjust the remark to say, "Mary, my friend from school, was driving to Oak Park Mall when she had a car accident." Hearing-impaired students frequently remain at a level of function similar to a much younger normal-hearing child; that is, one at which utterances are produced with little forethought as to the listener's perspective.

Adaptations such as these require sensitivity to the indicators of communicative breakdown. If the listener looks confused, raises an eyebrow, frowns, says "What?", or responds incorrectly, the speaker can assume that the message needs revision. Learning to read these signals, though, takes practice. Further, knowing *why* the message is inadequate comes after experiencing many examples of breakdown that successfully resolve. Due to many instances when their own verbal interactions have failed, hearing-impaired children may have learned a set of rules that only marginally meet the requirements of the general population.

By the early elementary years, most normal-hearing children are aware of conversational conventions because of the gradual shaping process imposed by their parents. Although three- and four-year-olds are allowed to violate many conversational taboos, such as interrupting, shifting topics randomly, and not responding in obligatory contexts, thereafter most parents gradually stop tolerating this behavior, which in turn modifies the child's interactive style.

Many such conventions are regionally specific. For example, in the New York City area it is considered acceptable in conversation to interrupt or minimally begin one's response before the speaker has finished as long as the breach continues on the same topic. A slow, thoughtful answer, appropriate in the Midwest, is considered disruptive to the flow of conversation in the fast-paced interaction style of the Northeast.

These conventions, so easily learned (though selectively used) by normal-hearing children, elude a hearing-impaired student for several reasons. First, due to reduced access to sound, he or she is less likely to be as readily aware of these instances of conversational shaping. Second, parents of hearing-impaired children are less likely to apply restrictions stringently, if at all, due to their joy in the child's ability to communicate through spoken language. Therefore, when hearing-impaired children enter school, they may seem at a conversational disadvantage relative to normal-hearing peers. Remaining at an immature level of conversational competence may disrupt peer relationships, as classmates object to the insensitive, egocentric style the child utilizes.

Classroom Management

The student who does not understand the verbal adaptations for group interaction is ill-prepared for the classroom experience. No longer can he or she concentrate on and monitor the conversational and pragmatic nuances of a single speaker. The group setting requires cognizance of all the potential speakers and a readiness to shift reference, style, and register as the speaker changes. Conversational adaptability is especially important in the seminar or discussion classes typical of secondary education. The classroom teacher becomes a conversation facilitator by monitoring the appropriateness of the hearing-impaired student's responses and providing constructive feedback regarding maladaptive behavior.

Hearing-impaired students may present as belligerent, flippant, or rude due to unawareness of registers that should be differentially applied. Instead of penalizing the student for what appears to be maladaptive behavior, the teacher can pull the child aside, explain the reason for the abrupt reaction to the utterance, and demonstrate a more appropriate way of saying the same thing. Support personnel should be notified so that individual sessions can include practice in utilizing appropriate registers during simulated situations.

Students who lack the social language required for effectively initiating social interactions may find themselves isolated from their peers and feeling ostracized from the group. It takes only a few rejections or failed overtures to convince one of these students that he or she is unworthy to be a friend. As support personnel work on improving initiation strategies, the classroom teacher can engineer positive interaction through class projects and team responsibilities. For example, the hearing-impaired student could be put in charge of a team and given responsibility for organizing members and parceling out duties. As with normal-hearing classmates, this student additionally would require assistance in carrying out leadership duties in a nonconfrontational manner.

Misperceptions and half-heard comments can give hearing-impaired students the impression that other students are making negative comments about them or calling them names. The student can choose to confront the alleged tormentor or ignore the remarks. The former approach (i.e., directly dealing with the students involved) can lead to unfortunate misunderstandings. The hearing-impaired student, lacking flexibility or variety in language, may not have the necessary conversational sophistication to convey angry thoughts. At this point the teacher should intervene, before students resort to physical means of expressing themselves. Support personnel should be notified if this behavior occurs regularly and begin practice sessions on verbally expressing emotional extremes.

The ineffective respondent in class discussions or exercises poses a somewhat different problem for the classroom teacher. Full participation in all classroom activities is certainly a goal, but when the student volunteers answers that are not just wrong but on a different topic, then the teacher has a responsibility to focus the situation. Comments such as "We're not talking about the assembly now. The topic is ___ " serve to direct the student's attention. Further, using visual support, such as writing key words on the board, may reduce the chances for this off-topic behavior to occur.

Explaining verbal classroom routines becomes the teacher's duty during the first week. Some teachers adopt an indirect approach that lets the student decipher these routines through experience. As the weeks and months progress and the teacher reacts negatively to calling out answers and talking among peers during lessons, students deduce the implied limitations. However, a teacher who offers direct concrete guidelines reduces the potential for confusion in the mind of the hearing-impaired student.

Valuable prognostic information comes from one-to-one presentations. Poor test scores in general usually suggest the child needs an intensive preview and review paradigm, which familiarizes the child with lesson content and specific vocabulary prior to the classroom presentation and then gives him or her an opportunity to review the lesson subsequently. The child's behavior when the test paragraphs become increasingly difficult often can help the teacher understand the genesis of problems such as inattentiveness, disruptiveness, and "borrowing" answers from the child in the next seat.

The language used for instructional purposes is more complex than conversational language. Not only is the vocabulary necessarily advanced, because the information relates to concept development, but the sentence structure often is difficult to decode. In addition, such language requires a level of abstraction missing from general conversation. Children listening must understand references to past topics, make predictions of outcome, or follow descriptions of relationships. When hearing-impaired children listen to a lecture on an unfamiliar topic, they not only confront the lesson's content but also the unknown vocabulary and complicated syntax used to express it. When prepared for the topic through vocabulary preview, they can expend more effort later in processing the lecture's content.

12
_____

Educational and Psychosocial Management

Mainstreaming hearing-impaired students into regular education classrooms assumes they can benefit from contact with normal-hearing peers. The associated advantages must be sufficient to override any
potential negative factors, such as the acoustic environment, the teacher/
student ratio, and untrained teachers. The anticipated communicative,
social, and academic benefits derive from the behavioral models and expectations of the regular classroom.

Hearing-impaired students placed in regular education settings should
arrive with entry skills that enable them to learn from the examples provided by peers. Communication skills can advance by listening to and
interacting with normal-hearing students. Social skills can develop by comparing responses to those of others, judging their appropriateness, and
modifying behaviors accordingly. Academic performance can improve by
catching the competitive spirit of the classroom and striving to emulate
classmates' accomplishments.

Expectation plays a large role in the benefits derived from a regular
classroom experience. The mainstreamed hearing-impaired student with
the requisite entry skills should establish a higher functional level of academic performance as a result of these increased expectations. The oppor-

tunity to participate in age-appropriate activities and social routines should result in a level of communicative and social interactions that might not occur in a more restricted learning environment. Over time these expectations should help establish higher levels of habitual performance from these students.

EDUCATIONAL MANAGEMENT

The educational management of mainstreamed hearing-impaired students can be approached in a manner similar to communication management; that is, direct remedial work on deficit areas as well as concentration on the child's performance in the classroom. Both the regular educator, accountable for the child's primary education, and the special educator, responsible for remediating documented weaknesses, share equal responsibility in this management process. The commitment of both these educators will determine if the educational management program is to succeed.

Although the special educator typically will participate in IEP development sessions, the regular educator often cannot be freed from teaching responsibilities to attend these meetings. This void becomes even more pronounced when the student reaches middle school or junior high and many teachers share the educational responsibility. In addition to the difficulty freeing them all to attend the meetings, it is hard to gain the same level of commitment from each. If the classroom teachers cannot attend the planning meeting, they should provide written observations and recommendations. The program subsequently developed, as well as notations of concerns and specific management needs, can be conveyed to the entire regular education staff at a later time. This pattern of communication allows all who are involved and responsible to understand the conditions necessary for success in the mainstream experience.

According to Birch (1976), every successful mainstream program for hearing-impaired students includes an academic support component. The academic support staff has a multifaceted job: to support the regular class curriculum through a preview/review strategy, to teach strategies for approaching the academic material, and to fill in missing information from the subject areas. This supportive service derives from the premise that the hearing-impaired child being educated in the regular classroom requires supplemental support in order to participate fully in classroom activities.

Normal-hearing students can listen to a teacher's presentation and glean the general concept of the lesson without having to decode each word in the sentence. They apply their familiarity with language to the job of learning content-specific vocabulary. Their rich associations allow them to determine meaning by tapping their knowledge of similar-sounding or related words. The hearing-impaired student, on the other hand, enters the learning situation at a disadvantage because of communication deficits due to reduced language input. This student must work to understand the overall intent of the lesson or the concept being presented and at the same time discern the meaning of the topic-related vocabulary and the more general words that make up the material. Having restricted word associations causes the hearing-impaired student to attack each word as a totally new vocabulary item, thereby increasing the processing time and decreasing the possibility of comprehending the total concept in the depth achieved by the other children.

The following statement from a lecture about the stars succinctly illustrates the problem: "It is possible to experience the excitement of astronomy by visiting a planetarium." The normal-hearing student, perhaps familiar with other words ending in *-rium* could deduce that a *planetarium* is a "room" for *planets* just as a *solarium* is a sunroom and an *aquarium* is a place for water. He or she also can figure out that the word *astronomy* must be the "the study of ___" from the knowledge of other *-onomy* words *(economy, autonomy)* and that related *astro-* words *(astrology, astronaut)* have to do with "star." The student likely would already be familiar with one of the topic-related words *(astronomy)* and could then use that knowledge to search for the meaning of the other key word *(planetarium)*.

The hearing-impaired student, however, must first decide what the sentence is saying before beginning to decipher the meaning of the topic-related vocabulary. The process goes as follows:

Original Phrase		*Simplified Meaning*
"It is possible"	means	you can
"to experience"	means	feel
"the excitement"	means	how exciting
"by visiting"	means	by going to

After decoding the basic sentence, the meaning of the unfamiliar topic-related vocabulary can be addressed. Two clues as to the meaning derive from the linguistic structure of the sentence: (a) the word *astronomy* must be a noun (thing), and (b) *planetarium* must be a singular noun referring to a nonspecific place or person. As the student probably does not have a fund of related words to draw on, he or she will have to acquire the meaning of the key words by nonverbal means such as pictures or charts. Thus, using the previous example, the words *astronomy* and *planetarium* could be taught by using visual aids.

Previewing the content material to familiarize the student with the lesson-vocabulary and to introduce associated words will reduce the effects of the communication problem on academic performance. In the preceding example, the academic support staff would replicate the process that normal-hearing students use to discern meaning; that is, apply prefixes and suffixes to generate related words. For example, the following word relationships could be developed: planet—planetarium; astro—asteroid, astronaut, astronomy, astronomer, astrology. Richness of meaning can be generated not only by defining the actual word that will appear in the lesson (e.g., *astronomy*) but also by discussing many words associated with it (e.g., *space, planets, aliens, rockets, lunar modules, sun spots, atmosphere, astronaut, astronomer*).

Syntactic structures can be used to expand vocabulary. The *-er* ending indicates people who do something (*astronomer, painter, astrologer*), as does *-ist* (*pianist, chemist, cellist*). The *-naut* ending indicates people who travel, as in *astronaut, aquanaut,* and *cosmonaut.*

Previewing vocabulary and concepts allows hearing-impaired students to compete on a more equal footing with their peers during the presentation of a lesson. After the topic has been presented, a review should follow in order to solidify the student's understanding. Rather than reviewing the concepts and vocabulary only within the context used in class, they should be generalized to other situations. Minimally, they should appear in discussions of other topics being introduced and should be listed on cards for random review during the next few weeks and months. Having learned the topic-related vocabulary, the student will have strong associations of concepts and prefixes and suffixes to apply to the process of deriving meaning from new vocabulary.

In general, the academic tutor reviews prospective lessons with the classroom teacher and then previews them with the student, discussing content and emphasizing new concepts and new language with simplified examples. After the classroom teacher has presented the lessons, the tutor reviews the material with the student to ensure mastery. The new language and concepts must be used frequently by the support staff as other topics are discussed to ensure that the new material becomes "automatic" and available for retrieval on demand. Subjects such as language arts (literature, grammar), social studies (history, civics, ethnology, geography), science, and math (word problems) usually need previewing, due to the dependence on language to convey their content.

The preview/review approach to academic support may prove difficult to implement because of the time required for coordination. Coordination time should be written into the IEP under the section labeled "management needs." Support staff and the regular educator must designate a time to meet each week to review upcoming material in all language-based subjects. The support teacher will need to digest the material and ascertain those areas of potential difficulty for the hearing-impaired student. Specific concepts and vocabulary will become the basis of the preview/review program. Additional areas will be targeted as the previewer notices student deficits.

The success of the support program rests largely on the coordination between the special and regular educator. The more information the classroom teacher can give regarding the student's knowledge of the topic, the easier it will be for the academic support staff to specifically adapt the program. However, the special educator must realize that the hearing-impaired student is just one of about 25 in the class, making it exceedingly difficult for the teacher to recount all the details of a particular student's grasp of a topic. The preview/review approach to academic support offers students a comprehensive understanding of topic areas.

Another approach to academic support entails surveying homework assignments to determine areas of difficulty. Although this approach does address some of the most obvious deficits, it is merely a surface analysis and less effective than preview/review.

The most prevalent version of academic support focuses on helping the student study for quizzes and tests. The service provider can implement this approach easily, and it requires only minimal contact with the classroom teacher. However, it represents a "band-aid" approach, resulting in short-term learning rather than long-term mastery.

Support programs often take on an identity of their own, with separate curricula designed to remediate particular academic deficits. Instead of using the regular classroom curriculum and analyzing it for particular pitfalls, the special educator may spend time teaching strategies for test taking, for solving math word problems, for using context to gain meaning, and for general problem solving. Though these skills may be useful, teaching them in isolation does not help the student take full advantage of the regular classroom learning environment. A combination of the two approaches—academic support and skill remediation—may be the most effective assistance outside of the regular classroom.

CLASSROOM ACADEMIC MANAGEMENT

The academic support program comprises only one part of educational management. Mainstreamed students receive their primary education in the regular classroom, following the curriculum prescribed for that class. As long as they are mainstreamed with normal-hearing students, their academic performance must justify this placement. This does not mean that these students will demonstrate average achievements in all subjects, but they should mesh with existing groups within the classroom.

Major curriculum changes should not be necessary, given the prerequisite entry skills discussed earlier. The need for such changes would bring into question the suitability of a child's mainstream placement. Within each regular classroom the range of academic performance typically spans 2 years above and below the stated grade level. The appropriately placed hearing-impaired child should be able to function adequately within this range of performance.

When teachers present content material, they assume that normal-hearing students have understood most of what was presented. With hearing-impaired students, however, one can assume that they have not received the same amount of information as their normal-hearing peers, automatically leading to learning less of the material. The special and regular educator must jointly establish some system for tracking content learning. Herein lies one of the potential pitfalls of mainstreaming, as being aware of each student's learning rate is difficult for the regular educator except through tests. Yet waiting for the results of quizzes and tests takes too long. Intervention must occur during the period between the initial introduction of the material in the classroom and the final test on the topic. At this early stage in the process the academic support staff can facilitate the expected learning by the time the class completes the unit.

When mainstreamed children perform satisfactorily, school administrators often suggest withdrawing services (because the student's problems have been eliminated). They instead should view the fact the student is doing well as a demonstration of the efficacy of the total support program; withdraw one component of it and performance will decrease. Unlike normal-hearing students, who once their deficits have been remediated may function with the rest of the class unassisted, hearing-impaired students' needs persist through high school. Regardless of the intensity of the remedial program, hearing loss is not going to improve. These children will continue to miss portions of the orally presented material and thus will require continued compensatory programs.

Certain school activities/environments seem especially problematic for the hearing-impaired student (see Table 12.1). The underlying reasons that inappropriate behaviors occur primarily involve auditory, social, and communicative factors, any of which can be affecting the student at a particular time. Effective in-service training of the classroom teacher can resolve many such problems. Others require more direct intervention.

Many potential problems can be avoided prior to the first day of school by offering an in-service program on the unique needs of the mainstreamed hearing-impaired student. This preliminary exposure helps teachers develop an initial set of expectations that will affect the way they feel about having the student in class and how they present the situation to the other students. If teachers feel comfortable and supported in this

TABLE 12.1 Potential Problem Areas During Regular Classroom or School Activities

Situation	Problems	Cause	Solution
Hallway	Takes off amplification after every class No response to greetings	Embarrassment over wearing personal or classroom amplification Unable to hear in noisy reverberant hallways	Purchase the least obvious form of FM unit Peers and teachers need to be in close proximity to converse Inservice peers as to function and purpose of amplification
Changes in teachers	Does not attend to a specific speaker Does not perform for a specific teacher Refuses to use classroom amplification	Teacher presentation style may interfere Seating varies Classroom acoustics may vary Knowledge of subject may vary	Each teacher needs inservice training regarding class presentation and use of FM Analysis of classroom acoustics for each room Provide in-depth tutoring in subject areas
Spelling	Poor performance after studying Has words numbered wrong	Does not hear the word or all of its components Studied visually while test was presented orally Words presented without linguistic context	Use word-context-word approach during test Student should study how the words sound and how they are spelled Teacher should present words close to the child or use FM system

TABLE 12.1   (Continued)

Situation	Problems	Cause	Solution
Spelling (cont.)			Give the student a chance to look up by saying "number six is—"
Language-based subjects	Does excellent special projects, but poor daily work in social studies and science Does well in selecting correctly spelled words, but poor in understanding what they mean Does well in reading, but poor on questions related to passage	Poor reading comprehension affects all subjects requiring reading Underdeveloped vocabulary Limited experiential base	Preview or review vocabulary and concepts during support period Work on language comprehension during speech or language sessions and academic support Material used in subject areas can be adapted for remedial purposes and will help carryover
Class discussion	Unaware of previous answers given Asks the same question again Does not participate	Problem determining who is speaking By the time the student has turned to the speaker, he may have missed a portion of the answer Reticent to speak in class Has not understood the discussion	Designate speaker by name Reiterate the pertinent answers given in class Summarize discussion at conclusion Preview vocabulary in support program

TABLE 12.1 (Continued)

Situation	Problems	Cause	Solution
Test taking	Poor performance in comparison to class participation Does whole page wrong Asks many questions regarding what is expected	Has had assistance in preparing for class from resource teacher Wording of the question is different than child is used to Looks at the page and guesses at what he is supposed to do Not read or understood instructions	Give test outside of class with extended time Keep questions short and succinct Allow support personnel to reword questions using simplified vocabulary and syntax Have student demonstrate that he understands instructions
Reading group	Does not know where to begin reading when another child has finished Repeats the same answer already given by another child Reluctant to read out loud	Difficulty following auditorily along, since his eyes are on the printed page Speech intelligibility poor	Aim the microphone at the child who is reading Reiterate the last sentence or phrase that was read: "John—start after 'and he ran down the street'."
Classroom lecture on specific content material	Poor attention Offers inappropriate answers Gets related answers wrong on work sheets or tests	Difficulty hearing due to speaker-listener distance or noise Poor language skills	Use of FM unit to counteract the negative effects of noise and distance Teacher can use visual support in the form of demonstration or writing key words or topic changes on the blackboard

TABLE 12.1 (Continued)

Situation	Problems	Cause	Solution
Classroom lecture (cont.)			Give child an outline with main ideas portrayed that provide him with the framework for understanding
Independent desk work	Wants teacher's help Does not know what to do on his own Does not complete work Copies from seatmate	Used to having an adult assist in resource room Poor reading skills affecting the understanding of instruction No confidence in own ability Takes longer to process the language or reading material due to immature language system	Work on the vocabulary of directions during support program Support personnel and parents should be aware of problems and encourage independent work done with maximum effort
Group projects	Does not offer ideas Not selected as group member	Poor speech intelligibility Prior failure during group interaction causes reticence Difficulty following group discussion, especially during planning sessions when the pace of information sharing is rapid	Teacher can assign students to groups to eliminate selection process Support personnel can prepare student for the topic and assist as a resource for information

TABLE 12.1 (Continued)

Situation	Problems	Cause	Solution
Peer-peer social interaction	Isolated Class clown On periphery of social groups Physical interaction rather than verbal	Poor self-image Difficulty following conversation with 2 or more people	Practice verbal conversational entry skills Encourage activities or sports in which one-to-one is possible Provide opportunities for interaction with other hearing impaired, to discuss problems
Homework	Does wrong assignment Does not do assignment Gets all homework correct, but all class work wrong	Difficulty hearing the assignment due to paper shuffling and talking Not aware that an assignment has been given Assistance with homework in resource room or at home Did not choose to do assignment	Write all assignments on the board to prevent confusion Help student set priorities so he can find time for homework and extracurricular activities When student has had help with homework, it should be so indicated
Announcements over loudspeaker	Not aware of announcements, i.e., changes, etc. Asks question later on the same information already presented	Difficulty hearing poorly amplified speech Has to rely on auditory information alone	Assign a "buddy" who can explain announcements face-to-face Teacher can reiterate pertinent information when it is completed

TABLE 12.1 (Continued)

Situation	Problems	Cause	Solution
Assembly	Inattentive to speaker At conclusion, does not know content	Difficulty hearing due to speaker-listener distance Distance from the speaker prohibits speech reading Limited language competency affects understanding of lecture	Primary speaker can use FM microphone in addition to PA microphone Student should sit as close as possible to the speaker Preview of assembly content by support personnel
Physical education	Trouble understanding instructions Always follower Does not know game rules	Acoustic conditions poor Difficult hearing the instructions Never heard rules explained close up	Teacher should stand close to the student during the instructions to counter the poor listening conditions Use FM system whenever the activity allows Preview rules and vocabulary by support personnel

Note. From "The Hearing-Impaired Child in Regular Schools" by A. B. Maxon and D. Brackett, 1987, *Seminars in Speech and Language, 8*, pp. 402–403. Copyright 1987 by Thieme Medical Publishers. Reprinted by permission.

effort, they will transmit an aura of acceptance to all their students. If, however, uncertain of their responsibilities teachers react in a "different" way to the hearing-impaired student, a pattern of behavior may take hold that will be difficult to modify in the future.

Specifically, teachers bear the same responsibility for educating the hearing-impaired student as the other students in the class; therefore, the same level of expected performance, including grading, must be applied to each. By establishing this common reference for the parent and teacher (i.e., that the student will be compared to normal-hearing classmates), all participants in the process will understand the comments made by the teacher on the child's progress. Ultimately this information is much more useful than comments such as "Justin is doing wonderfully for a hearing-impaired child."

The initial orientation to these management needs should be only the first of regularly scheduled in-service sessions for the teachers who have direct contact with the student throughout the school year. Having an "expert" available for consultation on an as-needed basis can relieve teachers' anxiety over tackling a new situation for which they may feel unprepared. (A complete description of in-service training is presented in chapter 13.)

PSYCHOSOCIAL MANAGEMENT

As noted previously, one of the benefits of a mainstreamed education lies in exposing the hearing-impaired child to the appropriate social models of normal-hearing students and to the age-appropriate social expectations of the teacher. The premise of social mainstreaming states that exposure to social behavior that is within normal range will cause the student to emulate this behavior rather than behavior idiosyncratic to a handicapped population. Direct and indirect intervention may be necessary to facilitate this social learning process. Paralleling the communication management model, psychosocial management requires remedial work to develop new skills and classroom management to foster the refinement and reinforcement of newly learned skills.

Direct work on social skill development can take two separate formats: group discussions and individual therapy. The first functions to increase self-awareness. The group most appropriately would include hearing-impaired students from similar educational settings who might be experiencing similar feelings of low self-esteem and confused identity. With a dynamic group leader, it is possible to share these feelings and generate potential solutions. Some commercially available social skills programs include pictures of difficult interactive situations that can apply to any child with a handicapping condition. The leader might start off with a statement explaining how this situation applied to him- or herself when young and then encourage children to respond by posing the question, "How about you?"

Children at the elementary level may have difficulty expressing their feelings due to language deficits unless concrete situations are used. Older students present a different set of problems. Although much more aware of their feelings and in many cases better equipped to express them (albeit simply), they may for adolescent reasons be reluctant to do so. One can glean some insight into their perception of the world and their place in it from the advice they give to others. Thus a project to develop an "advice" book for hearing-impaired students in the mainstream can prove enlightening as to their own feelings as well as potentially useful to others. The adult can "prime the pump" with statements such as "It must be difficult to hear everything that teachers say in the classroom." The concerns expressed can be translated into questions (e.g., "What should I do if the teacher writes on the board and talks at the same time?"). Multiple responses to each statement should be recorded so that the students realize more than one way exists to handle any given problem.

Service providers can help the student develop a realistic view of his or her strengths and weaknesses by discussing future plans and expectations. Students who have experienced only mainstreamed education may lack awareness of personal characteristics that could affect their ability to function in certain occupations. Most of these students have been encouraged for years to consider themselves on equal footing with their normal-hearing peers, a positive perception while trying to compete in school but not necessarily when trying to develop a realistic life view. For example, it is not uncommon to find an adolescent planning a career in an occupation that requires hearing (e.g., airline pilot). It is important to create a realistic outlook that can serve to redirect but not discourage the student's aspirations.

Parents and professionals, in an effort to protect children from the harsh realities of life, may avoid discussions about some of the more difficult aspects of being hearing-impaired, thereby depicting the world as more accepting of differences than it is. Using successful hearing-impaired adults as speakers, people who have experienced both the positive and negative aspects of life, provides students with effective role models. The experiences of these hearing-impaired adults can trigger discussions that otherwise may be awkward to introduce. Importantly, the discussion also must generate strategies for handling these painful situations when they arise.

In addition to the group discussion format, an individual counseling program can focus on practicing, in a nonthreatening setting, potentially difficult decision-making and interaction scenarios. In these sessions students can rehearse dialogues and have their body language and facial expressions critiqued. Social skills curricula can provide a place to begin, with other scenarios specific to the hearing-impaired population added as necessary. This direct approach allows participants to address issues such as independence and responsibility in learning and social situations. The degree of growth in any of these areas depends on the cooperation of the parents and other significant adults in the child's life. Once parents realize the need for this intervention, they can be allies, agents for change, sources of encouragement. With parental resistance, however, change may only be effected in the school environment.

Responsibility and independence take on a new role for older students as they prepare for adulthood in a hearing world. No longer can they be concerned only about themselves; they must become keenly aware of the way their behavior affects others at home, school, and in the workplace. How students view themselves can color their response to peer pressure and their career choice.

Helping hearing-impaired students avoid prolonged adolescence requires the joint efforts of parents and teachers, and begins when these children are preschoolers. Efforts at instilling independence, within the realm of the child's abilities, can commence at age 2 or 3 with home responsibilities. Making decisions and living by the results should start as soon as the concept is maturationally present. Understanding the logical consequences for unmet responsibilities produces adults who understand their role in the world of work and friendship.

A child's self-concept and feelings of belonging intertwine more closely with peer relationships than those established with teachers, particularly as he or she matures. When working with older hearing-impaired children, it is not unusual to have the best management frustrated because they feel that wearing a hearing aid or an FM system will set them apart and make them "different" from their peers. Objective demonstrations of superior auditory abilities with amplification carry very little weight compared to what the child believes his peers will think of him if he has to utilize some device.

Actually, the best time to observe interactions with classmates is not in the classroom but in the hall or at lunch, recess, or free play. These unstructured situations provide a vehicle for ascertaining group status as well as how the other children deal with and talk to the hearing-impaired child. Is he or she included as a full partner in the games? Does he or she have a special friend? Do normal-hearing students talk to the child at all? If so, is it in whispered or shouted monosyllables accompanied by gestures? Normal-hearing children may unconsciously develop a system of communication based on their experiences in trying to get a message across to a hearing-impaired child.

Teachers can assist in these peer interactions by opening the door for more to occur during classroom activities. Further, they can help normal-hearing students modify their speech to the hearing-impaired child through example and, if necessary, a frank discussion about any changes noted that are negative instead of positive.

Part of functioning in the classroom depends on the student's ability to understand the social routines that govern the orderly flow of activity.

The educational day divides unevenly into unstructured, transitional, and instructional activities. In addition to exhibiting socially appropriate behavior when direct instruction is the focus, the student also must become aware of acceptable interaction styles for transitional periods between lessons. Typically as the class moves from lesson to lesson, there is less formal time in which the students can interact verbally with one another, basically to "shift gears."

Usually in the first few days of school, the teacher demarcates the limits of behavior for the instructional, transition, and unstructured intervals. Acceptable interaction styles for instructional periods are usually the easiest for the hearing-impaired student to recognize, as the activities are primarily teacher-directed with structured student responses required. Teachers have requirements regarding how students acceptably gain attention, with handraising being the most often observed (with or without the teacher's name attached). Although calling out answers is unacceptable in many large class situations, it becomes necessary when signaled by the teacher through questions without a person designated ("The first astronaut to walk on the moon was who?") or an unnatural pause combined with expectant look ("The composer of the "1812 Overture" was [pause/look]?"). Unless the teacher nonverbally indicates a particular student, anyone in the class can accept the invitation to answer it. If the teacher frames the question so that only one person in the class can answer ("Who knows the name of the first astronaut to walk on the moon?"), then calling out an answer is inappropriate.

Teachers also use attention-focusing rituals that students must recognize if they are expected to integrate behaviorally with the class. During unstructured intervals throughout the day, the teacher may employ visual attention-getters such as standing up at the front of the room or flicking the lights. Auditory signals include clearing the throat, banging on the desk, whispering, or elevating the intensity level of his or her voice.

In the upper grades, the constraints of the subject matter may impose an unusual structure on the classroom. Science labs, foreign language class, shop/home economics, and seminars have a built-in structure that the student must grasp, either through observation, peer query, or direct teacher questioning. When students apply previous knowledge regarding instructional periods to these unconventional structures, their behavior is viewed negatively by teachers and peers. Support personnel may need to heighten their students' awareness of the differences among classroom organizations. Flexibility on the student's part becomes a necessary characteristic if he or she will be able to adjust to different teachers' styles, classroom formats, and instructional demands.

Socially appropriate behavior is intricately conjoined with social communication skills. If hearing-impaired students do not overhear the comments of peers or misinterpret their meaning, they may be unaware of the social hierarchy that exists in the classroom. Cliques commonly structure the social dynamics of the classroom. Although it would be better for all children if these exclusionary groups did not exist, the reality says they do; therefore, the hearing-impaired student must recognize them for harmony to exist in the classroom. This observation does not suggest that hearing-impaired students should ingratiate themselves to all factions in order to feel a part; instead, they must be aware of the undercurrents that may affect their interactions.

The hearing-impaired student may seem to exhibit physically aggressive tendencies when placed in an adversarial relationship with a peer. Rather, as noted previously, the student simply may lack the communicative sophistication to express arguments or displeasure adequately in an other than physical way. In less confrontational situations, hearing-impaired students also may employ physical means, emulating the strategies normal-hearing students use with them (i.e., touching to get attention).

Being aware of acceptable social overtures, entry into games, and organizational strategies can facilitate the student's integration into the social aspects of classroom life. If the teacher observes socially isolating behaviors, he or she can model acceptable techniques in a way that does not point to the hearing-impaired student yet makes the required behavior noticeable. Teachers can help the student identify classroom teaching styles by pointing out the most salient features to the entire class, as in the following examples:

> "When I stand up here quietly, it means that I want your attention."
>
> "Unless I indicate otherwise, you are to raise your hand before answering a question."
>
> "Don't ask to go to the bathroom unless it is an emergency."
>
> "In this seminar, you will be expected to answer without raising your hand. Make sure only one person talks at a time."

Teachers should be prepared by support staff to always include this information.

Implementation of quality management requires knowledge on the part of all school personnel who come in contact with the hearing-impaired child. Although some will have prior experience, all will need to become familiar with the particular child. Quality in-service training provides the key.

13

In-service Training

In-service training, a concept in existence for many years, should be considered an integral part of any hearing-impaired child's educational planning as a result of two issues. The first relates to the diversity of potential and skills among hearing-impaired children in regular education settings. This heterogeneity means that no one professional can meet all the needs of all hearing-impaired children. No matter what the area or degree of expertise that a professional brings to a particular educational setting, working with hearing-impaired children always turns up situations that require more information. Often the best way to obtain that information is through in-service training.

Secondly, undergraduate and graduate-level preservice training programs in speech, language, and hearing cannot provide students with all of the information needed to completely manage a hearing-impaired child. When considering the rate at which new assessment tools and techniques for management are developed, obviously even the best trained professional has to update previous knowledge and acquire new information. Recent literature has reported on the needs of regular and special educators with respect to managing hearing-impaired children: selection, purchase, and use of wireless FM systems (Maxon, Brackett, & van den Berg, in press); knowledge of and exposure to hearing aids (Lass et al., 1989); and knowledge of hearing, hearing loss, and noise effects (Martin, Bernstein,

Daly, & Cody, 1988; Lass et al., 1990). Furthermore, Martin et al. (1988) found that regular education teachers are more comfortable having a hearing-impaired child in class if in-service training is provided.

Too often in-service training is conceptualized along a traditional lecture-type model that provides generalizations about hearing loss and its effects to school personnel. Although this type of training has its place, faculty can take in the information they require to work with a hearing-impaired child in a number of ways. In addition, families and peers of the hearing-impaired child must not be overlooked. Often just the acknowledgment that a particular child must use classroom amplification, for example, and a brief explanation of what it does can defuse a potentially difficult acceptance situation. In-service training takes major consideration in planning for a mainstreamed hearing-impaired child's success.

In the same way that educational placement and service delivery options vary, so should in-service training. Further, just as IEPs vary from child to child, so should the training program for a particular person. This concept has been referred to as the Individual In-service Plan (IIP; Maxon, 1991). Guidelines for developing IIPs and for making in-service training an informative and pertinent experience follow:

1. *Formal in-service training:*

   a. *General.* Although not always most crucial, it is often beneficial to provide school personnel with general information about hearing loss and its effects. This type of program for all direct service personnel instills confidence in applying the suggestions made through the child's IEP. For the sake of relevance, the presenter must be aware of the personnel attending the session, the number of hearing-impaired children in the school, the type of programming in which the children are enrolled, and the level of expertise of the participants.

   b. *Specific.* Formal presentations can take on more specific overtones when the presenter relates general information to a specific child. Therefore, if there is one hearing-impaired child in the school, and that child has a bilateral, profound sensorineural hearing loss, it may be more appropriate to have a workshop that talks directly to the auditory, amplification, language, and academic needs of that type of child, rather than to spend time on the effects of mild and/or conductive hearing losses. With several hearing-impaired children, however, or a resource room for the hearing-impaired in a school, this specific sort of workshop must become more diverse. A one-time presentation may not sufficiently cover all of the issues for a larger number of children, in which case a series of workshops should be developed.

   c. *Specific concerns.* Even more focused is the workshop that develops out of the concerns of professionals working with a particular child or group of children. Such a session may result from questions presented to the case manager by other direct service personnel, regular education teachers, children, or families. For example, the concerns may reflect uncertainty about the need for so many services, or the use of classroom amplification. Conversely, school personnel may feel that the child is not receiving enough special services. In any case, this type of in-service program requires careful development and input from the case manager and the interdisciplinary team.

d. *Theoretical.* Just as with general information, participants also may need one or more theoretically based programs. For example, regular education preschool teachers may benefit from information about language acquisition, including communicative intent. This could serve as a good base for future formal or informal child-specific in-service programs. In addition, many aspects of working with these children require separating the effects of hearing loss from those of general maturation and development. Without an understanding of the theoretical material, the professionals and families involved may have a very difficult time making that separation. It is unlikely, however, that a theoretical workshop conducted once a year, with no connection made either to hearing loss or a given child, will provide the type of information that educators and parents need to carry out their daily responsibilities.

e. *Applied.* Armed with the theoretical framework, direct service personnel will want a program that applies that material to the children with whom they are working. Like the specific workshops described previously, these should be based on a particular child or children and address their specific needs. However, not all applied programs must be preceded by a theoretical one. Often topics, such as troubleshooting amplification, directly relate to the child's daily education but do not have complex underlying issues. Such a workshop could easily be introduced with basic information, such as the reason for monitoring amplification equipment on a daily basis. Typically very practical, these workshops are best scheduled at the very beginning of the school year. In this way pertinent information gets disseminated quite early, school personnel have an opportunity to become familiar with it, and questions can be addressed before too much of the school year has passed. Such a strategy implies, of course, that planning must take place before the close of the previous school year.

2. *Informal in-service training:*

a. *On-site, "on the spot."* Even when the formal in-service programming has covered the necessary theoretical and applied information, questions and concerns will continue to arise. Often these problems require immediate consultation with the case manager. One such example occurs when the hearing-impaired child misperceives what another child has said and either a verbal or physical dispute ensues. Although the classroom teacher may not feel comfortable in dealing with this particular problem, it does need direct attention. The case manager should either talk directly with the hearing-impaired children or ask another professional, like the school psychologist, to address the issues. The in-service aspect of handling this particular problem would be to explain to the classroom teacher the reason for the misunderstanding and help the school psychologist separate issues of hearing from those more socially based.

b. *Weekly meetings.* Another form of on-site in-service could occur in a regularly scheduled meeting. In this case, a formal agenda does not exist; rather, the meeting becomes a forum for direct service personnel and regular education faculty to ask questions and present concerns. The case manager can use this opportunity to provide pertinent information and to plan for more formal meetings and presentations.

c. *Planning team meetings.* Often a planning team meeting offers a means of providing crucial information to direct service personnel, classroom teachers, and families. For example, sometimes parents make decisions about their child's needs through the help of outside professionals. In such cases school personnel must know the reasons for these decisions and determine how to implement them. This type of situation often arises when a new child enters a particular school or the school system. Although this child may have undergone an early intervention program, it may have been provided outside the specific school system (e.g., through a regional program). When the child is ready for home-school kindergarten, the school planning team may be unfamiliar with him or her. Further, they may find themselves confronted with recommendations made by educational and clinical personnel from the regional program or an outside agency. In such situations, clinical audiologists can provide information about how the child's hearing loss will affect classroom performance. Even when personnel in a school system have had experience with other hearing-impaired children, a different child brings new and different skills and problems, perhaps requiring new and different programming. The in-service program provided at this point must address the fact that children with hearing loss differ from one another, even when they have the same type and degree of loss.

d. *From outside agencies.* One of the most obvious but typically overlooked opportunities for informal in-service training comes from the written and oral reports from professionals in outside agencies. The results and implications of their assessments can enhance the child's educational program. For example, in the report from a child's annual audiological evaluation, the clinical audiologist should be willing to comment on how the child's aided performance could affect both receiving and perceiving verbally presented material in the classroom. He or she might also reiterate the reasons for using a wireless FM system, even when the child's personal hearing aids are functioning properly and providing appropriate amplification. When children receive some aspect of management outside the regular education setting (e.g., auditory training at a private agency), thorough reports can offer an excellent source of informal in-service training (particularly if they describe the type of management being conducted and the way in which the child's skills will impact on the educational program). In fact, reports from outside agencies should regularly incorporate information and suggestions to help broaden the knowledge base of the school personnel. School staff members should feel comfortable telephoning the outside professional to clarify anything questionable.

e. *To outside agencies.* School personnel also should take on the responsibility of providing information to outside agencies, to assist clinical personnel in assessing a particular child appropriately and in considering the educational implications of their results. For example, although clinical audiologists are well aware of the effects of hearing loss on language development, they need to know about the language skills of the children they test. Such information helps them choose the most effective method for assessing receptive speech intelligibility, the results of which help determine if the child is making maximal use of residual hearing. An audiologist also would benefit from knowing what auditory and communicative demands the educational setting places on the child, so that he or she can include suggestions for classroom modifications in the report.

3. *Providers of in-service training:*

a. *Outside speech, language, and hearing professionals.* The services of an outside professional should be sought whenever necessary information cannot be covered by someone within the school system. Ongoing developments in assessing and managing hearing-impaired children demand keeping school personnel current. When a new child enters the school system, educators may find themselves ill-equipped to plan an educational program although previously they adequately accommodated another hearing-impaired child. For example, the child with a severe sensorineural hearing loss who had been partially mainstreamed in the fourth grade in a rural elementary school likely required different services than the new mildly hearing-impaired, fully mainstreamed child in the same grade and school. The fact that the second child exhibits more intelligible speech, better use of hearing, and better language may even erroneously induce school personnel to develop an IEP that lacks speech and language management. An in-service training program dealing with mild hearing loss and its effects on language, with implications for classroom performance, would help ensure a well-developed IEP that does include work on communication. Having only worked previously with a more severely hearing-impaired child, the school personnel may be unfamiliar with the implications of mild hearing losses and therefore must acquire that information from an outside source. Further, as few school systems have audiologists working for them, issues such as noise, amplification, and speech acoustics definitely will require the services of an outside provider.

b. *Case manager.* The case manager routinely provides in-service training in the course of assisting with emergency situations; however, such should not be the only time he or she acts as an in-service trainer. As the case manager has been selected as the professional with the most knowledge about hearing impairment and the particular child, he or she presents a key training resource in the school. The case manager may feel quite comfortable covering certain theoretical as well as applied programs and should be called upon to do so. When, however, the areas of interest necessitate a greater expertise, the case manager likely will be the person who organizes an in-service training program conducted by other professionals. As mentioned earlier, specific questions and concerns about a particular hearing-impaired child should go directly to the case manager, as should reports from outside agencies and requests to make contact with them. He or she therefore stays an integral part of virtually all aspects of in-service training related to the hearing-impaired child.

c. *Other direct service personnel.* At times school personnel other than the case manager will provide the in-service training, particularly when the desired topics have implications for managing hearing-impaired children but do not relate directly to hearing and hearing loss (e.g., workshops on cognition or motor development, or concomitant effects of other handicapping conditions).

d. *Regular education personnel.* Special educators often become so immersed in managing children with delays and/or disorders that they lose sight of the typical behaviors and difficulties that normally developing children display and experience. They would benefit from greater familiarity with expectations in the regular education classroom and "specials." The physical education teacher, for example, can reveal a great deal about how much children are expected to know about rules of games. The school speech-language pathologist, well aware of a particular hearing-impaired child's reduced language skills, may be quite unaware of how ignorance of the rules for dodgeball can keep that child from doing well in physical education class. In this example, in-service material from the child's physical education teacher can be used to help the child learn the vocabulary and language of the rules for dodgeball.

e. *Parents.* Often the parents of a hearing-impaired child can impart knowledge about hearing loss and amplification to school personnel. They certainly can provide very specific information about their child and the problems that he or she brings to the educational setting. School personnel should not be threatened by parental expertise, but open to it. Difficulties can arise, however, when a parent crosses, or is perceived as crossing, the fine line between helping and interfering.

4. *Recipients of in-service training:*

a. *Regular educators.* All regular educators who come in contact with the hearing-impaired child during the school day should have information about hearing loss and amplification. The depth of the presentation relates directly to the amount of time spent with the child and the accommodating modifications expected to be made. All formal presentations should conclude with an invitation to direct all questions and concerns to the case manager, so that informal training can go on throughout the year. At the preschool and elementary levels, it will be the teacher with a hearing-impaired child enrolled in the class who receives the bulk of in-service training. For junior high and high school faculty, all classroom teachers should be carefully in-serviced, with particular care taken to address issues arising in certain subjects. For example, the high school French teacher must become knowledgeable about FM microphone technique so that he does not try to "get away" with placing the transmitter on his desk and expecting the hearing-impaired child to learn French as easily as normal-hearing classmates.

b. *Direct service providers.* The school psychologist, speech-language pathologist, teacher of the hearing-impaired, social worker, reading teacher, and so forth all have particular areas of expertise and abilities in working with special needs children. Yet they should also know how a hearing impairment affects a child's development. Further, the specifics of a particular child's impairment can make the difference between that child's success or failure. Assessment in any area that requires the use of language, spoken or written, requires modifications of assessment procedures for hearing-impaired children. The pros and cons of using tests normed on normal-hearing children also presents an important area to explore. Special educators' exposure to each of these items leads to appropriate assessments, IEPs, and educational management.

c. *Non-teaching school personnel.* Although not responsible for providing services or traditional education to a hearing-impaired child, the school's paraprofessional, clerical, cafeteria, and maintenance staff do interact with and therefore educate the child about school life. These individuals should be aware of the child's hearing loss and the optimal way to communicate with him or her. They can benefit from strategies for coping with communication situations, such as getting the child's attention, confirming that he or she understands what is being said, and understanding what the child says in return.

d. *Administrators.* As indicated previously, school administrators have very specific concerns in the planning of the child's educational program. Because of their budgetary responsibilities they may focus on justification for services rather than the theoretical bases for specific recommendations. Therefore, if the in-service program will discuss the purpose and effects of wireless FM systems, administrators in attendance will also want information that enables them to justify the cost of providing one for a single child.

　　e. *Peers.* All the normal-hearing peers of the hearing-impaired child should receive information about hearing and amplification, though not in formal workshops. This training can be incorporated into the curriculum of the regular class, be part of health and/or science, or can be a class presentation made by the hearing-impaired child. Demonstrations of FM systems always offer an interesting way to make the equipment familiar, and sometimes popular, with normal-hearing classmates. For example, the hearing-impaired child and the case manager can demonstrate how an FM system works through a "mind reading" act, where the child goes out of the room with the FM receiver and the adult makes a few statements into the microphone. When the hearing-impaired child returns to class, he or she can repeat all of the adult's comments. A basic understanding of why the hearing-impaired child uses the equipment and gets special attention may head off confrontations. A fine line exists, however, between explaining about hearing impairment and making the hearing-impaired child seem an oddity in the class. In-servicing the normal-hearing classmates, and helping the hearing-impaired child understand his or responsibility in reacting to the normal-hearing classmates, should result in better integration. This important aspect of the IIP can be critical to the hearing-impaired child's feeling of social competence and academic equality.

　　f. *Families.* Hearing-impaired children exist as part of a family unit, and the in-service plan must reflect this. PL 99-457 requires that the management plan be family directed, empowering the family to provide the best for their child. Although the Individual Family Service Plan (IFSP) is not concerned directly with in-service training, the latter is implied in the required provision of information to parents. Parents tend to get much of their initial information about hearing loss and amplification from the clinical audiologist who originally saw their child. Further material may come through support groups or early intervention/parent programs. By the time the hearing-impaired child enters school, even preschool, the parents should possess a great deal of knowledge about hearing impairment and its possible impact upon their child. School personnel can then expand this background with information about the educational implications of the hearing loss.

　　In-service training is an aspect of working with hearing-impaired children that deserves a great deal of careful planning. Such training can and should cover a wide variety of topics. Table 13.1 offers some ideas for in-service training and links them to the corresponding chapters within this book where the reader can find pertinent content material. As with a good

TABLE 13.1 Potential Topics for In-service Training and Their Location Within This Text

Topics	Corresponding Chapters
1. Troubleshooting:	
Hearing aids	9
FM systems	9
2. Classroom selection:	
Noise levels	8
Teachers	3
Demands	3, 10
3. Management options:	
Auditory	8, 9, 10, 11
Communication	10, 11
Social	12
4. Educational modifications:	
Teaching	3, 12
Physical	8
Curriculum	7, 12
5. Hearing impairment:	
Hearing loss	2, 4
Effects on communication	2, 5
Effects on education	2, 6
6. Language:	
Normal development	2, 5
Effects of hearing loss	2, 5
Classroom demands	3, 10, 11
Various modes	2
7. Speech:	
Normal development	2
Effects of hearing loss	2
8. Educational management:	
Classroom modifications	8, 9, 12
Use of tutor/interpreter	12
Use of amplification	8, 9
Classroom acoustics	8, 9

TABLE 13.1 (Continued)

Topics	Corresponding Chapters
9. Audiological issues:	
Assessment	4
Amplification	8, 9
Speech perception	2, 8
Maximizing residual hearing	2, 8, 9
10. Amplification:	
Hearing aids	8
FM systems	9
Use of amplification	8, 9
Effects on speech perception	8, 9, 10, 11
11. Auditory training:	
Use of residual hearing	8, 9, 10, 11
Effects on communication	10, 11
12. Socialization:	
Effects of hearing impairment	6, 12
Effects of language	6, 12
Problems in school setting	3, 6, 12
13. Heterogeneity of hearing-impaired children	2, 3
14. Vocational issues:	
Language	2, 3
Use of hearing	8, 9
Mode of communication	2, 10
Communication demands	3, 10
15. School transitions:	
Educational placement options	3
Demands of various grade levels	3

IEP, the development of an appropriate, flexible, comprehensive Individual In-service Plan hinges on knowing the needs of the recipients—professionals, children, and families. Often the best way for the case manager to assess areas of need starts with eliciting questions from the other direct service personnel and the regular educators involved. This informal survey can be integrated with the extant information about the individual child so that the IIP can cover all critical areas.

Table 13.2 presents suggestions for workshops that can be developed from the topics in Table 13.1. Specific materials for in-service training, including suggestions for other workshops, and specific guidelines for developing an IIP can be found in Maxon (1991).

TABLE 13.2 In-service Workshop Models

Title	Type	Provider	Recipient
"FM Troubleshooting"	Formal/Specific	Audiologist	Case manager & teacher
"Classroom Acoustics"	Formal/General	Audiologist	All regular & special ed. faculty
"Oral/Aural Communication"	Formal/ Theoretical	Speech-language pathologist	Classroom teachers
"Teaching Modifications"	Formal/Specific	Case manager	All regular ed. faculty
"Hearing Loss"	Formal/General	Case manager & child	Peers
"Effects of Hearing Loss on Language"	Formal/Specific	Speech-language pathologist	All regular ed. faculty
"Normal Speech Development"	Informal/Plan-ning Meeting	Speech-language pathologist	Team & parents
"Role of a Tutor"	Informal/On-site	Case manager	Classroom teacher
"Speech Acoustics"	Informal/Weekly Meeting	Case manager	Team & teacher
"Why an FM System?"	Formal/ Theoretical	Audiologist	Administrators
"Maximizing Residual Hearing"	Formal/Applied	Speech-language pathologist	Teachers

(Continued)

TABLE 13.2 (Continued)

Title	Type	Provider	Recipient
"Socialization of Hearing-Impaired Children"	Formal/Specific Concerns	Counselor	All faculty
"Hearing-impaired Children"	Formal/General	Audiologist	All special ed. faculty & administrators
"Vocational Education"	Informal/Planning Team Meeting	Vocational ed. counselor	
"Demands of the Junior High"	Formal/Specific	School administrator	Parent group & planning team

14

Case Studies

Case studies can effectively synthesize a broad, complicated, and multifaceted process such as mainstreaming. The following cases of David, Michael, and Monique, three children of different ages, skills, potential, deficits, and needs, illustrate the message of the preceding chapters and demonstrate how evaluations yield a diagnostic picture that suggests various levels of service.

CASE 1

NAME: David
AGE: 10 years, 11 months
GRADE: Completing 5th grade

Figure 14.1 displays the results of David's audiological evaluation, showing a severe to profound, relatively flat hearing loss by air conduction. Bone conduction measurements were not made, but normal immittance results demonstrate the hearing loss is sensorineural.

David uses binaural ear-level hearing aids as personal amplification that provide him with good functional gain across frequencies. An aided speech discrimination score of 76% demonstrated that David has minimal difficulty perceiving the various speech sounds at a comfortable listening level. When his responses were scored according to phoneme errors, the

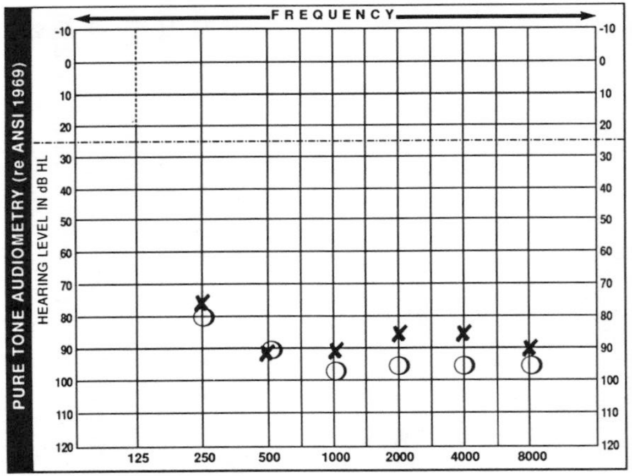

X left ear, unaided

O right ear, unaided

IPSILATERAL ACOUSTIC REFLEX
Absent bilaterally

OTOSCOPIC
Unremarkable bilaterally

SPEECH AUDIOMETRY

	UNAIDED					
	RIGHT	HL	LEFT	HL	SOUNDFIELD	HL
SAT		dB		dB		dB
SRT		90 dB		85 dB		dB
WORD RECOG.	68 % at	115 dB	64 % at	115 dB	% at	dB
	% at	dB	% at	dB	% at	dB
	% at	dB	% at	dB	% at	dB
	% at	dB	% at	dB	% at	dB
MASKING		dB		dB		dB
MCL		115 dB		115 dB		dB
UCL		dB		dB		dB
MATERIALS						

DESIGN BY BOB ESSMAN

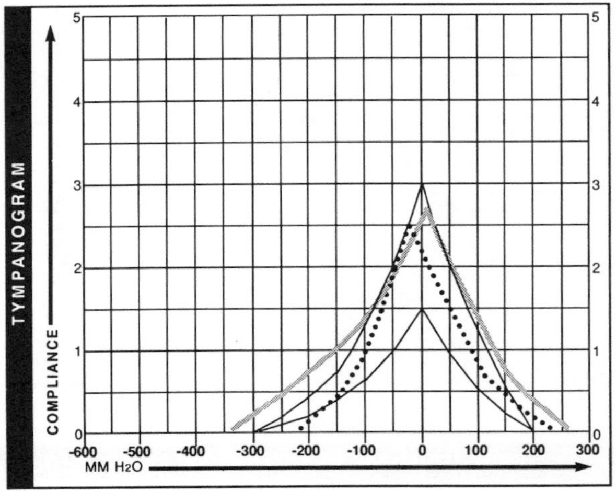

FIGURE 14.1 David's unaided audiological results.

FIGURE 14.2 David's aided audiological results.

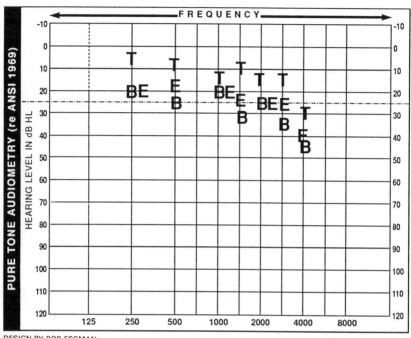

DESIGN BY BOB ESSMAN

B binaural, aided

E environmental
   microphone

T transmitter/microphone

BINAURAL AIDED
SPEECH DISCRIMINATION
84% at 50 dB

STIMULUS	ERROR
p	t
f	s
g	d
ae	uh
ee	oo
p	k
s	sh

pattern showed predominantly high-frequency phonemes. Figure 14.2 demonstrates the errors on the aided speech discrimination testing as a function of aided thresholds. When analyzed according to the speech acoustic method, one can see clearly that the errors occurred because of David's inability to hear the various cues. The fact that he heard /p/ when a /t/ was the stimulus is explained by the overlapping lower frequency components. David does not hear the higher frequency distinguishing acoustic cues (refer to Table 8.4).

Such an obvious high-frequency error is readily understood, even without plotting it on the audiogram, but the substitution of /u/ for /i/ may not be. Professionals often assume that vowels are readily available to hearing-impaired children because of their primarily low-frequency energy; however, vowel discrimination occurs on the basis of relative frequency differences between F1 and F2. Table 8.1 demonstrated that the F2 for /i/ is above 2000 Hz while the F2 energy for /u/ hovers around 900 Hz. David has easy access to F2 for /u/ but not F2 for /i/; because he did not readily hear the critical distinguishing feature, he substituted a more audible vowel.

Figure 14.2 also displays David's aided results using his FM system (E = environmental microphones, T = transmitter); functional gain is good across frequencies. His thresholds were better when using the microphone/transmitter than when using the environmental microphones because of the positioning of the transmitter within a few inches of the loudspeaker.

The true advantage of an FM system cannot be demonstrated by measuring aided thresholds in a soundproof booth. The degree of benefit David derives from using the FM system is reflected in the functional listening assessment results shown in Table 14.1. In all listening conditions, the FM system tended to be superior to the hearing aid conditions. Differences are particularly apparent for the consonant sounds, which are most affected by noise and distance. Table 14.1 also presents David's scores on sentence and paragraph perception using his hearing aids and FM system in different listening conditions. Sentence scores were better than the individual words in all of the conditions, which is expected because of the linguistic information carried by the sentence. The poorer paragraph scores are most likely a function of the low number of items (five questions) and the fact that the response had to be based on hearing specific words within the context of the paragraph.

Table 14.2 presents David's communication assessment results. With the exception of single-word receptive vocabulary, David's language is excellent. Closer consideration of the various test scores reveals that he has less difficulty with semantics when words are used in a context. This difficulty with understanding the meaning of individual words could negatively affect David's classroom performance. New concepts and vocabulary are likely to be more difficult for him than for his normal-hearing classmates. It would be helpful for his speech-language pathologist to obtain a list of new vocabulary words from the classroom teacher and familiarize David with their meanings prior to presentation in class.

David can easily express his intent in syntactically and grammatically correct sentences. There is, however, a discrepancy between his spoken and written language structure. He omits many unstressed morphological endings and relies primarily on simple sentence types. His speech-language

TABLE 14.1 Results of David's Functional Listening Evaluation Using Personal Hearing Aids and FM System

A. CVC words (AB lists) scored as percent correct phonemes:

Condition	Scores		Condition	Scores	
QUIET—AUDITORY ONLY					
HA/CLOSE	Vowels:	100%	FM/CLOSE	Vowels:	100%
	Consonants:	70%		Consonants:	80%
	Total:	75%		Total:	80%
HA/FAR	Vowels:	90%	FM/FAR	Vowels:	100%
	Consonants:	50%		Consonants:	80%
	Total:	63%		Total:	83%
NOISE—AUDITORY ONLY					
HA/CLOSE	Vowels:	90%	FM/CLOSE	Vowels:	100%
	Consonants:	65%		Consonants:	80%
	Total:	76%		Total:	83%
HA/FAR	Vowels:	90%	FM/FAR	Vowels:	90%
	Consonants:	30%		Consonants:	60%
	Total:	50%		Total:	73%
QUIET—AUDITORY + VISUAL					
HA/CLOSE	Vowels:	90%			
	Consonants:	100%			
	Total:	96%			

B. Monosyllabic words scored as percent word correct:

Condition	Scores		Condition	Scores	
HA/CLOSE	Quiet:	50%	FM/CLOSE	Quiet:	65%
	Noise:	60%		Noise:	65%
HA/FAR	Quiet:	30%	FM/FAR	Quiet:	60%
	Noise:	10%		Noise:	50%

C. Sentences scored as perent of words correct within the sentence:

Condition	Scores		Condition	Scores	
HA/CLOSE	Quiet:	95%	FM/CLOSE	Quiet:	100%
	Noise:	75%		Noise:	96%
HA/FAR	Quiet:	91%	FM/FAR	Quiet:	100%
	Noise:	54%		Noise:	82%

TABLE 14.1 (Continued)

D. Paragraph comprehension scored as percent questions answered correctly:

Condition	Score	Condition	Score
HA/CLOSE	Quiet: 100% Noise: 50%	FM/CLOSE	Quiet: 100% Noise: 100%
HA/FAR	Quiet: 60% Noise: 20%	FM/FAR	Quiet: 100% Noise: 90%

TABLE 14.2 Results of David's Communication Evaluation

Test	Score	Percentile
PPVT	7–10	6th
TACL (GM)	8.9–9.11	53rd
TAC (paragraphs)	100%	—
EOWPVT	12–11	87th
Word Test		
Associations	13–6	95th
Synonyms	6–0	6th
Semantic Absurd.	10–6	47th
Antonyms	11–5	71st
Definitions	10–8	45th
Multiple Def.	9–9	28th

PLE: distorted high frequency phonemes (s,sh,f,c,ch,dg,z)

LANGUAGE SAMPLE:

1. I don't know why, but I don't like baseball that much.

2. Last Monday was another hearing test and I guess I don't know what this is all about.

3. I do waterskiing when I go on vacation up the cabin in New York.

4. They can play while they're out.

5. The trouble is that it's hard to get up on the water skis.

pathologist has been assisting him in learning "proofreading" skills, which, when applied aloud, give him a chance to hear the errors.

David's speech is highly intelligible to the naive listener, with only a few distortions present on the high-frequency phonemes. This pattern is not surprising given his auditory perception capabilities. The fact that his aided thresholds are worse in the higher frequencies and that high-frequency sounds are less intense play a role in David's speech production. This clearly demonstrates the relationship between David's speech production and auditory self-monitoring of speech.

The need to carefully assess academic performance and cognitive potential is well documented by David's scores on the *Stanford Achievement Test* (SAT) and the *Wechsler Intelligence Test for Children–Revised* (WISC-R) (Table 14.3). His academic achievement scores are good except for those tests affected by his slightly immature language (e.g., Vocabulary, Reading Comprehension, and Math Application [word problems]). David's score on the more concrete tasks, like Spelling and Math Computation, rise well above grade level. Similar effects can be seen in the "Typical Profile" that he presents on the WISC-R. Even his Verbal scores show good skills except for Vocabulary, corroborating the delay revealed in the communication assessment. When judging David's capabilities, his Performance scores (all within or above normal limits) indicate that he should be very able to function on a par with his normal-hearing peers.

David has reached an age where he is conscious about his appearance. Recently he has expressed to his parents feelings of frustration over having a hearing loss and wearing hearing aids. Although he complains about the cosmetics of wearing visible classroom amplification equipment, he realizes the benefits he derives and becomes furious when it breaks down. David's circle of friends, though smaller than when he was younger, remain loyal. Many of them share his interest in Boy Scouts and band. Only recently had David begun to notice the girls in his class; he primps before school each day in an effort to impress them. His parents have expressed concern about David's social life, particularly as he enters middle school.

David's case manager integrated the information derived from the formal assessments with those obtained from a classroom observation and produced the results seen in Table 14.4.

David is a willing participant in his class, following the teacher's presentation and interacting with her and his peers. He attempts to answer questions, although he is not always correct. He tries to keep up with events in the class through unobtrusive methods, such as visually scanning the room and checking with his friend about something the teacher said. In his efforts to "fit in," though, he does not ask questions even when uncertain of some of the material.

TABLE 14.3 Results of David's Educational and Psychological Evaluations

SAT (grade equivalent)	Score	WISC-R (10 ± 3 = normal range)	Score
Vocabulary	3.4	VERBAL	
Reading Comprehension	3.6	Information	10
Word Study Skills	4.8	Comprehension	8
Math Concepts	5.6	Similarities	6
Math Computation	6.0	Arithmetic	7
Math Application	3.7	Vocabulary	4
Spelling	8.1	PERFORMANCE	
Language	4.7	Picture Completion	14
		Picture Arrangement	15
		Block Design	11
		Object Assembly	13
		Coding	9

David's teacher has made some good efforts to provide the special kind of help that he needs in order to work to potential in the classroom. There were still some areas that could improve, such as indicating when David's answers are not correct and asking him to repeat when his speech is not understood. The teacher also needs to know that although David makes good use of his hearing and has good communicative skills, he can still benefit from seeing her when she is speaking. Incorporating visual aids for subjects with a lot of new vocabulary is also an area in which she requires more information.

David's program includes the use of a notetaker and an FM system to overcome some potential problems. It was observed, however, that his teacher often leaves the transmitter on when she is speaking directly to another child or talking privately (e.g., when the school secretary came in to pass on a message). The teacher did not seem to realize the problem, but more importantly, David did not tell her that he could hear what she was saying during times when he should not have been listening.

David's case manager did not measure the noise levels in the classroom, but a relatively high ambient noise level was noted that appeared to be related to a poor physical environment. The high ceilings and wooden floors have no acoustical tiles and the high windows have no covering. The combination of these reflective surfaces causes a lot of reverberation, mak-

TABLE 14.4   Results of Classroom Observation (David)

Item	Observer Notes
Participation	Raises hand with answer when appropriate to do so Attends to teacher for most of the lecture Offered to take a note to another teacher in another room
Child/teacher interaction	Teacher did not tell him that his answer was incorrect Teacher did call on him regularly Teacher seemed reluctant to have him repeat when his speech was not completely intelligible
Classroom modifications	Used FM during teacher-directed activity Teacher called on other children by name during class discussion No obvious checking of comprehension by the teacher Teacher did glance at his book to see if he was on the correct page A notetaker was available for social studies Teacher wrote on the board and talked at the same time, with her back to the class Limited visual aids were used during social studies
Child/child interaction	Stopped at a friend's desk and talked to him In a group, laughed when his friends laughed but appeared to be on the periphery "Borrowed" answers from his friend's paper Several times he was not aware that he was spoken to
Learning strategies	He made no attempt to write down what the teacher was saying Did not ask any questions during a class presentation, even when the teacher specifically asked for them Asked friend what the teacher said when he did not understand Seemed to rely on visual scanning of the room to note if there was any change

TABLE 14.4 (Continued)

Item	Observer Notes
Use of FM	Teacher left the transmitter turned on during lecture, independent seatwork, and an adult/adult conversation Child did not respond well to other children's asides Child did not ask the teacher to turn off the transmitter when he was doing independent seatwork, or when she was having a private conversation
Analysis of noise sources	Presence of hall noise High ambient room noise due to reflective, non-sound-treated surfaces Hiss from the radiator

ing the listening conditions difficult. Therefore, the need to use the FM appropriately becomes critical in this particular classroom.

At the planning team meeting, questions arose about continuing David's mainstream setting. David is moving from a regular elementary school curriculum with one teacher for all his academics to a middle school setting with greater communicative demands in the classroom and several different teachers with whom to interact. Some team members felt that his less than perfect language skills would cause him significant problems in accessing the academic material. They suggested he might be better off in a program for the hearing-impaired where the level of material and expectations would be reduced. There was some consideration given to providing David with an oral or sign language interpreter because of concerns about the increased rate at which new material would be presented along with the decreased sensitivity to individual needs of each student. The consensus was to table the decision until mid-year when David's progress could be reevaluated and the program modified if necessary. The case manager used this opportunity to provide some informal in-service training about David's potential and the benefits he reaps from higher level, rather than reduced, expectations.

Using this information and the results from the formal and informal evaluations, the multidisciplinary team developed David's IEP. Table 14.5 presents some of the goals and objectives from David's plan. The team also

TABLE 14.5 Sample Components From David's IEP

Classification: Deaf

Extent of participation in regular education: Full mainstreaming

Services: Speech-language management: 2/week, individual 45-minute sessions

Management needs: FM unit for all academic subjects; notetaker; amplification monitoring program

Objectives will include:
—improve vocabulary related to subject areas
—improve flexibility of his vocabulary through synonyms, antonyms, and multiple definitions
—improve in use of grammar in written language
—improve written language as used to compare and contrast
—extended time for standardized tests
—individually administered standardized tests

---

developed an in-service plan for the faculty who work with David that included the following suggestions:

1. Workshop on appropriate FM use presented by an audiologist
2. Classroom modifications specific to David's needs
3. Material for David to help him understand his responsibility in acquiring the information during classroom presentations

CASE 2

NAME: Michael
AGE: 4 years, 11 months
GRADE: Preschool

Figures 14.3 and 14.4 show the results of Michael's audiological and amplification evaluation. He has a severe, flat, sensorineural hearing loss confirmed by the normal immittance measures. When using his personal binaural ear-level hearing aids, the functional gain is appropriate across frequencies. Aided speech discrimination was assessed using the PB-K lists, and the resulting score of 80% reflects the good use that Michael makes of his residual hearing, particularly in the higher frequencies.

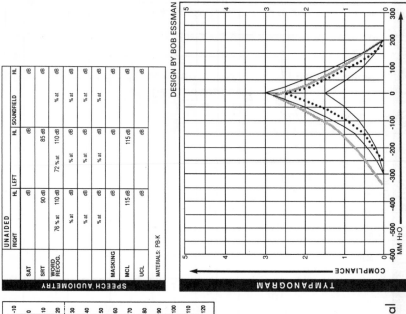

FIGURE 14.3 Michael's unaided audiological results.

FIGURE 14.4 Michael's aided audiological results.

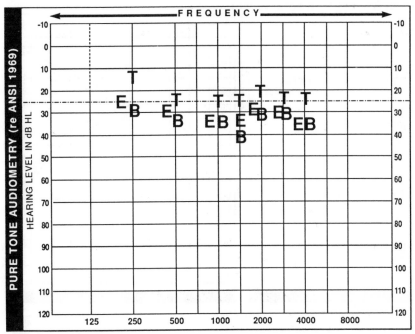

DESIGN BY BOB ESSMAN

B binaural, aided

E environmental
    microphone

T transmitter/microphone

BINAURAL AIDED SPEECH
DISCRIMINATION
80% at 50 dB

Michael has not used an FM system in his preschool class, but there is an interest in considering one for his kindergarten placement. Michael therefore has used a unit on trial at home, and an evaluation was conducted after 1 month of use. The aided (FM) warble tone thresholds demonstrate that in the optimal listening conditions of the soundproof booth, Michael receives appropriate functional gain from the environmental microphones as well as the transmitter. The true benefit that he receives in difficult listening conditions can be seen in the functional listening measures (Table 14.6).

TABLE 14.6 Results of Michael's Functional Listening Evaluation Using Personal Hearing Aids and FM System

A. CVC words (AB lists) scored as percent correct phonemes:

Condition	Scores		Condition	Scores	
	QUIET—AUDITORY ONLY				
HA/CLOSE	Vowels:	100%	FM/CLOSE	Did not test	
	Consonants:	75%			
	Total:	83%			
HA/FAR	Did not test		FM/FAR	Vowels:	100%
				Consonants:	70%
				Total:	80%
	NOISE—AUDITORY ONLY				
HA/CLOSE	Vowels:	100%	FM/CLOSE	Did not test	
	Consonants:	75%			
	Total:	83%			
HA/FAR	Vowels:	100%	FM/FAR	Vowels:	100%
	Consonants:	45%		Consonants:	70%
	Total:	63%		Total:	80%
	QUIET—AUDITORY + VISUAL				
HA/CLOSE	Vowels:	100%			
	Consonants:	75%			
	Total:	83%			

B. CVC words scored as percent word correct:

Condition	Scores		Condition	Scores	
HA/CLOSE	Quiet:	50%	FM/CLOSE	Quiet:	DNT
	Noise:	30%		Noise:	DNT
HA/FAR	Quiet:	DNT	FM/FAR	Quiet:	30%
	Noise:	10%		Noise:	40%

C. Paragraph comprehension scored as percent of questions answered correctly:

Condition	Scores
FM/AUDITORY + VISUAL without PICTURES	66%
FM/AUDITORY + VISUAL with PICTURES	100%
FM/AUDITORY—CLOSE, QUIET without PICTURES	66%
FM/AUDITORY—CLOSE, QUIET with PICTURES	77%

Michael does well with his hearing aids as long as the listening conditions are optimal (close, quiet). The introduction of noise and distance from the speaker does, as expected, cause a decrease in his consonant and total phoneme scores. The implications for the classroom are quite significant because the acoustic environment in the preschool class is considerably less than optimal. Although the kindergarten class Michael will attend has not yet been evaluated, similar problems are known to exist because of noise levels generated by the other children and the physically open setting. Therefore, an FM is strongly indicated for Michael during teacher-directed activity.

Michael's language easily can be described as better than average. In fact, the results presented in Table 14.7 show that considering the degree of hearing loss and his age, his language could be described as exceptional. The language sample demonstrates that Michael's command of language goes well beyond his ability to perform on standardized tests; he uses language quite easily and has a good deal of flexibility. This proficiency gives Michael the ability to interact with ease in school and may account for the potential problems noted during the observation.

Michael has been quite indulged by his parents, who have also gone to great lengths to improve his linguistic skills. As a result, Michael fully expects to be understood by everyone and to receive their total, immediate attention whenever he demands it. Although his good language will benefit him as he moves into the regular school setting, his attitude may cause some significant problems as teachers have less time to address his requests for individual attention and as classmates are less likely to be "amused" by his attempts to be the center of attention. These areas should be carefully monitored as Michael moves into kindergarten.

As Michael is still a preschooler, no formal academic assessment was conducted. He is an exceptionally bright child who performs well within and above normal limits on the *Wechsler Preschool and Primary Scale of Intelligence* (WPPSI). He has shown a significant improvement in his language skills, demonstrated by the decrease in the difference between his Performance and Verbal IQ scores. At his prekindergarten screening, Michael knew the alphabet and sound symbol associations. He possessed number concepts to 10 and could count to 20.

At the classroom observation several potential problem areas emerged (see Table 14.8). Despite being in this class for 7 months, Michael has yet to learn to comply with classroom routines. This behavior that is considered marginal in preschool will quickly become unacceptable when the demands of kindergarten are imposed. The communication assessment results (Table 14.7) illustrate that Michael is a child with good abilities who also has a strong ego. His personality and high-level skills should serve as a good base for entrance into school, but his performance must continue to be monitored carefully.

TABLE 14.7   Results of Michael's Communication Evaluation

Test	Score	Percentile
PPVT	4-3	47th
TACL		
Total	4-3 to 4-5	32nd
Word Class & Relations	4-6 to 4-10	42nd
Grammatical Morphemes	4-0 to 4-3	28th
Elaboration Sentences	4-2 to 4-5	32nd
EOWPVT	5-8	83%
SPELT-II	50% correct	—
Preschool Language Scale		
Language Age	4-9	—
Auditory Comprehension	4-9	—
Verbal Abilities	4-9	—

CID Phonetic Inventory: Primarily place of articulation errors

CID Picture Spine: 70% correct

Goldman-Fristoe Test of Articulation: Uses back sounds for tongue tips; final sounds deleted

LANGUAGE SAMPLE:
 1. I make a different color.

 2. Can I help you?

 3. How do you stop it?

 4. Your turn, Mom.

 5. You can't do that.

The IEP planning team meeting was composed of professionals from the home school where Michael will attend kindergarten, his clinical audiologist, a speech-language pathologist, the preschool teacher, and his parents. Results of the assessment were integrated with information about conditions and options in the new school during the writing of goals and objectives. Table 14.9 provides some examples of those items.

Because Michael will be attending a new school in the fall and the school system has not yet mainstreamed a hearing-impaired child, the in-

TABLE 14.8 Results of Classroom Observation (Michael)

Item	Observer Notes
Participation	During group, talks out without being recognized by teacher Wants to be the center of attention of adults Volunteers for calendar and snack help, even when not his turn
Child/teacher interaction	Demands immediate attention to his questions Teacher does not attempt to make Michael do anything he balks about Teacher gives group instruction on the playground and in the "motor room" when the other children are making noise
Classroom modifications	A large open room with no attempts made to ensure that Michael hears all he needs to A teacher aide has been assigned to check on Michael during the day
Child/child interaction	Attempts to tell the other children what to do Definitely a part of the social group Makes the other children laugh by being "funny"
Learning strategies	No attempts are made to ask for help Does not consider that he does not understand something Good language and routines allow him to predict much of what is happening in the room
Use of FM	No FM is being used in school at this time
Analysis of noise sources	A lot of noise is generated by the children Poor room acoustics created by open space and reflective surfaces make listening conditions less than optimal External noise generated by another group on the playground

TABLE 14.9 Sample Components From Michael's IEP

Classification: Deaf

Extent of participation in regular education: Full mainstreaming

Services: Academic support: 2x/week, 40 minutes, individual
  Speech-language management: 2x/week, 40 minutes, individual

Management needs: FM unit; all academic classes; amplification monitoring program

Objectives will include:
  —improve vocabulary related to readiness activities, categories, and childhood games
  —facilitate development of higher level verb tenses and complex sentences
  —improve his use of socially appropriate language during peer and adult interaction
  —improve production of lingua-alveolar phonemes /t,d,n,l/ as a group
  —facilitate self-monitoring of newly acquired /s/ in plural contexts
  —extended time for standardized tests
  —individually administered standardized tests

---

service training program must be quite extensive. The following topics were suggested for that training, which will take place prior to Michael's entrance into the school:

1. The purpose of FM systems
2. The effects of hearing loss on language and academics
3. Modifications of teaching style to accommodate a hearing-impaired child

It was also recommended that the troubleshooting designee receive special training in the daily monitoring of personal and classroom amplification. A program was designed for Michael's normal-hearing peers so that they could become familiar with the FM system. The school speech-language pathologist had acquired experience working with hearing-impaired children while employed in another school system. He was designated as the case manager and asked to be ready to provide "on-site" in-service training as the occasion arose.

CASE 3

NAME: Monique
AGE: 14 years, 7 months
GRADE: Entering 10th grade

Monique has a bilateral, mild to profound sensorineural hearing loss that drops off at 1000 Hz. Figure 14.5 displays the unaided results of Monique's audiological evaluation. She has some history of recurrent negative middle-ear pressure that affects her low-frequency hearing slightly, but at the time of this evaluation, all immittance measurements registered within normal limits. The slightly elevated stapedial reflex thresholds at 500 Hz reflect the good hearing in that frequency range, while the absent reflexes in the high frequencies are consistent with the significantly poorer hearing. Unaided speech audiometry measures also reflect the configuration of the audiogram. Monique's speech recognition thresholds (SRT) are within the mild range as a result of good hearing at 500 Hz. However, her reduced speech discrimination scores are due to the limited availability of the higher frequency consonant cues.

Monique benefits greatly from the wireless FM system that she has always used in school (Figure 14.6). She changed from a traditional unit to one that uses direct audio input (DAI) when she entered middle school. Monique's clinical audiologist was directly involved in the recommendation for the hearing aids she uses with the system, so care has been taken to ensure that the frequency response, gain, and output are appropriate. Monique's case manager keeps a record of the settings of all amplification and knows the correct wire and boot for FM coupling.

Monique makes good use of her aided residual hearing as noted in the results of functional listening evaluation (Table 14.10). Her clinical audiologist, who has worked closely with the school system since Monique entered kindergarten, conducted this testing during the annual audiological evaluation. Although she realizes the importance of unaided information, she also is aware that school personnel want to know how a child functions with amplification in a variety of listening situations. Following identification at 4 years, 6 months, Monique received intensive speech-language management for 4 years to remediate the effects of the hearing loss on her communication skills. Currently she shows little residual communication deficit (Table 14.11). In social conversation, Monique uses colloquial expressions and slang similar to her peers. She is fortunate to have an older sister who keeps up with the newest expressions. Monique's love of horseback riding and her demonstrated expertise have given her a close circle of friends with similar interests.

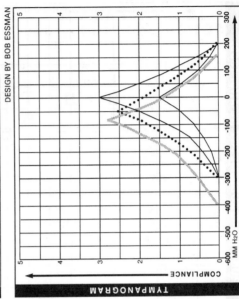

SPEECH AUDIOMETRY

	UNAIDED					
	RIGHT	HL	LEFT	HL	SOUNDFIELD	HL
SAT		dB		dB		dB
SRT		40 dB		40 dB		dB
WORD RECOG.	76 % at	75 dB	72 % at		80 dB	80 % at
		dB		dB		% at
	% at	dB	% at	dB		% at
	% at	dB	% at	dB		% at
MASKING		dB		dB		dB
MCL		75 dB		75 dB		80 dB
UCL		dB		dB		dB

MATERIALS: Campbell

TYMPANOGRAM

COMPLIANCE

MM H₂O

DESIGN BY BOB ESSMAN

PURE TONE AUDIOMETRY (re ANSI 1969)

HEARING LEVEL IN dB HL

FREQUENCY

X left ear, unaided

O right ear, unaided

IPSILATERAL ACOUSTIC REFLEX
Present = 500 Hz bilaterally
Absent = 1000 - 4000 Hz bilaterally

OTOSCOPIC
Unremarkable bilaterally

FIGURE 14.5 Monique's unaided audiological results.

FIGURE 14.6 Monique's aided audiological results.

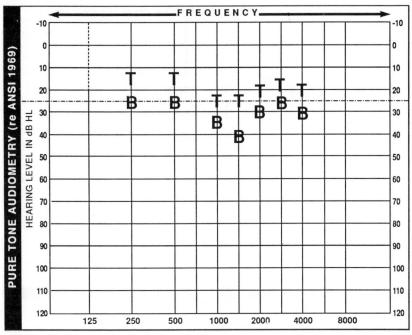

DESIGN BY BOB ESSMAN

B binaural, aided
E environmental
   microphone
T transmitter/microphone
BINAURAL AIDED SPEECH
DISCRIMINATION
84% at 50 dB

Monique's academic work is outstanding, primarily because of her maturation and careful preparation. (Table 14.12 displays her performance on standardized tests.) She uses reading to supplement the information she misses during classroom lectures. Two years ago, when the services of a notetaker were added to the IEP, Monique was relieved because it enabled her to give full attention to the classroom teacher instead of dividing her focus between notes and the teacher. When Monique entered high school she requested that academic support be eliminated from her program because she did not want to miss any classwork. At the present time she can request the service for a particular problem area whenever needed.

TABLE 14.10 Results of Monique's Functional Listening Evaluation Using Personal Hearing Aids and FM System

A. CVC words (AB lists) scored as percent correct phonemes:

Condition	Scores		Condition	Scores	
	QUIET—AUDITORY ONLY				
HA/CLOSE	Vowels:	100%	FM/CLOSE	Did not test	
	Consonants:	74%			
	Total:	80%			
HA/FAR	Vowels:	100%	FM/FAR	Vowels:	100%
	Consonants:	60%		Consonants:	74%
	Total:	68%		Total:	86%
	NOISE—AUDITORY ONLY				
HA/CLOSE	Vowels:	100%	FM/CLOSE	Did not test	
	Consonants:	50%			
	Total:	60%			
HA/FAR	Vowels:	90%	FM/FAR	Vowels:	100%
	Consonants:	30%		Consonants:	74%
	Total:	60%		Total:	86%

B. Sentences scored as percent of words correct within the sentence:

Condition	Scores	Condition	Scores
HA/CLOSE	Quiet: 100%	FM/CLOSE	Quiet: 100%
	Noise: 80%		Noise: 100%
HA/FAR	Quiet: 100%	FM/FAR	Quiet: 100%
	Noise: 60%		Noise: 100%

C. Paragraph comprehension scored as percent questions answered correctly:

Condition	Scores	Condition	Scores
HA/CLOSE	Quiet: 100%	FM/CLOSE	Quiet: 100%
	Noise: 70%		Noise: 100%
HA/FAR	Quiet: 70%	FM/FAR	Quiet: 100%
	Noise: 20%		Noise: 100%

TABLE 14.11 Results of Monique's Communication Evaluation

Test	Score	Percentile
PPVT	14-1	45%
EOWPVT	17-2	81%
Fullerton	± 1 std. dev.	

Speech production: distortion on high frequency phonemes /s,z/

LANGUAGE SAMPLE:

1. I was so excited about going to the movies with him, but I was also very nervous.

2. Don't you think that is the dumbest thing you've ever heard?

3. Did you go to the fair after school yesterday?

4. I hate that teacher because she always gives us tons of homework.

5. I don't think I want to get married unless I can keep being a lawyer, too.

TABLE 14.12 Results of Monique's Educational and Psychological Evaluations

SAT (grade equivalent)	Score	WISC-R (10 ± 3 = normal range)	Score
Vocabulary	8.9	VERBAL	
Reading Comprehension	9.9	Information	11
Word Study Skills	9.8	Comprehension	10
Math Concepts	10.3	Similarities	10
Math Computation	10.5	Arithmetic	12
Math Application	9.6	Vocabulary	9
Spelling	10.0	PERFORMANCE	
Language	9.3	Picture Completion	15
		Picture Arrangement	16
		Block Design	13
		Object Assembly	14
		Coding	13

Classroom observation demonstrated that Monique's difficulties are related to teacher presentation rather than her skills. She makes the most of the situations that occur and attempts to make some suggestions to her teachers (see Table 14.13).

Monique presents an excellent example of a student who derives maximum benefit from the support services provided. At the present time she is able to maintain her skills without these services. Table 14.14 shows some of the areas covered in Monique's IEP prior to her entrance into 10th grade. The annual review will permit her case manager to monitor Monique's level of performance and determine if a need arises to reinstate services in the future. In-service training will be considered because of the problems observed in Monique's classes. The French teacher needs more instruction on the proper use of the FM, while her algebra teacher would benefit from information about classroom modifications.

TABLE 14.13 Results of Classroom Observation (Monique)

Item	Observer Notes
Participation	Raises her hand to correctly answer questions (A)* Readily follows teacher's presentation (A) Asks for clarification of topic (F)**
Child/teacher interaction	Teacher gives assignments orally (A) Teacher allows Monique to write on the board but not give oral answers (F) Teacher used a lot of class discussion (F) Teacher wrote homework assignments on the board (F) Teacher gave lengthy explanations about what would be on the final exam (A)
Child/child interaction	Chatted easily with classmates before the period began (A & F) Asked for repetition when she did not hear something Had difficulty talking while changing classes because she unplugged the DAI in the hallway

TABLE 14.13 (Continued)

Item	Observer Notes
Learning strategies	Listened to the teacher and had a "buddy" take notes (A) Used a dictionary when new vocabulary was written on the board (F)
Use of FM	Teacher placed transmitter on the desk and did not wear it (F) Monique reminded teacher about using the microphone after class (F)
Analysis of noise sources	Classroom is next to music room (A)

*Algebra class
**French class

TABLE 14.14 Sample Components From Monique's IEP

Classification: Hard of hearing

Extent of participation in regular education: Full mainstreaming

Management needs: FM use in all academics; amplification monitoring program; notetaker for English, French, algebra, European history; extended time for standardized tests; individually administered standardized tests

Services: Academic support as needed

15

Summing Up

Mainstreaming as an educational concept was not invented in 1975 with the passage of PL 94-142. Although the term defining to an educational practice may be of relatively recent origin, the concept itself was applied to hearing-impaired children nearly two centuries ago. In a fascinating article, Gordon (1885) reviewed attempts to educate hearing-impaired children in regular schools from the first written record in 1815 to 1885.

Among the first publications on the topic appeared in 1819, entitled *The Art of Instructing the Infant Deaf and Dumb* (Arrowsmith, cited in Gordon, 1885). This book was written in England by a man with a deaf brother, whose mother took the responsibility of educating her child rather than sending him away to be educated. According to the report, she developed educational material and approaches that she shared with her child's teachers in the regular schools. Her hearing son, the author of the book, became a strong advocate of educating deaf children alongside their hearing counterparts. Others in England took up the challenge but soon abandoned the effort as generally impractical and unsuccessful.

Shortly after this large-scale efforts arose in France and Germany (perhaps stimulated by the Arrowsmith book) to educate deaf children in regular schools. In spite of the fact that many educational authorities supported the concept and conscientiously implemented it, by the end of the century it too was abandoned in these countries as unsuccessful. It is instructive, however, to review some of the comments on "mainstreaming" made by the educators of the period. The practice was recommended for much the same reasons as today; that is, children would be able to remain within the family setting, be exposed to normal behavioral and language models in a regular school, and have greater diversity of educational opportunities. They believed that the eye could substitute for the ear, and that all that was necessary to integrate deaf children successfully would be for the regular teachers to "talk more slowly and distinctly" (Gordon, 1885, p. 124). Educational insights and suggestions made at the time (from 1815 to 1885) include the following:

1. Early education in a special school, to lay the educational groundwork, and later transfer to a regular school

2. Early education in a regular school, to be with family and learn good work habits, and then later transfer to a special school

3. "Units" in a regular school, and partial integration into the regular classes

4. In-service training for the regular teachers

5. Better training for the special teachers

6. Recognition that adventitiously deaf children had different needs than those who were congenitally deaf

7. Recognition that children differed in their degree of hearing loss (the Arrowsmith boy could "hear" when someone talked directly into his ear)

8. Formal parent education programs, using a natural language approach

9. Concern that true "assimilation" between deaf and normal-hearing children did not take place, judging from their interactions on playgrounds

These predecessors of ours knew what they were doing; they just did not have the technical and educational resources to implement their knowledge. Regional day programs were not possible because of transportation limitations, and, of course, the existence of hearing aids and FM systems could not even be imagined. We, on the other hand, possess these formerly unimaginable resources; our challenge is to employ them effectively.

Unlike our colleagues of 150 years ago, the question we face is not whether mainstreaming is possible. We know the answer to this question. Not only is it possible, but—like it or not—it undoubtedly will remain a permanent fixture on the educational landscape. The questions we face are somewhat more subtle: Who should be mainstreamed? When should it happen? How should it be implemented? What are the necessary conditions to ensure its success?

GENERAL PRINCIPLES

Means and Ends

Our goal is to ensure the *appropriate* education of a child, not mainstreaming per se. Mainstreaming in its various manifestations presents a process, a means by which this goal can be reached for some hearing-impaired children. The physical placement of such a child in a regular classroom is not an educational success criterion. Chapter 3 emphasized that educational alternatives should be viewed as horizontal, equal value choices, not as a vertical display (the higher up, the least restrictive, the "better"). This is not to denigrate mainstreaming; when it offers the correct choice for a child, it can pay academic and communicative dividends not possible with more restrictive educational placements. But the educational perspective must consider the unique needs of a child and not the commitment of some educators to an abstract notion.

Mainstreaming Varieties

Mainstreaming is not a polar phenomenon, where children are either mainstreamed or not. As we view the concept, the gradations extend beyond the usual range of educational models. Within a school setting, any social, communicative, or academic interactions between hearing-impaired children and normal-hearing peers or teachers can be considered mainstreaming. We know of one young lady who is a fully enrolled student in a school for the deaf but goes to a regular high school, accompanied by an interpreter, for one course 3 days a week. She has very few interactions with either the teacher or the other students in the class, although these are increasing as time goes by. Is this mainstreaming? We would argue yes, albeit very limited in scope. She is taking a course not available in the special school, is slowly gaining confidence in her ability to relate to the "hearing world," has piqued her hearing classmates' interest in sign language, and is sensitizing them to the problems of deafness. In spite of its limited scope, we view this as a very successful example of mainstreaming.

Child Assessment

One cannot develop a valid individual educational plan without a careful, comprehensive assessment of the child's limitations and capabilities. Many dimensions of performance, such as a child's communicative motivation (Pflaster, 1981), do not lend themselves easily to quantification but have been found to be crucial determiners of academic success in the mainstream. Because they are difficult to quantify does not mean that they are unimportant and can be ignored. Indeed, we believe that the most sensitive evaluation "tool" is the gut impression of the experienced, skilled, and sensitive examiner. At the same time, it is also vital to administer standardized tests of academic, communicative, and psychosocial performance, which can be quantified.

A comprehensive assessment is not required only to determine the appropriate educational placement for a child, but the resulting scores can measure the child's progress over time. The emphasis we place on evaluation is reflected in its detailed coverage in the foregoing chapters. Moreover, we have stressed that no one examiner can possibly provide all the information necessary to plan a program and chart a child's progress. Although the "educational team" may appear to be an overworked cliché, it nonetheless validly describes the comprehensive assessment of hearing-impaired children. The case manager is responsible for coordinating the activities of the team and for ensuring that all the components have been considered.

The Hearing Component

All the components of a comprehensive evaluation are necessary, and all are important. Of them all, however, we view the auditory factor as particularly significant. The children are in our care and receive our concern precisely because they have a hearing loss. It is their hearing impairment that generates the communicative, academic, and psychosocial problems we attempt to document with our evaluations. Much of the rationale for the management program rests on the fact that hearing loss is rarely total, and the most effective therapeutic approach exploits this hearing residuum. Our first priority, therefore, is to minimize the impact of a hearing loss as much as possible through the effective use of amplification. Easier said than done, as it requires knowledge of the variables that can affect the full realization of residual hearing (see chapter 8). There is no easy way to acquire this knowledge, but one cannot ignore it. Speech-language pathologists, teachers of the hearing-impaired, and audiologists require such mastery, not only for use when working directly with the children but also when providing support and in-service training to classroom teachers.

Supportive Assistance

Rarely if ever are support services *not* necessary for mainstreamed hearing-impaired children, particularly those with more severe hearing losses. The fact that a child functions academically at grade level does not indicate that support can be withdrawn; it may well explain why the child is performing satisfactorily. If such help is withdrawn, the strong possibility exists that academic deficiencies will soon become apparent. Continual monitoring is necessary to determine what services the child still requires (e.g., focus on articulation skills may be phased out, with changing pragmatic requirements becoming the new emphasis of therapy).

Similarly, following up a child's use of amplification is always necessary. While children can be expected to troubleshoot their own systems as they grow older, they cannot know about amplification developments more suited to their needs in changing educational circumstances. Deplorably, some hearing-impaired students enter college with little information about their hearing losses, the most suitable type of hearing devices for their needs, and the value of an FM system in large classes (Flexer, Wray, & Black, 1986). Even at the college level, support services help these young men and women understand more about their hearing losses, themselves, and the kinds of strategies they can use to minimize the effects of a hearing loss.

Psychosocial Considerations

Various criteria can help judge whether mainstreaming has been successfully accomplished. We would place the psychosocial dimension at the top of the list. The evidence (reviewed in chapter 2) clearly demonstrates that in terms of oral communication and academic skills, mainstreamed hearing-impaired children are superior to their peers in special schools. The reasons for this observed superiority are speculative, although we hold that the increased expectations and demands of a regular setting play a stimulatory role in this finding. We do not have any convincing large-scale evidence, one way or another, regarding the differences in the psychosocial dimension between mainstreamed and segregated hearing-impaired children. For individual children—and all education ultimately reduces to a particular child—we would be remiss if superiority in academic and communication performance occurred at the expense of a child's psychosocial adjustment. This consequence is far from inevitable; otherwise we would not be exponents of mainstreaming. However, a hearing-impaired child's psychosocial adjustment in school cannot be left to chance; there are many ways to increase a child's social adjustment and self-esteem in the school setting (Schwartz, 1990). An unhappy, isolated child is too high a price to pay for academic "success." All school personnel must be sensitive to this factor, and it must be an explicit topic raised in the team meetings.

In-service Training

Our predecessors of 150 years ago recognized the need for in-service training for the same reason we do now: If these children are to be placed in a regular classroom, the classroom teacher must be prepared to deal with them. The classroom teacher is the central educational figure in mainstreaming. He or she is the one involved with the children for most of the day, and the skills that he or she brings to bear will, in large part, determine how well the children perform. The curriculum for training regular classroom teachers does not include information on the effects of hearing loss and how to circumvent these effects in a classroom. Therefore, when a hearing-impaired child is placed in a regular classroom, there is no alternative to an in-service program if the child is to receive an appropriate education.

The issue, then, revolves not around such a program's necessity, but rather its content, how and when it is to be scheduled, and who will be responsible for conducting it. Furthermore, as the child will be exposed to many teachers while progressing through school, in-service programs must persist throughout the child's school years. The most effective program focuses on the specific problems and needs of a particular child, with generalities emerging and discussed as necessary (e.g., dimensions of auditory management). The trainer should be a staff member in the school system (speech-language pathologist, teacher of the hearing-impaired, educational audiologist) and available for classroom visits and consultations.

"Listening" to the Children

We should need no reminder that children are not "objects" that we service, manipulate, or control, even with the best of intentions. True, we use our knowledge and professional skills to plan the best program we can for a child. But there is always going to be a reaction, not necessarily verbal. The reaction can be seen behaviorally or through changes in a performance dimension. The point is our sensitivity to these changes, which is what we mean by "listening."

Some changes may have nothing to do with a child's hearing loss but simply be an example of a child growing up in a particular environment. The professional who is "listening" will be able to separate out these instances from changes that relate somehow to the hearing loss. As these children grow up, questions about their hearing losses inevitably arise. Sometimes they want to know when they can discard their hearing aids, as no adults in their life wear them. Often they resent being the only one in class must wear a visible hearing device. Most hearing-impaired children eventually need some help in dealing with the fact of their hearing losses. "Rap" groups with other children (beginning when in the early teens) can prove very helpful. Children who never refer to their hearing losses and who resent being the recipients of special services are also telling us something we must "hear." This behavior cannot be ignored. The hearing loss will not go away, and thus we must try to help the children accept its reality *but not limit their eventual possible accomplishments.*

"Listening" to the Parents

Parents of hearing-impaired children come with the territory. There is no way we can, or should, provide therapeutic services to their children without involving them to one extent or another. By law parents must be consulted before an IEP can be accepted and implemented. This is a given. "Listening" to them, however, means going beyond the legal requirements. A relationship must exist between professionals and parents in which the professionals explicitly offer their "ears" to the parents as they express their hopes, concerns, and anxieties.

The IEP process is not often conducive to this relationship. The IEP itself is a very dry document, reviewed by the parents in the (unintended) intimidating presence of the interdisciplinary team. Not many parents can open up in this atmosphere. There is another "team" involved here, however, the one comprised of the parents and each individual professional concerned with their child. Each must give the parents an opportunity to discuss the child in an open, nonthreatening atmosphere. The insights gained in these exchanges will not only help the professionals round out their picture of the child but will help the parents accept the reality of their child's condition.

THE EDUCATIONAL AUDIOLOGIST

Rationale

A pervasive theme in this book has been the necessity to provide mainstreamed hearing-impaired children with knowledgeable and continuing auditory management. In our judgment, this can be implemented most effectively by educational audiologists. These professionals' specialized competencies make them most suitable to oversee a school-based audiological management program. In the past few years, an increasing number of audiologists are being employed by public school systems. This heartening development must be nurtured and encouraged—most effectively by the actual demonstration of their contributions to the education of mainstreamed hearing-impaired children. It must be understood, however, that their contributions cannot be fully realized unless these educational audiologists have the appropriate facilities and equipment readily accessible in the school setting.

The alternative to an on-site educational audiologist entails depending on outside facilities for these services. Ordinarily in such situations a great deal of effort is expended in trying to work out a mutually acceptable working relationship. Although such models can and have worked, they embody inherent contradictions that no amount of goodwill or skill can overcome completely.

The child has to be taken from the school and transported to the audiology center. There he or she has to be "registered"; many forms must be filled out and ongoing records kept in several of the center's offices; arrangements must be made through one or more agencies to pay for the services, often with the time-consuming help of a social worker; a communication exchange (written, phone, or personal visits) must be initiated between the center and the school. These requirements add a financial burden to society, with no consequent benefits and indeed a loss of efficiency for the child receiving the services. This occurs because we engage an administratively separate agency to provide what are basically educational, not clinical, services.

There are other disadvantages in depending on outside centers to provide audiology services to hearing-impaired children. The children may not be able to bring their FM systems to the clinic because school officials are often reluctant to permit school property to be taken home. Often, too, clinic-based audiologists will not know that a child uses such a unit unless they specifically query the parents and the child. Some clinical audiologists make an effort to visit the schools of the children they serve, but these visits are difficult to arrange. Schools must compensate the center for the visit and are often reluctant to include travel time in the compensation. Because an audiologist will have to cancel several appointments when scheduling a visit, the cost can easily become an issue. Rarely, therefore, are such visits scheduled on an ongoing basis.

The day-to-day audiological emergencies that never cease (e.g., the sudden onset of feedback, a nonfunctioning hearing aid or auditory trainer, a change in a child's auditory responsiveness) require that a knowledgeable person be available almost immediately. The speech-language pathologist or the teacher of the hearing-impaired should be able to resolve some of these crises. The more involved problems (such as the need to fashion a new earmold, make minor repairs, or run an electroacoustic analysis of the amplification system) require on-site audiological expertise.

Clinic-based audiological management of children was not a planned event or a deliberately created model of care for the audiological needs of hearing-impaired children. The situation evolved as an outgrowth of the development of audiology centers that focused mainly on adults. Children were simply plugged into existing possibilities while all concerned did the best they could under the prevailing constraints. Now, however, we must acknowledge the technological developments of a new era and marshall them for the benefit of hearing-impaired children. In our judgment, this is difficult to accomplish without trained on-site personnel. We must, in other words, organize a new programmatic model, one that brings current technological developments right into the schools. The full educational implications of proper audiological management cannot be realized in absentia.

Organization, Activities, and Demographics

The audiological management of hearing-impaired children begins once these children are detected. The effects of a hearing loss for deaf children becomes apparent early, but confirmation of a hearing loss for hard-of-hearing children often occurs only after they begin school. The educational audiologist is the logical person to supervise the school system's identification audiometry program (Wilson & Walton, 1978). This function should not be underestimated, particularly now that we have more insight into the potential effects of mild, unilateral, and fluctuating hearing losses (Bess, 1988; Kavanagh, 1986).

A properly organized hearing conservation program—incorporating as it does personnel training, equipment calibration, appropriate record-keeping, and follow-up efforts—is a time-consuming and involved process. The educational audiologist's contributions to such a program can serve as an entree to convince school officials of the need to employ a school-based professional. The economics of the situation can help lend additional weight to this argument.

Each child who fails the screening examinations must receive a more comprehensive audiometric evaluation. The school often bears the cost for these evaluations, at least when testing is required by the IEP. In this category there may be children with a history of chronic otitis media and those exhibiting other "special" needs (developmentally disabled, emotionally disturbed, etc.). The IEPs of children with significant hearing losses, whether or not they wear hearing aids, should require a yearly comprehensive audiological evaluation. Though we doubt that educational audiologists will ever recoup their costs by administering such tests under the aegis of a school system, nevertheless the expense will not be as high as it might at first appear. Ultimately, of course, the most urgent justification is educational; if we cannot defend such a position on educational grounds, no other reasoning would be acceptable.

The greatest initial expense in employing an educational audiologist comes with providing this person with the tools necessary for the job. The extent to which an audiologist can carry out his or her detailed responsibilities depends on the equipment and facilities available. The less adequate the facilities available in the school system, the more contracting with outside centers will be necessary. Although a little unwieldy, this arrangement can be moderately effective because the on-site audiologist can collaborate on equal professional terms with a clinic-based audiologist. In these instances, the school audiologist acts as the initiater, controller, traffic manager, interpreter, and gadfly regarding any outside audiological assistance required.

A complete public school audiological center should be indistinguishable from the average outside clinic. It should include a sound-treated two-room testing suite, a two-channel clinical audiometer, several portable audiometers, a middle-ear immittance testing device, a probe-tube microphone unit, an electroacoustic hearing aid analyzer, a sound-level meter (incorporating audiometer calibration capacities), a stock of loaner hearing aids and FM auditory training systems, earmold impression material, battery testers, and hearing aid stethoscopes. Some of these devices (the audiometer and the probe-tube microphone system) may include computer capability for data storage and analysis. Most of these tools represent capital expenses; once purchased, they should last for years (provided the budget includes maintenance expenditures). It is not necessary to duplicate the medical audiology capacity of outside centers by including electrophysiological testing devices.

The actual delivery of audiological services can be expedited, at a great savings of time, efficiency, and convenience, if the audiological equipment and facilities are incorporated in a mobile audiometric van. This permits services to be brought to the children rather than the other way around. Such a van is useful not only in rural areas but in urban centers as well, particularly if the children are not located in one immediate geographic area (such as an educational "park"). The school system's hearing conservation program is also greatly simplified if a mobile van is employed.

We suggest that any school system that enrolls 8,000 or more pupils can gainfully employ a full-time educational audiologist. About 2,000 of the children will receive a hearing screening each year. The personnel who actually perform the screening must be supervised, the equipment must function properly, and detailed records of failure and referral must be kept. Of the 2,000, perhaps 5–10% will fail the screening tests and need to be rescreened later. Somewhat less than half, or about 60–100 children, will fail the rescreening and must then receive an individual audiometric evaluation by the audiologist.

The demographic data reviewed in chapter 1 reveal that 15 to 30 per 1,000 schoolchildren will have a hearing loss in excess of 16 dB in their better ear. Taking the minimum figure, we can estimate that about 120 children (in our hypothetical school system of 8,000 pupils) will show this degree of hearing loss and will require individual audiometric testing each year. This population will overlap only in part with those identified through hearing screening. Thus, we can conservatively estimate that about 150 complete evaluations must be conducted each year. In addition, many of the younger children with known hearing losses should be monitored more often.

Of this population of 8,000 children, demographic data indicate that approximately 80–100 will have or require amplification, many using binaural fittings. The educational audiologist therefore will need to administer about 150 behavioral and electroacoustic hearing aid evaluations each year. All the children who wear amplification systems are potential candidates for an FM system, which also must be checked behaviorally and electroacoustically.

Visits must be scheduled to all the children's classrooms to ensure that FM systems are being used properly, to monitor the acoustical conditions, and to consult with the classroom teachers. All staff members concerned with a hearing-impaired child should receive periodic in-service training programs, ideally conducted by the educational audiologist. The latter is also the logical case manager, which in itself can be a time-consuming task.

What we have outlined is clearly a full-time job. Moreover, it is not a clinical position, as the term is generally understood, but one that primarily emphasizes the communicative and educational needs of hearing-impaired children. Certainly, educational audiologists cooperate with their medical colleagues. When a child fails a school screening, when the hearing loss appears to be progressive, when immittance testing suggests a middle-ear problem, they make a medical referral and then follow up on the recommendations. Although their primary purpose is defined in medical terms, their specialty is the nonmedical habilitation of hearing-impaired children. Among their responsibilities is the sensitization of their medical colleagues to the communicative, educational, and psychosocial implications of a hearing loss. The educational audiologist is an *educator*, one who specializes in reducing the impact of a hearing loss by maximizing the use of residual hearing.

Professionals working with hearing-impaired children should understand that, of all the children manifesting linguistic disturbances, functionally hard-of-hearing children probably have the best prognosis. The cause of their difficulties is known and remediation measures clear-cut.

Their problem derives not from some faulty "wiring" in their brains but from damage to the peripheral nerve of hearing. Technology has offered us possibilities for treatment inconceivable years ago and, one hopes, will offer us more in the years to come.

In the past, many hard-of-hearing children were overlooked (except by themselves and their parents, of course) and caught between two worlds, the deaf and the hearing. We maintain that these children are more like hearing children than deaf ones and that, allowing for minor modifications, curriculum and expectations should be patterned on their normal-hearing peers. Given appropriate management, hard-of-hearing children are capable of a normal range of achievements and a normal range of contributions to our society. Our hope is that the professionals involved can manifest the same capacity for growth inherent in these children, and that they will employ this book effectively for that purpose.

APPENDIX A:
Letter to Classroom Teacher

Dear ____,

Your student, _____, appears to be in a classroom situation that would benefit from physical modifications to improve the classroom acoustics. Such modifications include carpeting on the floor, drapes on the windows, and acoustical tiles on the walls and ceiling. It should be noted that while the average ambient noise level in a classroom is typically 60 dB SPL, the noise level measures that were made in _____'s classroom on ____(date) demonstrated noise levels of ____. The higher levels make it difficult for him/her to receive a good auditory signal.

Another recommendation from improving _____'s listening environment is the use of a wireless FM system. This system, used only in school, enables a child to receive direct auditory stimulation from the teacher while suppressing some of the environmental noise. In light of _____'s hearing loss and his/her dependence on proper amplification for receiving a strong auditory signal, an FM system is highly recommended.

Although the hearing aids _____ uses provide him/her with appropriate amplification in many situations, the noise levels in the school setting make it difficult to hear even when using the hearing aids. Through the use of an FM system, _____ will be better able to attend to the teacher and other students.

I hope this information is of benefit to you in meeting _____'s unique educational needs.

APPENDIX B:
Definition of and Competencies for Aural Rehabilitation Position Statement[1]

The following Committee on Rehabilitative Audiology Report was adopted by the ASHA Legislative Council in November, 1983. Present and past committee members responsible for the development of this statement include O. T. Kenworthy, past Chair; James McCartney, current Chair; Evelyn Cherow, ex officio; Jaclyn Gauger, Robert Hinkle, Antonia Maxon, Mary Pat Moeller, Mary Jo Osberger, Thomas Rees, Jan Colton, Cheryl Deconde, Gene Del Polito, William Haas, Gerri Kahn, Dorothy Stein, Dean Garstecki, and Vice Presidents for Clinical Affairs, Hughlett Morris and David Yoder.

The following Definition of and Competencies for Aural Rehabilitation Position Statement and the Guidelines for Graduate Training in Amplification were each developed by a separate standing committee of the Association in response to a charge formulated by the Legislative Council. In November, 1983, the Legislative Council adopted the products of both committees. In addition, a recommendation was made that these be published together in order to convey to the membership that the content of the two documents is viewed by Council to be significantly interrelated.

E. Cherow, Director
Audiology Liaison Branch

BACKGROUND

Some apparent contradictions among ASHA policies, as well as discrepancies between those policies and clinical practice, have obscured who should provide services in aural rehabilitation and who should supervise those services.

- A position paper adopted by Legislative Council in 1973 (*Asha*, 1974), The Audiologist: Responsibilities in the Habilitation of the Auditorily Handicapped, indicated that the audiologist is the main provider and supervisor of aural rehabilitation.
- A resolution by the American Board of Examiners in Speech-Language Pathology and Audiology (ABESPA) (ABESPA, 1979), now the

1 From *ASHA*, 26(5), pp. 37–41. Copyright 1984 by the American Speech-Language-Hearing Association. Reprinted by permission.

Professional Standards Council, specified some supervisory roles in aural rehabilitation: audiologists supervise assessment procedures, including hearing aid selection and fitting, and speech-language pathologists supervise speech and language assessment of the hearing-impaired clients. No position was taken about supervision of intervention.

- Meanwhile, in actual practice, many speech-language pathologists provide services to hearing-impaired clients, particularly in settings where such services by an audiologist are not available.
- There continued to be differences among audiologists and differences among speech-language pathologists in their interests, training, experience, and competencies in aural rehabilitation.

The apparent discrepancies between Association policy and clinical practice led this Committee to shift the focus of debate over who should provide aural rehabilitation services. Rather than endorse either audiologists or speech-language pathologists as the primary service provider, the Committee chose to delineate comprehensive service delivery as a set of proposed minimal competencies (Committee on Rehabilitative Audiology, 1980). Those minimal competencies however, did not offer a corresponding definition of aural rehabilitation and did not address current variations in clinician's skills, interests, and training. Therefore, this report proposes:

- a revised definition of aural rehabilitation that is consistent with the proposed minimal competencies and complements the definition provided in the 1973 Position Statement; and,
- a revision of the minimal competencies that subdivides the required body of special knowledge into areas of expertise consistent with present clinical practice.

DEFINITION OF AURAL REHABILITATION

Aural rehabilitation refers to services and procedures for facilitating adequate receptive and expressive communication in individuals with hearing impairment. These services and procedures are intended for those persons who demonstrate a loss of hearing sensitivity or function in communicative situations as if they possess a loss of hearing sensitivity. The services and procedures include, but are not limited to:

I. Identification and Evaluation of Sensory Capabilities
   A. Identification and evaluation of the extent of the impairment, including assessment, periodic monitoring and re-evaluation of auditory abilities.

B. Monitoring of other sensory capabilities (e.g., visual and tactile-kinesthetic) as they relate to receptive and expressive communication.

C. Evaluation, fitting and monitoring of auditory aids and monitoring of other sensory aids (e.g., visual and vibrotactile) used by the auditorily handicapped person in various communicative environments (e.g., home, work and school). Such auditory and sensory aids are taken to include all amplification systems (group and individual), as well as such supplementary devices as telephone amplifiers, alarm systems and so on.

D. Evaluation and monitoring of the acoustic characteristics of the communicative environments confronted by the hearing-impaired person.

II. Interpretation of Results, Counseling and Referral

A. Interpretation of audiologic findings to the client, his/her family, employer, teachers, and significant others involved in communication with the hearing-impaired person.

B. Guidance and counseling for the client, his/her family, employer, caregiver, teachers and significant others concerning the educational, psychosocial and communicative effects of hearing impairment.

C. Guidance and counseling for the parent/caregiver regarding:
- educational options available;
- selection of educational programs; and
- facilitation of communicative and cognitive development.

D. Individual and/or family counseling regarding:
- acceptance and understanding of the hearing impairment;
- functioning within difficult listening situations;
- facilitation of effective strategies and attitudes toward communication;
- modification of communicative behavior in keeping with those strategies and attitudes; and,
- promotion of independent management of communication-related problems.

E. Referral for additional services (e.g., medical, psychological, social, and educational), as appropriate.

III. Intervention for Communicative Difficulties

A. Development and provision of an intervention program to facilitate expressive and receptive communication.

B. Provision of hearing and speech conservation programming.

C. Service as a liaison between the client, family and other agencies concerned with the management of communicative disorders related to hearing impairment.

IV. Re-evaluation of the client's status
V. Evaluation and modification of the intervention program

PROPOSED MINIMAL COMPETENCIES FOR THE PROVISION OF AURAL REHABILITATION

Definition of Terms:

The terms *basic knowledge, basic understanding,* and *special knowledge* require some specification before proceeding to the proposed competencies. Considered relative to the familiar taxonomy of Bloom (1956; Bloom, Hastings, & Madaus, 1971) we would define these terms as follows:

- Basic knowledge incorporates what Bloom refers to as *knowledge.* It involves the "recall of specifics and universals, recall of methods and processes, or recall of a pattern, structure or setting (Bloom et al., 1971; p. 271)."
- Basic understanding may be equated with Bloom's category of *comprehension.* "This represents the lowest level of understanding or apprehension such that the individual knows what is being communicated and can make use of the material or idea . . . without necessarily relating it to other material or seeing its fullest implications (p. 272)." This may involve the processes of translation, interpretation and/or extrapolation.
- Special knowledge refers to the remainder of Bloom's categories which include *application, analysis, synthesis,* and *evaluation.* It is at this level that the learner is expected to not only possess knowledge but also to demonstrate the ability to apply and elaborate upon the knowledge.

Basic Knowledge and Basic Understanding

Persons providing aural rehabilitation should demonstrate:
I. A basic knowledge of general psychology, sociology, mathematics, general physics, zoology, human anatomy and physiology.
II. A basic understanding of normal communication processes, including:
A. Anatomic and physiologic bases for the normal development and use of speech, language and hearing; such as, anatomy, neurology, and physiology of speech, language and hearing mechanisms;
B. Physical bases and processes of the production and perception of speech and hearing; such as, (a) acoustics or physics of sound, (b) phonology, (c) physiologic and acoustic phonetics, (d) perceptual processes, and (e) psychoacoustics; and,

C. Linguistic and psycholinguistic variables related to the normal development and use of speech, language, and hearing; such as, (a) linguistics (historical, descriptive, sociolinguistics, urban language), (b) psychology of language, (c) psycholinguistics, (d) language and speech acquisition, and (e) verbal learning and verbal behavior.

Special Knowledge

III. A special knowledge of the following areas should be demonstrated, depending upon whether the chosen area of expertise is to be adults (A), children (C) or hearing aid selection (H):

Area of Expertise

A. As regards *auditory system disorders*, persons should be able to:

ACH
   • identify, describe and differentiate the various disorders of auditory function such as disorders of the outer, middle and inner ear, the auditory nerve and the associated neural and central auditory system pathways.

B. As regards *audiologic assessment procedures*, persons must be able to:

ACH
   • provide and interpret pure-tone and speech audiometric measures used to evaluate peripheral and central auditory functions including, but not limited to, measures of threshold sensitivity and measures to differentiate sites of auditory dysfunction.

ACH
   • identify and perform screening examinations for speech and language problems.

ACH
   • determine the need for referral to other medical and nonmedical specialists for appropriate professional services.

C. As regards *evaluation of personal and group amplification, and other sensory aids*, persons must be able to:

ACH
   • perform and interpret measures of amplification-system characteristics.

ACH
   • provide and interpret behavioral measures of listener performance with amplification.

ACH
   • demonstrate skills in the fitting and adjustment of amplification (e.g., modifying tubing, manipulating controls, and fitting earmolds).

ACH
   • plan and implement a program of orientation to hearing aid use as a means of improving communicative function.

ACH	• evaluate and describe the effects of amplification use on communicative function.
ACH	• evaluate and describe the influences of environmental factors on communicative function.
ACH	• describe the availability and use of sensory aids, as well as telephone and telecommunication devices, for hearing-impaired persons.
ACH	• design and implement a program for monitoring and maintaining both personal and group amplification systems.
ACH	• describe alternate methods of hearing aid selection and procurement.

D. As regards *normal communicative development and the effects of hearing impairment on communicative development*, persons must be able to:

C	• describe the semantic, syntactic, pragmatic and phonologic aspects of human communication as they relate to normal communicative development both in terms of comprehension and production.
C	• describe the effects of hearing impairment on the development of semantic, syntactic, pragmatic and phonologic aspects of communication, both in terms of comprehension and production.

E. As regards the *assessment of and intervention upon communicative skills* of hearing-impaired individuals, persons must be able to:

AC	• administer or provide for the administration of all assessment measures in the client's preferred mode of communication.
AC	• administer and interpret appropriate standardized and nonstandardized measures of speech and voice production.
AC	• administer and interpret appropriate standardized and nonstandardized measures of language comprehension and production skills and/or alternate communicative skills, such as signing.
AC	• administer and interpret appropriate standardized and nonstandardized measures of auditory, visual and combined auditory-visual communicative skills.
AC	• describe communicative skills based upon a comprehensive assessment of communicative abilities.
AC	• determine and describe communicative needs of the hearing-impaired individual.

AC   • develop and implement a rehabilitative intervention plan based on considerations of communicative skills and communicative needs of the hearing-impaired individuals.

AC   • develop and implement a system for measuring and monitoring the appropriateness of the rehabilitative intervention plan.

F. As regards *conservation of hearing and prevention of communicative problems*, persons must be able to:

ACH   • plan and implement a program of periodic monitoring of auditory abilities and communicative function.

ACH   • describe the effects of environmental influences, hearing aid use, and sources of trauma on residual auditory function.

ACH   • evaluate measures of environmental acoustic conditions and relate that evaluation to effects upon communicative skills.

G. As regards the *psychological, social, educational, and vocational ramifications of hearing impairment*, persons must be able to:

ACH   • describe normal aspects of psychosocial development.

ACH   • describe the impact of hearing impairment on psychosocial development.

CH   • describe the effects of hearing impairment on learning.

CH   • describe, in general terms, systems and methods of educational programming.

ACH   • identify the need for and availability of psychological, social, educational and vocational counseling.

H. As regards *communicative-rehabilitative case management*, persons must be able to:

ACH   • describe various techniques of interviewing and interpersonal communication.

ACH   • demonstrate skills in interviewing and interacting with communicatively-impaired individuals and their families.

C   • plan and implement inservice and public-information programs for allied professionals and other interested individuals concerning the prevention, identification, assessment and management of hearing impairment and resulting communicative disorders.

C   • plan and implement parent-education programs concerning the management of hearing impairment and resulting communicative disorders.

H   • plan and implement inservice and public-information
             programs for allied professionals, parents and other
             interested individuals concerning the prevention, iden-
             tification, assessment and management of auditory dis-
             orders only.
ACH   • demonstrate the ability to communicate case informa-
             tion to allied professionals and others working with
             communicatively-impaired individuals.
AC   • plan and implement service programs with allied profes-
             sionals who serve hearing-impaired persons.

DISCUSSION

Terminology

This Committee recommends use of *aural rehabilitation* as the appropriate
descriptive term for the following reasons:

1. With the accompanying definition as supporting documentation,
   the term *aural rehabilitation* is no longer as restrictive as was con-
   tended in the 1973 position statement.
2. The term *audiologic habilitation* is potentially viewed as discipline
   specific and, therefore, more restrictive. By incorporating specific
   reference to audiology this term potentially limits both service
   provision and supervision to audiologists. As noted previously, this
   is inconsistent with present practice and with at least one aspect of
   Association policy (ABESPA, 1979).
3. The term habilitation suggests skill establishment and skill replacement rather than elaboration of existing skills. Such a view is inconsistent with existing literature on normal language acquisition
   (Fletcher & Garman, 1979) and language development of the hearing impaired (e.g., Curtiss, Prutting & Lowell, 1979; Skarakis &
   Prutting, 1977). As defined above, aural rehabilitation addresses
   communicative skills which are known to exist in some form.
   Therefore, the process becomes a rehabilitative one rather than
   habilitative. Furthermore, the orientation implied by the term habilitation potentially disregards the fact that the majority of auditory
   disorders are adventitious in nature and are suffered primarily by
   adults with an established set of communicative skills.
4. The term rehabilitation is better recognized by third-party payers
   and others not familiar with this profession's terminology.

Training Implications

As a clinical service, aural rehabilitation occupies a unique position. The duties of the aural-rehabilitation service provider cover a broad range of specialized skills that may be addressed by speech-language pathologists, audiologists, teachers of the hearing impaired, psychologists, counselors and physicians. Cross-disciplinary training, therefore, seems requisite to properly prepare clinicians to provide aural rehabilitation. To be maximally effective, training programs may need to draw upon courses in several areas and departments. The proposed minimal competencies may provide training programs with guidelines in the selection, evaluation and monitoring of coursework and clinical experiences. Furthermore, a competency-based approach may allow training programs to indicate more clearly to potential employers what to expect from graduating students. This not only increases the credibility of the training program but may also improve student performance for at least two reasons. First, employers may be less inclined to impose unrealistic expectations upon the clinician. Second, if the content of the training is properly specified, the clinician should be better prepared to meet the critical demands of the work setting (Northcott, 1973). From the clinician's perspective, such shifts in job-readiness and employer attitudes should lead to increased credibility, effectiveness and job satisfaction. More importantly, from the client's perspective these shifts should facilitate improved service delivery.

A repeated concern is that the implementation of competencies will necessarily increase the time required for students to matriculate. This is a legitimate point in view of rising educational costs and declining enrollments at the graduate level. Such a concern, however, is predicated on the assumption that all training occurs at the preservice level. It seems unreasonable, though, to expect any preservice training program to be the complete source of knowledge in any profession. We should only expect that preservice training will provide the emerging professional with the skills for meeting a limited set of client and employer needs and the strategies for acquiring new knowledge and skills on the job.

From this viewpoint, then, continuing education assumes a prominent role in training clinicians. It, therefore, becomes critical that we delineate training and service-delivery guidelines that extend beyond the preservice level. As such, the proposed minimal competencies are intended to delineate comprehensive service delivery independent of training method or level.

Continuing Education

The need for and utility of inservice training in aural rehabilitation is well documented in the literature (Davis, 1977; Garstecki, 1978; Hochberg,

Levitt & Osberger, 1980; Davis & Shepard, 1983; Hochberg & Schmidt, 1983; Maxon & Brackett, 1983). For example, studies by Hochberg et al., (1980) and Hochberg & Schmidt (1983) examined the need for inservice training to upgrade speech-language pathologists' skills in teaching speech to hearing-impaired children. Based on a questionnaire survey, they found that a large percentage of speech-language pathologists learned such speech-training techniques from outside reading and from inservice training. This survey further revealed that 95% of the clinicians surveyed felt they would benefit from continuing professional education designed to improve their competence in providing speech and language services to hearing-impaired children.

Although the need for continuing education is clearly established, the most effective method for implementing such training is open to further study. In fact, the National Commission on Allied Health Education (1980) recommended that participants carefully examine the issue of delivery systems for continuing education. The question arises, then, whether a competency-based approach might be effectively applied to continuing education in our field. An example of a successful application of this approach is a project conducted by Hochberg & Schmidt (1983). After intensive inservice training, speech-language pathologists and teachers of the hearing impaired completed a rating scale designed to identify their relative degree of confidence in various areas of competence. Competencies were classified relative to direct provision of services or implementation of inservice training for other staff. The results indicated that, after training, the participants felt more confident in those activities related to direct provision of services. They felt less confident in presenting didactic materials and demonstrating the application of the methods to their colleagues. Although more rigorous evaluation procedures may be needed to assess training effects, this study demonstrates the feasibility of identifying and teaching specific competencies utilizing inservice training.

Consumer and Professional Needs

Competency-based training may also service as a mechanism for meeting some consumer and professional needs that appear to be interdependent. For instance, a number of reports in the literature have identified the following concerns:

1. Public information relative to the services we provide and the impact/importance of those services is lacking (Stream & Stream, 1980; Smaldino & Sahli, 1980; Sweetow & Barrager, 1980). This lack of awareness has been identified in both large metropolitan areas

(Pearlstein, Russell & Fink, 1977) and in rural areas (Kellarney & Lass, 1981).

2. Hearing aid orientation programs are not always offered to hearing-impaired clients by audiologists or speech-language pathologists (Barrager, 1978; Brooks, 1979; Sweetow & Barrager, 1980; Stevenson & Dawtry, 1980).

3. Most programs in aural rehabilitation do not target specific goals and objectives relative to counseling of clients. Yet, such counseling has been shown to have a significant impact upon prognosis (Oyer, Freeman, Dixon, Donnelly, Goldstein, Lloyd & Mussen, 1976; Brooks, 1979; Sweetow & Barrager, 1980; Flahive & White, 1981).

It is reasonable to expect that, if we re-oriented our certification and training to reflect the consumer needs and concerns expressed in points two and three above, that customer satisfaction and the credibility of our profession might concomitantly improve. This, in turn, would address the professional concerns raised in point one. In an era of declining resources, such consumer support represents a crucial element of professional survival. It is noteworthy that the proposed competencies specifically address the consumer concerns raised relative to counseling and hearing aid orientation.

Certification Standards

How then might we reorganize our present training and certification standards to meet these consumer and professional needs? In examining the present certification standards, it is this Committee's opinion that they do not require sufficient training of either audiologists or speech-language pathologists to meet the minimal competencies as proposed. For instance, many audiologists who meet current standards might have difficulty demonstrating even a basic understanding of language development or language intervention. Similarly, speech-language pathologists might encounter difficulty in demonstrating competency in such content areas as amplification systems and implications of audiologic assessment.

What remains before our profession then is the task of specifying how the current standards might align with the proposed competencies. Clearly, that process will require lengthy and detailed study. In the course of that study, however, this Committee recommends that we consider:

- the unique status of aural rehabilitation as a cross-disciplinary area of service provision;
- the need for clear role definitions in the provision of aural rehabilitation to reduce duplication of service and increase cost effectiveness;

- the utility of balancing our training expectations between preservice and continuing education efforts;
- the consumer needs underlying the proposed minimal competencies;
- the need for an official Association policy that addresses both the consumer and professional needs raised here; and,
- the potential utility of addressing the issue of who should provide aural rehabilitation by specifying what services should be provided.

REFERENCES

ABESPA resolution. (1979). *Asha, 21,* 931.

Barrager, D. (1978). A professional hearing aid plan for audiologists in private clinics. *Audiology and Hearing Education, 4,* 12–14.

Bloom, B. S., Hastings, J. T., & Madaus, G. F. (1971). *Handbook on formative and summative evaluation of student learning.* New York: McGraw Hill Inc.

Bloom, B. S. (Ed). (1956). *A taxonomy of educational objectives: The classification of educational goals* (Vols. 1–3). New York: David McKay Co., Inc.

Brooks, D.N. (1979). Counseling and its effects upon hearing aid use. *Scandinavian Audiology, 8,* 101–107.

Committee on Rehabilitative Audiology. (1980). Proposed minimal competencies necessary to provide aural rehabilitation. *Asha, 22,* 461.

Curtiss, S., Prutting, C., & Lowell, E. (1979). Pragmatic and semantic development in young children with impaired hearing. *Journal of Speech and Hearing Research, 22,* 543–552.

Davis, J. (1977). Personnel and services. In J. Davis (Ed.). *Our forgotten children: Hard of hearing pupils in the schools.* Washington, DC: Division of Personnel Preparation, BEH, HEW.

Davis, J., & Shephard, N. (1983). The use of questionnaire data as a basis for inservice planning. In I. Hochberg, H. Levitt, & M. J. Osberger, *Speech of the hearing impaired: Research, training, and personnel preparation.* Baltimore, MD: University Park Press (in press).

Flahive, M., & White, S. (1981). Audiologists and counseling. *Journal of the Academy of Rehabilitative Audiology, 14,* 274–283.

Fletcher, P., & Garman, M. (Eds.). (1979). *Language acquisition: Studies in first language development.* London: Cambridge University Press.

Garstecki, D. (1978). Survey of school audiologists. *Asha, 20,* 291–296.

Hochberg, H., Levitt, H., & Osberger, M. J. (1980). Improving speech services to hearing-impaired children. *Asha, 22,* 480–484.

Hochberg, H., & Schmidt, J. (1983). A modern inservice-preservice training program to improve the speech of hearing-impaired children. In I. Hochberg, H. Levitt, & M. J. Osberger (Eds.). *Speech of the hearing impaired: Research, training and personnel preparation.* Baltimore, MD: University Park Press.

Kellarney, G., & Lass, N. (1981). A survey of rural public awareness of speech-language pathology and audiology. *Asha, 23,* 415–420.

Maxon, A., & Brackett, D. (1983). Inservice training for public school speech-language pathologists in the management of mainstreamed hearing-impaired children. In I. Hochberg, H. Levitt, & M. J. Osberger (Eds). *Speech of the hearing impaired: Research, training and personnel preparation.* Baltimore, MD: University Park Press.

National Commission on Allied Health Education. (1980). The future of allied health education: New alliances for the 1980's. San Francisco: Jossey Bass Publishers.

Northcott, Winifred. (1973). Competencies needed by teachers of hearing-impaired infants, birth to three years, and their parents. *Volta Review, 75,* 532–544.

Oyer, H. L., Freeman, D., Hardick, E., Dixon, J., Donnelly, K., Goldstein, D., & Mussen, E. (1976). Unheeded recommendations for aural rehabilitation: Analysis of a survey. *Journal of the Academy of Rehabilitative Audiology, 9,* 20–30.

Pearlstein, E., Russell, L., & Fink, R. (1977). *Speech-language pathology and audiology: The public's view.* Paper presented at the Annual Convention of the American Speech-Language-Hearing Association, Chicago, IL.

Skarakis, E., & Prutting, C. (1977). Early communication: Semantic functions and communicative intentions in young children with impaired hearing. *American Annals of the Deaf, 122,* 382–391.

Smaldino, J., & Sahli, J. (1980). A litany of needs of hearing impaired customer. *Journal of the Academy of Rehabilitative Audiology, 13,* 109–115.

Stevenson, J., & Dawtry, L. (1980). A study of private hearing aid users in London. *British Journal of Audiology, 14,* 105–114.

Stream, R., & Stream, K. (1980). Focusing on the hearing needs of the elderly. *Journal of the Academy of Rehabilitative Audiology, 13,* 104–108.

Sweetow, R., & Barrager, D. (1980). Quality of comprehensive audiological care: A survey of parents of hearing-impaired children. *Asha, 22,* 841–847.

The audiologist: Responsibilities in the habilitation of the auditorily handicapped. (1974). Report of the committee on Rehabilitative Audiology. *Asha, 16,* 68–70.

References

Allen, T., & Osborn, T. (1984). Academic integration of hearing impaired students. *American Annals of the Deaf, 129,* 100–113.

Allen, T. E. (1986). Patterns of academic achievement among hearing impaired students: 1974 and 1983. In A. N. Schildroth & M. A. Karchmer (Eds.), *Deaf children in America* (pp. 161–206). Austin, TX: PRO-ED.

American National Standards Institute (ANSI). (1982). *American national standard specifications for hearing aids* (S3.22). New York: American National Standards Institute.

American Speech-Language-Hearing Association. (1982). Joint Committee on Infant Hearing statement. *ASHA, 24,* 1017–1018.

Ammons, R. B., & Ammons, H. S. (1948). *Ammons Full-Range Vocabulary Test.* Missoula, MT: Psychological Test Specialists.

Baker, H. J., & Leland, B. (1967). *Detroit Tests of Learning Aptitude.* Austin, TX: PRO-ED.

Bess, F. (1986). The unilaterally hearing-impaired child: A final comment. *Ear and Hearing, 7,* 52–54.

Bess, F. H. (Ed.). (1988). *Hearing impairment in children.* Parkton, MD: York Press.

Blank, M., Rose, S. A., & Berlin, L. J. (1978). *Preschool Language Assessment Instrument.* San Antonio, TX: Psychological Corporation.

Binnie, C. A., Montgomery, A. A., & Jackson, P. L. (1974). Auditory and visual contributions to the perception of consonants. *Journal of Speech and Hearing Research, 17,* 619–630.

Birch, J. W. (1976). *Hearing-impaired children in the mainstream* (Publication of the Leadership Training Institute/Special Education). Reston, VA: University of Minnesota & Council for Exceptional Children.

Boehm, A. (1967). *Boehm Test of Basic Concepts.* San Antonio, TX: Psychological Corporation.

Boney, S. J., & Bess, F. M. (1984, November). *Noise and reverberation effects in minimal bilateral sensorineural hearing loss.* Paper presented to the American Speech-Language-Hearing Association, San Francisco.

Boothroyd, A. (1978). Speech perception and sensorineural hearing loss. In M. Ross & T. G. Giolas (Eds.), *Auditory management of hearing-impaired children* (pp. 117–144). Baltimore, MD: Park Press.

Boothroyd, A. (1982). *Hearing impairments in young children.* Englewood Cliffs, NJ: Prentice-Hall.

Boothroyd, A. (1984). Auditory perception of speech contrasts by subjects with sensorineural hearing loss. *Journal of Speech and Hearing Research, 27,* 134–144.

Boothroyd, A. (Ed.). (1988). Auditory and tactile presentation of voice fundamental frequency as a supplement to speech reading [special issue]. *Ear and Hearing, 9* (6).

Boyle, P. (1977). Psychology. In B. Jaffe (Ed.), *Hearing loss in children* (pp. 266–282). Baltimore, MD: University Park Press.

Brackett, D. (1982). Language assessment protocols for hearing-impaired students. *Topics in Language Disorders, 2*(3), 46–55.

Brackett, D. (1983). Group communication strategies for the hearing impaired. *Volta Review, 85*(5), 116–128.

Brackett, D. (1990). Developing an individual educational plan (IEP). In M. Ross (Ed.), *Hearing-impaired children in the mainstream* (pp. 81–94). Parkton, MD: York Press.

Brackett, D., & Maxon, A. B. (1986). Service delivery alternatives for the mainstreamed hearing-impaired child. *Language, Speech and Hearing Services in the Schools, 17,* 115–125.

Brandes, P., & Ehinger, D. (1981). The effects of early middle ear pathology on auditory perception and academic achievement. *Journal of Speech and Hearing Disorders, 46,* 250–257.

Brannon, J. B. (1968). Linguistic word classes in the spoken language of normal, hard of hearing, and deaf children. *Journal of Speech and Hearing Research, 11,* 279–287.

Brannon, J. B., & Murry, T. (1966). The spoken syntax of normal, hard of hearing, and deaf children. *Journal of Speech and Hearing Research, 9,* 604–610.

Byers, V. B. (1973). Initial consonant intelligibility by hearing-impaired children. *Journal of Speech and Hearing Research, 16,* 48–55.

Carrow-Woolfolk, E. (1985). *Test for Auditory Comprehension of Language–Revised.* Allen, TX: DLM Teaching Resources.

Chaiklin, J. (1959). The relation between three selected auditory speech thresholds. *Journal of Speech and Hearing Research, 2,* 237–243.

Clopton, B. M., & Silverman, M. S. (1977). Plasticity of binaural interaction: II. Critical period and changes in midline response. *Journal of Neurophysiology, 40,* 1275–1280.

Clopton, B. M., & Winfield, J. A. (1976). Effect of early exposure to patterned sound on unit activity in rat inferior colliculus. *Journal of Neurophysiology, 39,* 1081–1089.

Cone, B. K., & Gerber, S. E. (1980). Impedance measurements. In S. E. Gerber (Ed.), *Audiology in infancy* (pp. 99–116). New York: Grune & Stratton.

Cox, R. M. (1979). Acoustic aspects of hearing aid canal coupling systems. In D. M. Schwartz & F. H. Bess (Eds.), *Monographs in Contemporary Audiology, 1*(3), 22–27.

Dalsgaard, S. C., & Jensen, O. D. (1976). Measurement of the insertion gain of hearing aids. *Journal of Audiological Techniques, 15,* 170–183.

Danhauer, J. L., Abdale, C., Johnson, C., & Asp, C. (1986). Perceptual features from normal-hearing and hearing-impaired children's errors on the NST. *Ear and Hearing, 7,* 318–322.

Davis, H., & Silverman, S. R. (1960). *Hearing and deafness.* New York: Holt, Rhinehart & Winston.

Davis, J. (1974). Performance of young hearing-impaired children on a test of basic concepts. *Journal of Speech and Hearing Research, 17,* 342–351.

Davis, J. (1981a). Psychosocial considerations and evaluation. In M. Ross & L. W. Nober (Eds.), *Educating hard of hearing children* (pp. 42–50). Washington, DC: A.G. Bell Association.

Davis, J. (1981b). Utilization of audition in the education of the hearing-impaired child. In F. H. Bess, B. A. Freeman, & J.S. Sinclair (Eds.), *Amplification in education* (pp. 109–120). Washington, DC: A. G. Bell Association.

Davis, J. (Ed.). (1990). *Our forgotten children: Hard-of-hearing pupils in the schools* (2nd ed.). Washington, DC: Self-Help for the Hard of Hearing.

Davis, J., & Blasdell, R. (1975). Perceptual strategies employed by normal hearing and hearing-impaired children in the comprehension of sentences containing relative clauses. *Journal of Speech and Hearing Research, 18,* 281–295.

Davis, J., Shepard, N., Stelmachowicz, P., & Gorga, M. (1981). Characteristics of hearing impaired children in the public schools: II. Psychoeducational data. *Journal of Speech and Hearing Disorders, 46,* 130–137.

De Filippo, C. L., & Sims, D. G. (Eds.). (1988). New reflections on speechreading [special issue]. *Volta Review, 90* (5).

deVilliers, J. G., & deVilliers, P. A. (1978). *Language acquisition.* Cambridge, MA: Harvard University Press.

DiCarlo, L. M. (1968). Speech, language, and cognitive abilities of the hard of hearing. In *Proceedings of the Institute on Aural Rehabilitation* (pp. 45–66). Denver, CO: University of Denver.

Dirks, D. D., Morgan, D. E., & Dubno, J. R. (1982). A procedure for quantifying the effects of noise on speech recognition. *Journal of Speech and Hearing Disorders, 47,* 114–122.

Dodd, B., & Burnham, D. (1988). Processing speechread information. *Volta Review, 90,* 45–60.

Dubno, J. R., Dirks, D. D., & Langhofer, L. R. (1982). Evaluation of hearing-impaired listeners using a nonsense-syllable test: II. Syllable recognition and consonant confusion patterns. *Journal of Speech and Hearing Research, 25,* 141–148.

Duffy, J. K. (1967). *Audio-visual speech audiometry and a new audio-visual speech perception index* (Maico Audiological Series, Vol. 5, Report No. 9).

Dunn, L. M., & Dunn, L. M. (1981). *Peabody Picture Vocabulary Test–Revised.* Circle Pines, MN: American Guidance Service.

Durost, W., Bixler, H., Wrightstone, J., Prescott, G., & Balow, I. (1971). *Metropolitan Achievement Test.* San Antonio, TX: Psychological Corporation.

Elliot, L., & Katz, D. (1980). *Development of a new children's test of speech discrimination.* St. Louis, MO: Auditec.

Elliot, L. L. (1967). Some possible effects of the delay of early treatment of deafness. *Journal of Speech and Hearing Disorders, 10,* 209–224.

Elser, R. P. (1959). The social position of hearing handicapped children in the regular grades. *Exceptional Children, 25,* 305–309.

Elssmann, S. F., Matkin, N. D., & Sabo, M. P. (1987). Warning: A unilateral hearing loss may be detrimental to a child's academic career. *Hearing Instruments, 40,* 18–22.

Erber, N. P. (1974). Visual perception of speech by deaf children: Recent developments and continuing trends. *Journal of Speech and Hearing Disorders, 39,* 178–185.

Evans, W., Webster, D., & Cullen, J. U. (1983). Auditory brainstem responses in neonatally sound deprived CBA/J mice. *Hearing Research, 10*, 269–277.

Fairbanks, G. (1958). Test of phonemic differentiation: The Rhyme Test. *Journal of the Acoustical Society of America, 30*, 596–600.

Farrar, C., Francis, J., Owens, S., Schepard, D., Thies, T., Witlen, R., & Faist, L. (1976). *Test of Auditory Comprehension*. North Hollywood, CA: Foreworks.

Feagans, L., Blood, I., & Tubman, J. G. (1988). Otitis media: A model of effects and implications for intervention. In F. Bess (Ed.), *Hearing impairment in children* (pp. 347–374). Parkton, MD: York Press.

Finitzo-Hieber, T., & Tillman, T. W. (1978). Room acoustics effects on monosyllabic word discrimination ability for normal and hearing-impaired children. *Journal of Speech and Hearing Research, 21*, 440–458.

Flexer, C. (1989). Turn on sound: An odyssey of sound field amplification. *Educational Audiology Association Newsletter, 5*(5), 6–7.

Flexer, C., Wray, D., & Black, T. (1986). Support group for moderately hearing-impaired college students: An expanding awareness. *Volta Review, 88*, 223–229.

Friel-Patti, S., Finitzo-Hieber, T., Conti, G., & Brown, K. (1982). Language delay in infants associated with middle ear disease and mild fluctuating hearing impairment. *Pediatric Infectious Disease, 1*, 104–109.

Fry, D. B. (1978). The role and primacy of the auditory channel in speech and language development. In M. Ross & T. G. Giolas (Eds.), *Auditory management of hearing-impaired children* (pp. 15–44). Baltimore, MD: University Park Press.

Gabbard, S. A. (1982). References for communication disorders related to otitis media. *Seminars in Speech Language and Hearing, 3*, 351.

Gardner, M. F. (1979/1981). *Expressive One-Word Picture Vocabulary Test*. Austin, TX: PRO-ED.

Gardner, M. F. (1983). *Expressive One-Word Picture Vocabulary Test–Upper Extension*. Austin, TX: PRO-ED.

Gardner, M. F. (1985). *Receptive One-Word Picture Vocabulary Test*. Austin, TX: PRO-ED.

Garstecki, D. (1988). Speechreading with auditory cues. *Volta Review, 90*, 161–178.

Geers, A., & Moog, J. (1989). Factors predictive of the development of literacy in profoundly hearing-impaired adolescents. *Volta Review, 91*, 69–86.

Gemmill, J. E., & John, J. E. J. (1975). A study of samples of spontaneous spoken language from hearing-impaired children. *Teacher of the Deaf, 75*, 193–201.

Gengel, R. W. (1974). Mean intelligibility functions of nine sensorineural hearing-impaired Ss for vowels and consonants. In R.E. Stark (Ed.), *Sensory capabilities of hearing-impaired children* (pp. 129–132). Baltimore, MD: University Park Press.

Gerber, S. (1974). *Introductory hearing science*. Philadelphia, PA: W. B. Saunders.

Gilman, L. A., & Danzer, V. (1989). *Use of sound field amplification in regular classrooms*. Unpublished manuscript. Portland, OR: Portland Public Schools.

Gordon, J. C. (1885). Deaf-mutes and the public schools from 1815 to the present day. *American Annals of the Deaf, 30*, 121–143.

Gordon, T. G. (1987). Communication skills of mainstreamed hearing-impaired children. In H. Levitt, N. McGarr, & D. Geffner (Eds.), *Development of language and communication skills in hearing-impaired children* (ASHA Monograph No. 26, pp. 108–122). Washington, DC: American Speech-Language-Hearing Association.

Gottlieb, M. E., Zinkus, P. W., & Thompson, A. (1979). Chronic middle ear disease and auditory perceptual defects. *Clinical Pediatrics, 18,* 725–732.

Gravel, J. (1990, April). *Assessment of hearing in infants.* Paper presented to the Connecticut Pediatric Audiology Study Group, Hartford, CT.

Hamp, N. W. (1972). Reading attainment and some associated factors in deaf and partially hearing children. *Teacher of the Deaf, 70,* 203–215.

Hamilton, P., & Owrid, H. L. (1974). Comparison of hearing impairment and socio-cultural disadvantage in relation to verbal retardation. *British Journal of Audiology, 8,* 27–32.

Hawkins, D. B., & Schum, D. J. (1985). Some effects of FM-system coupling on hearing aid characteristics. *Journal of Speech and Hearing Disorders, 50,* 132–141.

Hawkins, D. B., & Van Tassell, D. J. (1982). Electroacoustic characteristics of personal FM systems. *Journal of Speech and Hearing Disorders, 47,* 355–362.

Hedrick, D., Prather, E., & Tobin, A. (1975/1984). *Sequenced Inventory of Communication Development.* Seattle, WA: University of Washington Press.

Heller, P. (1990). Psycho-educational assessment. In M. Ross (Ed.), *Hearing-impaired children in the mainstream* (pp. 61–80). Parkton, MD: York Press.

Hieronymus, A., & Lindquist, E. (1974). *Iowa Tests of Basic Skills.* Chicago: Riverside Publishing.

Hine, D. W. (1970). The attainments of children with partial hearing. *Teacher of the Deaf, 68,* 129–135.

Hodgson, W. R. (1985). Testing infants and young children. In J. Katz (Ed.), *Handbook of clinical audiology* (3rd ed., pp. 642–645). Baltimore, MD: Williams & Wilkins.

Hodgson, W. R. (1986). *Hearing aid assessment and use in audiologic rehabilitation* (3rd ed.). Baltimore, MD: Williams & Wilkins.

Jackson, P. L. (1988). The theoretical minimal unit for visual speech perception: Visemes and coarticulation. *Volta Review, 90,* 99–115.

Jensema, C. J. (1975). *The relationship between academic achievement and the demographic characteristics of hearing impaired children and youth* (Series R, No. 2). Washington, DC: Gallaudet College, Office of Demographic Studies.

Jensema, C. J., Karchmer, M. A., & Trybus, R. J. (1978). *The rated speech intelligibility of hearing-impaired children: Basic relationships and a detailed analysis* (Series R, No. 6). Washington, DC: Gallaudet College, Office of Demographic Studies.

Jerger, J. (1970). Clinical experience with impedance audiometry. *Archives of Otolaryngology, 92,* 311–312.

Jerger, S., Jerger, J., Alford, B. R., & Abrams, S. (1983). Development of speech intelligibility in children with recurrent otitis media. *Ear and Hearing, 4,* 138–145.

Jorgenson, C., Barrett, M., Huisingh, R., & Zackman, L. (1981). *The Word Test.* Moline, IL: LinguiSystems.

Katz, D., & Elliot, L. (1978, November). *Development of a new children's speech discrimination test.* Paper presented at the American Speech and Hearing Association Convention, San Francisco.

Katz, J. (1985). *The handbook of clinical audiology* (3rd ed.). Baltimore, MD: Williams & Wilkins.

Kavanagh, J. E. (Ed.). (1986). *Otitis media and child development.* Parkton, MD: York Press.

Kennedy, P., Northcott, W., McCauley, R., & Williams, S. N. (1976). Longitudinal sociometric and cross-sectional data on mainstreaming hearing-impaired children: Implications and preschool programming. *Volta Review, 78,* 71–82.

Kessler, M., & Randolph, K. (1979). The effects of early middle ear disease on the auditory ability of third grade children. *Journal of the Academy of Rehabilitative Audiology, 12,* 6–20.

Killion, M. C. (1980). Problems in the application of broadband hearing aid microphones. In G. Studebaker & I. Hochberg (Eds.), *Acoustical factors affecting hearing aid performance* (pp. 219–266). Baltimore, MD: University Park Press.

Kirkwood, C. R., & Kirkwood, M. E. (1983). Otitis media and learning disabilities: The case for a causal relationship. *Journal of Family Practice, 17,* 219–227.

Klee, T., Kenworthy, O. T., Riggs, D., & Bess, F. H. (1984, November). *Reverberation times for speech and discrete signals.* Paper presented at the American Speech-Language-Hearing Association Convention, San Francisco.

Kleffner, R. R. (1973). Hearing losses, hearing aids, and children with language disorders. *Journal of Speech and Hearing Disorders, 38,* 232–239.

Kodman, J. (1963). Educational status of hard-of-hearing children in the classroom. *Journal of Speech and Hearing Disorders, 28,* 297–299.

Lass, N. J., Carlin, M. F., Woodward, C. M., Campanelli-Humphreys, A. L., Judy, J. M., & Hushion-Stemple, E. A. (1985). A survey of classroom teachers' and special educators' knowledge of and exposure to hearing loss. *Language, Speech, and Hearing Services in the Schools, 16,* 211–222.

Lass, N. J., Tecca, J. E., & Woodford, C. M. (1987). Teachers' knowledge of, exposure to, and attitudes toward hearing aids and hearing aid wearers. *Language, Speech, and Hearing Services in the Schools, 16,* 211–222.

Lass, N. J., Woodford, C. M., Pannbacker, M. D., Carlin, M. F., Saniga, R. D., Schmitt, J. F., & Everly-Myers, D. S. (1989). Speech-language pathologists' knowledge, exposure to, and attitudes toward hearing aids and hearing aid wearers. *Language, Speech, and Hearing Services in the Schools, 20,* 115–132.

Lass, N. J., Woodford, C. M., Schmitt, J. F., Pannbacker, M., Lundeen, C., & English, P. J. (1990). Health educators' knowledge of hearing, hearing loss, and hearing health practices. *Language, Speech, and Hearing Services in the Schools, 21,* 85–90.

Leckie, D. (1979, May). *Pilot study of the effects of early auditory training on speech perception by profoundly deaf children.* Paper presented to the Voice Conference, Toronto.

Lee, L. (1974). *Developmental sentence analysis.* Evanston, IL: Northwestern University Press.

Lemay, M., & Maxon, A. B. (1991). *Alternative FM coupling: Some effects of changing transmitter settings.* Unpublished manuscript. Storrs, CT: University of Connecticut.

Lenneberg, E. H. (1967). *Biological foundations of language.* New York: John Wiley & Sons.

Levitt, H. (1978). The acoustics of speech production. In M. Ross & T. G. Giolas (Eds.), *Auditory management of hearing-impaired children* (pp. 45–116). Baltimore, MD: University Park Press.

Levitt, H. (1987). Development of syntactic comprehension. In H. Levitt, N. McGarr, & D. Geffner (Eds.), *Development of language and communication skills in hearing-impaired children* (ASHA Monograph No. 26, pp. 47–78). Washington, DC: American Speech-Language-Hearing Association.

Levitt, H., McGarr, N., & Geffner, D. (Eds.). (1987). *Development of language and communication skills in hearing-impaired children* (ASHA Monograph No. 26). Washington, DC: American Speech-Language-Hearing Association.

Levitt, H., Youdelman, K., & Head, J. (1990). *Fundamental Speech Skills Test.* Englewood, CO: Resource Point.

Liberman, A. M., Cooper, F. S., Shankweiller, D. P., & Studert-Kennedy, M. (1967). Perception of the speech code. *Psychological Review, 7,* 431–461.

Ling, D. (1976). *Speech and the hearing-impaired child: Theory and practice.* Washington, DC: A.G. Bell Association.

Ling, D. (1978a). Auditory coding and recoding: An analysis of auditory training procedures for hearing-impaired children. In M. Ross & T.G. Giolas (Eds.), *Auditory management of hearing-impaired children* (pp. 181–218). Baltimore, MD: University Park Press.

Ling, D. (1978b). Discussion summary. In M. Ross & T.G. Giolas (Eds.), *Auditory management of hearing-impaired children* (pp. 295–332). Baltimore, MD: University Park Press.

Ling, D. (1978c). *Aural habilitation.* Washington, DC: A. G. Bell Association.

Ling, D. (1980). Integration of diagnostic information: Implications for speech training in school-aged children. In J. Subtelny (Ed.), *Speech assessment and speech improvement for the hearing impaired.* Washington, DC: A. G. Bell Association.

Ling, D., Leckie, D., Pollack, D., Simser, J., & Smith, A. (1981). Syllable reception by hearing-impaired children: Training from infancy in auditory-oral programs. *Volta Review, 83,* 451–457.

Ling, D., & Ling, A. G. (1977). *Basic vocabulary and language thesaurus for hearing-impaired children.* Washington, DC: A. G. Bell Association.

Longhurst, T., & Grubb, J. (1974). A comparison of language samples collected in four situations. *Language, Speech, and Hearing Services in the Schools, 5,* 71–78.

Longhurst, T. M., Briery, D., & Emery, M. (1975). *SKI-HI Receptive Language Test.* Logan, UT: Utah State University, Project SKI-HI.

Lynch, O. C., & Ross, M. (1988). *Current FM listening systems: A primer.* Unpublished manuscript. Storrs, CT: University of Connecticut.

Madden, R., Gardner, E., Rudman, H., Karlsen, B., & Merwin, J. (1973). *Stanford Achievement Test.* San Antonio, TX: Psychological Corporation.

Markides, A. (1970). The speech of deaf and partially hearing children with special reference to factors affecting intelligibility. *British Journal of Disordered Communication, 5,* 126–140.

Markides, A. (1978). Whole-word scoring versus phoneme scoring in speech audiometry. *British Journal of Audiology, 12,* 40–50.

Markides, A. (1986). Speech levels and speech-to-noise ratios. *British Journal of Audiology, 20,* 364–368.

Martin, F. N. (1987). Speech tests with preschool children. In F. N. Martin (Ed.), *Hearing disorders in children* (pp. 265–302). Austin, TX: PRO-ED.

Martin, F. N., Bernstein, M. E., Daly, J. A., & Cody, J. P. (1988). Classroom teachers' knowledge of hearing disorders and attitudes about mainstreaming hard-of-hearing children. *Language, Speech, and Hearing Services in the Schools, 19,* 83–95.

Maxon, A. B. (1982, November). *Speech acoustics: A model for managing hearing-impaired children.* Miniseminar presented at the American Speech-Language-Hearing Association, Toronto.

Maxon, A. B. (1990). Implementing an in-service training program. In M. Ross (Ed.), *Hearing-impaired children in the mainstream* (pp. 257–274). Parkton, MD: York Press.

Maxon, A. B., & Brackett, D. (1983). In-service training for public school speech-language pathologists in the management of mainstreamed hearing-impaired children. In I. Hochberg, H. Levitt, & M. Osberger (Eds.), *Speech of the hearing impaired* (pp. 379–388). Baltimore, MD: University Park Press.

Maxon, A. B., & Brackett, D. (1987). The hearing-impaired child in regular schools. *Seminars in Speech and Language, 8,* 393–413.

Maxon, A. B., Brackett, D., & van den Berg, S. (1991). Self-perception of socialization: The effect of hearing status, age, and gender. *Volta Review, 98*(1), 5–8.

Maxon, A. B., Brackett, D., & van den Berg, S. (in press). Classroom amplification use: A national long-term study. *Language, Speech, and Hearing Services in the Schools.*

Maxon, A. B., & Mazor, M. (1977). The effects of microphone spacing on auditory localization. *Audiology, 16*(5), 438–445.

McCauley, R. J., & Swisher, L. (1984a). Psychometric review of language and articulation tests for preschool children. *Journal of Speech and Hearing Disorders, 49,* 34–42.

McCauley, R. J., & Swisher, L. (1984b). Use and misuse of norm-referenced tests in clinical assessment: A hypothetical case. *Journal of Speech and Hearing Disorders, 49,* 338–348.

McClure, A. T. (1977). Academic achievements of mainstreamed hearing-impaired children with congenital rubella syndrome. *Volta Review, 79,* 379–384.

McDermott, R. P., & Jones, T. A. (1984). Articulation characteristics and listener's judgment of the speech of children with severe hearing loss. *Language, Speech, and Hearing Services in the Schools, 15,* 110–126.

McGarr, N. S. (1987). Communication skills of hearing-impaired children in schools for the deaf. In H. Levitt, N. McGarr, & D. Geffner (Eds.), *Development of language and communication skills in hearing-impaired children* (ASHA Monograph No. 26, pp. 91–107). Washington, DC: American Speech-Language-Hearing-Association.

Moeller, M. P. (1988). Combining formal and informal strategies for language assessment of hearing impaired children. In R. Kretschmer & L. Kretschmer (Eds.), *Communication assessment of hearing impaired children: From conversation to classroom* (JARA Monograph #21, pp. 73–100).

Monsen, R., Moog, J., & Geers, A. (1988). *CID Picture Spine: Speech Intelligibility Evaluation*. St. Louis, MO: Central Institute for the Deaf.

Monsen, R. B. (1978). Toward measuring how well hearing-impaired children speak. *Journal of Speech and Hearing Research, 21,* 197–219.

Montgomery, G. W. G. (1967). Analysis of pure-tone audiometric responses in relation to speech development in the profoundly deaf. *Journal of the Acoustical Society of America, 41,* 53–59.

Moog, J. S., & Geers, A. E. (1979). *Grammatical analysis of elicited language*. St. Louis, MO: Central Institute for the Deaf.

Morgan, D., Dirks, D., & Bower, D. (1979). Suggested threshold sound pressure levels for frequency modulated tones in the sound field. *Journal of Speech and Hearing Disorders, 44,* 37–54.

Nabalek, A. K., & Robinson, P. K. (1982). Monaural and binaural speech perception through hearing aids under noise and reverberation with normal and hearing-impaired listeners. *Journal of Speech and Hearing Research, 17,* 724–739.

Neuman, A. C., & Hochberg, I. (1983). Children's perception of speech in reverberation. *Journal of the Acoustical Society of America, 73,* 2145–2149.

Newcomer, P., & Hammill, D. (1977). *Test of Language Development–Primary*. Austin, TX: PRO-ED.

Nober, L. W. (1981). Developing IEP's for hard of hearing children. In M. Ross & L. Nober (Eds.), *Educating hard of hearing children* (pp. 51–58). Washington DC: A. G. Bell Association.

Oller, D. K., & Kelly, C. A. (1974). Phonological substitution processes of a hard of hearing child. *Journal of Speech and Hearing Disorders, 39,* 64–74.

Olmstead, T. (1986, June). *Making miracles happen: Effective mainstreaming*. Paper presented at the 1986 Convention of the A. G. Bell Association, Chicago.

Olsen, W. O. (1977). Acoustics and amplification in classrooms for the hearing-impaired. In F. Bess (Ed.), *Childhood and deafness: Causation, assessment, and management* (pp. 251–256). New York: Grune & Stratton.

Olsen, W. O. (1988). Classroom acoustics for hearing-impaired children. In F. H. Bess (Ed.), *Hearing impairment in children* (pp. 266–277). Parkton, MD: York Press.

Owens, E. (1978). Consonant errors and remediation in sensorineural hearing loss. *Journal of Speech and Hearing Disorders, 43,* 331–347.

Owens, E., & Schubert, E. D. (1977). Development of the California Consonant Test. *Journal of Speech and Hearing Research, 20,* 436–474.

Oyler, R. F., Oyler, A. L., & Matkin, N. D. (1988). Unilateral hearing loss: Demographics and educational impact. *Language, Speech, and Hearing Services in the Schools, 19,* 201–209.

Paradise, J. L. (1981). Otitis media during early development: How hazardous to development? A critical review of the evidence. *Pediatrics, 68,* 869–873.

Pascoe, D. P. (1975). Frequency responses of hearing aids and their effects on the speech perception of hearing-impaired subjects. *Annals of Otology, Rhinology, & Laryngology, 84* (Suppl. 23).

Patchett, T. A. (1977). Auditory pattern discrimination in albino rats as a function of auditory restriction at different ages. *Developmental Psychology, 13,* 168–169.

Paul, R. I., & Young, B. (1975). *The hard of hearing child in the regular classroom* (ESEA Title Project). Pontiac, MI: Oakland Schools.

Peckham, C. S., Sheridan, M., & Butler, N. R. (1972). School attainments of seven-year-old children with hearing difficulties. *Development Medical Child Neurology, 14*, 592–608.

Pflaster, G. (1981). A second analysis of factors related to the academic performance of hearing-impaired children in the mainstream. *Volta Review, 83*, 71–81.

Pickett, J. M. (1980). *The sounds of speech communication.* Baltimore, MD: University Park Press.

Pollack, M. C. (1988). *Amplification for the hearing impaired* (3rd ed.). Orlando, FL: Grune & Stratton.

Pressnell, L. (1973). Hearing-impaired children's comprehension and production of syntax in oral language. *Journal of Speech and Hearing Research, 16*, 12–21.

Preves, D. A., & Griffin, T. S. (1976). In-the-ear aids: Parts I–IV. *Hearing Instruments, 77* (3), (5), (7), & (9).

Quigley, S. P. (1978). Effects of hearing impairment on normal language development. In F. Martin (Ed.), *Pediatric audiology* (pp. 35–63). Englewood Cliffs, NJ: Prentice-Hall.

Quigley, S. P., Smith, N. O., & Wilbur, R. B. (1974). Comprehension of relativized sentences by deaf students. *Journal of Speech and Hearing Research, 17*, 325–341.

Quigley, S. P., Steinkamp, M. W., Power, D. J., & Jones, B. (1978). *Test of Syntactic Abilities.* Beaverton, OR: Dormac.

Quigley, S. P., & Thomure, R. E. (1968). *Some effects of hearing impairment upon school performance.* Urbana, IL: University of Illinois, Institute for Research on Exceptional Children.

Ray, H. (1989). Project Marrs—An update. *Educational Audiology Association Newsletter, 5*(5), 4–5.

Reich, C., Hambleton, D., & Houldin, B. K. (1977). The integration of hearing impaired children in regular classrooms. *American Annals of the Deaf, 122*, 534–543.

Richard, G., & Hanner, M. (1985). *Language Processing Test.* Moline, IL: LinguiSystems.

Richards, D. L. (1973) *Telecommunication by speech: The transmission performance of telephone networks.* New York: John Wiley & Sons.

Rintelmann, W. F., & Bess, F. H. (1988). High-level amplification and potential hearing loss in children. In F. H. Bess (Ed.), *Hearing impairment in children* (pp. 278–309). Parkton, MD: York Press.

Rogers, W. T., Leslie, P. T., Clarke, B. R., Booth, J. A., & Horvath, A. (1978). Academic achievements of hearing impaired students: Comparisons among selected populations. *British Columbia Journal of Special Education 2*(3), 183–209.

Rosenberg, P. E. (1966). Misdiagnosis of children with auditory problems. *Journal of Speech and Hearing Disorders, 31*, 279–283.

Ross, M. (1976). Assessment of the hearing impaired prior to mainstreaming. In G. Nix (Ed.), *Mainstream education of hearing impaired children and youth* (pp. 101–110). New York: Grune & Stratton.

Ross, M. (1978a). Classroom acoustics and speech intelligibility. In J. Katz (Ed.), *Handbook of clinical audiology* (2nd ed., pp. 469–478). Baltimore, MD: Williams & Wilkins.

Ross, M. (1978b). Mainstreaming: Some social considerations. *Volta Review, 80,* 21–30.

Ross, M. (1980). Binaural vs. monaural amplification. In C. Libby (Ed.), *Binaural hearing aids* (pp. 1–22). Chicago: Zinetron.

Ross, M., & Calvert, D. R. (1967). The semantics of deafness. *Volta Review, 69,* 644–649.

Ross, M., Duffy, R. J., Cooker, H. S., & Sergeant, R. J. (1973). Contribution of the lower audible frequencies to the recognition of emotions. *American Annals of the Deaf, 118,* 37–42.

Ross, M., & Giolas, T. G. (1971). Effect of three classroom listening conditions on speech intelligibility. *American Annals of the Deaf, 116,* 580–584.

Ross, M., & Giolas, T. G. (1978). Issues and exposition. In M. Ross & T.G. Giolas (Eds.), *Auditory management of hearing-impaired children* (pp. 255–294). Baltimore, MD: University Park Press.

Ross, M., Giolas, T. G., & Carver, P. (1973). The effect of classroom listening conditions on speech intelligibility: A replication in part. *Language, Speech, and Hearing Services in the Schools, 4,* 72–76.

Ross, M., Kessler, M. E., Phillips, M. E., & Lerman, J. W. (1972). Visual, auditory, and combined mode presentations of the WIPI test to hearing impaired children. *Volta Review, 74,* 90–96.

Ross, M., & Lerman, J. W. (1970). A picture identification test for hearing impaired children. *Journal of Speech and Hearing Research, 13,* 44–53.

Ross, M., & Madell, J. R. (1988). The premature demise of body worn hearing aids. *ASHA, 30,* 29–30.

Ross, M., & Matkin, N. (1967). The rising threshold configuration. *Journal of Speech and Hearing Disorders, 32,* 377–382.

Ross, M., & Randolph, K. (1987, November). *A test of the auditory perception of alphabet letters.* Paper presented at the American Speech-Hearing-Language Association Convention, New Orleans.

Ross, M., & Seewald, R. F. (1988). Hearing aid selection and evaluation with young children. In F. H. Bess (Ed.), *Hearing impairment in children* (pp. 190–213). Parkton, MD: York Press.

Ross, M. (in press). Amplification for the profoundly hearing impaired. In G. A. Studebaker & E. Hochberg (Eds.), *Acoustical factors affecting hearing aid performance* (2nd ed.). Austin, TX: PRO-ED.

Ruben, R. J., & Rapin, I. (1980). Plasticity of the developing auditory system. *Annals of Otology, 89,* 303–311.

Samar, V. J., & Sims, D. G. (1983). Visual evoked-response correlates of speechreading performance in normal-hearing adults: A replication and factor analytic extension. *Journal of Speech and Hearing Research, 26,* 2–9.

Sanders, D. (1965). Noise conditions in normal school classrooms. *Exceptional Child, 31,* 344–353.

Sarff, L. S. (1981). An innovative use of sound field amplification in the classroom. In R. Roeser & M. Downs (Eds.), *Auditory disorders in school children* (pp. 263–272). New York: Thieme-Stratton.

Sarff, L. S., Ray, H., & Bagwell, C. (1981, October). Why not amplification in every classroom? *Hearing Aid Journal*, pp. 11, 44–50.

Schildroth, A. N., & Karchmer, M. A. (Eds.). (1986). *Deaf children in America*. Austin, TX: PRO-ED.

Schwartz, S. (1990). Psycho-social management of hearing-impaired children. In M. Ross (Ed.), *Hearing-impaired children in the mainstream* (pp. 159–180). Parkton, MD: York Press.

Seewald, R., Ross, M., Giolas, T. G., & Yonovitz, A. (1985). The primary modality for speech perception in children with normal and impaired hearing. *Journal of Speech and Hearing Research, 28*, 36–46.

Seewald, R., Ross, M., & Stelmachowicz, P. (1987). Selecting and verifying hearing aid performance characteristics for young children. *Journal of the Academy of Rehabilitative Audiology, 20*, 25–37.

Seewald, R. C. (1981). *The interrelationships among hearing loss, utilization of auditory and visual cues in speech reception and speech production intelligibility in children.* Unpublished doctoral dissertation, University of Connecticut, Storrs, CT.

Semel-Mintz, E., & Wiig, E. (1982). *Clinical Evaluation of Language Functions.* San Antonio, TX: Psychological Corporation.

Shepard, D. C. (1982). Visual-neural correlate of speechreading ability in normal-hearing adults. *Journal of Speech and Hearing Research, 25*, 521–527.

Shepard, D. C., DeLavergne, R. W., Frueh, F. X., & Clobridge, C. (1977). Visual-neural correlate of speechreading ability in normal hearing adults. *Journal of Speech and Hearing Research, 20*, 752–765.

Shepard, N., Davis, J., Gorga, M., & Stelmachowicz, P. (1981). Characteristics of hearing impaired children in the public schools: I. Demographic data. *Journal of Speech and Hearing Disorders, 46*, 123–129.

Silva, P. A., Chalmers, D., & Stewart, I. (1986). Some audiological, psychological, educational and behavioral characteristics of children with bilateral otitis media with effusion: A longitudinal study. *Journal of Learning Disabilities, 19*, 165–169.

Silverman, M. S., & Clopton, B. M. (1977). Plasticity of binaural interaction: I. Effect of early auditory deprivation. *Journal of Neurophysiology, 40*, 1266–1274.

Simon, C. (1979). *Communicative competence: A functional-pragmatic approach to language therapy.* Tucson, AZ: Communication Skill Builders.

Simon, C. S. (1981). *Communicative competence: A functional-pragmatic approach to language therapy* (rev. ed.). Tucson, AZ: Communication Skill Builders.

Skinner, M. W. (1988). *Hearing aid evaluation.* Englewood Cliffs, NJ: Prentice-Hall.

Snow, C. (1977). The development of conversation between mothers and babies. *Journal of Child Language, 4*, 1–22.

Stark, R. E. (1974). *Sensory capabilities of hearing-impaired children.* Baltimore, MD: University Park Press.

Steer, M. D., Hanley, T. D., Speuhler, H. E., Barnes, N. S., Burk, K. W., & Williams, W. G. (1961). *The behavioral and academic implications of hearing loss among secondary school children* (Purdue Research Foundation, Project No. P.U. 2040). West Lafayette, IN: Purdue University.

Subtenly, J. (1975). An overview of the communication skills of NTID students with implications for planning of rehabilitation. *Journal of the Academy of Rehabilitation Audiology, 8,* 33–50.

Sumby, W. H., & Pollack, I. (1954). Visual contributions to speech intelligibility in noise. *Journal of the Acoustical Society of America, 26,* 212–215.

Swisher, M. V., & Thompson, M. (1985). Mothers learning simultaneous communication: The dimensions of the task. *American Annals of the Deaf, 130,* 212–217.

Tees, R. C. (1967). Effects of early auditory restriction in the rat on adult pattern discrimination. *Journal of Comparative Physiological Psychology, 63,* 389–393.

Thompson, M., Biro, P., Vethivelu, S., Pious, C., & Hatfield, N. (1987). *Language assessment of hearing impaired school age children.* Seattle, WA: University of Washington Press.

Tiegs, E., & Clarke, W. (1970). *California Achievement Test.* Monterey, CA: CTB/Macmillan/McGraw-Hill.

Tillman, T., Carhart, R., & Olsen, W. (1970). Hearing aid efficiency in a competing speech situation. *Journal of Speech and Hearing Research, 13,* 789–811.

Tonelson, S., & Watkins, S. (1979). *The SKI-HI Language Development Scale.* Logan, UT: Utah State University, Project SKI-HI.

Trammel, J. (1977). *Test of Auditory Comprehension.* North Hollywood, CA: Foreworks.

Trybus, R. J., & Karchmer, M. A. (1977). School achievement status of hearing impaired children: National data on achievement status and growth patterns. *American Annals of the Deaf, 122,* 62–69.

U.S. Public Health Service. (1964). *Demographics of hearing loss* (Public Health Service Publication No. 1227). Washington, DC: Government Printing Office.

Ventry, I. M. (1980). Effects of conductive hearing loss: Fact or fiction. *Journal of Speech and Hearing Disorders, 45,* 143–156.

Wallace, I. F., Gravel, J. S., McCarton, C. M., & Ruben, R. J. (1988). Otitis media and language development at 1 year of age. *Journal of Speech and Hearing Disorders, 54,* 245–251.

Warner, E. O'H., & Kresheck, J. (1983). *Structured Photographic Expressive Language Test-II.* Sanwich, IL: Janelle Publications.

Watkins, S. (1987). Long term effect of home intervention with hearing-impaired children. *American Annals of the Deaf, 132,* 267–275.

Webster, D. B. (1983). Effects of peripheral hearing losses on the auditory brainstem. In E. Lasky & J. Katz (Eds.), *Central auditory processing disorders: Problems of speech, language, and learning* (pp. 185–202). Austin, TX: PRO-ED.

Webster, D. B., & Webster, M. (1977). Neonatal sound deprivation affects brain stem auditory nuclei. *Archives of Otololaryngology, 103,* 392–396.

Webster, J. C., & Snell, K. B. (1983). Noise levels and the speech intelligibility of teachers in a classroom. *Journal of the Academy of Rehabilitative Audiology, 16,* 234–255.

West, J. J., & Weber, J. L. (1973). Phonological analysis of the spontaneous language of a four-year-old hard-of-hearing child. *Journal of Speech and Hearing Disorders, 38,* 25–35.

White, S. J., & White, R. E. C. (1987). The effects of hearing status of the family and age of intervention on receptive and expressive oral language skills in hearing-impaired infants. In H. Levitt, N. McGarr, & D. Geffner (Eds.), *Development of language and communication skills in hearing-impaired children* (ASHA Monograph No. 26, pp. 9–24). Washington, DC: American Speech-Language-Hearing Association.

Whitehead, R. L., & Jones, K. O. (1976). The influence of consonant environment on duration of vowels in the speech of normal hearing, moderately deaf hearing impaired and deaf adults. *Journal of the Acoustical Society of America, 60,* 513–515.

Wilcox, J., & Tobin, H. (1974). Linguistic performance of hard of hearing and normal hearing children. *Journal of Speech and Hearing Research, 17,* 286–293.

Wilson, G. W., Ross, M., & Calvert, D. R. (1974). Experimental study of the semantics of deafness. *Volta Review, 76,* 408–414.

Wilson, W. R., & Walton, W. K. (1978). Public school audiometry. In F. N. Martin (Ed.), *Pediatric audiology* (pp. 389–445). Englewood Cliffs, NJ: Prentice-Hall.

Wolk, S., Karchmer, M., & Schildroth, A. (1982). *Patterns of academic and non-academic integration among hearing impaired college students in special education* (Series R, No. 9). Washington DC: Gallaudet College, Center for Assessment and Demographic Studies.

Wolk, S., & Schildroth, A. N. (1986). Deaf children and speech intelligibility: A national study. In A. N. Schildroth & M. A. Karchmer (Eds.), *Deaf children in America* (pp. 139–160). Austin, TX: PRO-ED.

Woodford, C. M. (1987). Speech-language pathologists' knowledge and skills regarding hearing aids. *Language, Speech, and Hearing Services in the Schools, 18,* 312–322.

Ying, E. (1990, March). *Aural habilitation procedures for children with cochlear implants.* Paper presented at Cochlear Implants in Children: Rehabilitation Techniques Conference (N.Y. League for the Hard of Hearing), New York.

Young, D., & McConnell, F. (1957). Retardation of vocabulary development in hard of hearing children. *Exceptional Child, 23,* 368–370.

Zinkus, P. W., & Gottlieb, M. I. (1980). Patterns of perceptual and academic deficits related to early chronic otitis media. *Pediatrics, 66,* 246–253.

Author Index

Abdale, C., 26
Abrams, S., 8
Alford, B. R., 8
Allen, T., 54, 55
American Board of Examiners in
Speech-Language Pathology and
Audiology (ABESPA), 373, 380
American National Standards
Institute (ANSI), 207
American Speech-Language-Hearing
Association, 6, 17, 373
Ammons, H. S., 36
Ammons, R. B., 36
Arrowsmith, 359
Asp, C., 26

Bagwell, C., 258
Balow, I., 44, 144
Barrager, D., 382, 383
Bernstein, M. E., 18, 321
Bess, F., 3, 45, 195, 196, 197, 210, 259,
367
Binnie, C. A., 34
Birch, J. W., 304
Biro, P., 113
Bixler, H., 44, 144
Black, T., 363
Blasdell, R., 40, 41
Blood, I., 8
Bloom, B. S., 376
Boehm, A., 37
Boney, S. J., 196, 197, 259
Booth, J. A., 48
Boothroyd, A., 4, 12, 21, 24, 26, 28,
34, 47, 48, 118
Bower, D., 228
Boyle, P., 148
Brackett, D., 15, 20, 36, 42, 45, 76, 82,

106, 109, 113, 150, 237, 263, 271,
280, 283, 292, 299, 314, 321, 382
Brandes, P., 8
Brannon, J. B., 48
Brooks, D. N., 383
Brown, K., 8
Burnham, D., 34, 35
Butler, N. R., 42
Byers, V. B., 22, 23

Calvert, D. R., 2, 4
Carhart, R., 196
Carver, P., 231, 232
Chalmers, D., 8
Clarke, B. R., 48
Clarke, W., 144
Clobridge, C., 32
Clopton, B. M., 7, 205
Cody, J. P., 18, 322
Committee on Rehabilitative
Audiology, 374
Cone, B. K., 101
Conti, G., 8
Cooker, H. S., 4, 189
Cooper, F. S., 33
Cox, R. M., 104
Cullen, J. U., 7, 205
Curtiss, S., 380

Dalsgaard, S. C., 213, 214
Daly, J. A., 18, 322
Danhauer, J. L., 26
Danzer, V., 258, 259–260
Davis, H., 91
Davis, J., 3, 11, 15, 37, 38, 40, 41, 43,
48, 82, 381, 382
Dawtry, L., 383
De Filipo, C. L., 31

Delavergne, R. W., 32
Deutsch, L. J., 202
DeVilliers, J. G., 9
DeVilliers, P. A., 9
DiCarlo, L. M., 29
Dirks, D. D., 26, 196, 199, 228
Dixon, J., 383
Dodd, B., 34, 35
Donnelly, K., 383
Dubno, J. R., 26, 27, 196
Duffy, L. M., 91
Duffy, R. J., 4, 189
Dunn, L. M., 124
Dunn, L. M., 124
Durost, W., 44, 144

Ehinger, D., 8
Elliot, L., 10, 22, 91, 117
Elser, R. P., 64
Erber, N. P., 33
Evans, W., 7, 205

Fairbanks, G., 22
Farrar, C., 127
Feagans, L., 8
Finitzo-Hieber, T., 8, 196, 197
Fink, R., 383
Flahive, M., 383
Fletcher, P., 380
Flexer, C., 258, 260, 363
Freeman, D., 383
Friel-Patti, S., 8
Frueh, F. X., 32
Fry, D. B., 21

Gabbard, S. A., 8
Gardner, E., 143
Garman, M., 380
Garstecki, D., 33
Garstecki, H., 381
Geers, A., 46, 61, 138
Geffner, D., 12, 24, 41, 49, 50
Gemmill, J. E., 48
Gengel, R. W., 196
Gerber, S., 101, 189, 191
Gilman, L. A., 258, 259
Giolas, T. G., 5, 185, 196, 231, 232
Gold, 28

Goldstein, D., 383
Gordon, T. G., 24, 28, 29, 30, 359, 360
Gorga, M., 15, 82
Gottlieb, M., 8
Gravel, J., 8, 101
Griffin, T. S., 203

Hambleton, D., 55, 113
Hamilton, P., 36
Hamp, N. W., 42, 43, 48, 59
Hastings, J. T., 376
Hatfield, N., 113
Hawkins, D. B., 236, 237
Head, J., 138
Heller, P., 148
Hieronymus, A., 144
Hine, D. W., 42, 43, 48
Hochberg, I., 195, 381, 382
Hodgson, W. R., 6, 207
Horvath, A., 48
Houldin, B. K., 55, 113

Jackson, P. L., 35
Jensema, C. J., 47, 48, 49, 54, 55, 56,
    57, 58, 59, 61
Jensen, O. D., 213, 214
Jerger, J., 8, 95
Jerger, S., 8
John, J. E. J., 48
Johnson, C., 26
Jones, B., 41
Jones, K. O., 30
Jones, T. A., 29

Karchmer, M. A., 15, 20, 42, 47, 48,
    54, 55, 56, 59, 62, 113
Karlsen, B., 143
Katz, D., 22, 91, 117
Katz, J., 95
Kavanagh, J. E., 367
Kellarney, G., 383
Kelly, C. A., 29
Kennedy, P., 64
Kenworthy, O. T., 195, 259
Kessler, M., 8, 22, 33
Kirkwood, C. R., 8
Kirkwood, M. E., 8
Klee, T., 195, 196, 259

Kleffner, R. R., 10
Kodman, J., 42, 43, 44

Lairidsen, 107
Langhofer, L. R., 26
Lass, N., 17, 18, 321, 322, 383
Leckie, D., 33
Lemay, M., 237
Lenneberg, E. H., 9
Lerman, J. W., 22, 33, 91, 117
Leslie, P. T., 48
Levitt, H., 12, 21, 24, 28, 40, 41, 42, 47, 49, 50, 138, 188, 382
Liberman, A. M., 33
Lindquist, E., 144
Ling, A. G., 288
Ling, D., 21, 33, 91, 136–137, 288
Lloyd, L., 383
Lowell, E., 380

Madaus, G. F., 376
Madden, R., 143
Madell, J. R., 202
Markides, A., 28, 36, 47, 91, 194, 196
Martin, F. N., 18, 89, 93, 321, 322
Matkin, N. D., 3, 10
Maxon, A. B., 15, 20, 36, 42, 45, 76, 82, 86, 105, 106, 109, 113, 150, 202, 227, 237, 314, 321, 322, 331, 382
Mazor, M., 202
McCarton, C. M., 8
McCauley, R., 64, 124
McClure, A. T., 46
McConnell, F., 36
McDermott, R. P., 29
McGarr, N., 12, 24, 41, 49, 50
Merwin, J., 143
Moeller, M. P., 113, 124, 126, 131
Monsen, R., 28, 47, 48, 138
Montgomery, A. A., 34
Montgomery, G. W. G., 28, 47
Moog, J., 46, 61, 138
Morgan, D. E., 196, 228
Murry, T., 48
Mussen, E., 383

Nabalek, A. K., 195

National Commission on Allied Health Education, 382
Neuman, A. C., 195
Nielsen, 107
Nober, L. W., 13
Northcott, W., 64, 381

Oller, D. K., 29
Olmstead, T., 46
Olsen, W. O., 196, 198
Osberger, M. J., 382
Osborn, T., 54, 55
Owens, E., 24, 25, 26, 27
Owrid, H. L., 36
Oyer, H. L., 383
Oyler, A. L., 3
Oyler, R. F., 3

Paradise, J. L., 8
Pascoe, D. P., 212
Patchett, T. A., 7
Paul, R. I., 42, 44, 45, 194, 196
Pearlstein, E., 383
Peckham, C. S., 42
Pflaster, G., 362
Phillips, M. E., 22, 33
Pickett, J. M., 191
Pious, C., 113
Pollack, D., 33
Pollack, I., 35
Pollack, M. C., 207
Power, D. J., 41
Prescott, G., 44, 144
Pressnell, L., 48
Preves, D. A., 203
Prutting, C., 380

Quigley, S. P., 3, 39, 41, 42, 43, 44

Randolph, K., 8, 93
Rapin, I., 7
Ray, H., 258
Reich, C., 55, 59, 60, 61, 64, 113
Richards, D. L., 186
Riggs, D., 195, 259
Rintelman, W. F., 210
Robinson, P. K., 195
Rogers, W. T., 48, 61

Rosenberg, P. E., 10
Ross, M., 2, 4, 5, 10, 11, 22, 33, 48, 55, 63, 91, 93, 117, 184, 185, 189, 196, 202, 205, 210, 229, 231, 232
Ruben, R. J., 7, 8
Rudman, H., 143
Russell, L., 383

Sahli, J., 382
Samar, V. J., 32
Sanders, D., 194, 196
Sarff, L. S., 3, 258, 259
Schildroth, A. N., 15, 20, 28, 48, 54, 55, 62, 113
Schmidt, J., 382
Schubert, E. D., 25
Schum, D. J., 237
Schwartz, S., 363
Seewald, R. F., 5, 106, 184, 210, 229, 230
Sergeant, R. J., 4, 189
Shankweiller, D. P., 33
Shepard, D. C., 32
Shepard, N., 15, 82, 229
Sheridan, M., 42
Silva, P. A., 8
Silverman, M. S., 7, 91, 205
Sims, D. G., 31, 32
Simser, J., 33
Skarakis, E., 380
Skinner, M. W., 207, 212
Smaldino, J., 382
Smith, A., 33
Smith, N. O., 41
Snell, K. B., 194
Stark, R. E., 4, 47, 48
Steer, M. D., 42
Steinkamp, M. W., 41
Stelmachowicz, P., 15, 82, 229
Stevenson, J., 383
Stewart, I., 8
Stream, K., 382
Stream, R., 382
Studert-Kennedy, M., 33
Subtelny, J., 138
Sumby, W. H., 35
Sweetow, R., 382, 383
Swisher, L., 124

Tecca, J. E., 18
Tees, R. C., 7
Thompson, A., 8
Thompson, M., 113
Thomure, R. E., 42, 43, 44
Tiegs, E., 144
Tillman, T. W., 196, 197, 196
Tobin, H., 39, 40
Trybus, R. J., 42, 47, 48, 54, 56, 59
Tubman, J. G., 8

U.S. Public Health Service, 3

Van den Berg, S., 150, 237, 321
Van Tassell, D. J., 236
Ventry, I. M., 8
Vethivelu, S., 113

Wallace, I. F., 8
Walton, W. K., 367
Watkins, S., 11
Weber, J. L., 30
Webster, D., 7, 205
Webster, J. C., 194
Webster, M., 7
West, J. J., 30
White, R. E. C., 11–12
White, S., 11–12, 383
Whitehead, R. L., 30
Wilbur, R. B., 41
Wilcox, J., 39, 40
Williams, S. N., 64
Wilson, G. W., 2
Wilson, W. R., 367
Winfield, J. A., 7
Wolk, S., 28, 48, 54, 55
Woodford, C. M., 17, 18
Wray, D., 363
Wrightstone, J., 44, 144

Ying, E., 273
Yonovitz, A., 5
Youdelman, K., 138
Young, B., 42, 44, 45, 194, 196
Young, D., 36

Zinkus, P. W., 8

Subject Index

AB Isophonemic Word Lists, 118
Academic achievement. *See also* Education; Performance
 educational setting and, 56–63
 evaluation of, 142–146, 172
 research on, 42–46
Academic communication, 262–263
Academic management, 307–315
Achievement. *See* Academic achievement
Acoustic reflex thresholds, 94, 97–101
Acoustics. *See* Classroom acoustics; Speech acoustics
Aided audibility, 212–213
Aided residual hearing
 phoneme error analysis, 226–227
 plotting of, 221–230
 sound pressure levels, 227–230
 unaided and aided thresholds, 221–226
American National Standards Institute (ANSI), 102
Ammons Full-Range Vocabulary Test, 36
Amplification assessment
 behavioral amplification analysis, 104–107
 communication of results of, 108–111
 electroacoustic analysis, 102–104
 probe microphone measurements, 107–108
ANSI. *See* American National Standards Institute (ANSI)
APAL. *See Auditory Perception of Alphabet Letters* (APAL)
Assessment. *See* Amplification assessment; Audiological evaluation; Communication assessment; Evaluation
Audibility
 aided audibility, 212–213
 definition of, 221
 effects of distance on, 198–199, 231
 effects of noise on, 194–198
Audiologic habilitation, 380
Audiological evaluation
 communication of results of, 108–111
 immittance measurements, 94–101
 importance of, 362
 in Individualized Education Plan (IEP), 172
 pure tone measures, 85–89
 speech audiometry, 89–94
Audiologists, 17, 257, 331–332, 362, 365–370, 381
Audiovisual perception of speech, 31–36
Auditory impairments. *See* Hearing-impaired children
Auditory management
 classroom acoustics, 194–199
 educational audiologist and, 365–370
 electroacoustic considerations, 199–219
 FM sound-field amplification, 258–260
 model of, 181–183
 organization of, 367–369
 phoneme error analysis, 226–227
 plotting aided residual hearing, 221–230
 sound pressure levels, 227–230
 speech acoustics, 183–194

troubleshooting, 251–258
unaided and aided thresholds,
251–258
Auditory Perception of Alphabet Letters
(APAL), 93
Auditory sensory deprivation, 6–9
Auditory trainers, 200
Aural rehabilitation
background on, 373–374
certification standards on, 383–384
consumer and professional needs
concerning, 382–383
continuing education concerning,
381–382
definition of, 374–376
minimal competencies for provision of, 376–380
position statement on, 373–384
terminology concerning, 380
training implications concerning,
381

Behavioral amplification analysis,
104–107
Behavioral anomalies, 10–11
Behind-the-ear (BTE) aids, 202–203
BICROS (bilateral routing of signals)
hearing aids, 204–205
Binaural amplification, 205–206
Body aids, 201–202
Boehm Test of Basic Concepts, 37
BTE aids. *See* Behind-the-ear (BTE)
aids

California Achievement Test (CAT),
144, 145
Case studies, 333–357
CAT. *See California Achievement Test*
(CAT)
Classroom academic management,
307–315
Classroom acoustics, 194–199
Classroom performance evaluation,
151–156
Classroom teachers. *See* Teachers
Classrooms. *See also* Education

academic communication in, 262–
263
academic management in, 307–315
arrangement of, for FM systems,
244–251
communication skills needed in
regular classroom, 68–69
effect of educational setting on performance, 54–63
language usage remediation in, 299,
301–302
letter to classroom teacher, 371
potential problem areas in, 308–314
social communication in, 262–263
speech production remediation in,
280, 281
speech reception remediation in,
271, 277–278
syntax/morphology remediation
in, 292, 296–297
vocabulary remediation in, 283,
289–290
Cloze procedures, 273
Cochlear implants, 206–207
Communication assessment
comprehension of spoken language, 122–127
importance of, 113–114
speech articulation/intelligibility,
136–139
speech reception, 116–122
spoken language production,
127–134
test selection and general procedures for, 114–116
written comprehension/produc-
tion, 134–136
Communication management
general principles of, 263–267
generalization in, 266–267
importance of, 261–262, 269
language usage, 297–302
practice in, 265–266
selection of targets in, 264
social and academic communication, 262–263
speech production, 278–281

hard-of-hearing children compared with, 2–3, 19
historical perspectives on, 359–360
in-between children compared with, 5–6
intervention strategies for, 12–14
language abilities of, 36–42
"least restrictive educational setting" for, 1, 54, 69–70
"most appropriate educational setting" for, 1, 54
performance evaluation of, 14–17
preschool children, 74–76
professional personnel working with, 17–18
psychosocial considerations for, 63–65, 363
in regular classrooms, 19–20, 54–63, 67–69, 113–114
relationship of hearing loss to performance of, 46–54
sensory deprivation in, 6–9
speech perception of, 20–28
speech production of, 28–31
support services for, 76–83, 362–363
supporting evidence for early management, 11–12
therapeutic objectives for, 14–17

IEP. *See* Individualized Education Plan (IEP)
IFSP. *See* Individual Family Service Plan (IFSP)
IIP. *See* Individual In-service Plan (IIP)
Immittance measurements, 94–101
In-service training
in aural rehabilitation, 381–382
formal in-service training, 322–323
guidelines for, 322–328
importance of, 321–322, 364
informal in-service training, 323–325
providers of, 325–326
recipients of, 327–328
topics and workshops for, 328–332
In-the-ear (ITE) aids, 203–204

Individual Family Service Plan (IFSP), 76, 328
Individual In-service Plan (IIP), 322
Individualized Education Plan (IEP)
annual goals in, 172–173
classification of handicapping condition in, 162–163
components of, 162
extent of participation in regular education, 163–164
legal requirement for, 13, 14
management needs in, 164–166
multidisciplinary evaluations and, 157, 158–159, 161
objectives in, 173–179
parent involvement in, 161, 365
performance level in, 171–172
placement options in, 70–74
regular classroom teacher and, 304
service options in, 76, 82–83, 166–171
standardized testing and, 143
troubleshooting of acoustic devices and, 256–257
Intelligence (IQ) tests, 146–148
Intelligibility. *See* Speech articulation/intelligibility
Interference, speech reception and, 119–120
Intervention strategies, 12–14
Iowa Test of Basic Skills (ITBS), 144, 145
IQ tests, 146–148
ITBS. *See Iowa Test of Basic Skills* (ITBS)
ITE aids. *See* In-the-ear (ITE) aids

Language abilities. *See* headings beginning with Speech
Language development. *See* Speech/language development
"Least restrictive environment" (LRE), 1, 54, 69–70
Legislation. *See* Education for All Handicapped Children Act (PL 94–142); Education of the Handicapped Act: Amendments (PL 99–457)
Lipreading. *See* Speechreading

Listening activities, 273–274
Loudness, 212
LRE. *See* "Least restrictive environment" (LRE)

Mainstreamed hearing-impaired children. *See* Hearing-impaired children
Mainstreaming. *See also* Education for All Handicapped Children Act (PL 94–142); Education of the Handicapped Act: Amendments (PL 99–457); Individualized Education Plan (IEP)
   attitudes toward, 169–170
   auditory evaluation and, 362
   challenges for hearing-impaired children, 67–69
   child assessment for, 361–362
   costs of, 171
   educational audiologist and, 365–370
   educational placement alternatives, 70–74
   extent of, 163–164
   facilitation of, 72–73
   full mainstreaming, 70–72, 74–75
   general principles of, 361–365
   goals of, 361
   historical perspectives on, 359–360
   in-service training and, 321–332, 364
   "least restrictive environment," 69–70
   listening to the children and, 364–365
   parents and, 365
   partial mainstreaming, 71, 72, 74–75
   of preschool children, 74–76
   psychosocial considerations for, 363
   requisite entry skills for, 303–304
   service options for educational programming, 76–83
   social mainstreaming, 71, 74
   support services for, 362–363
      varieties of, 361
Management. *See also* Auditory management; Communication management; Early detection and management
   classroom academic management, 307–315
   considerations for mainstreaming, 79–81
   educational management, 304–307
   management needs indicated in IEP, 164–166
   psychosocial management, 315–319
MAT. *See Metropolitan Achievement Test* (MAT), 144
MCL. *See* Most comfortable loudness (MCL) measurement
Metropolitan Achievement Test (MAT), 44, 144, 145
Mixed hearing loss, 88–89
Morphology. *See* Syntax/morphology
"Most appropriate educational setting," 1, 54
Most comfortable loudness (MCL) measurement, 93–94

National Technical Institute for the Deaf, 138
Noise, in classrooms, 194–198
Northwestern University Children's Perception of Speech (NU-CHIPS), 91, 92, 117
NU-CHIPS. *See Northwestern University Children's Perception of Speech* (NU-CHIPS)
Nurses, 256–257

Objectives
   in Individualized Education Plan (IEP), 173–179
   therapeutic objectives, 14–17
Otitis media, 8
Output, of hearing aids, 209–211

Paragraphs
   speech reception of, 121–122

spoken language comprehension
of, 126–127
spoken language production of, 133
Parents, 161, 168–169, 262, 300, 316,
317, 326, 328, 365
Peabody Picture Vocabulary Test
(PPVT), 124
Performance. *See also* Academic
achievement
academic achievements, 42–46
audiovisual perception of speech,
31–36
classroom performance evaluation,
151–156
educational setting and, 54–63
evaluation of, 14–17, 171–172
in Individualized Education Plan
(IEP), 171–172
language abilities, 36–42
level of, 171–172
psychosocial status and, 63–65
in regular classrooms, 19–20, 54–63
relationship of hearing loss to,
46–54
speech perception, 20–28
speech production, 28–31
syntax, 39–42
vocabulary, 36–39
Personnel. *See* Audiologists; Speech-
language pathologists; Teachers
Phoneme error analysis, 226–227
PPVT. *See Peabody Picture Vocabulary
Test* (PPVT)
Preschool children, 74–76, 343–350
Probe microphone measurements,
107–108
Production of spoken language. *See*
Speech production
Professional personnel. *See*
Audiologists; Speech-language
pathologists; Teachers
Psychological evaluation, 146–148. *See
also* Social adjustment evaluation
Psychosocial considerations, 63–65,
363. *See also* Social communica-
tion; Social skills development
Psychosocial management, 315–319

Pure tone measures, 85–89

Receptive language. *See* Speech
reception
Recruitment, 212
Rehabilitation. *See* Aural rehabilita-
tion; Speech/language therapy
Residual hearing. *See* Aided residual
hearing
Reverberation time, 195–196

SAT. *See* Speech awareness threshold
(SAT); *Stanford Achievement Test*
(SAT)
Saturation, 209
Schools for the deaf, 74
Selective amplification, 211–212
Sensorineural hearing loss, 88, 99
Sensory deprivation, 6–9
Sentences
speech articulation of, 137–138
speech reception of, 121–122
spoken language comprehension
of, 125–126
spoken language production of,
130–132
Service options for educational pro-
gramming, 76–83, 166–171
Social adjustment evaluation, 148–
150, 172. *See also* Psychological
evaluation
Social communication, 262–263. *See
also* Psychosocial considerations
Social skills development, 315–319. *See
also* Psychosocial considerations
Sound pressure levels (SPL), 227–230
Speech acoustics, 183–194
Speech articulation/intelligibility
assessment of, 136–139
intelligibility, 138–139
sentence level, 137–138
syllable level, 136–137
word level, 137
Speech audiometry, 89–94
Speech awareness threshold (SAT),
89–90
Speech comprehension

assessment of, 122–127
  paragraph level, 126–127
  sentence level, 125–126
  word level, 123–125
Speech discrimination tests, 90–93
Speech Intelligibility Evaluation
  (SPINE), 138–139
Speech/language development
  critical period for, 9–10
  elements of, 261–262
  via single or combined sensory
    modality, 34
Speech-language pathologists, 17–18,
  170, 257, 269, 285, 331, 362, 381
Speech/language therapy
  language usage, 297–300
  speech production, 278–280
  speech reception, 270–277
  syntax/morphology, 290–296
  vocabulary, 282–289
Speech perception
  audiovisual aspects of, 31–36
  components of, 20–21
  of deaf children, 24
  error patterns in, 22–27
  of hard-of-hearing children, 24
  of hearing-impaired children,
    21–28
  of normal-hearing listeners, 21
  tests for, 22
Speech production
  assessment of, 127–134
  classroom management, 280, 281
  language usage, 133–134, 297–302
  language use, 133–134
  paragraph level, 133
  performance of mainstreamed
    hearing-impaired children,
    28–31
  remediation considerations and
    activities, 278–280
  sentence level, 130–132
  syntax, 39–42
  vocabulary, 36–39
  word level, 129–130
Speech reception
  assessment of, 116–122

classroom management, 271,
    277–278
  error patterns in, 120–121
  interference and, 119–120
  primary modality for, 118–119
  remediation considerations and
    activities, 270–277
  sentences and paragraphs, 121–122
Speech recognition thresholds (SRTs),
  89–90, 91
Speech tracking, 273
Speechreading, 31–33
SPELT-II. *See Structured Photographic
  Elicited Language Test-II* (SPELT-II)
SPINE. *See Speech Intelligibility Evaluation* (SPINE)
SPL. *See* Sound pressure levels (SPL)
SRTs. *See* Speech recognition thresholds (SRTs)
Stanford Achievement Test (SAT), 43–
  44, 143, 144, 145, 339, 340
Static immittance, 94, 95–97
*Structured Photographic Elicited Lan-
  guage Test-II* (SPELT-II), 130–131
Syllables, speech articulation of,
  136–137
Syntax/morphology
  classroom management, 292,
    296–297
  performance of mainstreamed
    hearing-impaired children,
    39–42
  remediation considerations and
    activities, 290–296

TAC. *See Test of Auditory Comprehension* (TAC)
TD. *See* Threshold of discomfort (TD)
Teachers. *See also* Classrooms; Com-
    munication management;
    Management
  classroom academic management
    and, 314–315
  classroom acoustics and, 194,
    198–199
  classroom performance related to,
    151–154

and early detection and management of hearing impairments,
18
in-service training for, 321–332
letter to classroom teacher, 371
troubleshooting of acoustic devices
by, 257
Test of Auditory Comprehension (TAC),
127
Test of Syntactic Ability (TSA), 41,
134–135
Tests. *See* Communication assessment; and names of specific tests
Therapeutic objectives, 14–17
Threshold of discomfort (TD), 93–94
Training. *See* In-service training
Troubleshooting, 251–258
TSA. *See Test of Syntactic Ability* (TSA)
Tympanometry, 94, 95

University of Connecticut Mainstream Project, 20, 194

Vocabulary. *See also* Words
classroom management, 283,
289–290

performance of mainstreamed
hearing-impaired children,
36–39
remediation considerations and
activities, 282–289

*Wechsler Intelligence Test for Children–
Revised* (WISC–R), 339, 340
WIPI. *See Word Intelligibility by Picture
Identification* (WIPI)
Wireless FM systems. *See* FM systems
WISC–R. *See Wechsler Intelligence Test
for Children–Revised* (WISC–R)
*Word Intelligibility by Picture Identifica-
tion* (WIPI), 22, 91, 92–93, 117
Words. *See also* Vocabulary
speech articulation of, 137
speech reception of, 116–118
spoken language comprehension
of, 123–125
spoken language production of,
129–130
Written language
assessment of, 134–136
comprehension of, 134–135
production of, 135–136